IDS DEVELOPMENT STUDIES SERIES

States or Markets?

IDS Development Studies Series

The Institute of Development Studies at Sussex University was established in 1966 as the British national research and training centre in development studies. In this series members of the Institute aim to bring the results of their most interesting research projects to the widest possible audience. The books will be drawn from a number of social science disciplines and will have their origins in research projects, reflective work by IDS Fellows, or conference papers. The series will reflect the broad range of IDS Fellows' expertise on development and will encompass both the traditional concerns of this interdisciplinary area of study and new theoretical debates.

States or Markets?

Neo-liberalism and the Development Policy Debate

edited by

CHRISTOPHER COLCLOUGH

and

JAMES MANOR

CLARENDON PRESS · OXFORD

Oxford University Press, Walton Street, Oxford OX2 6DP

Oxford New York Toronto
Delhi Bombay Calcutta Madras Karachi
Kuala Lumpur Singapore Hong Kong Tokyo
Nairobi Dar es Salaam Cape Town
Melbourne Auckland Madrid
and associated companies in
Berlin Ibadan

Oxford is a trade mark of Oxford University Press

Published in the United States
by Oxford University Press Inc., New York

First published in new as paperback 1993

British Library Cataloguing in Publication Data
Data available

Library of Congress Cataloging in Publication Data
States or markets? : neo-liberalism and the development policy debate
/ edited by Christopher Colclough and James Manor.
p. cm.—(IDS development studies series)
Result of a workshop held at the Institute of Development Studies.
Sussex University in Dec. 1988.
Includes bibliographical references and index.
1. Economic development—Congresses. 2. Economic policy—
Congresses. 3. Free enterprise—Congresses. 5. Developing countries—
Social policy—Congresses. I. Colclough, Christopher. II. Manor,
James. III. Sussex University. Institute of Development Studies.
IV. Series.
HD73.S73 1991 338.9—dc20 91–9512
ISBN 0–19–828376–8
ISBN 0–19–828811–5

1 3 5 7 9 10 8 6 4 2

Printed in Great Britain
on acid-free paper by
Biddles Ltd,
Guildford and King's Lynn

This book is dedicated to Richard Jolly and Hans Singer, in warm appreciation of their contribution to development studies.

Preface

During 1988 a number of us at the Institute of Development Studies began to feel that the work of a prominent group of 'neo-liberal' economists, who exercised increasing influence during the 1980s on both development theory and policy, deserved systematic assessment. Many of the well-established tenets of development theory had been attacked by this group of writers. Some of the earlier theories in the 'structuralist' tradition were in any case looking vulnerable in the face of widespread dissatisfaction with the economic and social results of state intervention in countries of both north and south. Nevertheless the iconoclasm which attended some of the neo-liberal attacks looked likely to replace earlier false idols with a heavily entrenched set of new ones. It therefore seemed to be the right moment to attempt a synthesis of lessons from the neo-liberal critique of theory, together with an examination of the coherence—in both theoretical and empirical terms—of their proffered alternative.

We therefore embarked upon a rather ambitious project to provide an interdisciplinary analysis of the achievements and limitations of neo-liberalism. A seminar series during the autumn of 1988 provided a forum for discussion of first drafts. In addition a number of distinguished academics from outside the IDS were invited to participate, and to lead some of the discussions. Further drafts were presented and discussed during the annual Retreat Conference, which in December 1988 was devoted entirely to a three-day workshop on neo-liberalism. The discussion at the workshop, together with commentaries from the editors, led to further amendments to most of the chapters during 1989.

This book is the result. It attempts to provide a coherent and interdisciplinary assessment of the contribution to development studies made by leading neo-liberal authors. In many ways, it also represents a statement on the condition of development studies from the IDS Fellowship providing an appropriate way to launch the IDS/OUP series of volumes on development.

Brighton   C.C.
June 1990   J.M.

Contents

Tables

Figure

1
Structuralism versus Neo-liberalism: An Introduction

CHRISTOPHER COLCLOUGH

1. Development Theory and the Limits to Economic Liberalism: 1950–1980

The history of economic thought is, to an important extent, a history of the fortunes of economic liberalism. We refer here to the doctrine that economic life should be as untrammelled by constitutional, legal, and administrative constraints as it is possible to achieve, consistent with the maintenance of a stable society and market-place. The case for this was first set out at length by Adam Smith. He showed how, under free competition, the operation of the market continually tends to produce prices as low as is consistent with supplying the product, whilst yielding a fair return on the effort expended in its production. Freedom of exchange produces a natural harmony of interests, which needs to be let alone in order to produce as much economic advantage to everyone as the circumstances permit. Thus, according to Smith, freely working markets produce outcomes which maximize both individual and social benefits. The struggles to define the precise conditions which have to be satisfied in order to achieve those results, and to explain, predict, and control outcomes where the conditions are absent, have dominated economic enquiry ever since.

Central parts of the neo-classical analysis, for example, are about ways in which markets would work if perfect competition were to prevail. Much of its power and influence, however, derives from its ability to explore the ways in which output, employment, and pricing outcomes vary in the presence of a determinate range of market imperfections—including non-constant returns to scale, externalities, collusion in pricing or purchasing decisions, and many others. Even in diversified capitalist economies, it is worth remembering that with more than one imperfection in the market-place, the welfare

This chapter has benefited from discussions with and comments from a number of colleagues in IDS. Suggestions from Philip Daniel, David Evans, Martin Greeley, Stephany Griffith-Jones, Michael Lipton, Mick Moore, Hans Singer, John Toye, and Adrian Wood were particularly helpful.

implications of attempts to make the market work better remain uncertain (Lipsey and Lancaster 1956–7). But here, it is at least intuitively plausible that anti-trust legislation, laws against pollution and in favour of union ballots, would, in combating some forms of monopoly, negative externality, and restrictive practice be promotive of both greater efficiency and greater welfare. Such an outcome is, however, less certain in cases where market imperfections are more pervasive. Laws against monopoly in very small or poor states may mean that domestic production might never begin. Ballots presuppose full and fair access to information if they are justly to reflect people's perception of their own interests. Environmental protection lobbies can be seen as undermining the prospects for a Brazil or Malaysia to industrialize. Similarly, minimum wage legislation underpinned by social security provision may be a means of protecting the interests of a vulnerable minority in states where full employment in the formal sector is possible. Yet in states where that is not possible it may be a means of protecting the interests of a relatively small élite, and of helping to keep more people from gaining access to wage employment. Thus, if one does not recognize the context and use it in the analysis, unintended outcomes will result.

structuralists

These kinds of consideration have been central to the evolution of the dominant intellectual paradigm in the economics of developing countries over the years 1950–80. Most major contributors to this subset of economic theory have shared the view that the structures of most developing countries are significantly different from those of industrialized countries, to such an extent that economic outcomes in response to similar events in each environment will systematically reflect such differences. It is not that these 'structuralist' writers have rejected neo-classical theory. Rather, they have applied neo-classical (and other) tools selectively, within an analytic framework which attempts to recognize and integrate the specific characteristics of the case to which it is being applied. A contingent, but frequently repeated, conclusion of such exercises is that the market in 'typical' developing countries tends to be more imperfect—and hence less socially efficient in allocating goods and services—than in more industrialized societies. The idea that governments will need to intervene in order to help, support, or 'stand in for' the market more substantially in developing than in more developed societies often follows from this diagnosis. This is not, however, a tradition which is bent upon *replacing* the market. Most writers would not have disagreed with Arthur Lewis, in claiming:

the case against detailed central planning is that it is undemocratic, bureaucratic, inflexible and subject to great error and confusion. It is also unnecessary. There is a much better case for piece-meal planning; that is to say for concentrating on a few matters which it is particularly desired to influence, such as the level of exports, or of capital formation, or of industrial production, or of food production . . . Some planning is necessary, since the results of demand and supply are not socially acceptable in their entirety; but planning can be confined to those spheres where it is considered most important to modify the results that market forces, acting alone, would yield. (Lewis 1955: 384)

This 'structuralist' tradition, then, has tended to be interventionist—albeit with strong differences in the emphasis given to market failure between individual writers.[1] There has, however, been some evolution in attitudes towards the desirability of a stronger state role. This happened particularly during the 1970s, when structuralist writers, having concentrated heavily upon the analysis of constraints on economic growth in developing countries, shifted their attention increasingly towards questions of income distribution and poverty alleviation. Earlier work by Kuznets (1955) had suggested that the economic growth of the industrialized countries had been associated, initially, with a deterioration in the size distribution of income, and only later with its improvement. Did this imply that relative poverty in developing countries would initially worsen and that absolute poverty would remain unaffected by economic growth? If so, the prospects for development—on most sensible definitions of this term (Seers 1969)—seemed bleak. Although the experience of some developing countries during the 1950s and 1960s appeared consistent with this hypothesis (Oshima 1962) its automaticity came to be questioned on both theoretical and empirical grounds. The *locus classicus* for this argument (Chenery *et al.* 1974), outlined a strategy of 'redistribution with growth', and provided positive case-study evidence for its achievement in countries as diverse, politically and economically, as Cuba, Tanzania, Sri Lanka, South Korea, and Taiwan. By implication, early capitalist development, if untrammelled, may be characterized by deteriorating income distribution. But history also showed that it was possible, in both capitalist and socialist states, to avoid the unwelcome trade-off and achieve both growth and distributional objectives at the same time. Purposive government policies were needed to secure access to and maintain direction on this path.

Two important characteristics of this structuralist tradition have been criticized by analysts from each end of the spectrum stretching from Marxist to mainstream. The first is the extent to which it de-emphasized the importance of relative prices as means of affecting both distributive and productive outcomes. Their neglect by structuralists arose partly from growing evidence of the importance of non-price variables in affecting (or in explaining the absence of) economic responses in developing countries. The ideas of capital, foreign exchange, and manpower 'constraints', which could not be solved by relative price changes (Nurkse 1953, Chenery and Strout 1966, Harbison and Myers 1964) of inter-industry integration, big investment 'pushes', and planning based upon fixed coefficients (Rosenstein-Rodan 1943, 1957, Tinbergen 1958), of secular declines in terms of trade arising from structural features of and relationships between countries of the north and south (Prebisch 1950, Singer 1950), of vicious circles of poverty and the cumulative causation of inequality (Myrdal 1957), and much else, indicated that it was along this non-price axis that the central insights of structuralism were being revealed. It was also a reflection of the problems of development increasingly being seen in dynamic terms. The existing structure of relative prices reflects a particular set of relative scarcities and expectations. These signals were believed by structuralists to provide an incomplete—sometimes a misleading—guide to resource allocation, since the complementary inputs required for structural change were not in elastic supply. Thus, pricing policy—and, particularly, the defence of freely determined market prices— was assigned lower priority than was the manipulation of other macro-economic instruments. There is no doubt that the comparative silence of structuralists over matters of price has proved to be a weakness.[2] But this lacuna does not begin to justify—as this book will show—the single-mindedness with which some critics of structuralism have reasserted market pricing strategies as the central and overriding concern of development policy.

The second characteristic focused upon by critics is the role envisaged for the state. The style and extent of interventionism favoured by structuralists has been especially criticized, as has their apparent belief that governments would and could intervene in order to improve the incomes and welfare of the poor. Critical reaction to the former—the nature of desirable government intervention—is discussed at length later in this chapter. As to the latter, structuralists' optimism that reformist states exist was judged by many political scientists and some economists to be naïve. Some, using a Marxist framework, argued that such reformism was generally unrealistic since the redistribution of income would be against the interests of the owners of capital (Leys 1975). Others developed parallel non-Marxist critiques (Bates 1981, 1983), arguing that governments have to reward the interest groups that keep them in power; whatever the nature of such alliances, to assume that they can be ignored or transformed at will, without jeopardizing the political status quo, would thus be a mistake.

It is important to notice that this latter kind of attack does not, even if successful, reveal analytic 'errors' in the theoretical framework offered by structuralists. Rather, it presents concrete obstacles to the implementation of structuralist *policies*. Theorists can reasonably claim the importance of identifying the kinds of policy that would be necessary if the poor were to be made better off, even if its practical possibility turned out to be remote. More fundamentally, even at the practical level, these criticisms are not decisive. We find, for example, one of the co-authors of *Redistribution with Growth* examining ways in which discriminatory action to improve the lot of the poor can be made consistent with the interests of richer and more powerful groups (Jolly 1975). Thus—even accepting a Bates/Leys critique —prospects for reform would become contingent upon new alliances being forged between interest groups comprising a larger proportion of the population, ultimately including interests compatible with, if not identical with, those of the peasants. These kinds of outcome are not inconceivable (particularly where both commercial farmers and peasants grow the same crops), and thus they do not present an insurmountable obstacle to the analytic integrity of reformism.

Compared with the pre-packaged solutions which have been advocated as desirable policy reforms for the south during the 1980s, the structuralist literature is markedly more eclectic and less dogmatic. This follows from the basic building blocks of the structuralist approach: an emphasis upon the importance of initial conditions, of national resources, of the size of the country and its relations with the international economy, as variables which must influence the appropriate balance and composition of policies aimed at higher growth and a better distribution of its fruits. Thus, prescriptions for the detailed content of policy tended to be avoided except when analysis was conducted in a particular country context (as with the ILO employment 'missions' of the 1970s to Colombia, Sri Lanka, and Kenya). What may be appropriate in one case may be highly inappropriate in another.[3] There was, however, agreement about the need for governments to intervene, about the set of instruments that might be utilized, and about the need to bring the objective of poverty alleviation to the centre of the stage.

These arguments seemed gradually to be won. The ideas that 'development' meant something closer to the alleviation of poverty than to the mere achievement of aggregate economic growth, and that the latter would not necessarily deliver the former, became widely accepted in academic circles and within the international community of development 'professionals'. By the mid-1970s the President of the World Bank had announced that the development record should be judged not by economic growth but by the extent to which poverty was reduced in the world. A consensus emerged: the World Bank and the British and other Western governments reorientated their aid policies so as to focus them explicitly upon the poorest peoples, regions, and countries. Moreover, the introduction of government policies in the south aimed directly at alleviating poverty whilst maintaining growth became the orthodoxy of development theory and practice, as preached by the governments and institutions of the north, during the second half of the decade.

2. The New Liberal Challenge

The consensus did not last for long. The major challenge to structuralism came not from the left, but from a group of economists who have sought to reassert the major tenets of economic liberalism in the analysis of development. The most influential of these critics have been Balassa, Bauer,

Krueger, Lal, and Little, each of whom have written extensively and combatively on these matters, mainly in the academic press, since the early 1970s. In identifying this group of writers as the leading purveyors of a particular mode of analysis two types of rough justice must be acknowledged: first, there is a risk of caricature—whilst there are some central ideas which each of these writers share, there are, of course many others about which they disagree. Thus in picking out their common ground—be it for praise or criticism—the intellectual richness and diversity of each individual may be missed. Second, identifying leadership is a matter of judgement, which is vulnerable to dissent as much on account of whom one chooses to exclude as of its attribution. It should be noted, therefore, that there are many other writers who have had major influence of a 'neo-liberal' kind in particular areas of theory or policy. These would include Schultz on agricultural incentives, Becker on human capital and the economics of the household, Mirrlees on project appraisal, Scitovsky, Bhagwati, Srinivasan on trade, industrialization, and outward orientation. These and others continue a tradition of economics whose origins lie in Chicago, and whose pre-eminent post-war exponent has been Harry Johnson.[4] However, when generalizing about neo-liberal opinion we shall be referring to the five authors mentioned earlier, unless otherwise indicated.

Neo-liberals, then, deny many of the main ideas of structuralist orthodoxy. They have been revisionist in reasserting the primacy of economic growth amongst policy objectives, believing poverty will thereby be most effectively reduced. Moreover, they have been radical, both in their diagnoses of the major causes of development problems, and their proposed solutions. As to the former, these economists share the view that the slow progress made by developing countries has been mainly caused by excessive economic intervention by their own governments. The costs of this intervention have been typically much greater than its benefits in terms of both production and distribution. New kinds of efficiency costs—most notably, rent-seeking (see below)—have been identified which become, in some states, a dominant form of bureaucratic activity. Moreover, the direct and indirect impact on prices of a wide variety of state interventions has resulted in a sharp difference emerging between market and 'shadow' prices, resulting in the market not being able to facilitate efficient resource allocation. Market failure is thus seen as mainly caused by excessive intervention, rather than as providing a case for its further, even more pervasive, extension.

As for solutions, this group of economists have advocated market-orientated principles and policies which echo those of the early liberal economists from Smith to Marshall. Their central thesis is that long-run growth and development will proceed provided everything possible is done to achieve short-run allocative efficiency: although such a result will not necessarily be delivered by freely working markets since initial imperfections are (often grudgingly) acknowledged, the market nevertheless provides the best way of approximating it, and conventional interventionist strategies will almost always be even less satisfactory in that regard.

During the early 1980s, these criticisms of the excessive costs of intervention were already finding favour outside the academic world as the climate of political opinion shifted to the right in the industrialized societies of the US and Western (and, more recently Eastern) Europe. Reductions in state expenditure and emphasis on the importance of incentives and of 'getting prices right' became increasingly a unifying message for economic policy reform in the countries of the north. Northern opinion was therefore particularly open to the view that similar strictures should be aimed at the countries of the south. The fact that neo-liberals argued thus, and pointed to some apparent (but misleadingly labelled) success stories for such policies in the newly industrialized countries of South East Asia, captured the attention of bilateral and multilateral development agencies and banks, who were searching for stronger guarantees of repayment for new monies advanced to an increasingly indebted developing world. Some neo-liberal economists secured strategic advisory or executive posts in government and international agencies.[5] Accordingly, packages of policy reforms, attached as conditions for advancing new loans to the south, were increasingly influenced by their analyses and prescriptions. Thus, although the influence of neo-liberals has been partly a function of these and other historical coincidences, their critique of development theory and practice has become powerful in both intellectual and practical terms. An examination of the general validity of their case is the principal aim of this book. The remainder of this introduction provides a summary overview and assessment of the contribution made by neo-liberals, referring, where relevant, to themes raised in later chapters. Reference to the papers is made in a sequence which suits the argument in hand, rather than that in which they subsequently appear in the book.

3. An Assessment

If there were to be a single statement which symbolized the fundamental message of neo-liberalism, it would be this: in settling matters of resource allocation, imperfect markets are better than imperfect states.[6] Neo-liberals are *not* asserting that markets are perfect—rather that, warts and all, they will allocate resources more efficiently than alternative mechanisms.

It is important, for our purposes, to recognize on what grounds such an assertion could be validly based. As neo-liberal economists themselves remind us (Lal 1983: 15), there is a well-established methodology provided by welfare economics for dealing with deviations from the optimum as a result of market imperfections. This involves comparing the welfare gain from correcting the initial distortion with the inevitable welfare loss that is caused by the intervention itself. The latter is related to the costs of government action. These include not merely the direct costs (e.g. the wages and salaries of those who are required to take that action) but the indirect costs arising from the distorting of relatives prices elsewhere in the economy consequent upon (say) the revenue raising measures to finance the government actions concerned. In the light of such a careful comparison, the proposed action may be judged second best (first best being unattainable) if the welfare benefits are judged to outweigh the costs. It follows that whether government actions *generally* have costs exceeding their attendant welfare benefits is an empirical question which, strictly, would need to be based upon careful measure in each and every case. Thus, the generalization that imperfect markets are better than imperfect states cannot be adduced using purely theoretical argument. It is, rather, a statement about the way things have worked out in the world. For one to accept it as correct would thus require a fairly formidable empirical treatment covering a large number of country cases in considerable detail.

Although such a comprehensive empirical treatment does not exist, and would even in principle, be very difficult to achieve, there is one area of economic policy which has been closely studied by neo-liberals. Since the late 1960s five major inter-country studies of the effects of different trade policy regimes on economic growth, income distribution, and a range of other development indicators have been completed. Data for twenty countries have been included, and a number of the major neo-liberal writers have been involved in this work (Little, Scitovsky, and Scott 1970; Balassa and Associates 1971, 1982; Donges 1976; Krueger 1978; Bhagwati 1978). This empirical work informs and underpins neo-liberal prescription. Trade policy is the core area for neo-liberal reform and whilst for some writers it defines its extent, others (including the five 'leaders' mentioned earlier) branch out from this base to generalize about the whole of macro-economic policy. Setting aside for the moment the question as to whether or not this is justifiable, it is clear that this empirical work—and trade policy in general— needs to occupy an important place in the minds of critics of neo-liberalism.

Neo-liberal economists put great emphasis upon their statistical demonstration that export expansion has been associated with rapid economic growth: countries that have tended to do well in terms of one of these variables have also tended to do well in terms of the other (Michaely 1977, Balassa 1978). At first sight, there is nothing very unexpected about this statement. Since exports account for a high proportion of the income of developing countries—even many of the poor ones—it is not surprising that strong growth of one of these variables should be associated with strong growth of the other. However, the non-trivial aspect is the assertion by neo-liberals of a causal linkage between export growth and that of total output, which, by implication, is not so strongly true of the other items of total demand—consumption, investment, and government expenditure.

Theoretical explanations for this relationship are less strong than one might expect. As David Evans's chapter in this volume points out, the intellectual pedigree of the theory of trade policy, and the principle of comparative advantage from which it is derived, is long and controversial. He argues that the principle of comparative advantage, almost by default, has been captured by neo-liberal writers on trade theory and policy, to the detriment of its judicious application in the context of the structures and institutions prevailing in developing countries. This leads neo-liberals into a number of pitfalls, which he elaborates. Krueger (1980) does acknowledge that available trade and growth models provide little indication of the quantitative importance of trade as a contributor to growth and still less insight into the probable orders of magnitude of the losses in attainable growth rates that may be incurred with departures from free trade. But Balassa's explanation rests—as (from a very different perspective) did Kaldor's—upon the dynamic benefits expected from trade, the facts that specialization is limited by the extent of the market and that, by widening the market, economies of large scale (increasing returns) can be exploited (Balassa and Associates 1982: 59; Kaldor 1972). Thus, whilst export fetishism may be unjustifiable for a range of empirical and theoretical reasons, autarkic solutions are likely to involve serious economic costs.

As to the question of how rapid export growth has been achieved in some countries but not in others, a range of contingent explanations seems possible—that 'better' (in some sense) products were chosen to export than those chosen to replace imports, or that other characteristics of successful exporting countries happened to be more favourable (policies, resources, the reactions of international markets, or other exogenous events).

Amongst this list of possible contingent explanations, neo-liberals focus almost all of their attention upon policy differences amongst countries. Specifically, they argue that export success was a product of the trade-policy regime employed by the governments concerned. This conclusion is based upon the results of the five research studies listed earlier, which, for twenty countries, described the different trade regimes holding between the 1950s and the early 1970s, and attempted to assess their consequences. The Krueger/Bhagwati research was concerned to investigate the effects of moving from quantitative controls on imports to a price-regulated trading system. Balassa, on the other hand, was concerned to categorize countries according to their degree of outward orientation, which depends 'on whether sales in domestic and in foreign markets receive similar incentives in terms of effective subsidies, or whether the system of incentives favours domestic sales over foreign sales . . . in short an anti-export bias' (Balassa and Associates 1982: 38). This work is said to justify the conclusion that countries operating a liberal trading regime—a set of policies which approximated free trade—did best in economic and export growth.

There are at least three important sets of problems involved in making the jump from the results of this empirical work on trading regimes to the conclusion that 'free' market outcomes are the desirable mechanism for trade.

First there is some disagreement in the neo-liberal camp about what free trade (or, more commonly, 'nearly' free trade) means. For Balassa it is certainly not 'production on the basis of the unassisted market price' (or *laissez-faire*): his explanation for the dynamic benefits of trade rests upon the existence of scale economies, as we have seen; for consistency he therefore allows protection, since domestic production in either export or import-competing industries might not otherwise occur. He further allows it to compensate for the presence of distortions in factor markets, external economies, and other imperfections (Balassa and Associates 1982: 68–9). Thus, for Balassa, nearly free trade is consistent with interventionism, being merely concerned with relative incentives to produce for domestic and foreign markets. Little's earlier (1970) definition seems at first sight more demanding of non-intervention: 'virtual free trade . . . means that exporters could obtain inputs (including tradeable domestic inputs) at world market prices, while the effective exchange rate for exporters was close to that which would have ruled under free trade'. This must surely mean applying no domestic protection in the context of a market-determined exchange rate. Lal, too, denies the wisdom of ever using tariffs (Lal 1983: 28) and argues in the case of Korea (as an example of one of the newly industrializing countries (NICs)) that 'success has been achieved *despite* intervention' (Lal 1983: 46). It is, then, not easy to establish what particular set of policies is implied by the apparently agreed target (amongst neo-liberals) of 'nearly free trade'.

Second, as the paper by Evans shows, the meaning of 'outward orientation', the determining variable in neo-liberals' analysis of export success, is also far from clear. Although it is referred to as a continuous variable (with the generally agreed conclusion amongst neo-liberals being: the more of it the better) in practice it appears in the analysis as a 'dummy', having four or five values, each of which is a composite of nominal protection, effective protection, and effective subsidies (Balassa and Associates 1982, chapter 3) or, in the case of the World Bank (1987) of effective protection, of the use of quantitative restrictions, of export incentives, and of the degree of exchange rate overvaluation. These variables are, like apples and pears, very different, and cannot easily be added together. Determining the membership of country groups (each implying a similar degree of outward orientation) thus becomes as much a matter of judgement as of measurement. On this important empirical question, Evans concludes that the link between trade policy, rapid growth, and economic efficiency cannot be strongly established.

The third, and probably the most important problem associated with the neo-liberal conclusions on trade policy, concerns the number of variables which are omitted from their analysis. It is not that the strength of the relationship between the growth of exports and total output is in contest. It is that neo-liberals attribute export and output success to a fairly narrow set of policy instruments being manipulated in a tightly defined way. Their analysis takes account of very little else. This involves two important categories of oversimplification. First, it ignores all of the other policies utilized by successfully industrializing exporters, many of which have been highly interventionist in neo-liberal terms (see White and Wade in White 1988). Second, it implies that both the initial conditions of these countries immediately prior to their export success and the international environment within which they were beginning to trade had few if any implications for the success of their endeavours. These two sets of assumptions are completely unsatisfactory. As A. K. Sen has pointed out in a similar context, 'To what extent fast growth is possible, with export industries taking the lead, is a question that can be answered for any particular country only by looking at the details of its economic circumstances . . . The lessons to be drawn have to concentrate on understanding the *functional roles* of various instruments rather than on blind imitation of the instruments themselves' (1980: 63).

The dangers inherent in this kind of 'blind imitation' are illustrated by a number of papers in this book. As will now be clear, neo-liberals argue that production consistent with, and capitalizing upon, the comparative advantages of nations will bring most potential benefit to all, and will be attainable only if market prices which truly reflect opportunity costs rule. Even where authors permit intervention, this would only be to the extent that freely working market prices do not, or would not, do so. Two such cases, which frequently arise in developing countries, are those of the market wages paid to unskilled labour by formal sector employers and the cost disadvantages faced by new entrants to industries which are characterized by economies of large scale.

In the case of the former, where market imperfections lead to a differential between the market and the 'shadow' wage rate—as witnessed, perhaps, by the persistence of unemployment at the social minimum wage—corrective action would be justifiable: not a tariff (which would provide incentives to increase the use of all factors rather than labour alone and would discriminate against exports) but a uniform labour subsidy. This is generally proposed in the form of a reduction in social security charges (where relevant) or, oddly, as a subsidy for staples (Balassa and Associates 1982: 65–6)—thereby, presumably, encouraging real wage reductions—rather than the more obvious approach, seldom used outside the UK, of providing recurrent subsidies to defined categories of worker (Little, Scitovsky, and Scott 1970; Little 1982: 143). Raphael Kaplinsky, however, analyses the effects of one such scheme in Botswana. Designed closely according to neo-liberal principles, a labour subsidy scheme was introduced for new, or expanding, ventures, in order to bring the cost of labour down towards what was thought to be its shadow price, thereby to stimulate manufacturing output and employment. The paper shows that this intervention failed to achieve its expected results:

rather than stimulating additional manufacturing activity, it provided increased profitability to entrepreneurs who would have invested in any event; moreover, within projects it seemed not to succeed in influencing the choice of technique in the direction of greater labour use. Thus, direct employment and output outcomes were unaffected by the subsidy, even though private profitability was enhanced. Kaplinsky's explanation for this is that the type of intervention needed to promote Botswana's manufacturing sector was of a quite different kind. Although the country surely had a comparative advantage in manufacturing (given that agricultural potential is climatically constrained) its major constraint in the labour market was the quality of labour rather than the level of unskilled labour costs. Action was needed to upgrade the knowledge and skills available. Price intervention in the labour market proved inadequate to accommodate this type of structural constraint.

A similar kind of lesson emerges from the case study of the computer industry in Brazil by Hubert Schmitz and Tom Hewitt. Neo-liberals are unanimous in their criticism of quantitative controls as a means of protecting domestic industry, pointing to the efficiency costs associated with the use of such a blunt instrument. Schmitz and Hewitt demonstrate for one part of the computer industry how such controls appear to have succeeded in helping to establish a locally owned, increasingly efficient subsector. Their point is that the creation of a 'market reserve' open only to Brazilian nationals succeeded in capturing a range of externalities which would probably have been lost if a form of protection based only on prices had been used.

Other examples of the potential costs of 'blind imitation' are not difficult to find. Some of the most heavily indebted developing countries provide examples of cases where packages of neo-liberal reforms have been introduced at the behest of northern interests and institutions. On the one hand, as argued by Stephany Griffith-Jones in this volume, their present predicament has, to an important extent, resulted from a massive increase in the share of credit from the private banks in total lending to developing countries during the 1970s. Such lending was, she argues, caused by market failure: bankers possessed imperfect information about borrowers and incorrectly believed that national default would not occur. The need for more, rather than less regulation of international transfers is here implied: the privatization of international financial flows, contrary to the neo-liberal view, provides an important part of the explanation for the debt crisis.

As for the impact of neo-liberal reforms in these countries there is now a series of evaluations which point to their mixed, rarely very successful and sometimes damaging impact in particular country settings (Killick 1984; Cornia, Jolly, and Stewart 1988; Taylor 1988; Colclough and Green 1988). Charles Harvey's paper in this volume draws upon these and other country-based analyses. He examines the experience of seven countries in Sub-Saharan Africa which have introduced neo-liberal reforms—usually, but not entirely at the behest of the IMF—in response to acute macro-economic problems. Some have had moderate success in terms of their objectives, but most have failed. He finds that partial implementation of reform packages can lead to early demise—devaluation, for example, without civil service reform further undermines public service efficiency. Equally, implementing all the reforms quickly can generate such strong political opposition that they risk being overthrown before positive achievements can be secured.

This and other work show that liberalization, in the context of a seriously overvalued exchange rate, initially makes almost everyone worse off than before. The only exceptions are traders or producers with high levels of unsold stocks, who are often few in number during times of economic austerity. Delays in supply response (but not in price rises) in aid disbursements, and changes in the power/income of the most articulate citizens make for a very difficult time. Liberalization might work better only where the adjustment challenge is small and where the distributive changes needed are not acute. Thus, one of the critical differences between liberalization as applied in South-East Asia and as it has been applied in Sub-Saharan Africa, lies in the initial conditions. Introducing a liberal regime in the context of impoverishment is very different from a setting (or early prospect) of dynamic growth. All of this evidence strengthens the case for what we have argued is the central tenet of structuralism: the context within which particular policies are applied exerts a major influence upon their outcomes, such that different national contexts often require different policies to secure similar objectives.

It is in many ways surprising that the work of Anne Krueger does not acknowledge this insight. Her contributions have included, centrally, a study of over twenty liberalization attempts in ten countries between 1950 and 1972 (Krueger 1978). Most of these reforms were introduced in response to balance of payments crises or to the need to reschedule debt. Only one country (Korea) was judged completely successful, in that it eliminated anti-export bias. Elsewhere, failure was usually judged to arise from insufficient government commitment, bad luck, or extensive political opposition. There is not much that separates Krueger from later commentators on the reasons for liberalization failure. What differs are the sets of implications that are subsequently drawn: that the fault lies with the governments, rather than with either the nature or the inherent practicability of the policies themselves.

The advocacy of price liberalization in foreign trade—and, by implication, throughout the economy—is only half of the neo-liberal message. The other part concerns the role of government. The two are, of course, related in that 'non-liberalized' prices are regulated or determined by the state. Arguments in favour of liberalization thus imply the need to reduce or stop some types of intervention. As Michael Lipton in this volume shows, however, this does not necessarily entail a *generally* reduced role for government. Indeed if price liberalization—nationally or sectorally—were to occur its success may depend upon the government actually increasing its activities to ensure that effective market allocation were to happen. In this connection, Lipton shows the ways in which price liberalization in agriculture (which in modified form he supports) would usually require an extended and changed rather than merely a reduced state role in extension, research, marketing, and infrastructure support.

The neo-liberal case against government would accept the above argument in principle: that is, price liberalization and smaller government, like love and marriage, are separable, and are desirable on different grounds. Thus, the neo-liberal case for reduction in state activity is based not only upon what is necessary to secure the benefits bestowed by the market, but also upon analysis which demonstrates that non-market allocation attracts a specific and important set of costs. The classic example again comes from trade policy. Krueger (1974) noted that import licensing creates scarcity rent, i.e. the difference between the value of an imported good at world prices converted through an equilibrium exchange rate, and its cost in terms of the overvalued domestic currency. This difference accrues to the licence holder as a windfall gain. Capturing such rents becomes the object of competition within and without the bureaucracy, and thus the locus for a range of directly unproductive activities which secure remuneration but produce nothing and use up real resources.

This has proved to be a fertile idea which some see as forming the core of a whole new social scientific paradigm created by applying the methods of economics to the study of politics. As Mick Moore's chapter in this volume puts it, the unifying feature 'is the attempt to see how far one can explain political phenomena by exploring the assumption that political decisions are the product of the interactions of individual agents each rationally pursuing individual material self-interest'. Application of this method has led to a large and rapidly developing literature on 'rational choice', as Moore's paper indicates. Nevertheless this application of economics to the study of politics has not yet captured the interest of many political scientists who study politics in the Third World. James Manor in this volume argues that this is because it focuses upon a narrow range of political variables and pays insufficient attention to the complexities within and the variations among political regimes in developing countries. John Toye's paper, however, demonstrates that, even in its own terms, the 'new political economy' is badly flawed: it adopts a profoundly cynical view of the state, which appears to countermand the practical possibility of liberalization experiments, not-withstanding its own advocacy of them; furthermore it ignores consideration of international factors as potential cause of economic and political change. Toye also argues that the 'new political economy' derives less from the logic of rent-seeking than it does from the older neo-Marxist political economy, with which it shares more than its advocates either admit or realize. In considering the concept of 'rent-seeking', our task in what follows is the narrower one of assessing the extent to which this concept truly adds strength to the case for minimizing state functions in market economies in the interests of efficiency, as neo-liberal economists argue is the case.

The central economic concept underlying rent-seeking analysis is that of monopoly. Rents are necessary to economic life in market economies. When they appear they provide incentives for others to produce the item in question which, in turn, reduces the size of the rents obtained until they become 'normal profits'. This process does not happen if free entry is prevented. Here, there will be no dissipation of rents, no shift of resources towards producing the product in question, no increase in output and no fall in the price. People then have to use other means of securing access to these monopoly profits which may include both legal and illegal means. This process of non-productive competition is rent-seeking (Bauer (1984) terms it 'the politicisation of economic life').

In one sense these are merely additional distributive costs which are unnecessary and inefficient. It should be noted, however, that for the argument to hold that such behaviour represents a net additional cost equal to the size of the rent (as opposed to merely a different distributional outcome) a number of conditions must hold. First, it is necessary that the labour involved in these rent-seeking activities would not otherwise be unemployed: it has to be diverted towards these activities from other productive work. Thus, the assumption of full employment of the category of labour concerned has to be made, or at least that, at the margin, labour use carries a social opportunity cost fully equal to the market wage. This, of course, is a hazardous assumption in many developing countries. In such cases the cost of rent-seeking would depend critically upon the skill levels of the labour involved (whether educated bureaucrats, scarce entrepreneurs, or opportunists who would otherwise be unemployed). Second, if the cost of rent-seeking were to equal the full value of the rent, the allocation of the sought after opportunities would need to occur entirely on the basis of competition rather than of corruption, nepotism, etc. Paradoxically, then, the cost of rent-seeking (in the Krueger/Bhagwati sense) is inversely rather than directly related to the extent of corrupt non-competitive allocation. This is counter-intuitive and risks offending more basic notions of productive efficiency championed by neo-liberals. Third, the impression is falsely given that power to allocate rents exists only in the hands of those who work in the public sector. Although there are some categories of rent-associated scarcity that are peculiar to public sector action (e.g. the regulation of production by granting business licences) there are many others which are not: those responsible for awarding subcontracts in private sector firms, for example, may be as likely to dispose of rent-earning opportunities as their public sector counterparts.

The above arguments indicate that securing access to rents is not necessarily costly, and is not necessarily confined to the public sector. Whether this constitutes a major problem is an empirically testable matter, rather than an inevitable correlate of public action. It is nevertheless potentially costly, in ways which were unnoticed until neo-liberals pointed to them. Such potential costs do not, however, provide decisive injury to the case that public allocation and regulation of some goods and services remain important. Mechanisms are required here, as with all publicly financed action, in order to secure efficiency and fight corruption. Where rent-earning opportunities exist and where free entry to secure their removal is not possible—for whatever reason—the costs of their allocation can be minimized by auction, ballot, or other rationing systems, and—as illustrated by Moore's paper in this volume—by making bureaucracies more accountable for their actions and costs.

Although the general dislike of the public sector is informed, for all neo-liberal writers, by this analysis of rent-seeking, their advocacy of the need for state contraction is not based only upon its implications. There are other practical and theoretical considerations which underpin their position. Some of these—for example the extensiveness and expensiveness of past policy 'mistakes', particularly in the field of trade—have already been discussed. In addition, however, neo-liberals believe that, in many countries, 'the public sector is over-extended . . . which has resulted in slower growth than might have been achieved with available resources, and accounts in part for the current crisis' (World Bank 1981: 5). Thus, they believe that the state is doing too much, that public expenditures must be reduced if growth is to accelerate.

The empirical evidence does not support this contention. There is no significant difference between the proportion of GDP accounted for by public spending in Sub-Saharan African countries (the region about which the above-quoted generalization was made) and those in other parts of the world; nor is the functional breakdown of public spending significantly different. Equally, amongst SSA countries there is no apparent relationship between GDP growth rates achieved and the proportional importance of public spending (data are shown in Colclough 1983). A recent, more comprehensive study shows that across the world government size is *positively* associated with economic growth performance. This is so in the overwhelming majority of country cases (more than 100 time-series regressions) especially in developing countries (Ram 1986).

In spite of this lack of evidence, the desirability of achieving a reduction of state spending in developing countries is a constant neo-liberal theme, as indicated by a number of the papers in this book. In the social sectors neo-liberal analysts have advocated both the introduction of user charges for education and health services and the encouragement of their private provision. The papers by Gerald Bloom and Christopher Colclough analyse some of the dangers of this kind of strategy, arguing that in each case, equity and efficiency costs would be substantial, and that the problem of funding the social sectors needs to be set in the context of national spending priorities and of fiscal policy more generally. In view of the fact that more than 10 per cent of national budgets are typically spent on defence, Reginald Green argues that the silence of neo-liberal voices about the need to cut spending on armaments is both unaccountable and reprehensible, given their willingness to articulate the details of expenditure reductions elsewhere in the budget. There is a similar silence in neo-liberal writings on the matter of gender. Naila Kabeer and John Humphrey argue that this stems from the neo-liberal belief that the market can resolve the problems of gender and development. This emphasis on market forces contradicts earlier welfare-based interventions on behalf of women. Whilst the recognition of women's contribution to production may be welcome, Kabeer and Humphrey argue that the matter of gender subordination is ignored in the neo-liberal stance: women may be needed for development, but its achievement does not necessarily improve their condition. Thus, the vulnerability of women is likely to be increased by such trends. The key issue, they argue, is how to use the power of the state to act in women's interests rather than against them. Here, as in the concerns to tackle agricultural production and rural poverty expressed in the papers by Michael Lipton and Robert Chambers, government expenditures will need to increase—albeit with new emphases and some restructuring—rather than the reverse over the coming decade. For Chambers, 'reversals' are a major theme. Analysis and policy which put the needs of the poor, and particularly those of poor farmers first imply a major restructuring of development actions. The task, he argues, is to dismantle those parts of the state apparatus which exploit individuals and prevent production at the base. But equally, it is to create an enabling, efficient, and equitable state infrastructure where, in the past it has been absent in each of these respects.

The main neo-liberal authors discussed above have extended their analysis from the area of trade policy to advocate a much more generalized economic strategy. The watchwords of this strategy are a reduced role for the state and an increased dependence upon free market allocation mechanisms. The question arises as to whether this new and growing tradition of writings is distinguishable from orthodox neo-classical analysis and if so, whether the difference is one of kind or merely of degree. As we have tried to indicate, there are dangers involved in labelling intellectual movements, and people within them. The reality is that of a spectrum of ideas and assumptions which by no means all share. Are there then useful and important dividing lines which separate neo-liberalism from neo-classicism—accepting that each of these boxes contains a variety of opinion, assumption, and modes of analysis?

One difference that is easily detectable is a neo-liberal willingness to draw policy implications of a concrete kind whilst remaining at a very general level of analysis. Neo-classicals, structuralists, and—particularly—neo-Marxists have traditionally been much less willing to engage in specific policy advocacy. This has partly reflected a view that each country circumstance is specific, requiring particular analysis before detailed prognoses can be offered. Others may have believed, with Keynes, that 'the theory of economics does not furnish a body of settled conclusions immediately applicable to policy'. Held back by neither reticence nor modesty, however, neo-liberals do not hesitate to advocate policy reforms of a very specific kind.

In the attempt to identify both common themes and differences, it may be useful to summarize, by way of a list of propositions, the important tenets, beliefs, and conclusions of this group of writers. This now follows. Whilst the literature indicates that some neo-liberals would disagree with some of the propositions, it is a summary of the majority position as evidenced by their writings. In order to provide a bridge with what follows, some sectoral detail is provided which is taken up in later chapters.

Underlying economic assumptions

1. Systems of production in developing countries, taking account of capital stock, skills and knowledge, resource endowments and market size—all of which may be small—are nevertheless more closely approximated by flexible than by fixed coefficients.

2. There are no structural reasons to suppose that the size and role of government should be different between developing and industrialized societies.

3. Government activity should be limited to the provision of public goods—definitions of which, at the margin, vary—and to the correction of market distortions where justified by the balance of costs and benefits. Redistribution is a valid objective, but in practice it affects incentives and brings efficiency costs.

4. Continually reallocating resources in the short run in ways which maximize profits on the basis of freely determined market prices will maximize short-run efficiency (subject to (3) above) and provides the single best means of maximizing long-run growth.

Agriculture

5. Production problems in agriculture primarily stem from inappropriate pricing policies. The major reform requirements are to close the gaps between domestic and international prices by reducing currency overvaluation and other forms of foreign-exchange intervention and by reducing the burden of taxation on agriculture (often implicit via marketing boards). Profitability will then dictate optimal production patterns.

6. Non-price constraints on agricultural output have traditionally been exaggerated and are seldom important in the long run. For instance, inadequacies in research, extension, transport, marketing, and input supply will often be ameliorated by competitive private sector provision to agriculture,

provided that the state does not so act as to make this provision insufficiently profitable.

7. Fallacy of composition arguments based upon low world price and income elasticities of demand are misdirected. Price declines for particular crops would indicate the need for the least efficient world producers to shift into other products, in line with their longer-run comparative advantage.

Industry and trade

8. Failures of import substitution are primarily a result of 'price blindness' by protecting states.

9. All direct state actions to promote industrialization (protection, licensing, reserved markets, subsidies to labour or other inputs (but see (10) below), state-led research and development) divert resources away from more ultimately profitable uses. Privatization of state production and some service provision would increase efficiency and output growth.

10. Protection in the form of quantitative restrictions is always undesirable Tariffs should usually be avoided. It is better (*a*) to adjust domestic to international prices (i.e. devalue in most cases) and (*b*) to subsidize inputs if their market prices incorrectly reflect opportunity costs.

11. Concern for intermediate or appropriate technologies is usually unhelpful and at best irrelevant. Such technologies would be adopted without government action if they were profitable.

12. Payments deficits sustained over a number of years are mainly the result of internal policies failing to adjust to cyclical or other externally induced shocks. Stagnant or declining export revenues are also the result of 'bad' internal policies.

13. Declining terms of trade are an indication of the need to restructure into other export lines. They provide no justification for compensatory real resource transfers.

Finance and aid

14. External finance is unimportant for development, since foreign exchange or savings 'bottlenecks' can be removed by desirable changes to domestic policy. In particular, interest rate subsidies, which have depressed the supply of savings and have had little impact on real investment rates, should be removed.

15. Debt burdens, though high, could be further increased if the market identifies good cause. This would be unlikely, however, in the absence of policy reform. IMF and World Bank conditionality to achieve this is fully justified in 'bad debt' country cases.

16. The fundamental argument for aid is 'moral', not economic. There is

also a 'political' case—not only in a strategic sense, but to provide leverage for the achievement of reforms as in (15) above.

17. Aid diverts resources from more to less profitable uses. Thus its short-run impact, in a global sense, is usually negative. Its maximum benefit to recipients is the avoided cost of borrowing.

Social sectors

18. The social efficiency of service provision by the public sector can be increased by introducing user charges for recipients, subject to minimal welfare conditions being satisfied.

19. The labour market is highly responsive. Income differentials provide an efficient proxy for productivity differentials at the margin.

20. Manpower constraints are not important in the long run owing to substitutability obtaining between people with different skills and educational backgrounds and in different occupations.

21. Employment growth is important as a social goal. But policies to maximize labour absorption beyond the short run can be efficiently proxied by policies to maximize economic growth. The two concerns entirely overlap.

The twenty-one propositions set out above illustrate the extent to which a strategy of economic liberalism defines the purpose and intent of these recent critics of structuralist development theory. The intellectual foundations of their position are provided by orthodox neo-classical economic theory: they employ choice-theoretic analysis, and the overriding concern is to achieve efficiency in the distribution of resources. However, they differ from many careful neo-classical analysts in two very important ways. First, they give much less serious attention to the analysis of market failure than to that which is caused by the government. This makes it difficult for neo-liberals not to be hoist by their own petard: much neo-liberal analysis points to the costs imposed by ill-advised interventionism; yet precisely the same methodology demonstrates the costs of imperfections which are not policy induced. Thus where there *are* serious imperfections in the market, liberalizing could actually make matters worse (depending upon whether the net effects of policy-induced and other imperfections had been compensatory or complementary). To avoid this trap, neo-liberals need to hold that the only *important* forms of imperfection are policy induced. Some of these writers do, it seems, believe this to be true (particularly Bauer, Little, and Lal, but Balassa slightly less so). This, however, is an empirical, rather than a logical point, and they provide no satisfactory evidence to assess the balance of this argument.

Second, neo-liberal writers appear to claim more for the long-run correlates of short-run optimization than both classical and other neo-classical writers would presume. Variables with enormous influence upon long-run outcomes —technology, labour supply and quality, capital stock, natural resources and their replacement—are relegated, in these recent writings, to a category which will look after itself. The long run is no more than a series of short runs. It is not that these variables are judged unimportant—it is rather that they need no separate attention other than that which they merit, and will get, by consequence of short-run price signals. By contrast, the classical economists were more subtle. Smith, for example, was already clear about the damaging impact of natural monopoly, and the need to prevent its emergence (Book I, chapter 7), of the important role for government in providing public works and services 'which it can never be for the interest of any individual . . . to erect and maintain, because the profit could never repay the expense . . . though it may frequently do much more than repay it to a great society' (Book IV, chapter 9). In addition, Smith saw a strong requirement for the state to provide the regulatory framework within which capitalism could do its benign work. He stressed the importance of a strong institutional structure for promoting justice, protecting the individual, providing education, and strengthening morality (via the church). These were all necessary if long-term prosperity were to be secured. Smith's 'invisible hand' could work only in the presence of a not-so-invisible state. By contrast, latterday 'neo-liberals' often appear to be more minimalist on this matter than even Adam Smith would have allowed.

Most neo-classical writers, on the other hand, are cautious to exclude from their prognoses issues of long-run growth and development. There are, of course, neo-classical theories of growth. These, however, most commonly set out to explain the possibility of steady growth, under conditions of full employment (Meade 1961 provides an excellent early example). They typically investigate the conditions influencing output growth given certain propensities to save, technological possibilities, and growth in the labour force. Now, it is not that the determinants of output growth under such circumstances are uninteresting. It is just that a different set of determinants would apply if (for example) there is no domestic capital goods industry; if choices of technique are, in practice, limited; if physical shortages (of food, spare parts, machinery) interrupt production in ways which are unresponsive to changes in the prices of inputs or outputs; if wages are higher than the opportunity costs of labour; or if unemployment cannot be eliminated by any feasible redistribution of resource use in the short run. These and other commonly observed features in developing countries may be sufficient seriously to impede a market-driven process of growth. Liberalizing may not help because, under such circumstances, the market itself is precisely the problem to be addressed.

In these two respects, then, neo-liberals have been particularly uncautious, and lay themselves open to attack from more careful analysts working within the orthodox tradition. Furthermore, economists who are more comfortable with structuralist assumptions will find themselves disagreeing with many, and probably most, of the twenty-one propositions given above. We should grant that neo-liberals have done at least two important things. They have identified—and analysed seriously—some economic aspects of government failure, pointing out new aspects of the costs of intervention at the same time. This is the area where they have been most innovative, in both theoretical and empirical terms. Second, the writings of neo-liberals have reminded other theorists and policy-makers of the power and importance of price as an allocation mechanism. In both of these senses, the list of propositions deserves close attention. It falls far short, however, of providing the new overall policy and research agenda which is claimed by its advocates. As the papers in this book demonstrate, the reality remains much more complex: desirable reforms to development policy are not—either in theory or in practice—so simple as neo-liberals wish to make them sound.

Notes

1. In addition to Arthur Lewis, a list of major contributors to the structuralist economic theory of development would include Chenery, Hirschman, Myrdal, Nurkse, Prebisch, Rosenstein-Rodan, Seers, Singer, Streeten, and Tinbergen. There is, of course, a large 'second generation' of structuralist writers, although to select individuals for particular mention would be both invidious and more contentious.
2. The extent to which pricing policy was ignored in some prominent structuralist writings is examined—for the important case of agricultural products—in an earlier paper (Colclough 1985). In addition to factors already mentioned, it appears either that structuralists overlooked the typical extent of agricultural price repression by developing country governments, or that it was viewed—misguidedly—as a necessary means of raising investible resources for industrialization.
3. In that context, the diversity of structuralist strategy in comparison with that of orthodoxy can be seen by comparing the very different recommendations of the employment missions to Colombia and Kenya (ILO 1970, 1972) with the startingly similar advice which was proffered to these two countries—and, of course, many others—by the international financial institutions (IFIs) a decade later (World Bank 1988).
4. John Toye, who provides an important analysis of the intellectual genealogy of neo-liberalism (which he terms 'the counter-revolution in development theory and policy') attributes a central role in its early influence to the writings of Harry Johnson (Toye 1987).
5. Bela Balassa, Anne Krueger, and Deepak Lal each held senior posts at the World Bank during this period. Elliot Berg led a team which produced the World Bank's first major neo-liberal applied policy statement. It addressed the growing development crisis in Sub-Saharan Africa, attributing its emergence over-whelmingly to domestic policy mistakes, rather than to world recession, declining terms of trade, drought, war, or other exogenous factors (World Bank 1981).

Alan Walters, so influential with the new Conservative Prime Minister in Britain, had—jointly with Peter Bauer—strongly criticized leading development economists (Bauer and Walters 1975), and had advised the World Bank, *inter alia*, on the privatization of transport systems in developing countries (Walters 1979).

6. This, for example, is the most prominent conclusion in Lal's pamphlet (Lal 1983: 106); it encapsulates the whole thrust of Little's critique of structuralism (Little 1982) and of Bauer's fulminations about 'the state of economics' (Bauer 1981: 255–66).

References

Balassa, B. (1978), 'Exports and Economic Growth: Further Evidence', *Journal of Development Economics*, 5 (June): 181–9.

—— and Associates (1971), *The Structure of Protection in Developing Countries*, Johns Hopkins University Press, Baltimore, Md.

—— —— (1982), *Development Strategies in Semi-Industrial Economies*, Johns Hopkins University Press, Baltimore, Md. (for the World Bank).

Bates, R. H. (1981), *Markets and States in Tropical Africa*, University of California Press, Berkeley, Calif.

—— (1983), *Essays on the Political Economy of Rural Africa*, Cambridge University Press, Cambridge.

Bauer, P. T. (1981), *Equality, the Third World and Economic Delusion*, Weidenfeld & Nicolson, London.

—— (1984), 'Remembrance of Studies Past: Retracing First Steps', in Meier and Seers (1984): 27–43.

—— and Walters, A. A. (1975), 'The State of Economics', *Journal of Law and Economics* (Apr.): 1–23.

Bhagwati, J. N. (1978), *Foreign Trade Regimes and Economic Development: Anatomy and Consequences of Exchange Control Regimes*, Ballinger, Cambridge, Mass.

Chenery, H. B., and Strout, A. M. (1966), 'Foreign Assistance and Economic Development', *American Economic Review*, 56: 680–733.

—— *et al.* (1974), *Redistribution with Growth*, Oxford University Press, Oxford and London.

Colclough, C. (1983), 'Are African Governments as Unproductive as the Accelerated Development Report Implies?', *IDS Bulletin*, 14/1: 24–9.

—— (1985), 'Competing Paradigms in the Debate about Agricultural Pricing Policy', *IDS Bulletin*, 16/3: 39–46.

—— and Green, R. H. (1988), *Stabilisation—for Growth or Decay?*, *IDS Bulletin*, 19/1.

Cornia, G., Jolly, R., and Stewart, F. (1988), *Adjustment with a Human Face*, ii: *Ten Country Case Studies*, Oxford University Press, Oxford.

Donges, J. B. (1976), 'A Comparative Survey of Industrialisation Policies in 15 Semi-industrial Countries', *Weltwirtschaftliches Archiv*, 112/2: 627–59.

Harbison, F., and Myers, C. (1964), *Education, Manpower and Economic Growth*, McGraw-Hill, New York.

ILO (1970), *Towards Full Employment: A Programme for Colombia*, Geneva.

—— (1972), *Employment, Incomes and Equality: A Strategy for Increasing Productive Employment in Kenya*, Geneva.

Jolly, R. (1975), 'Redistribution with Growth: a Reply', *IDS Bulletin*, 7/2: 9–17.

Kaldor, N. (1972), 'The Irrelevance of Equilibrium Economics', *Economic Journal*, 82 (Dec.): 1237–55.

Killick, T. (1984), *The IMF and Stabilisation: Developing Country Experiences*, Gower, in Association with the Overseas Development Institute, London.

Krueger, A. O. (1974), 'The Political Economy of the Rent-seeking Society', *American Economic Review*, 64/3 (June): 291–303.

—— (1978), *Foreign Trade Regimes and Economic Development: Liberalisation Attempts and Consequences*, Ballinger, Cambridge, Mass.

—— (1980), 'Trade Policy as an Input to Development', *American Economic Review*, Papers and Proceedings, 70 (May): 288–92.

Kuznets, S. (1955), 'Economic Growth and Income Inequality', *American Economic Review*, 45 (Mar.): 1–28.

Lal, D. (1983), *The Poverty of 'Development Economics'*, Institute of Economic Affairs, London.

Lewis, W. A. (1955), *The Theory of Economic Growth*, Allen & Unwin, London.

Leys, C. (1975), 'The Politics of Redistribution with Growth', *IDS Bulletin*, 7/2: 4–8.

Lipsey, R. G., and Lancaster K. (1956–7), 'The General Theory of Second Best', *Review of Economic Studies*, 26 (Dec.): 11–32.

Little, I. M. D. (1982), *Economic Development: Theory, Policy and International Relations*, Basic Books, New York.

—— Scitovsky, T., and Scott, M. F. G. (1970), *Industry and Trade in Some Developing Countries*, Oxford University Press, London, Oxford, New York.

Meade, J. (1961), *A Neo-classical Theory of Economic Growth*, Unwin, London.

Meier, G., and Seers, D. (1984), *Pioneers in Development*, Oxford University Press, Oxford.

Michaely, M. (1977), 'Exports and Growth: An Empirical Investigation', *Journal of Development Economics*, 4 (Mar.): 49–53.

Myrdal, G. (1957), *Economic Theory and the Underdeveloped Regions*, Duckworth, London.

Nurkse, R. (1953), *Problems of Capital Formation in Under-developed Countries*, Oxford University Press, Oxford.

Oshima, H. (1962), 'The International Comparison of Size Distribution of Family Incomes with Specific Reference to Asia', *Review of Economics and Statistics*, 44 (Nov.): 439–45.

Prebisch, R. (1950), *The Economic Development of Latin America and its Principal Problems*, United Nations, New York.

Ram, R. (1986), 'Government Size and Economic Growth', *American Economic Review*, 76/1 (Mar.).

Rosenstein-Rodan, P. (1943), 'Problems of Industrialisation of Eastern and South-Eastern Europe', *Economic Journal*, 53 (June–Sept.): 202–11.

—— (1957), 'Notes on the Theory of the "Big Push"', MIT Centre for International Studies, Cambridge, Mass.

Seers, D. (1969), 'The Meaning of Development', *International Development Review*, 11/4.

Sen, A. K. (1980), 'Levels of Poverty: Policy and Change', World Bank Staff Report, 401, Washington, DC.

Singer, H. (1950), 'Distribution of Gains between Investing and Borrowing Countries', *American Economic Review*, Papers and Proceedings, 40 (May): 473–85.

Smith, A. (1970), *The Wealth of Nations*, Penguin, Harmondsworth.

Taylor, L. (1988), *Varieties of Stabilization Experience*, Clarendon Press, Oxford.

Tinbergen, J. (1958), *The Design of Development*, Johns Hopkins University Press, Baltimore, Md.

Toye, J. (1987), *Dilemmas of Development*, Blackwell, Oxford.

Walters, A. A. (1979), 'Costs and Scale of Bus Services', World Bank Staff Working Paper, 325, Washington, DC.

White, G. (ed.) (1988), *Developmental States in East Asia*, Macmillan, London.

—— and Wade, R. (1988), 'Developmental States and Markets in East Asia: An Introduction', in White (1988): 1–29.

World Bank (1981), *Accelerated Development in Sub-Saharan Africa: An Agenda for Action*, Washington, DC.

—— (1987), *World Development Report*, Oxford University Press, New York.

—— (1988), 'Adjustment Lending: An Evaluation of Ten Years of Experience', Policy and Research Series, 1, Country Economics Department, Washington, DC.

2
Market Relaxation and Agricultural Development

MICHAEL LIPTON

> There, at one Passage, oft you might survey
> A Lye and Truth contending for the way;
> And long 'twas doubtful, both so closely pent,
> Which first should issue through the narrow Vent:
> At last agreed, together out they fly,
> Inseparable now, the Truth and Lye.
>
> (Pope 1710: ii. 489–94)

1. Introduction

Neo-liberalism in developing countries (LDCs) comprises market relaxation (MR) 'closely pent' with state compression (SC). The case for agro-rural MR needs to be moderated and modified, in particular by shifting the emphasis from corrected prices towards derestricted exchanges, but is in essence a truth (section 2, below). It is shown elsewhere (Lipton 1989) that the case for agro-rural SC, while it contains sensible ideas, is in essence a lie. Liberalizing 'adjustment' packages have disappointed (section 3, below), in part because the truth has been impeded, in its useful application to agriculture, by the 'inseparable' lie.

It is above all the benefits for agriculture that are stressed by neo-liberal arguments for MR, especially for relaxing foreign trade and exchange rate regimes. Such arguments make little sense as pleas to 'get the prices right' in isolation—let alone to leave it to market forces to *let* them come right. Many features of LDC agriculture render such formulas unfeasible, undesirable, or sometimes meaningless. However, substantial—not total—relaxation of many agro-rural (AR) factor and product markets will, if carefully phased, eventually bring some improvement in growth, efficiency, and equity to most LDCs. This is usually done more effectively by relaxation of constraints on exchange than by price relaxation alone (section 2, below).

Yet MR has often produced disappointing results, because linked—initially by ideology, more recently by fiscal crisis—to agro-rural SC. The arguments for such linkage do not stand up. It is false that state commodity provision in LDCs (*a*) as such, rather than monopoly power, tends to increase rents, inefficiency, or inequity (Nellis and Kikeri 1989: 66); (*b*) has been growing rapidly; (*c*) is substantially to blame for fiscal crises; (*d*) crowds private enterprise out (much more than in); (*e*) retards GNP growth; (*f*) causes, rather than embodies or redirects, urban bias; (*g*) is justified only (or, indeed, necessarily) for public, merit, and/or basic goods (Lipton 1989).

Indeed, MR requires that states bear much of the cost of market development. Just as there is no free lunch, so there is no free market; markets are expensive. Agricultural risk and information are so structured that growing state involvement is usually a prerequisite of effective MR. Yet declines in state activity in LDCs—whether brought about by adjustment programmes stressing SC or by fiscal pressures—have borne disproportionately upon outlays for agriculture and rural development (Mosley and Smith 1988: 11–13, 25; Faaland *et al.* 1988: III. 18–20, 66; Pinstrup-Andersen 1989: 99) and investment (World Bank 1988*a*: 42, 62; Commander 1989: 129, 150, 170, 177, 195, 233). This directly undermines the bases for response to agro-rural MR (Lipton 1987, Lipton and Longhurst 1989). This is sufficiently obvious that we must seek deeper reasons for the neo-liberal 'yoking' of truth to lie, of MR to undermining SC; two such reasons, public-sector deficits and centralized repression, are briefly examined in section 4, and alternatives are proposed to a fruitless quest for 'smaller states'.

2. Market Relaxation (MR) and Agriculture

In any case, who would seriously think of minimizing the role of the *market*? . . . The market spells liberation, openness, access to another world. It means coming up for air. (Braudel 1985: 26)

Policies that ignore or fight the incentives provided by, and the options for, market exchange sometimes help the poor for a while, but normally fail, and retard development in the attempt. However, markets, while lethal opponents and excellent if sometimes risky servants, are doubtful masters. Hence MR that relies on letting prices return to levels uninfluenced by state action—even if, as is doubtful, that is feasible for a state with significant income or outlay—is less clearly justified than MR that seeks to remove 'artificial' barriers, and stimuli, affecting exchanges.

Market relaxation is the removal of restraints upon movement of relative prices, quantities, and qualities of commodities and factors exchanged towards levels that clear the markets. Neo-liberals have emphasized that MR can contribute significantly to agricultural performance in many LDCs, and that government actions to affect macro-economic variables, especially exchange rates (Krueger, Schiff, and Valdes 1988), often do more to impede MR—and to harm agro-rural performance—than direct interventions in agricultural micro-markets. Neo-liberals have developed these important points with new rigour, detail, and sophistication.

However, the points themselves are not new. When the damage to agriculture in many LDCs from foreign-exchange management, especially overvaluation, was reviewed fourteen years ago, Lipton (1977: 321–3) could draw on an already substantial literature. It included numbers for the 'damage' in Kenya and Argentina, and pioneering work by Little *et al.* (1970), Balassa *et al.* (1971), Lewis (1972), and others.[1]

Market suppression (MS) has harmed rural people by distorting the structure of their outputs and incomes and by discouraging exchanges. However, the problems about treating agro-rural MS as the main disease affecting LDC agricultures, and MR via state deregulation of price as its main cure, are also familiar.

First, agro-rural MS is in most LDCs only a small part of state actions and inactions by which, in order to increase urban income, rural income or output is (often unintentionally) reduced. Zaïre's government spends less than 3 per cent of its outlays on agriculture and rural development, yet donors felicitate it for abandoning forms of MS that, fortunately, it never had the power or will to enforce.

Second, much anti-agricultural MS takes place through private actions, ranging from locally monopsonistic trading or credit to quasi-feudal extraction. Public-sector legal or market interventions—public MS—may then be needed to *reduce* private, and hence overall, MS. They may involve new distortions among prices facing farmers, and/or new corruptions or inefficiencies. These consequences of public MS, however, *may* reduce farmers' income by less than they gain from the alleviation of private MS.

Third, where state power is persuaded or compelled to diminish its own anti-agricultural MS, the national balance of power will often ensure compensating rural-to-urban transfers. These will often prove more harmful to farmers, and/or less avoidable, than the MS they replace. Such new harms are especially likely if the MR takes place in a context of scarce public-sector resources and SC. Then, powerful urban interests will accept the MR only if the costs of SC—reduced public outlays on health, education, roads, etc.— are borne largely by rural people (see section 1 above for references).

Fourth, numerous and dispersed small farmers come to understand MS, and rationally to anticipate its operations and fluctuations. They thus trade in parallel markets; or switch to products, inputs, or services where MS is absent, and/or expensive or difficult to enforce; or consume more of what they produce. Even allowing for the new costs[2] of such avoidance of MS, as a rule it greatly reduces net costs from MS before liberalization. Since MS was less effective than it seemed, gains from MR are less than reformers anticipate.

Fifth, in small part for the above reason,[3] *total* farm output, unlike single-crop output, is usually highly price-inelastic, especially in the short term (during which the political viability of MR packages is tested), but even in the longer term (Binswanger 1989, Chibber 1989, Lipton 1987). A 10 per cent rise in farm output prices, relative to all other prices, normally generates much less extra farm output than a 10 per cent rise in the rate of technical progress (due, say, to agricultural research),[4] or even in general government expenditure on agriculture (Cleaver 1985).

Sixth—although the last point invites the retort that MR is 'free', as extra government expenditure on agriculture is not—MR for agriculture in fact has costs. GNP gain, from aggregate farm supply response to better relative prices, is partly[5] offset by GNP loss from aggregate non-farm supply response to relative prices.[6]

Seventh, improved LDC incentives to grow crops in world-wide price-inelastic demand may, if successful in raising supply, transfer income from developing to developed countries.

Eighth, MR often takes the form of reduced subsidies to farm inputs. Such subsidies, however, may be justifiable to encourage risk-taking,[7] or to correct, in part, for economic interventions damaging to farmers.

Ninth—although MR induces farmers who are X-efficient, technically efficient, and price-efficient to move closer to the 'correct' point on their production possibility surface, and to exchange 'correct' amounts of farm products—MR need not do anything, statically, to move farmers closer to that surface (to reduce X-inefficiency); nor to provide them with correct and timely information about technical options for reaching (or moving on) that surface, or about relative prices of factors and products. If MR, by reducing income (even extractive income) of parastatals, denies a genuinely developmental state resources to improve agricultural extension or market information, it might bring *increases* in technical, price, or X-inefficiency.

Tenth, MR need not help to raise the potential rate of growth of outward movement of the economy's production possibility surface. Indeed, since $g = sc$—growth is the product of the savings ratio and the marginal output/capital ratio—MR that reduces the tax take by lowering farm price repression (while otherwise justified) may on its own reduce public savings (by more than any induced rise in private savings). This offsets its effect in raising farm efficiency. The impact on growth is indeterminate.

Finally, unless price distortions are substantial, governments and their agencies may lack the information needed to 'correct' them. That is especially likely for a product which is an import in some years and an export in others;[8] or when world prices are fluctuating substantially, or are themselves distorted by actions of other countries that may change substantially (such as EEC cereals policy).

All these objections—not to MR, but to undue reliance on it as an agricultural cure-all—were familiar when summarized in Lipton (1987), Mosley and Smith (1988), and Commander (1989). So, of course, was the generally good case for MR. Must rural people suffer in each generation—

first from MS, later from naïve overconfidence in the effects of unassisted MR—'to save those who have no imagination'? Such lack of professional imagination arises because the market relaxers and the objectors are both essentially 'right, but . . .' in their views of agricultural development. Each side, 'knowing' it is right, mishears or misunderstands—and thus in effect ignores—the 'buts' of its opponents.

The market relaxers are right that restraints upon economic activity limit the long-term development of agriculture and the rural sector. But the market relaxers are wrong when, as often, they imply that MR usually (*a*) comprises mainly 'getting the prices right', (*b*) is achieved mainly by government abstention from 'distorting' markets (in farm output and input prices, and above all in foreign exchange), (*c*) can often achieve, on its own, large and rapid rises in total farm output, or (*d*) can substitute for, or induce, institutional (structural) or technical changes sufficient to permit a big response to market incentives.

Conversely, the objectors are right that—save in extreme cases like Ghana in 1975–81—MR does less for farm output, income, or growth than institutional or technical changes of comparable economic cost and political difficulty. But, if rural-to-urban resource extractors are strong enough to suppress or distort many agricultural markets, the objectors are wrong to expect technical or structural change (*a*) to happen, or (*b*) if it does, to bring major gains to many farmers, or, therefore, to induce or enable them to use the improved techniques or institutions.

Both market relaxers and objectors are wrong when (as often) they imply that state action or abstention is exogenous to intra-rural or rural-urban power relationships, yet can greatly affect them. It is these power-structures that largely determine whether rural people can obtain resources, to some extent at the cost of urban people—whether via better prices following MR, or via other means stressed by the objectors (irrigation, roads, land reform). If the state includes, or represents, mainly powerful interest groups, it will in the long run—after it has the adjustment loan—act accordingly. If the state is outside (or weak relative to) such groups, its 'concessions'— towards agricultural MR, or towards institutional reforms and public sector rural inputs stressed by the objectors—will be offset by other, rurally harmful, 'concessions' to the wealthy, the urban, the rent-seekers. Only a more active, balanced, probably open civil society can secure lasting reform—whether of rural-urban MS, or of public spending on rural life chances.

We must 'unpack' MR and MS to make further progress. MS is PS plus ES, price suppression plus exchange suppression. Neo-liberals have concentrated on the case against agricultural PS, and for price relaxation (PR). PR is the removal of PS: of actions, or inactions, inhibiting movement towards 'appropriate', or 'undistorted', prices. However, another component of agricultural MR is exchange relaxation, ER, which is the removal of ES: of actions, or inactions, inhibiting movement towards appropriate or undistorted *exchanges*.

The primary economic relationship is the offer to exchange. PS is only one way in which governments, monopolists, or others seek to 'distort' agricultural markets. ES—from interlocking factor markets and bond-slavery through import quotas to roadblocks—is in most LDCs harder to evade, and covers more commodities and factors, than PS. Although elementary economics ensures that ES normally affects prices as well as exchanged quantities and qualities (and that PS affects exchanged items as well as prices), there is a valid distinction between actions designed, or tending, mainly to alter prices and those affecting mainly options and conditions of exchange.

It is usually simpler to identify ES than PS. An indirect tax or tariff induces some economic relationships and deters others, and the net effect of what is apparently PS may *reduce* MS, if, say, pre-tax relationships were greatly influenced by monopoly power. Apparent ES, however, is more certain to be real ES and MS; a roadblock clearly distorts (by rendering fruitless) offers of exchange that potentially exchanging parties would otherwise have deemed desirable. This is not to say that all ER is desirable—exchanges can spread drugs or bombs—but only that there is more agreement about the definition, and the undesirability, of 'distortion' by ES than by PS.

For example, structures of incentives (except among pure tradables with zero transport costs) may be greatly influenced by 'landlord power and the importance of land rent' (Sarris 1987: 9), or by demands out of inherited (rather than earned) incomes; a price intervention could curtail such influences and actually help MR. Or 'distortions' from today's border prices may bring internal prices closer to tomorrow's border prices, or next year's. Hence, while second-bestness should not be used as a lazy excuse for large price 'distortions', it does cast doubt on policy conditions that imply confidence, within (say) 30 per cent, about where a price ought to be. And apparent price 'distortions' are usually likely to be reduced, by transactors in parallel markets, to well below 30 per cent of border prices (albeit at some cost). Moreover, the PS that does get corrected all too often concentrates on price 'distortions' that, prior to correction, had compensated farmers for other wrongs.

Probably for such reasons, in 1968–75 many economists—liberal and structuralist—emphasized the case for MR, by reducing not PS but state reliance on one form of ES: quotas and licences to import or invest. This earlier case for MS stressed the advantages of achieving a given set of goals by 'general controls' through price *policy* (Myrdal 1968, chapter 19 and appendix 8, especially p. 2077); quotas should give way to tariffs, or preferably indirect taxes, to the extent possible at uniform and low rates (Little *et al.* 1970; Balassa 1971). The neo-liberal approach in the 1980s instead emphasized price *mechanisms* (letting, rather than setting, the prices right), and PR rather than ER. This is not an improvement, especially for agriculture.

Knudsen and Nash (1989: 6–7) write:

60 percent of [World Bank] adjustment loans, and [all but one] agricultural sector [loans,] included agricultural pricing conditionality. [The grounds are that,] since prices are the primary determinant of the incentive structure for agriculture, an almost universal concern of adjustment loans has been to 'get the prices right'.

Hence in twenty-one agricultural sector loans in fiscal years 1980–8, product price reforms appeared before lending in seventeen cases and as loan conditions in fifteen; for input price reforms the numbers were fourteen and fifteen respectively; for deregulation—in essence ER—zero and three (ibid.). Market liberalizers may be wrong to focus on state actions disturbing farm prices, rather than on reducing physical barriers in the public-sector and private-sector environment that affect farm incentives to production and exchange.

The power of PR to reach farmers is weakened because—with incentives dependent on *relative* prices—at least three sets of ratios are involved; particular acts of PR can move them in different ways. The price of a farm product (or an index of farm product prices) can change relative to the price of (*a*) farm inputs, (*b*) consumer goods purchased by farming families, or (*c*) farm families' land, labour, and capital in alternative uses—including non-farm uses. Getting some of these price-ratios moving in the 'right' direction may not help other ratios to do so—may, indeed, make matters worse. Bell (1974), in a simple but instructive model, has traced very different effects on marketed surplus where big and small farmers face an improved (reduced) price ratio of inputs to outputs, (*a*) above, or of consumer goods to output, (*b*) above.

As for (*c*), prices of farm factors in alternative uses (relative to prices of some or all farm outputs), it is sometimes argued that within farming these need not complicate, let alone vitiate, a policy of PR. It is argued, for example, that accelerated food output normally accompanies accelerated non-food farm output. The cross-country evidence that 'export and food crops complement each other' (World Bank 1986: 78) is quite unpersuasive (Lipton 1987: 208; for the Ivory Coast, see Bassett 1988). Between farming and non-farming, increased price ratios can attract back some types of capital and of migrant workers to agriculture and increase its long-run price response; but the factor supply elasticities have never been carefully investigated. Food price rises temporarily raise relative rewards to farm labour—but are transmitted to industrial wage costs. That again reduces the relative attractiveness of farmwork. This offset does not apply to export-crop price rises (e.g. from government marketing agencies), but here the fiscal effects may alter relative factor rewards in farm and non-farm sectors.

Advocates of PR seek corrections of distortions in all four types of price affecting agriculture: of outputs, inputs (including interest rates), consumables, and factor rewards in alternative uses. If all four types of price become less distorted at about the same time, all might be well (although some of the *ratios* might actually become more distorted)—but for the fact that agriculture is not a point-input, point-output process. To take advantage of devaluation, farmers must often buy fertilizer (made dearer by devaluation) before they can sell extra crop (also made dearer by devaluation), and must meanwhile bear the extra cost of seasonal lending (often at interest rates raised by the adjustment conditions).

Anyway, the four types of price seldom improve at desired relative speeds (seldom specified, let alone justified, in PR conditions upon adjustment lending). Nor are all price changes equal in the speed of their effects. This has major, neglected policy consequences. When in the farming year should a 'one-season LDC' devalue? Before or after the seeds are planted, the basal or top dressing of fertilizer purchased, the crop sold? The effects of the choice on the short-run rates at which the four prices adjust, or at which farmers respond—and hence on farm incentives and profits—can be large.

In particular, budgetary realities render parastatals readier to cut input subsidies than to raise farm output prices to market levels, and conditions on the former in adjustment loans have been more fully implemented (Knudsen and Nash 1989: 9–10). This imbalance is increased by the fact that in much of Africa parastatals handle a much larger proportion of purchased farm inputs than of total, or even purchased, farm outputs. Governments are especially reluctant to maintain increases in farm-gate prices of food where, as in Zambia, urban consumers have the political clout to minimize offsetting rises in consumer prices, throwing the whole strain of improved farm-gate prices onto the budget. If domestic price reform, or devaluation, is timed before sowing, it might seem the best way to encourage farmers to grow more tradables; but that timing affects farm incomes via increased fertilizer prices now, via increased food prices only at harvest time and if the government dares, and via increased export crop prices at harvest and if world prices hold up. Selective PR can leave many farmers poorer and with worse incentives than before.

Even if all three ratios enjoy PR in parallel, it is not clear that 'prices are the primary determinant of the incentive structure for agriculture' (ibid. 7) except in the short run, for two reasons. First, the farmers' share of a border price depends on costs and competitiveness in marketing, not just on the degree of state PS. Second, profits per unit of an input, and hence the incentive to purchase units (and the total profits), depend not only on the price ratio of inputs to output(s), but also on the transformation ratio of inputs to outputs.

A switch to a dwarf cereal variety sometimes doubles output from a given set of inputs. If both farmer and country are price-takers, that doubles price-incentives, relative to other activities of production, input purchase, or consumption. Such a large change is unlikely to be achieved by any fiscally and politically sustainable set of PR decisions. These can help to stimulate adoption, or in some cases generation, of the technology to permit the big leaps in incentive—but, if feasible, an 'incentive-doubling technology' probably pays farmers (and stimulates researchers) despite the limited '15–30% PS' which is all that states can usually implement.[9]

Suppose, however, the prices to be relaxed are definable and are the main impact on farmers' incentives. What should governments do, or refrain from doing? The first attempt is often to reduce PS by parastatals—even to eliminate them. However, parastatals that greatly 'distort' farm prices have usually already lost most business to parallel markets. In Mali, OPAM at its high point handled 'merely 3–6% of total production' (Staatz *et al.* 1989: 705; compare Commander *et al.* 1989*b*, for Senegal). Green (1989: 40) writes:

A rough estimate for sub-Saharan Africa . . . is that 75 percent of domestic food is self-provisioning . . . About 13–15 percent relates to [products without] official prices, another 5 percent is parallel marketed . . . Trying to raise output by acting on [the remaining 5 to] 7 percent of output . . . is hardly likely to be spectacularly effective.

The second main attempt to implement PR is via real effective devaluation (RED). Just as farmers had avoided (via parallel markets) substantial PS by parastatals, so, before RED, they had avoided (by smuggling) substantial PS via currency overvaluation. However, RED benefits farmers over a wide range of economic activities, if tradables form a larger proportion of output, and smaller proportions of purchased inputs and consumption, for farmers than for non-farmers.

That is often asserted, but seldom are the inequalities proved. The proportion of purchased consumption comprising tradables is probably often larger for food-deficit farmers—often the majority—than for towns-people. Hence these poor farmers lose from RED, relatively to others and absolutely, as the price of their consumption bundle increases. Their ratio of input purchases to value-added is, especially in Africa, lower than for commercial farmers or for urban producers, so that they gain relatively as RED increases the price of tradable inputs—but they lose absolutely. As for outputs, many (though not most) African farmers grow mainly crops that are virtually non-tradable. Often, such items have weight/value ratios too high (given long distances and poor transport) to compete with grain imports in, or to be exported via, urban markets.

Nevertheless, RED is likely to favour farmers and to permit (via extra income) and encourage (via price incentives) higher levels of farm sales and probably outputs. But the extent of such effects (as with parastatal liberal-ization) is likely to be much smaller, slower, less sure, and less widely applicable than required to justify neo-liberals' strong emphasis on PR, especially RED, as a help to farmers by its impact on incentives to sell (and to grow?) tradables.

In addition, tradables and non-tradables often (*a*) are inputs into each other's production, or into intermediates for it; (*b*) compete with each other for consumers' outlays; (*c*) complement each other in crop rotations or labour timings; (*d*) provide incomes spent upon each other. Hence—even without introducing the most basic distinctions among tradable products (importable but quota-restricted; normally importable; normally exportable (Demery 1988); or marginal between importable in years of poor harvests and exportable, as with the main food staple in many African countries)—the simplistic textbook portrait of 'adjustment' is terribly misleading.

In this portrait, the relative price of tradables to non-tradables is increased via PR. That induces profit-maximizing farmers to select an operating point, on the production possibility frontier, from which (with trade) more goods can be commanded than before. Of course, sophisticated modelling of the gain from PR goes far beyond such textbook heuristics. Yet these underlie the propaganda of adjustment. Moreover, even the complex models seldom handle the above interactions between tradables and non-tradables. All four weaken the impact, on the ratio between their prices and therefore (via supply response) their net outputs, of RED.

In summary, tradable/non-tradable price-ratios are less, and less clearly, affected by RED than appears at first sight; and, even if affected, impinge less, and less universally, on farmers. Further, governments often cannot achieve RED. Nominal devaluations were implied or explicit conditions in thirty-eight of forty countries receiving adjustment loans from the World Bank (1988*a*: 55); yet RED averaged 21 per cent in 'strongly reforming' countries of sub-Saharan Africa between 1980–2 and 1986–7, little more than the 17 per cent in the countries with 'weak or no' programmes (World Bank and UNDP 1989: 29). Indeed, for sub-Saharan African LDCs 'as a whole the trend in real exchange rates is upward until 1985 (with a slight downward movement thereafter), although it is much more convincingly downward after 1983 for the IDA [subset]' (Mosley and Smith 1988: 11).

Hence neither raising (or even eliminating) parastatal prices, nor nominal devaluation, need raise farm prices, relative to other prices in which farmers transact. Only in sub-Saharan Africa did countries receiving World Bank adjustment loans improve this relativity (on a rather subtle index[10]) as compared with countries not entering into adjustment lending operations (World Bank 1988*a*: 73–4). Yet in Africa these countries were less successful than otherwise comparable non-recipients of Bank adjustment loans in improving their growth rates or investment/GDP ratios (though more successful on foreign-balance indicators) (ibid. 41). This underlines doubts about the wisdom, not of agricultural PR, but of emphasizing it above ER—and about its prospects for substantial success, at least where fiscal shortage (and sometimes lending conditions) are reducing governmental capacity to help farmers respond to ER *or* PR.

In that environment, governments find it easier to remove input subsidies than to increase output prices. Partial PR by removal of fertilizer subsidies has increased overall extraction from the farm sector, and harmed farm output (on Bangladesh see Faaland *et al.* 1988: I–60). Even if output prices rise, distributional and incentive effects of partial PR among farmers can be perverse; higher prices for marketed surplus grains in Mali transferred income from deficit areas to areas that were already better endowed and wealthier, partly due to continuing selective public sector support (Staatz *et al.* 1989: 711–13).

All this is not to oppose agro-rural PR—only to caution against undue expectations from it. Farmers often avoid price distortions; the state often cannot greatly reduce them; they comprise only a small part of anti-rural discrimination (unbalanced public expenditure being usually much more important); and *aggregate* farm supply response to better prices is normally low (and partly offset by negative non-farm response to worse prices). But there is a good case, of course, against adding state price distortion or suppression to the farmers' other problems. If it offsets them, that needs to be shown. Merely to invoke second-bestness is not good enough.

Yet there are fundamental difficulties with the 'price-auction model' (Thurow 1983), on which the strong case for price abstentionism by the state rests. First, concentration on micro-economic effects of adjusting farm and foreign exchange prices omits Walrasian general-equilibrium effects (Sarris 1987: 31, 81, 87, 89; Norton 1987: 34–7). Second, micromarket price-to-output effects are also altered by general-equilibrium interactions of a Keynesian or input-output nature (Lipton with Longhurst 1989, chapter 6). Third, leaving such effects aside, even micro-economic incentive effects look different to a pure producer and to a multi-product household firm (such as a family farm), which responds not only to better farm prices by substituting farm output for other production, but also to higher income by substituting leisure for it. Fourth, even with only pure agricultural producers —farmers plus their employees—Pareto improvement from reduced price 'distortion' is not clear in the absence of full employment of labour (Demery 1988: 12).[11] Finally, the Pareto-optimizing performance of a set of exchange transactions in many commodities at undistorted prices—even at full employment, among firms hiring all labour and selling all output and ignoring macro-economic effects—depends either on zero risk or on perfect markets in contingent commodities (the Arrow–Debreu theorem) (Killick 1989). Either assumption is remote from rural reality in LDCs, especially in remote unirrigated areas. Given positive absolute risk aversion, that justifies some state actions there, both to reduce risks, and to raise farm-gate prices for risky but profitable farm outputs relative to others—and for safe but marginally profitable farm inputs and techniques relative to others.

These and other facts mean low aggregate agricultural price-elasticity of supply (p. 28, above). However, that is only one of three key points. In equations such as

$$\log S_t = a + b \log P_{t-1} + \epsilon$$

where S_t and P_{t-1} are dated indices of aggregate farm output and prices respectively, the problem is not simply (1) that b is small, but—just as seriously—(2) that the level of statistical significance of b is often low, and (3) that r^2 is often very low, revealing that most determinants of aggregate agricultural supply are left out, yet in an equation that does not permit comparison of the effects upon it of price adjustment with those of other adjustments. Much more sophisticated supply-to-price equations (including standard Nerlovian improvements) have been tested, but without satisfactorily meeting the above criticisms.

What are we arguing about? Nobody believes that the extraction of large parts of farm income, to enrich an otherwise uncompetitive urban sector, is sensible. The question is: how are states, heavily reliant on such processes for both tax base and political viability, to be helped to find alternatives? It is unhelpful to exaggerate the extent to which: past farm prices were *effectively* distorted; such distortion was due to the state; distortion can be durably corrected (by state withdrawal or otherwise) at low political or economic cost; distortions cause most extraction from, or other inequity towards, farmers and rural people; or aggregate farm output will expand (or will do so rapidly, or with little cost to non-farm output) in response to the price stimuli. Unfortunately, PR has often been required in lending conditions, alongside rhetoric that aroused such exaggerated expectations. PR has suffered from too much PR.

Advocates of PR as the key to policy reform may reply that PS, especially through inefficient and extractive parastatals and through overvalued domestic currencies, is the main form of state action impinging on agriculture in many LDCs, and (being plainly wrong) is therefore the main focus for policy reforms. Such a response, apart from being factually doubtful, raises three deeper problems. It implies an odd theory of why states do what they do, and therefore of how outsiders can durably influence them. It neglects the *in*actions by non-developmental states (failures to interact constructively with rural technologies, institutions, societies, health, roads, etc.), which are their main bad rural effect. Third, where state *actions* inhibit rural growth and equity via MS, they do so more clearly, and less avoidably, by exchange suppression, ES, than by PS.

Often, geography renders ES almost inescapable by farmers. In Sierra Leone, there is no economic way to get rice from the main surplus area (the mangrove swamps around the Great Scarcies river) to the main market, Freetown, except on a metalled road which is blocked by the army at 'Mile 39', increasing the costs and delays upon exchange in obvious ways. Even in as 'liberal' a country as Botswana in 1978–9, any adviser on employment was bound to note the numerous legal restrictions—upon rural and urban builders, housedwellers, hawkers of local products, transporters, traders, employers, and employees—that impeded exchange, and therefore employment and efficiency, with no clear gain to health or safety.[12]

Many such restrictions are colonial relics. Some protect larger producers (supermarket owners can often influence the granting of hawkers' licences). All can contribute to 'employment' for regulatory officials. Yet state or societal interests (and the case, if any) for most such regulations are weaker than those for many price distortions which do less damage. Also, the losers from a licensing or regulatory restraint on exchange know it (or think they do), and are therefore a potential political force: whereas the losers from domestic currency overvaluation, and more generally from all but the most transparent price distortions, are probably unaware at least of the size of their net loss, often of its sign, and are diffuse and hard to inform and organize (which is precisely why politicians are not thrilled by advice to cease PS so as to render policy effects 'transparent'). Policy advisers (and conditions) on rural MR would in most LDCs be more effective, as well as more efficient in raising GNP per unit of 'effect', if they were substantially switched from PR to ER.

3. Agricultural Performance of SC-MR Packages

Have adjustment packages been damaged by the undermining of MR by SC, or by the concentration of MR on price rather than exchange relaxation? It is difficult to assess their performance overall. First, many other things affect any nation's agriculture than simply SC and MR, notably weather; technology; pre-liberalization policies, with a time-lag; rising person/land ratios; and world prices. Second, world prices are also affected by other countries' SC-MR packages; if Ghana's package succeeds in stimulating cocoa production, the Ivory Coast loses both market share and (as Ghana's extra supplies reduce prices) unit revenue—and vice versa. Third, if a country initially had a very distorted set of farm prices and exchanges—and a very corrupt, extractive, or inefficient state machinery—an SC-MR package does more good for agriculture than if distortions were minor and the state fairly efficient and intersectorally neutral. Fourth, a country can more readily respond to SC-MR if it enjoys spare land and labour, or highly income-elastic supplies of rural savings, or new farm technologies near the margin of profitability. Finally, SC-MR packages differ greatly across countries, times, and even crops.

Careful evaluations of the agricultural impact of SC-MR to date are mostly neutral or negative. 'Countries with strong reform programmes' in Africa appear to have improved their *overall* performance—though not their GDP growth rates—somewhat more than others from 1980–4 to 1985–7; agricultural growth accelerated from 1.1 per cent annually to 2.6 per cent for strong reformers, and only from 1.3 per cent to 1.5 per cent for others. But this brief spurt (on terrible output data) is inconclusive, especially since the reformers' faster-rising aid inflows probably outweighed non-reformers' more favourable terms-of-trade movements[13] (World Bank/UNDP 1989: 27–8, 30).

As between recipients and selected comparable non-recipients of World Bank adjustment loans and conditions within each of the three most critical country groups for SC-MR reforms—Sub-Saharan Africa, low-income countries, and highly indebted countries—no significant difference is discernible in respect of success or failure in improving past performance on key indicators (World Bank 1988*a*: 39–42, 47). Part of the problem is partial or total failure to implement 40 per cent of conditions in World Bank adjustment loans, during or before the period of lending (ibid. 89). Of 54 World Bank project or policy loans with agricultural price conditions, Completion Reports (or Performance Audits) did not even report on compliance in 44 cases (World Bank 1988*b*: pp. iv, ix, 64).

Optimistic reports on 'model' adjusters, when looked at more closely, reveal disappointing agricultural outcomes, except where technical progress preceded or accompanied price reforms. Thus Ghana has been cited as 'something of a model case, an example to other African economies of the virtues of managed adjustments' in 1983–9; yet by 1986, despite some uptrend after 1983 in the (far from reliable) output data for main food crops and cocoa, both remained 'below the peak levels of the late 1960s' (Commander *et al.* 1989*a*: 107, 114). By 1986–8 the volume of average gross farm output per person was 3 per cent above 1977–9 levels (FAO 1989: 8).

However—perhaps due to the induced shift to cash crops with 'soft' world prices—agriculture's GDP contribution in Ghana did much worse. The trend rate of growth of *total* agricultural value added in 1965–80 was 1.6 per cent per year (population, 2.2 per cent); in 1980–7 it was zero (population, 3.4 per cent) (World Bank 1989: 116, 214). The true growth of farm GDP in the 1980s must have been not zero but significantly negative; for the post-1983 recovery in *recorded* cocoa output was due in 'significant proportion . . . to return to official marketing channels' of cocoa previously smuggled (Commander *et al.* 1989*a*: 113). From the late 1960s to 1989 'there is no evidence of any underlying upward trend in productivity' in agriculture (ibid. 114). It remains to be seen whether price incentives, alongside privatized cocoa input supplies (ibid. 116), will move agriculture forwards. New cocoa plantings were induced—but at what *world* price will their products be saleable, once the world's cocoa growers; not just Ghana's, have responded to PR?

Senegal, too, 'is commonly held up by donors as a model case of adjustment', and 'since 1983 the government has fulfilled all lending conditions satisfactorily' (Commander *et al.* 1989*b*: 146). Yet investment has borne the brunt of the falls in absorption, and 'the third World Bank structural adjustment loan' is alleged to expose 'the underlying lack of any strategy [other than] pricing and budget conditions' (ibid. 170), i.e. MR and SC respectively. From 1977 to 1988, big fluctuations in reported agricultural output-per-person drown out any trend (FAO 1989: 8), though growth of real agricultural GDP seems to have accelerated from 1.4 per cent in 1965–79 to 4.2 per cent in 1980–7 (World Bank 1989: 166). Groundnut and millet yields vary mainly with rainfall, and (in these very risky environments) not significantly with prices. With 'capital expenditures as a share of GDP . . . projected to remain at below 2.9 percent' through 1989 (Commander *et al.* 1989*b*: 150–1, 157), it is hard to see how either safer technologies for improved farming, or stocks to encourage family farmers to take risks with available technical improvements, are to be built up. Areas planted can still respond to price expectations; for yields to respond, however, risk-taking (and purchased input use) need to increase.

Such circumstances create a strictly neo-classical case to encourage risk-taking (and raise GNP) via limited, non-discriminatory subsidies for fertilizer.[14] Yet the phasing out of all such subsidies was a condition of the second World Bank SAL to Senegal. Such PR drastically raised fertilizer prices, reduced offtake (ibid. 162–3), and in the medium term surely damaged agricultural growth. That can be quantified for donor-conditioned reductions of fertilizer subsidy in Bangladesh; there, each 10 per cent rise in fertilizer prices induces a 6½–7½ per cent fall in offtake and hence a 1–1½ per cent fall in farm output (Faaland *et al.* 1988: I–60). Removal of fertilizer subsidies also harmed farm output in Malawi—another frequently claimed success for economic liberalization—partly due to the absence of resources or pressures for concomitant improvements in the supply of smallholder credit (Lele 1987: 5, 35–9). The earlier blanket opposition to farm input subsidies in MR-SC packages—even if such subsidies respond to a sound neo-classical case for encouraging risk-taking and correcting anti-rural biases elsewhere in public policy—may have reduced the medium-term impact of many such packages on farm output. Fortunately, donors are increasingly taking a more pragmatic view—though many LDC governments could do more for farmers by ER to liberalize amount, timing, and variety of fertilizer supply than by increased subsidies.

Some claims for agricultural success with MR-SC packages are dubious. In Zaïre, where output data are worthless for most crops (and where their reported trends are anyway unfavourable), the liberalizing courage of the government has been praised by the IMF and donors. The facts that previous illiberal MS was seldom enforceable and that agriculture and rural development still absorb less than 3 per cent of public spending often go unrecorded. The effectiveness of adjustment is left to be inferred from anecdotes, supported by verbal reports of surveys of unknown typicality or statistical significance (Thomas and Reintsma 1988: 29–35).

Zambia, too, is often claimed as a successful case of agricultural liberalization, at least until derailed by urban food riots in 1987 (Thomas and Weidemann 1988: 51). Indeed, an unusual combination of spare land, spare labour (potential return migrants), and improvable technology (maize hybrids) gives parts of Zambia better prospects than most of Africa for fairly price-elastic medium-term aggregate agricultural supply. Yet the evidence of 'success' turns out to rest on maize, on marketings, and on a year of good rainfall (1986) (ibid. 56–7). Total farm output per person for 1986–8 is reported at 19 per cent below the pre-liberalization levels of 1977–9 (FAO 1989: 8), although data are poor and climate not strictly comparable even between these three-year averages.

Turkey received five structural adjustment loans from the World Bank up to 1985, and three sectoral adjustment loans (i.e. loans imposing conditions, not as a rule supplying imports, concentrated on a sector, one in agriculture). The Bank's excellent *Review of Adjustment Lending* describes Turkey's adjustment as 'undoubtedly successful'. Yet agricultural output per person in 1986–8 was 1.7 per cent below the 1977–9 average (FAO 1989: 9).

The shining example of successful agricultural liberalization is supposedly China. The move from the brigade system towards (in effect) family farming, together with major PR and ER, helped to produce a big rise in farm output per person—at 5.7 per cent per year for the seven years from 1977 to 1984 (ibid. 8). This unprecedented growth includes some shifting from unrecorded to recorded output, as it became legal to sell at more attractive prices; but even 5 per cent growth for seven years, the likely minimum, is striking. Is this a vast and imitable example of the prospects of SC-MR packages?

Not exactly so. First, PS and ES before 1977 had been much more substantial, effective, and hard to escape than in most 'softer' LDCs. Second, it is not clear that a lot of SC was going on in absolute terms. Third, hundreds of years of state action to create rural infrastructures, especially irrigation but also education, transport, and research, had produced agricultural systems ready to respond more rapidly than in most LDCs. Fourth, China by the mid-1970s was a world leader in generating and spreading new rice technologies, especially seeds. Fifth, the combined momentum of new biological methods and old hydraulic infrastructures—especially when made more attractive by PR and ER—was great, but apparently used up its prospects fast; from 1984 to 1988 farm output per person stagnated, with non-foods doing rather worse than foods (ibid. 8). MR *perestroika* apparently gave China seven years in which to learn to expect annual growth in farm output per head at 5 per cent, followed by four years of stagnation: not a very stable prospect, especially without political *glasnost*.

Reverting to the Western 'success stories', we find some common threads that run through the disappointments: excessive withdrawal of a rurally *under*active state, slashing of (partly compensatory, partly risk-stimulating) farm input subsidies, and declining investment. In part underlying these problems is the growth in the debt service ratio in adjusting countries; they received aid loans designed to disburse more swiftly than older project loans, but by that same token (given the grace period) also requiring to be repaid sooner. In Ghana, 'external borrowing has ratcheted up the DSR . . . by 1987 [to over] 61 percent' (Commander *et al.* 1989*a*: 111). Senegal's was only 20 per cent—reduced from 30 per cent only by 'substantial rescheduling' —but there was also a net outflow of resources on capital account (Commander *et al.* 1989*b*: 148). Morocco's DSR was over 40 per cent by 1983 (Seddon 1989: 176). Turkey's was 23 per cent in 1970, but 34 per cent in 1987 (World Bank 1989: 208).

In 1987 DSR obligations—not all met—for IDA countries in Sub-Saharan Africa rose to 49 per cent (World Bank and UNDP 1989: 17). SC-MR liberalizers have proved somewhat likelier to obtain softer terms on their past debts, but much better able to attract official lending (not all conces- sional). These countries are therefore exposed to continued drains of scarce government funds to meet (overseas) debt obligations. Paradoxically, this erosion of states' fiscal capacities to support agricultural development—due in significant measure, at least for non-IDA adjusters, to the need to service past adjustment/stabilization lending from the World Bank, USAID, and implicitly the IMF—is becoming clear just as these agencies are shifting away from SC and trying to persuade governments to increase rurally orientated public investment. Yet this seldom yields much foreign exchange in forms swiftly appropriable by governments for debt servicing—especially once the marketing of export crops has been liberalized. High DSRs thus make costly rural public investment, even if complementary with MR, less appealing to governments.

4. Conclusion

International agencies are retreating from the more strident forms of neo- liberalism: from forms of PR shading into pricism (Lipton 1987), and from misguided attempts to support MR by forms of SC shading into state minimalism or libertarianism. Increasingly, the non-observance of SC and MR loan 'conditions', as well as the disappointing (or, as with rapid removal of fertilizer subsidies, counter-productive: ibid. 35) effect of some conditions where observed, have been recognized within lending agencies.

But *why* had neo-liberalism yoked a severely overstated and oversimplified version of a 'Truth' (the developmental usefulness of agro-rural MR) to a 'Lye' (the developmental necessity for agro-rural privatization, in the context of an extreme version of SC)? Such yoking is due in part to versions of ideologies for the transfer, to LDCs, of perceived Western successes of liberalization (an especially crude version is Gilder 1981); in part to the misperception that SC marked the successful experiences in South Korea and Taiwan (refuted in White 1988); but increasingly to unmanageable LDC public sector deficits, rising from 3.5 per cent of Third World GDP in 1972 to 7.7 per cent in 1987 (World Bank 1989: 185). These were caused mainly by interest burdens—up from 6.3 per cent of CELR (central government expenditure, plus lending, less capital repayments) by non-oil LDCs from 1976 to 18.4 per cent in 1986—and not by state expansion; indeed, investment meanwhile plummeted from 19.3 to 12.0 per cent of CELR (and agricultural outlays by central governments, from 6.3 to 4.8 per cent of GDP) (IMF 1984: 52, 61–3; 1988: 67, 74–7, 91).

The deficits have proved difficult to correct by higher taxation during recession. Hence SC appeals to some LDC governments, just as international agencies resile from it and encourage them to raise public investment. This the World Bank is now pressing upon several Latin American governments, as they protest that they lack the counterpart funds.

Yet there is a deeper reason, especially important for the rural sector, for the persistence of SC in many adjustment packages, and for its likely revival in others. Many neo-liberals see states in LDCs as predatory and monolithic Leviathans, and argue that their performance can be improved if and only if they can be rolled back to their proper scope. At best, such states then become developmental; at worst, defanged. Underlying such hopes is a neo-liberal political economy of the state as main source of rent-seeking (for individual gain), to the disadvantage of agriculture. Does this implicit account of power structures in LDCs correctly explain much urban bias, inequality, and misappropriation of potential economic surplus? If so, then—notwithstanding the flimsiness of the purely economic case for SC and its conflict with effective rural MR—there may be a *political* need for SC, if the state is to be so transformed that private production and exchange are permitted to realize the possibilities created by MR.

This perspective convinces neo-liberals that substantial SC alongside MR is required to assault not only stagnation but also poverty, inequality, and centralized repression. However, the neo-Hobbesian political economy that underlies such advocacy of SC, while correct about the interests of large parts of the state and of its private backers and clients, is wrong about the functioning, especially rurally, of both the state and the development process, and hence about the prospects for change. A state now enriching its agents and backers by centralized repression—especially as powerful urban centres act on a weak and dispersed rural mass—will not durably shift to SC because of lectures from foreigners whose loans it seeks for a few years.

Moreover, big and strong—but non-monolithic and competitive—states are needed for effective development. The best hope of impeding centralized repression is not to keep the state small by compression of its functions to such areas as 'public goods', but to keep an enlarging state honest by popular overview.

Such approach to MR via 'civil society' can no more be principally a gene transplant from donors (whether 'carried' though aid conditionally, as in the 1980s, or otherwise) than can the approach via SC. But export of political liberalism, or assistance to participatory civil societies, is more credible than of economic liberalism in its export temporary mid-1980s guise of MR-SC extremism, or advocacy of an *a*social market economy: an ideology rightly characterized by the conservative British journalist Peregrine Worsthorne, commenting on attitudes in Britain's 1987 election, as bourgeois triumphalism.

Luckily, MR-SC extremism is in decline (Killick 1989). However, a revival of intelligent neo-liberalism is likely, and probably desirable. Otherwise, in the next major recession, policy advice in and to LDCs may swing back from unintelligent neo-liberalism to naïve bureaucratic centralism. An evolution of neo-liberalism should take the form of more careful MR, supported by a political economy, not of how to persuade the state to compress itself, but of how poor rural groups can effectively take part in civil society, and can thus influence an inevitably enlarging and mainly urban state.

Notes

1. Valdes and Pinckney (1987: 2) may thus be wrong to claim that 'emphasizing trade and macro-economic policies' impact on agricultural growth . . . on the premise that agricultural incentives are derived as much from foreign trade as from sector-specific interventions [has], with few exceptions, so far . . . remained outside the scope of the debate on development strategies'.
2. Costs to farmers (and to those who transact with them) are obvious. Also, it creates atmospheres of corruption; of doubtful legality or worse; and in extreme cases of withering away of effective rural action by, and respect for, the state.
3. The main reason is that, whereas a farmer can respond to rises in the price of a single crop by raising its output through shifts of land and labour to it, he can respond to rises in a farm price index by raising total farm output only to the extent that (*a*) land and labour can be increased in quantity, or shifted from other activities into agriculture; and/or (*b*) a technology exists (and is pushed by the rise in the index across the margin, into profitability) permitting more output to be produced from the same inputs of land and labour—via extra capital, and/or more input-intensive use of existing land, labour, and capital.
4. Agricultural research outlays—largely public-sector in LDCs—do themselves respond to price incentives in the long run. However, achieved outputs of national AR show much weaker response to LDC prices (Binswanger and Ruttan 1978). Such outputs depend mainly on scientific discovery, plus (trans-

ferred) international technology generation. These are mainly structured, respectively, by peer judgements (and pressures); and by farmers', processors', and consumers' demands in the developed world.

5. The definition of a static intersectoral price 'distortion' implies net loss of real national product—i.e. that the extra output, induced from the sector enjoying an incentive due to the 'distortion', adds less to GNP in 'undistorted' prices than is deducted by the reduced value-added, induced by the corresponding disincentives, from other sectors.

6. Also political concessions, in the form of higher farm prices, can often be wrung from powerful urban groups only at the cost of often *more* damaging rural-to-urban shifts, e.g. of doctors.

7. Especially fertilizer use in water-insecure areas.

8. Zimbabwe has sought to offer maize farmers, via the parastatal, world price *less* marketing costs (including normal profit). However, in some years, the import parity price was offered, and proved much too high in a 'good' year when Zimbabwe was a net exporter.

9. At the extreme, if input price were effectively distorted from 100 to 130 and output price from 100 to 70, a technology doubling the input–output transformation ratio would more than correct the damage to farm income. Farmers would vote for the technology, even at the cost of suffering the distortion!

10. Official farm producers' prices (deflated by the consumer price index), relative to international reference prices (deflated by the index of unit value of manufactures). True farm prices presumably rose less than official prices in both sets of countries.

11. There is a strictly classical possibility of unemployment in very poor societies. If an equilibrium corn-wage would be too low to permit workforce survival, the wage rate must, structurally, be too high to clear the labour market. Then the state does better by increasing price incentives to (Leontief) labour-intensive 'mixes' of methods and products than by seeking neo-classical 'right prices'.

12. See Appendices 8.3–8.6 ('Effects of the laws against business', 'Licensing, trading and industrial legislation', 'Road transport and permit regulations', and 'Building and planning laws') in Lipton 1978, vol. ii.

13. The terms of trade (not just the aid) may have moved partly in response to the strong reforms—if they stimulated output of a group of crops in price-inelastic world demand, for countries with significant combined market share.

14. Risk-averse farmers, if water is not certain, select fertilizer inputs well below levels that equate expected marginal revenue and expected marginal cost. Taking good years with bad, it would raise net social product if farmers brought fertilizer input up to those levels. A fertilizer subsidy to induce this should, as a rule, be applied only if the government also permits supplies to rise to market-clearing levels.

References

Balassa, B. and associates (1971), *The Structure of Protection in Developing Countries*, IBRD/Johns Hopkins University Press, Baltimore, Md.

Bassett, I. (1988), 'The World Bank in the Ivory Coast', *Review of African Political Economy*, 41 (Sept.).

Bell, C. (1974), 'A Note on "Perverse" Producer Response to Changes in Prices', in D. Lehmann (ed.), *Agrarian Reform and Agrarian Reformism*, Faber, London.

Binswanger, H. (1989), 'How Agricultural Producers Respond to Prices and Government Investments', 1st Conference on Development Economics, World Bank, Apr.

—— and Ruttan, V. (eds.) (1978), *Induced Innovation: Technology, Institutions and Development*, Johns Hopkins University Press, Baltimore, Md.

Braudel, F. (1985), *The Wheels of Commerce* (tr. Sian Reynolds), Collins, London.

Chibber, A. (1989), 'The Aggregate Supply Response: A Survey', in Commander 1989.

Cleaver, K. (1985), *The Impact of Price and Exchange Rate Policies in sub-Saharan African Countries*, Staff Working Paper, No. 728, World Bank.

Commander, S. (ed.) (1989), *Structural Adjustment and Agriculture*, ODI and James Currey, London.

—— Howell, J., and Seini, W. (1989a), 'Ghana 1983–7', in Commander (ed.) 1989: 107–26.

—— Ndoye, O., and Ouedragu, I. (1989b), 'Senegal 1979–88', in Commander (ed.) 1989: 145–74.

Demery, L. (1988), 'Structural Adjustment, Smallholders and the Rural Poor: Scope, Concepts and Method', mimeo, IFAD, Oct.

Faaland, J., *et al.* (1988), *Bangladesh Agriculture: Performance, Resources, Policies and Institutions*, UNDP Independent Group, Dhaka, Dec.

FAO (1989), *Quarterly Bulletin of Statistics*, 2/1.

Gilder, G. (1981), *Wealth and Poverty*, Basic Books, New York.

Green, R. (1989), 'Articulating Stabilization Programmes and Structural Adjustment', in Commander (ed.) 1989: 35–54.

IMF (1984), *Government Finance Statistics Yearbook 1984*, Washington, DC.

—— (1988), *Government Finance Statistics Yearbook 1988*, Washington, DC.

Killick, A. (1989), *A Reaction Too Far: Economic Theory and the Role of the State in Developing Countries*, ODI.

Knudsen, O., and Nash, J. (1989), 'Agricultural Sector Adjustment Lending and Agricultural Policy', mimeo, World Bank, Mar.

Krueger, A., Schiff, M., and Valdes, A. (1988), 'Agricultural Incentives in Developing Countries: Measuring the Effects of Sectoral and Economy-wide Policies', *World Bank Economic Review*, 2/3: 255–71.

Lele, U. (1987), 'Structural Adjustment, Agricultural Development and the Poor: Some Observations on Malawi', mimeo, World Bank, 14 Dec.

Lewis, S. R. (1972), *Pakistan: Industrialization and Trade Policies*, OECD, Oxford.

Lipton, M. (1977)), *Why Poor People Stay Poor*, Temple Smith/Harvard.

—— (1978), *Employment and Labour Use in Botswana*, Ministry of Finance and Development Planning, Gaborone.

—— (1987), 'Limits of Price Policy for Agriculture: Which Way for the World Bank?, *Development Policy Review*, 5 (June): 197–215.

—— (1989), 'State Compression: Friend or Foe of Agricultural Liberalization?', in M. Dantwala (ed.), *Indian Agricultural Economics 1939–1989*, Indian Society of Agricultural Economics, Bombay.

—— with Longhurst, R. (1989), *New Seeds and Poor People*, Unwin Hyman, London.

Little, I., Scitovsky, T., and Scott, M. Fg. (1970), *Industry and Trade in Some Developing Countries*, OECD, Oxford University Press, London, Oxford, New York.

Mosley, P., and Smith, L. (1988), 'Structural Adjustment and Agricultural Performance in Sub-Saharan Africa 1980–87', Discussion Paper no. 15, Institute for Devel. Policy and Management, Manchester.

Myrdal, G. (1968), *Asian Drama* (3 vols.), Pantheon, New York.

Nellis, J., and Kikeri, S. (1989), 'Public Enterprise Reform: Privatization and the World Bank', *World Development*, 17/5.

Norton, R. (1987), *Agricultural Issues in Structural Adjustment Programs*, Social and Economic Development Paper no. 66, FAO.

Pinstrup-Andersen, P. (1989), 'The Impact of Macro-economic Adjustment: Food Security and Nutrition', in Commander (ed.) 1989.

Pope, A. (1710), *The House of Fame*, London.

Sarris, A. (1987), *Agricultural Stablization and Adjustment Problems in Developing Countries*, Social and Economic Development Paper no. 65, FAO, Rome.

Seddon, D. (1989), 'Morocco in the 1980s', in Commander (ed.) 1989: 175–89.

Staatz, J., Dioné, J., and Dembélé, N. (1989), 'Cereals Market Liberalization in Mali', *World Development*, 17/5: 703–18.

Thomas, S., and Reintsma, M. (1988), 'Zaïre's Economic Liberalization and its Impact in the Agricultural Sector', *Development Policy Review*, 6/4 (Dec.).

—— and Weidemann, W. (1988), 'The Impact of Zambia's Reform Programme in the Agricultural Sector', *Development Policy Review*, 6/4 (Dec.).

Thurow, L. (1983), *Dangerous Currents: The State of Economics*, Oxford.

Valdes, A., and Pinckney, T. (1987), 'Trade and Macroeconomic Policies' Impact on Agricultural Growth: Evidence to Date', mimeo, IFPRI.

White, G. (ed.) (1988), *Developmental States in East Asia*, Macmillan, London.

World Bank (1986), *World Development Report 1986*, Washington, DC.

—— (1988a), *Report on Adjustment Lending*, R88–199, 8 Aug.

—— (1988b), *Conditionality in World Bank Lending: Its Relation to Agricultural Pricing Policies*, Report no. 7357 (OED), 29 June.

—— (1989), *World Development Report 1989*, Washington, DC.

—— and UNDP (1989), *Africa's Adjustment and Growth in the 1980s*, Mar.

3
Visible and Invisible Hands in Trade Policy Reform

DAVID EVANS

1. Comparative Advantage and Trade Policy

1.1. The theory of trade policy

The principle of comparative advantage, first enunciated by Ricardo and Torrens nearly 200 years ago, is the best known proposition in international economics. In its simplest form, the proposition says that, when two countries enter into voluntary trade using the market mechanism, there are potential gains from trade even when one country is absolutely more productive in every line of production. As Samuelson (1969) remarked, this is an example of a proposition from the social sciences which is both true and non-trivial. Yet despite 200 years of writing from eminent economists of all persuasions, from Marx and List to Ohlin, from Samuelson to Krueger and Little, this principle seems not to have convinced many participants in the development debate, let alone policy-makers in developed and developing countries alike.

The most enduring argument for protection—the temporary suspension of the principle of comparative advantage—is the infant industry argument.[1] Typically, a case for infant industry protection can be made when there are market imperfections in factor and product markets induced by:

- economies of scale such that a competitive market outcome cannot be achieved in product markets;
- a lack of perfect foresight in capital markets;
- external economies, such as in labour training, affecting labour markets;
- important producer goods such as knowledge and technology may have mixed public and private good attributes.

However, whilst the above arguments can underpin an interventionist industrial policy for both developed and developing countries, they do not

I am grateful to my colleagues at the IDS Retreat Conference for many helpful comments and suggestions. I am particularly grateful to Christopher Colclough, Haris Gazdar, Raphael Kaplinsky, Hans Singer, and Adrian Wood. I thank them all and implicate none.

make the case for quantitative restrictions on imports. It is well established that the best policy response, where revenue constraints allow, is usually to direct the policy intervention as closely as possible to the market failure, thus minimizing the introduction of other by-product distortions which may impose production and consumption costs. Almost invariably the application of this rule implies that the optimal intervention is not in trade policy, but through a direct production or some other subsidy. One case when the application of this rule requires a trade policy intervention is when a country faces a less than perfectly elastic demand for its exports. In this case, the best form of intervention from a single country perspective is an optimal export tax. Equally where there are scale economies, depending on the nature of the competition, it may be better to allow a domestic monopoly to reap the benefits of scale economies behind a tariff or export subsidy.[2]

The application of these arguments to developing countries implies that, unless revenue considerations are paramount, directly targeted industrialization and trade policies using subsidies rather than import controls or tariff protection will be best. This will be true both for the initial period of import substitution as well as for a more export-orientated development strategy. To the extent that other domestic market distortions exist, such as in factor markets, the appropriate policy response is to tackle directly the source of the market imperfection rather than to use trade policy to overcome the distortion. The application of this policy framework leads to more efficient growth and a higher level of GDP. In some circumstances, such as when there is either a dual economy or an institutionally fixed wage with unemployment or a reserve army of labour, the rate of growth of output under freer trade will also be the higher.

The above interventionist arguments are in the mainstream neo-classical tradition. They may be extended to encompass a view of the state as an economic agent with additional, if imperfect, knowledge and foresight. In this case the appropriate response is for indicative planning so that imperfect market signals are supplemented as far as possible through an indicative planning mechanism.

1.2. Trade policy and the post-war period

At first glance, it would seem that the post-war period has been an era in which the principle of comparative advantage has been increasingly respected. Until the 1970s, there was a series of major trade policy reforms under the auspices of the General Agreement on Tariffs and Trade (GATT) which affected mainly the developed countries. These reforms concentrated on the reciprocal and non-discriminatory reduction of barriers to trade in industrial goods, mainly affecting trade between developed countries, leaving intact widespread intervention and protection of agricultural trade in the world

economy.[3] At the same time, the expansion of developing country manufactured exports, particularly from the newly industrializing economies of the
Far East, began to make an impact on world trade. Since then, the post-war
moves towards freer world trade and the role of the GATT as negotiating
forum for international trade policy reform has been increasingly undermined
with the rise of protectionism and the use of such measures as voluntary
export restraints (VERs). The Uruguay round of GATT negotiations,
focusing on the reduction of protection in agricultural and service trade,
would be deemed successful if they did little more than arrest the protectionist
tide.[4]

Paradoxically, there is a sense in which mercantilism, the pursuit of a
trade surplus for its own sake or in the belief that a trade surplus maximizes
national wealth, has never been so central to the evolution of the world
economy (Srinivasan 1989)). In the post-war period, mercantilism appears
in the guise of the more extreme versions of export promotion or import
substitution. These have frequently been pursued as ends in themselves
owing to their expected impact on the earning or saving of foreign exchange.
Even the notion of reciprocity in the GATT itself, whereby a reduction in a
country's protection is offered as a negotiating concession in return for
reciprocal lowering of protection on its exports by its trading partners, is
fundamentally mercantilist in the following sense. If the principle of comparative advantage is correct and there are potential and mutual gains in
economic welfare to be realized from trade, then barriers to trade are
misconceived in the first place, both from an individual country viewpoint or
from a collective viewpoint. It would therefore make sense for trading
nations to reduce barriers to trade unilaterally without bargaining with their
trading partners for mutual trade liberalization.

2. Neo-liberal Views about Trade

Almost by default, the principle of comparative advantage has been captured
by neo-liberal trade theory and policy advocacy.[5] It is usually argued that
'liberalization' of the market is the key to development policy reform, and
that this will lead to the realization of comparative advantage and maximization of the gains from international trade. Two main arguments have been
deployed in support of this case.

First, in the presence of widespread market imperfections and distortions,
it may be preferable to remove as many restrictions affecting the free play of
market forces as possible rather than to retain some intervention in the
market in an attempt to overcome the consequences of some of the market
imperfections. This argument follows from the theory of the second best,
which suggests that intervention to counteract the effects of a market
distortion will have ambiguous effects in the presence of other market

distortions.[6] For example, Customs Union theory suggests that the extent to which removal of trade restrictions between two countries decreases or increases welfare depends on the relative importance of trade creation over trade diversion in each particular case. As noted by Toye (1987: 74), this implies that the argument for and against intervention has to be fought on empirical rather than theoretical grounds.

Second, when full account is taken of the fact that the government may lack perfect information, neo-liberals have argued that an imperfect market solution may be much better than imperfect government intervention. This view is influenced by the literature on rent-seeking behaviour and Directly Unproductive Profit-seeking Activities and on interest group politics.[7] Since such rent-seeking behaviour uses scarce resources, there is an additional resource cost of market intervention. Such costs may be net welfare decreasing, in some circumstances, when they are added to the cost of the original intervention. In other cases, the rent-seeking activity may sufficiently undermine the effects of the original distortions so that the final net welfare effect is positive.[8] When this happens, the original distortion might just as well be removed on the grounds that it was ineffective anyway. Thus, the neo-liberal empirical and political judgement is that imperfect markets are better than imperfect governments in the formation and realization of long-run comparative advantages and the gains from trade.

To what extent, then, are these neo-liberal arguments correct?

3. Alternative Perspectives on Trade and Development

3.1. Some theoretical considerations

In contrast to neo-liberal views on trade and development issues, it is more difficult to find a core set of ideas which can be accurately attributed to what might be called 'Alternative Perspectives on Trade and Development'.[9] This is an eclectic tradition drawing on neo-classical, Marxian, and structuralist-institutionalist perspectives which includes no common methodology. In opposition to the mainstream neo-classical tradition of Marshall and Pigou, and to the neo-liberal paradigm, a common theme in all of the 'Alternative Perspectives' literature is an emphasis on the importance of class relationships and of inequalities of income and power, both within and between developed and developing countries.

Within a broadly defined 'Alternative Perspectives' camp, there are some uncomfortable bedfellows who either do not respect or are sceptical about the application of the principle of comparative advantage in any sense or form. For example, writers such as Amin, Frank, and Wallerstein (the radical Dependency and World Systems schools[10]) argue against full participation in the international division of labour by developing countries on the grounds that such exchange relations are unequal and exploitative.[11] It remains the case, however, that not being exploited at all may be much worse than being exploited and reaping some of the gains from trade!

It would be easy to brush aside the radical Dependency and World Systems writers as an aberration, but the extent of rejection of comparative advantage based policies is more pervasive.[12] Consider, for example, the major trade policy initiative in the 1970s embodied in the call for a New International Economic Order (NIEO). One of the key NIEO policy packages affecting trade and development was the UNCTAD Integrated Programme on Commodities (IPC). This was intended to redress a number of difficulties facing developing country primary commodity producers, particularly as regards commodity price fluctuation and adverse long-run terms of trade movements. In its essence, the IPC emphasized redistribution from developed to developing countries rather than a set of mutually gainful policies with favourable productive and redistributive aspects, particularly for developing countries. By aiming to use international commodity agreements to raise primary commodity prices important to developing countries, such policies fail to take into account the cost of these price increases to other developing country users of these commodities or that some of the benefits would accrue to developed country producers. The most obvious example in this regard is that of oil—which provided the implicit model of the benefits of asserting Third World commodity power—but it applies to almost all primary commodity in the production of which developing countries have an important stake. In this sense, the IPC policies were inefficient. They were also impractical, given demanding levels of finance and foresight required to operate a commodity stablization scheme without going bankrupt.[13]

A characteristic of the NIEO policy discussion was a heavy emphasis upon the importance of the international context and class structure and the relative neglect of national policy issues. This is reflected in the above discussion of commodity policy. It is also more true of policy discussion in documents such as Brandt (1980, 1983), as well as in more recent discussion of Third World debt when the policy errors of debtor nations are given less prominence than the errors of the international agencies, developed country banks, private banks, and the macro-policy failures of the leading third world creditor countries such as the United States (see, for example, Cornia *et al.* 1987, introduction). The literature has also been relatively uncritical of the protectionist measures adopted in the quest for import substituting industrialization (ISI). This is reflected in the failure of developing countries to use GATT principles and fora for negotiation of their own trade policy reform whilst negotiating special access to development country matters such as the Generalized System of Preferences (GSP). When such policies lead to tariff jumping by Multinational Corporations (MNCs), often the symptoms were attacked—the MNCs themselves—rather than national government policies which induced the inward investment in the first place.[14]

Part of the reason why the NIEO literature emphasizes the international context stems from an emphasis on Keynesian demand side issues, captured by the metaphor suggesting that trade is the 'engine of growth', the connecting link between the rate of growth of industrial production in the developed countries and the rate of growth of output in developing countries.[15] This Keynesian demand side view is in contrast to the idea that trade is the 'handmaiden of growth' (Kravis 1970, Riedel 1984), where trade is regarded as a facilitating rather than driving force in the development process and where both supply and demand side factors are identified but no one-way causality is established. If the supply side factors are sufficiently favourable, as in the case of the East Asian Newly Industrialized Countries (NICs), there can be a very rapid rate of growth of exports from such countries against unfavourable world trade trends. What appears to be a demand side argument for export-led growth is, in fact, a supply side argument for setting up the conditions necessary to exploit the possibility of rapidly growing manufactured exports by small countries which have little effect on the total volume of world trade.

The Keynesian demand side view works reasonably well when developing countries are highly specialized in primary commodity exports, and the rate of growth of world demand exerts a strong influence on primary commodity export revenues. However, the 'engine of growth' breaks down when the supply side changes from the accumulation of capital lead to the growth of manufactured exports from developing countries, in which the rate of growth of world demand may be less important than for additional primary commodity exports. To make this point more precisely, when the rate of growth of the capital stock exceeds the rate of growth of primary factors (augmented to take technical change into account), manufactured commodities will tend to grow faster than primary commodities at constant commodity prices. Initially, such capital accumulation will permit import substitution and, depending on the relative size of the natural resource base, eventually lead to the possibility of manufactured exports.[16] The absence of a clear-cut theoretical case linking the growth of world trade to the growth of income of a particular group of countries, or a single country, is confirmed by the rich diversity of country and commodity experience analysed by Riedel. Moreover, overemphasis on trade as the 'engine of growth' leads to undue pessimism about the extent to which developing countries can participate in gainful trade when the 'engine' fails, a theme to which I will return.

The alternative perspectives literature often fails to distinguish between efficiency and growth.[17] Whether under autarky or under free trade, it is possible to design policies which redistribute income towards profit accumulation which leads to very high rates of growth of GDP. Whether or not such growth is efficient in the narrow economic sense is another matter. Theoretically such a growth process could not be regarded as efficient if it took place under autarky rather than free trade. This follows from the observation that, with an institutionally given wage and unemployed or underemployed labour, the rate of profit will be higher under free trade compared with autarky and therefore a higher rate of growth will be possible when an economy is open to trade. In the real world, there may be good political, historical, and institutional reasons for eschewing gains from trade, but it also needs to be recognized that this may not be economically efficient. In short, the achievement of the high rate of growth in itself says nothing about economic efficiency in a static or in a dynamic sense.

There is no intrinsic reason why economic efficiency should be eschewed by the 'Alternative Perspectives' camp. Rather, efficiency arguments, both in theory and in empirical judgements used in trade policy analysis, need to be rescued from the particular sets of biases and blinkers of the neo-liberal paradigm. This is also implicitly recognized by Singer (1988*b*). In reviewing the Brandt Report recommendations on industrialization and world trade in the light of current trends in the world economy ten years on, Singer calls for new policies of efficient import substitution. Although he does not spell out what elements need to be taken into account in formulating new policies of efficient import substitution, the above arguments provide at least part of the theoretical background against which such policies might be developed.

3.2. Some areas neglected in the neo-liberal paradigm

The particular set of efficiency arguments which are emphasized by the neo-liberal writers (and which are carefully set out within the neo-classical discussion of trade policy) should obviously be acknowledged and taken account of where relevant. Equally the omissions from the neo-liberal discussion of trade policy stemming from their narrow focus on market liberalization should not be overlooked. Some of these omissions are discussed with the 'Alternative Perspectives' tradition, and are identified in what follows:

(*a*) Some important economic efficiency arguments are given little or no weight by neo-liberals. For example, a number of writers focusing on the internal organization of the firm and the organization of work agree that there is a deep conflict between individual and collective rationality at the point of production in any social system.[18] This conflict arises because it is not possible to write a complete contract governing the transformation of labour power, the capacity to work, into work itself. To overcome this inherent imperfection in labour contracts, firms spend resources in a variety of ways including supervision and the use of machines to regulate the pace of work. In this context, profit or growth maximization is likely to conflict with welfare maximization and can lead to authoritarian forms of organization of production. For example, 'divide not rule' strategies towards workers may enhance profitability at the expense of worker welfare. Similarly, the machine pacing of work may maximize profits but may lead to Pareto inefficient technical change and suboptimal social welfare.[19]

The widespread reinforcement of the profit motive in the process of market liberalization often fails to recognize the conflict between profit maximization and welfare maximization. The formulation of policies and the building of institutions which lessen the force of this conflict are not a part of the market liberalization agenda when applied in their authoritarian forms, such as in Chile or, in a less extreme form, in the UK over the 1980s. Moreover, neo-classical economists usually ignore the direct welfare benefits deriving from work itself in their analysis of social welfare. This must combine with the indirect welfare benefits of work deriving from consumption out of income earned, and welfare derived from leisure, in a fuller micro-economic analysis of the firm.[20] Failure to take these issues into account may lead to economically inefficient choice of policy instruments and institutional reform when market liberalization is carried out. This is particularly so in the context of new forms of organization of production which facilitate the use of micro-electronics in product and process technology, sometimes referred to as flexible specialization or post-Fordism.[21] For example, 'divide and rule' strategies which maximize profits under Fordist mass-production methods may fail to do so under flexible specialization. The adoption of the new technologies requires rather less hierarchy in the organization of work and far more co-operation within the work-force than the older Fordist forms.[22]

Neo-liberals often reinforce the position of authoritarian forms of production with arguments for strongly centralized state power. This must be capable of operating against interest groups which successfully exploit democratic processes to obtain special market intervention to the benefit of their members and the cost of everybody else. Such centralized state power is often accepted, even if undemocratic, in the interests of market efficiency. There is no perceived contradiction between calling pro-market reforms 'economic liberalization' even when they are implemented by unpleasant military or civilian dictatorships. These observations underline the need to identify and define desirable and feasible forms of politics to go hand in hand with market and institutional reform and the redesign of interventionist trade and development policies.

(*b*) Both mainstream neo-classical and the neo-liberal views often ignore the central importance of ideology in the developmental state, emphasized by Gerschenkron (1966) and White (1984).[23] Bardhan (1984) argues that in many cases of state-directed industrialization, the leadership genuinely considers itself the holder of the nations' deeply held normative aspirations. In a world of international military and economic competition, these aspirations may often take the form of striving for industrialization and rapid economic growth. A strong developmental ideology might also do much to facilitate 'hands on' intervention without state employees engaging in significant rent-seeking behaviour. This seems to have happened in South Korea, to cite one example.[24] On the other hand, ideology should not be used as an excuse for failing to deal with significant rent-seeking behaviour through market and institutional reform as appears to be the case in a number of Sub-Saharan African states.

(*c*) Work on the developmental state tends to stress the importance of state intervention in the formation and execution of a development strategy. It focuses upon the importance of the class base and the relative autonomy of the state, its administrative capacity, its ability to make long-run strategic decisions, and the role of intermediate levels of state intervention in the formulation and execution of a selective industrial policy.[25] Some of this is recognized by analysts who characterize interventionist East Asian states as clearing houses for information and technology in the face of market failure.[26] Yet even this narrow economic interpretation of the role of the East Asian developmental state is resisted by neo-liberals, who remain highly sceptical of any non-market policy instruments.[27]

The experience of the developmental state in East Asia seems to have important implications for the choice of trade policy instruments. The standard ranking of trade policy instruments in order of least to most efficient are direct import controls, tariffs, and subsidies aimed at the point of the distortion.[28] However, the East Asian experience suggests that trade policy instruments cannot be ranked in these terms separately from the institutional context within which they were applied. For example, highly selective quantitative controls have always been important in the South Korean case.[29] Yet, associated rent-seeking behaviour has not been dominant, partly because of the role of a strong national development ideology in countering these effects discussed above. More potently, it appears that quantitative controls were often tied to crude incentives. Access to import licences, for example, was linked to the export performance of the firm. Thus, the state combined incentives with instruments of direct control to achieve its selective industrial policies which tariffs alone could not attain. In such cases, the standard ranking of interventions cannot be sustained. Quantitative controls tied to incentives, however crude, may emerge as superior to tariffs precisely because they provide the instruments for implementing an efficient interventionist industrial strategy.[30]

The above view of the role of the state in the formulation of an interventionist trade and industrial strategy is reinforced by a variety of studies which stress the role of sector-level co-operation between firms and intervention by central and local government in a small firm economy.[31] Such interventions draw on the economic rationale for an active industrial strategy outlined above, but translated to a small firm context. In effect, such an industrial strategy seeks to combine interventionist policies normally associated with central government with a small firm strategy designed to give the sector the type of benefits derived from the head office of very much larger firms. In the small firm case, this is achieved through networking between firms, joint venture co-operative arrangements, and may also involve significant local government involvement.

(*d*) The concept of class and the analysis of class relations is often central to understanding some aspects of the process of economic development. Nevertheless, class is often ignored in both the mainstream neo-classical tradition and its neo-liberal offshoot. This is in spite of the fact that class, and the associated patterns of ownership of productive assets, often have a crucial impact on both the level of production and its growth. Perhaps the classic example is provided by land ownership in many developing countries. Amongst other things, class relations and the pattern of ownership of productive assets may have an important, if not crucial, bearing on the way in which the comparative advantage of a particular country or region is developed, as is often emphasized in the structuralist-institutionalist, dependency, and Marxian traditions.[32] This observation cuts two ways. If class relations have had an important historical influence on the development of long-run comparative advantage, then future changes in a country's comparative advantage might well be blocked by the classes who benefit from the present arrangements. In this case, a new trade and development strategy can only proceed if the class forces that have shaped the historical development of the existing one are changed or transformed.[33] Note that it is the class forces which must be overthrown in this case, not the principle of comparative advantage as so often happens in the dependency and Marxian traditions.

The above discussion gives some indication of the theoretical problems and omissions from the neo-liberal analysis. Equally important in such an assessment, however, is the empirical record of developing countries in the external sector, to which I now turn.

4. A Review of the Empirical Evidence

4.1. Historical background

The empirical evidence against high levels of protection to sustain import substituting industrialization (ISI) compiled during the 1970s was based on case-study evidence covering a relatively small number of countries (see Little, Scitovsky, and Scott 1970, Krueger 1978, Bhagwati 1978, and Balassa and Associates 1982). This case-study evidence was used to support the theoretical case against ISI and in favour of export-orientated industrialization (EOI). It suggested that pessimism concerning export prospects for developing countries was unfounded, particularly for non-traditional primary commodities and manufactures. Further, it suggested that, by exploiting developing country comparative advantage through the market mechanism, EOI was more efficient, requiring lower capital/labour ratios to achieve high rates of growth. It was also argued that additional efficiency benefits were achieved from the realization of scale economies through sales on the world market and through induced efficiency benefits from international competition. Finally, the case-study evidence was used to support the theoretical contention that the export of labour intensive manufactures would improve the income distribution for wage earners in labour abundant economies.

4.2. Generalizing from case-studies

One of the problems with using case-study evidence to support the case for EOI, often pointed out by the critics of EOI, is that it is impossible to generalize from this evidence. One way of attempting to overcome this difficulty is through the statistical analysis of the effects of trade orientation on growth. One of the best examples is Syrquin and Chenery (1989). They used a sample of over a hundred countries over the period 1950–83, attempting to capture the effects of both resource endowments and trade orientation on growth. Their findings suggest that small outward and manufacturing-orientated countries had the highest growth rates of per capita income over the sample period, and that outward orientation led to faster rates of growth for large and small countries, whether orientated to primary or manufactured activities. Such statistical studies are useful in establishing common patterns and some key differentiating aspects of country experience. However, they do not directly relate the degree of primary orientation to resource endowments, or the degree of outward orientation to trade policy variables. Rather, the degree of primary or trade orientation is measured in terms of the deviation of country shares from the sample averages.

Reports of an early attempt to establish the relationship between policy-induced market price distortions, economic efficiency, and growth can be found in World Bank (1983, chapter 6) and Agarwala (1983). This study was based on a simple cross-section regression of the average growth performance over the 1970s of a sample of over thirty countries and an unweighted average of seven indices of price distortion. Of the seven indices of price distortion, only three related directly to trade policy regimes—an index of manufacturing protection, an index of agricultural price distortion, and an index of exchange rate distortion. The central finding of the study was that a third of the sample variance in growth performance of countries in the World Bank study was accounted for by the index of price distortion. This was seen at the time as providing confirmation of the earlier case-study findings in respect of the benefits of EOI (see World Bank 1983: 61, 63), that respect for price efficiency was one of the key variables in explaining differences in the growth performance of developing countries.

The World Bank study can be criticized on a number of grounds. For example, there is a lack of a clear correspondence between the measured price distortion and the underlying theoretical requirements of a distortion measure. Also, the use of a variety of *ad hoc* economic and non-economic explanations of individual country behaviour, where this deviated strongly from the sample average, is methodologically unsound. These criticisms suggest that there was too much weight given to the role of a general respect for price efficiency, as captured by the average distortion index, in accounting for differences in growth performance. Also, there was a lack of theoretical or empirical discussion of the role of non-economic determinants of growth performance.

An extensive series of statistical tests reported in Aghazadeh and Evans (1988), using the 1983 World Bank study as a starting-point but adding further economic and non-economic variables, confirmed these general criticisms. Aghazadeh and Evans found that only three of the seven indices of price distortion were important in accounting for the sample variance in growth performance, and that the least significant of these related to manufacturing protection. The important price variables included a signficant negative effect on the sample countries' growth from an appreciation of the real exchange rate over the 1970s, and the negative effects of real wage growth being higher than productivity growth. It is noteworthy that neither of the empirically important price variables relate to micro-economic efficiency, but point rather to the importance of macro-economic management of both the exchange rate and of income distribution.

The addition of other variables into the regression analysis increased the variance accounted for to over two-thirds. The most statistically significant set of new economic and institutional variables centred around the capacity of an economy to sustain a rapid rate of growth of investment, including the capacity of the state for giving strategic direction to development policies.[34] The findings suggested that one of the main effects of manufacturing protection was through a negative impact on agricultural growth. The study also found no evidence of export-led growth, a result also found in other recent studies.[35] In summary, the 1970s data suggest exchange rate depreciation, appropriate policies which allow for domestic savings, and investment growth with institutional support for this process, are the most important factors associated with rapid growth.

4.3. Recent world bank evidence

More recently, the World Development Report (1987: ch. 5) divided a sample of forty-one countries into four categories according to the degree of

inward and outward orientation. Four quantitative and qualitative variables
were used in this classification scheme, namely:

- effective rate of protection;
- use of direct controls such as quotas and import licensing schemes;
- use of export incentives;
- degree of exchange rate overvaluation.

These variables were combined with a large element of judgement when
dividing the sample countries into strong and moderate outward orientation,
strong and moderate inward orientation.[36] The growth performance and
other macro-economic indicators for these countries were then compared
for the periods 1963–73 and 1973–85. The countries in the sample and the
results of this exercise are summarized in figure 3.1 and table 3.1.

Taken at face value, the results lend strong support to the idea that the
more outward orientated countries have experienced a higher rate of
growth. There is also some evidence that the more outward orientated
countries have lower capital/output ratios, suggesting that outward orientation
may also have been more efficient. However, on closer inspection, the case
in favour of outward orientation is not so clear cut.

Part of the problem with figure 3.1 and table 3.1 stems from the importance
of judgement in deciding how individual countries should be classified. This
is evident in the inclusion with Hong Kong of South Korea and Singapore in
the 'strong outward orientation' category. As Greenaway (1986: 33) suggests,
an alternative narrow definition of 'strong outward orientation' based on
estimates of bias in the incentive structure between imports and exports
would leave only Hong Kong in this category. Another problem arises in the
comparison of the classification of South Korea and Brazil. South Korea is
shown as 'strongly outward orientated' in both time periods, based entirely
on the 1960s evidence reported in Greenaway (1986, table 6). In contrast,
with evidence from both time periods, Brazil is classified as moderately
inward orientated in the earlier time period and moderately outward
orientated in the second time period. Yet comparing the characteristics of
trade and exchange rate regimes for South Korea and Brazil in Greenaway
(1986, tables 6 and 7), the basis of this classification is not so clear cut. These
tables show that South Korea, with a low average rate of effective protection
of 10 per cent, a high dispersion of effective protection rates, and a realistic
to undervalued exchange rate, scores as 'strongly outward orientated'. On
the other hand, Brazil with an average level of effective protection of 44 per
cent, a moderate degree of dispersion of effective protection, and an
overvalued exchange rate is classified as 'moderately outward orientated' in
the second period. Without evidence on the extent of the undervaluation of
the South Korean exchange rate, compared with overvaluation of the
Brazilian exchange rate, the actual protective effects of the two average
rates of effective protection cannot be compared. Nor is it possible to assess

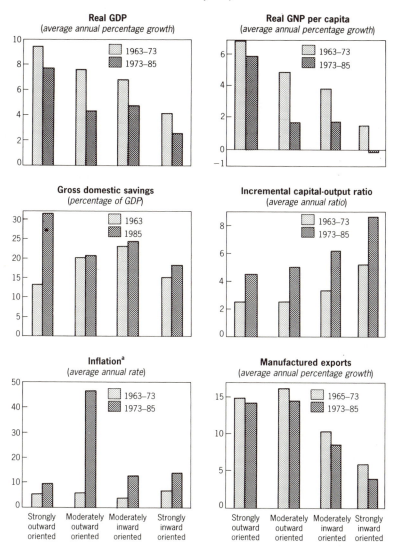

FIG. 3.1. Macro-economic performance of forty-one developing economies grouped by trade orientation

Note: Averages are weighted by each country's share in the group total for each indicator. See table 3.1 for a listing of the economies in each of the trade groups and for the source.

[a]Inflation rates are measured by the implicit GDP deflator. Values are group medians.

TABLE 3.1. *Forty-one developing countries, classified by trade orientation*

	Outward orientated		Inward orientated	
	Strong	Moderate	Moderate	Strong
1963–73	Hong Kong Republic of Korea Singapore	Brazil Cameroon Columbia Costa Rica Ivory Coast Guatamala Indonesia Israel Malaysia Thailand	Bolivia El Salvador Honduras Kenya Madagascar Mexico Nicaragua Nigeria Philippines Senegal Tunisia Yugoslavia	Argentina Bangladesh Burundi Chile Dominican Republic Ethiopia Ghana India Pakistan Peru Sri Lanka Sudan Tanzania Turkey Uruguay Zambia
1973–85	Hong Kong Republic of Korea Singapore	Brazil Chile Israel Malaysia Thailand Tunisia Turkey Uruguay	Cameroon Columbia Costa Rica Ivory Coast El Salvador Guatamala Honduras Indonesia Kenya Mexico Nicaragua Pakistan Philippines Senegal Sri Lanka Yugoslavia	Argentina Bangladesh Bolivia Burundi Dominican Republic Ethiopia Ghana India Madagascar Nigeria Peru Sudan Tanzania Zambia

Source: World Bank, *World Development Report 1987*, 83 and 84.

the importance of the differences in the degree of dispersion of effective protective rates, or the differential effects of import controls and export incentives, on the basis of the Greenaway data.

The inherent difficulties in assessing the protective effect of import controls have been reinforced by a recent study by Wade (1991, forthcoming).

He suggests that there has been an overestimation of the effects of the removal of quantitative restrictions in South Korea on the import side and that there has been much more import substitution in South Korea induced by targeted and made-to-measure protection than is captured by the available indices of protection.[37] It would seem, therefore, that there is a real danger that the set of judgements which were made in classifying countries by trade orientation in the Greenaway and the World Bank study was influenced by the attribution of a favourable growth performance of the countries in the sample to the degree of outward orientation. This point is reinforced by noting that there are no less than twelve alterations of country assignment by trade policy regime when the background paper by Greenaway (1986, tables 6 and 7) is compared with the final results in the World Bank (1987, figure 5.2), reproduced in figure 3.1.

Although Greenaway's data base was revised and extended, it is not clear how much of the revision of the country assignments by trade policy regimes were due to data revisions or to a different set of judgements. Other doubts arise from the data used in the country classification. Direct price comparisons often do not correspond with the measures of protection, and the reasons for the discrepancies are little understood.[38] Nor are the criteria by which the exchange rate is deemed 'realistic' at all clear.

Bearing these doubts in mind, it is not surprising that the results shown in figure 3.1 for the countries in the 'moderate inward' to 'moderate outward' orientation groups are ambiguous. It can readily be seen that, in terms of the growth of GDP, and of per capita GDP, domestic savings, and inflation, the moderately inward orientated countries did better than the moderately outward orientated countries in the period 1973–85. Other factors than those captured by the moderate inward/moderate outward classification have been influencing growth performance since the world economy began to slow down in the 1970s.[39]

In contrast to the above, the results shown in figure 3.1 seem to be unequivocal in relation to the strongly inward orientated category. It appears that the countries in this group did far worse than the other countries in the sample (with the exception of the inflation record), particularly when looked at in terms of per capita GDP in the period 1973–85. Yet, when examining the criteria used for assignment of countries to the strong inward orientation category, it is not immediately obvious how the final judgements were made in Greenaway (1986, tables 6 and 7). In some cases, the presence of an overvalued exchange rate and extensive import controls were present; in other cases not. In any event, other unidentified factors were obviously at work as well, a point also made by Singer (1988a). A similar criticism was made of the World Bank (1983) study discussed above.

4.4. Interpretation of the evidence: a summary

In view of these doubts on the evidence assembled in figure 3.1, the empirical case for arguing that a change in trade policy regime from strong inward orientation to one of the other categories is not as strong as it appears on first sight. Nor does the evidence cited in Aghazadeh and Evans (1988) support the proposition that trade policy *per se* is a central determinant of growth performance. In empirical terms, the link between trade policy, rapid growth, and economic efficiency cannot be strongly established. In this difficult and contentious area, perhaps the strongest empirical evidence is from the Syrquin and Chenery (1989) study described above, which suggested that, whatever it is that produces above average overall trade orientation and above average manufactured export orientation trade in small countries also produces above average growth performance.

5. Challenges for Trade Policy

5.1. The neo-liberal challenge

The lack of overwhelming empirical evidence to support trade policy reform has not lessened the widespread recognition that such reforms should nevertheless be a part of stabilization and adjustment policies for developing countries. Even if neo-liberal arguments can be faulted, they have certainly made the case for taking economic efficiency arguments seriously. The most important qualifications and adaptations necessary for the application of the principle of optimal policy choice by intervention at the point of distortion need to be taken into account. A central enabling ingredient for such a package to be successful will be the creation of an appropriate political and institutional environment for industrial and trade policy reform independent of international pressure for the implementation of (inappropriate) neo-liberal policies such as the timing of the reform of trade policy instruments discussed below.

5.2. Fallacy of composition

If successful, structural adjustment with trade policy reform may lead to increased traditional and non-traditional exports, including possibly manufactured exports, as well as more efficient import substitution. Should this implication of trade policy reform be resisted on the grounds that, if large numbers of developing countries are to be given the same policy advice, the policies will fail on fallacy of composition arguments?[40] In the case of primary exports, there are some commodities for which the fallacy of composition argument may hold. For example, Karunaskara (1984) identified eight possible primary commodities—coffee, cocoa, tea, bananas, bauxite, copper, tin, and tropical timber—where it may be possible to increase export revenue by applying a uniform export tax on all exporting countries. Some of these commodities are of importance to small and poor developing countries, particularly in Sub-Saharan Africa. Whilst an export tax would not be contrary to the specific provisions of GATT, inevitably there would be serious difficulties in administering such a scheme and distributing the revenues. Moreover, many of the commodities concerned are also produced by developed countries, and it may be an inefficient way to improve the export earnings of developing countries.

To the extent that the strongly inward orientated countries are precisely those countries which are benefiting least from trade, unilateral reforms which improved the export performance of these countries in the absence of a world export tax on relevant commodities would place some of the adjustment costs on existing exporters. To the extent that the more outward orientated countries have both a higher per capita income and a better growth performance, the costs of adjustment would fall on better-off developing countries. This observation is reinforced by studies which suggest that export supply side constraints such as those arising from the inward orientated trade regimes which existed for Sub-Saharan Africa as a whole during the 1970s led to falling world market shares even in those primary commodities where the fallacy of composition may have held.[41] Thus, whilst there are indeed cases where the fallacy of composition arguments may hold, it is very difficult in practice to design policies which take them into account. Worse, failure to reform trade policy regime on the grounds of the fallacy of composition runs the risk of overkill. In this case, the export demand elasticity for the single country concerned, or a subgroup of countries, may be greater than one so that their market shares fall without compensating benefits from the improvement in the terms of trade resulting from their action.

Similar arguments apply against attempts to take into account the fallacy of composition argument made in respect of manufactured exports.[42] Suppose that the price elasticity of demand for Third World manufactured exports was indeed less than unity. In this case, a new Third World manfactured exporter would still be able to increase its export revenue since the elasticity of demand for its manufactured exports, and for other new entrants, would undoubtedly be much greater than unity. The burden of adjustment would then fall on the established Third World manufactured goods exporters in both developed country and developing country markets.

How serious a problem is the fallacy of composition likely to be for manufactured exports from the Third World as a whole? There is some evidence to suggest that there is a strong downward bias in the estimated price elasticities of demand (Riedel 1988), so the fallacy of composition argument may have less force at the aggregate level on empirical grounds. Rather than eschew manufactured exports as a part of structural adjustment because of the uncertain consequences of the fallacy of composition argument, it would make more sense to explore the possibilities of manufactured exports even in the present unfavourable world trading environment. From a collective Third World perspective, the message is that it would make more sense to focus on trade policy reform amongst Third World countries as well as in the developed countries. It is not enough to focus attention on the protectionist policies of the industrial countries alone and their failure to achieve structural adjustment.

There is one important case where it may be possible to take into account the fallacy of composition argument. Consider the situation where an international agency such as the IMF, following a case-by-case approach, recommends price reform including devaluation to several countries who collectively face the fallacy of composition problem.[43] Should the countries involved resist the reform? On the face of it, the optimal policy would include an export tax on the relevant commodities administered by the IMF, so that the receipts from the tax could be distributed to the relevant countries as a part of the adjustment package.[44] Should the affected countries resist price reform and structural adjustment even if they are unable to persuade the IMF to collect an export tax on their behalf? In the short run, additional costs would indeed be incurred as a result of lost export revenue which would arise as other exporters undertake reforms which increase the supply of the relevant commodities on the world market. However, it may still be worth incurring these costs until the benefits of the structural adjustment in improving the growth performance of the economy as a whole come to fruition. Failure to undertake reforms essential to the long-run development prospects of the economy because of short-run costs, in this case exacerbated by the failure of institutions such as the IMF to take into account the direct way in which the policy reforms increase these short-run costs, may incur more substantial costs on the economy over the medium to long term. Worse, failure to adjust now may intensify the structural adjustment problem, affecting only the timing when the reforms must inevitably take place with or without international compensation for the short-run costs arising from the fallacy of composition.

The circumstances, timing, and sequencing of developing country trade policy reform which might be carried out will vary enormously. In the case of the NICs such as South Korea and Taiwan, the most important issues may relate to reform on the import side where high and selective levels of protection operate. For these countries, the key question is how much protection such import substituting industries should receive, and for how much longer, and whether the most appropriate form of intervention is through direct controls attached to crude incentives rather than direct subsidies targeted at the points of distortion. In other cases, trade policy reform is more likely to be carried out as a part of a wider process of stabilization and structural adjustment. In such cases, the timing and sequencing of the trade policy reform may be crucial.

5.3. Timing and sequencing of trade policy reform

A recent review of the theoretical and empirical issues and difficulties in the timing and sequencing of trade policy (Michaely 1986) suggests surprisingly few guide-lines without strong theoretical and empirical qualification. Few would disagree with his argument that, in a world where rigidities are ubiquitous, the reform process should be multi-staged with the speed of implementation depending on the degree of flexibility and adaptability of response. However, his description of the desirable components of the first stage of trade policy reform is more contentious. Michaely (1986: 56) suggests that this first stage of trade liberalization should entail a shift from quantitative restrictions to tariffs as the instrument of protection, accompanied with an appropriate exchange rate policy and, if possible, carried out under favourable circumstances. Yet for the reasons analysed in section 3.2 above, it may be appropriate to rank tariffs above import controls as a trade policy instrument. The application of the standard rule to the first stage of the process of reform may be unmanageable or undesirable for three reasons:

(a) Because of the difficulties in estimating the tariff equivalents of import controls, it is in fact very difficult to know what the reformed tariff rates should be. This will in turn make it impossible to estimate or predict what an appropriate new equilibrium exchange rate should be, whether or not it is to be administered or completely market determined.

(b) In the light of (a), it is likely to be very difficult to prevent a very rapid draining of foreign exchange reserves in the first stage of the reform process. This is particularly likely where it may be possible to use the removal of import restrictions to facilitate capital movements through transfer pricing when capital market restrictions remain intact.

(c) The removal rather than the reform of quantitative import controls may mean that a vital instrument for selective trade and industrial policy intervention is lost.

As argued above, it was through the reform of import controls that successful import substitution and export policies were executed in the cases of South Korea and Taiwan, rather than through the replacement of import controls by tariff equivalents. This interpretation of the South Korean and Taiwanese experience is consistent with Keesing (1979), who suggests that the first stage of the trade policy reform process should concentrate on direct intervention to stimulate exports without dismantling import controls.

Another case where trade policy reform is relevant is where there has been a long crisis and collapse of state power to regulate the economy, such as occurred in Uganda or in Ghana over the 1970s and much of the 1980s. In such circumstances, citizen survival depends on a combination of subsistence activities and the operation of markets, often black markets, in the parallel economy. Where the state is still able to intervene in the economy, either indirectly or through parastatal agencies such as marketing boards or directly through the foreign exchange and trade policy regime, it will usually be to the short-run advantage of some narrowly defined set of group, tribe, or class interests.[45] In these circumstances, the neo-liberal arguments in favour of breaking the remaining hold of the state over the operation of the market has some force. In the case of Ugandan small farmers and petty commodity producers described in Brett (1988), and the small firms in Ghana described by Schmitz (1989), the gains from getting state intervention 'off the backs of the people' are likely to be substantial. The more difficult question then arises: how is the political and institutional framework for longer-run policy reform to be generated? This point is illustrated by the case-study of industrial policy in a much more favourable environment in Botswana reported by Kaplinsky in this volume.

The Botswana industrial policy was built on careful cost–benefit principles, directly targeting assistance where possible and building in automatic tapers on the level of assistance to avoid the problem of infant industries which do not grow up. The rough rule of thumb used was broadly consistent with the conventional wisdom that not more than 10–20 per cent effective protection should be provided for more than 5–8 years (see for example Balassa 1975). However, as the Kaplinsky study shows, the industry policy was inappropriate, intervening in capital and commodity markets rather than the more important information and technology markets. The lesson to draw from the Botswana experience is not that the principles of optimal policy intervention in themselves were faulty, but that the policies failed because the wrong markets where chosen for intervention.

5.4. South–south trade

A final area where there is a very real need for trade policy reform lies in opening up south–south trade. In an open world economy with the rapid accumulation of capital in developing countries, it is likely that south–south trade would be the most dynamic component of world trade.[46] The reasons why this has not been the case are partly historical and institutional, the legacy of the colonial period which radically cut south–south trade links and opened up north–south trade,[47] and partly because of barriers to trade in the developing countries themselves. Moreover, in the context of the current debt crisis, there has been a dramatic fall in the capacity of the south to accumulate capital relative to the north. Not surprisingly, and in line with the predictions of the standard theory regarding south–south trade, there has been a sharper fall in the rate of growth of south–south trade than for north–south trade in the 1980s.[48] This suggests that a major part of any trade policy reform in developing countries as the debt crisis recedes should be the search for new opportunities for south–south trade. This could be achieved on the basis of bilateral negotiations either within or outside the context of structural adjustment reforms, as suggested by Parsan (1988) for the case of Trinidad and Tobago and Brazil. Whilst in principle the search for such trading links would be best facilitated in the context of multilateral trade reform, there is little point in waiting indefinitely for such reforms when the economic case for the opening of such trade is powerful enough.

5.5. Picking the winners

Trade policy reform and the associated industrialization strategies will inevitably involve the difficult task of picking the winners in many circumstances. Such decisions need to be made in regard to the reform of made-to-measure import substituting protection characteristics of countries such as South Korea and Taiwan. Picking which industries are to survive trade policy reform in the process of structural adjustment will also be unavoidable in many Latin American and African countries. The provision of a more consistent political and institutional framework for economic policies will be at least as important as trade policy reform itself and the answer given to the question 'how much protection, and for how long'.

6. The Wider Context and Conclusions

6.1. Trade and income distribution

Up to a point, outward orientation on the lines of the exemplary East Asian NICs has had favourable effects on the distribution of income. For these countries, there has been a measure of redistribution with very favourable growth. However, the consequences for the industrial countries of an open world economy may not have been so favourable. With very high rates of accumulation of capital, even in a small number of successful NICs, the employment of less skilled workers in the developed countries is threatened, the distribution of income between skilled and unskilled workers is likely to deteriorate, and the returns to capital increase.[49] These likely trends are not in themselves arguments for protection in the industrial countries, but have certainly increased the protectionist response on both mercantilist and interest group grounds. On this account, the prospects for a growing open world economy are not good. Should these, and other pressures and difficulties facing individual developing countries, and the world economy as a whole, alter the central thrust of the argument in this chapter? I think not.

6.2. Replication of the East Asian NICs?

The principle of comparative advantage and the associated theory of trade can help in the formulation of trade policy, particularly in the light of successful selective trade and industrial policies in the East Asian NICs. Replication of their experience is critically dependent upon the identification of the key market failures, the choice of trade and industrial policy instruments, and the institutional environment. Where the institutional prerequisites for a policy of selective infant industry protection cannot be met, it may be better on growth, equity, and efficiency grounds for the state to focus on macro policies and the improved functioning of markets. In such cases, there may be a measure of agreement on trade policy issues from a wide range of perspectives. However, the general neo-liberal view that imperfect markets do better than imperfect states in fostering infant industries must be strongly qualified. By no means can it be said that neo-liberal writers have a monopoly of either the efficiency or the empirical arguments. In particular, neo-liberals have not been able to grasp the lessons of the successful East Asian cases of selective interventionist trade and industrial policies, or of the potential for states to adapt and improve past protective policies designed selectively to enhance technological capability. Failure to grasp the lessons of this experience is likely to lead to poorly designed packages of trade policy reform which miss the interdependence between trade policy instruments and the institutional environment within which such instruments are deployed. Equally, failure of developing countries to recognize the importance of efficiency arguments may lead to missed opportunities for trade policy reform.

Notes

1. See Smith 1986 for a recent summary.
2. See Krugman 1986 and Neary 1988.
3. For a summary of trade policy reform in the post-war period, see Krueger 1984 and Baldwin 1984. See also World Bank, *World Development Reports*.
4. For a summary of the state of protection in the world economy as the Uruguay Round opened, see MacBean 1988. See also Erzan and Karsenty 1989.
5. For an overview of the neo-liberal paradigm, see the introductory chapter in this volume by Christopher Colclough.

6. For a statement of the theorem of the second best, see Lipsey 1957, and Lipsey and Lancaster 1956–7.
7. For a discussion of the original rent-seeking idea, see Krueger (1974). For a discussion and extension of the analysis of rent-seeking behaviour, see Bhagwati 1982, Bates 1981, 1983, Little 1982, Olsen 1982, Srinivasan 1986.
8. See Bhagwati 1982.
9. Much of the discussion in this section draws on Evans 1989*a*.
10. For a review of the writings of these schools, see Evans 1988; 1989*a* section 3.
11. For a discussion of the application of the general definition of exploitation in Roemer 1982 to exploitation in trade, see Evans 1989*a*, section 3 and the references cited therein. The particular definition of exploitation in trade used by the Radical Dependency and the World Systems schools is that exploitation takes place when productivity differentials between countries entering trade exceed wage differentials and that such trade with full international capital mobility is only entered into because of domination and coercion by developed 'imperialist' countries. This implausible definition of exploitation in trade denies the possibility of gains from trade because it implies that peripheral developing countries would be better off under autarky and capable of growing faster than with trade and international capital mobility.
12. For an elaboration of the arguments presented here, see Evans 1989*a*, section 5.
13. For a discussion of some of these issues, see Evans 1979. The International Tin Agreement is a case in point. In the 1970s this agreement was often cited as an example of a successful commodity agreement. However, this judgement ignored the key role of US strategic reserve stockpiles in supporting and underwriting this agreement. Without this support and without adequate finance, the International Tin Agreement was bankrupt by the mid-1980s. See Burke 1987.
14. For a further discussion of some of these issues, see Bhagwati and Ruggie 1984.
15. This idea was recently elaborated by Arthur Lewis in his Nobel Prize Lecture (Lewis 1980), where he suggested that, in the future, developing countries would have to look to south–south trade to provide the 'engine of growth'.
16. This point follows from an application of the Rybcynski theorem (Rybcynski 1955).
17. On this, see Bliss 1989.
18. See e.g. Williamson 1975, 1985; Lazear 1981; Bowles 1985; Pagano 1985; and the summary in Evans 1989*a*, section 4.
19. For an excellent summary and review of these arguments, see Bowles 1985.
20. See e.g. Pagano 1985.
21. For a summary of this literature in the context of the micro-economic theory of publication, see Evans 1989*a*, section 4.
22. See e.g. Hoffman 1988.
23. A notable exception within the neo-classical tradition is North 1981.
24. See e.g. White 1984 and 1988.
25. See in particular Bardhan 1984 and White 1988. My own attempt to summarize this literature is in Evans 1989*a*, section 4.3.
26. This view is reflected in World Bank (1987, Box 4.4. and p. 71) where some of the debates on industrial policy are surveyed. For an elaboration of the role of

the East Asian developmental state in developing technological capability through a selective industrial policy, see Pack and Westphal 1986.

27. See, for example, the discussion in the World Bank (1987, Box 4.4 and p. 71), where the text discussion appears to side with the neo-liberal view of East Asian industrial policy against the interventionist arguments summarized in Box 4.4.

28. For a summary of these arguments, see for example Michaely 1977.

29. See Luedde-Neurath 1986 and Wade 1991, (forthcoming).

30. See also Bhagwati 1982 for a discussion of the effect on economic efficiency of tying import licences to export performance.

31. This literature draws on both the experience of the dynamic export regions of Italy, sometimes called the Third Italy, as well at the literature on flexible specialization summarized in Evans 1989a, section 4. For a developing country application, see Murray *et al.* 1987.

32. On this, see for example Sideri 1970, De Janvry 1978, 1981 and Sheehan 1987.

33. For suggestions on these lines in the Nicaraguan case, see Fitzgerald 1986.

34. See Aghazadeh and Evans 1988, equation 2.1 and tables 3.3 and 4.2.

35. See e.g. the studies reported in Taylor 1986.

36. For details, including a discussion of the difficulties in measuring the degree of inward and outward orientation, see the background paper by Greenaway 1986.

37. Similar observations are made by Wade (1990, forthcoming) in relation to Taiwan. Although Taiwan is not in the above sample of countries, these observations nevertheless suggest that the successful non-city state East Asian NICs may have been less outward orientated than suggested by the statistics.

38. This observation is made in private exchanges with Robert Wade and is based on World Bank experience in trying to match tariff data with direct price comparisons.

39. See also Singer and Gray 1988.

40. See e.g. the news expressed in Singer (1988b). See also Sarker and Singer (1989a, 1989b, and 1989c).

41. See e.g. Riedel (1984).

42. There is some evidence to suggest that the aggregate elasticity of demand for Third World manufactured exports is less than one. See, for example, Goldstein and Khan 1985.

43. See Stewart 1987.

44. An alternative might be increased generosity in the provision ·of transitional support for structural adjustment from the international community in return for restraint from applying an export tax. However, it is difficult to argue that, as a general principle, compensation for not exercising collective monopoly power should be a criterion for the provision of international aid. The critical issue in the case discussed is that the countries affected are both poor and capital starved, and that the fallacy of composition increases the cost of adjustment which, in a more ideal world, would be financed at least in part by aid and international public capital provision.

45. See e.g. Brett 1988 and Schmitz 1989. A more general treatment of these issues is in Bates 1981, 1983, and 1986. See also the critical comments on Bates by Bienefeld 1986.

46. In a many-country Heckscher–Ohlin world with free trade, the most dynamic component of world trade may well be south–south trade rather than north–south trade when there is more rapid accumulation of capital in the south than in

the north. Thus suppose the world economy is divided into the 'north', the NICs and the rest of the 'south'. The most capital intensive commodities will tend to be produced and exported from the north and the most labour intensive commodities will tend to be produced and exported from the south. The NICs will tend to hold an intermediate position, exporting their most capital intensive commodities to the north and to the rest of the south in exchange for the most capital intensive commodities from the north and the most labour intensive commodities from the south. If growth is concentrated in the NICs and if total north–south trade is much larger than south–south trade, then the rate of growth of north–south trade may very well turn out to be less than the rate of growth of south–south trade. Additional dynamism may result from south–south trade because of the potential for trade in more appropriate commodities produced with more appropriate techniques. Other reasons for greater potential dynamism in south–south trade may arise from the application of the new theories of trade which have been developed to explain intra-north trade to intra-south trade. For an elaboration of these arguments, see Evans 1989*b*, section 7.6; Parsan 1988, ch. 2 and ch. 3; and Stewart 1984.

47. For a discussion of this in the context of British colonial monetary systems, see Narsey 1987. See also Roemer 1977.

48. For a useful recent summary of the evolution of south–south trade, see Parsan 1988, ch. 2.

49. See Beenstock 1984, Wood 1991, and Evans 1989*b*, ch. 7.

References

Agarwala, R. (1983), 'Price Distortions and Growth in Developing Countries', World Bank Staff Working Paper No. 575, Management and Development Series, International Bank for Reconstruction and Development, Washington, D.C.

Aghazadeh, E., and Evans, H. D. (1988), 'Price Distortions, Efficiency and Growth', mimeo, IDS, University of Sussex, Brighton.

Balassa, B. (1975), 'Reforming the System of Incentives in Developing Countries', *World Development*, 3/6: 365–82.

—— and Associates (1982), *Development Strategies in Semi-Industrial Economies*, Johns Hopkins University Press, Baltimore, Md. (for the World Bank).

Baldwin, R. E. (1984), 'Trade Policies in Developed Countries', in R. W. Jones and P. B. Kenen (eds.), *Handbook of International Economics*, vol. i, Elsevier, Amsterdam.

Bardhan, P. K. (1984), *The Political Economy of Development in India*, Basil Blackwell, Oxford.

Bates, R. H. (1981), *Markets and States in Tropical Africa: The Political Basis of Agricultural Policies*, University of California Press, Berkeley, Calif.

—— (1983), *Essays on the Political Economy of Rural Africa*, Cambridge University Press, Cambridge.

—— (1986), 'The Politics of Agricultural Policy—a Reply', *IDS Bulletin*, 17/1 (Jan.): 12–15.

Beenstock, M. (1984), *The World Economy in Transition*, Allen & Unwin, London.

Bhagwati, J. N. (1978), *Foreign Trade Regimes and Economic Development: Anatomy and Consequences of Exchange Control Regimes*, Ballinger Press for MBER, Cambridge, Mass.

—— (1982), 'Directly Unproductive Profit Seeking (DUP) Activities', *Journal of Political Economy*, 90/5 (Oct.): 988–1002.

—— and Ruggie, J. G. (eds.) (1984), *Power, Passions and Purpose: Prospects for North–South Negotiations*, MIT Press, Cambridge, Mass.

Bienefeld, M. (1986), 'Analysing the Politics of African State Policy: Some Thoughts on Robert Bates' Work', *IDS Bulletin*, 17/1 (Jan.): 5–1.

Bliss, C. J. (1989), 'Trade and Development Theoretical Issues and Policy Implications', ch. 23 in H. Chenery and T. N. Srinivasan (eds.), *Handbook of Development Economics*, vol. ii, North-Holland, Amsterdam.

Bowles, S. (1985), 'The Production Process in a Competitive Economy: Walrasian, neo-Hobbesian and Marxian Models', *American Economic Review*, 75/1 (Mar.): 16–36.

Brandt, W. (1980), *North–South: A Programme for Survival*, Pan, London.

—— (Brandt Commission) (1983), *Common Crisis North–South; Co-operation for World Recovery*, Pan, London.

Brett, E. A. (1988), 'Suppressing Agriculture Exports in Uganda: State Control Marketing Structures', mimeo, IDS, University of Sussex and Makerere Institute of Social Research, Makerere University.

Burke, G. (1987), 'The Rise and Fall of the International Tin Agreements', mimeo, IDS, University of Sussex.

Cornia, G., Jolly, R., and Stewart, F. (eds.) (1987), *Adjustment with a Human Face, i: Protecting the Vulnerable and Promoting Growth*, Oxford University Press, Oxford.

De Janvry, A. (1978), 'Social Structure and Biased Technical Change in Argentinian Agriculture' in Binswanger *et al.*, *Induced Innovation: Technology, Institutions and Development*, Johns Hopkins University Press, Baltimore, Md.

—— (1981), *The Agrarian Question and Reform in Latin America*, Johns Hopkins University Press, Baltimore, Md.

De Melo, J. (1988), 'Computable General Equilibrium Models for Trade Policy Analysis in Developing Countries: A Survey', mimeo, Trade Policy Division, Country Economics Department, The World Bank.

Erzan, R., and Karsenty, G. (1989), 'Products Facing High Tariffs in Major Developed Market-Economy Countries: An Area of Priority for the Developing Countries in the Uruguay Round', *UNCTAD Review*, 1/1: 51–74.

Evans, H. D. (1979), 'International Community Policy: UNCTAD and NIEO in Search of a Rationale', *World Development*, 7/3: 259–79.

—— (1988), Review of H. Addo (ed.) (1985), *Transforming the World Economy? Nine Critical Essays on the New International Economic Order*, Hodder and Stoughton, London: Westview Press (in association with United Nations University, Tokyo), Boulder, Colo.; *Journal of Development Economics*, 28/2 (Mar.): 280–3.

—— (1989a), 'Alternative Perspectives on Trade and Development', ch. 24 in H. Chenery and T. N. Srinivasan (eds.), *Handbook of Development Economics*, vol. ii, North-Holland, Amsterdam.

—— (1989*b*), *Comparative Advantage and Growth: Trade and Development in Theory and Practice*, Harvester-Wheatsheaf, Hemel Hempstead.

Fitzgerald, E. V. K. (1986), 'The Problem of Balance in the Peripheral Socialist Economy', in K. Martin (ed.), *Readings in Capitalist and Non-Capitalist Development Strategies*, Heinemann, London.

General Agreement on Tariffs and Trade (GATT) (1986–7), *International Trade Year Book*, Geneva.

Gerschenkron, A. (1966), *Economic Backwardness in Historical Perspective: A Book of Essays*, Belknap Press of Harvard University Press, Cambridge, Mass.

Goldstein, M., and Khan, M. (1985), 'Income and Price Effects in Foreign Trade', in R. W. Jones and P. B. Kenen (eds.), *Handbook of International Economics*, vol. ii, North-Holland, Amsterdam.

Greenaway, D. (1986), 'Characteristics of Industrialization and Economic Performance under Alternative Development Strategies', mimeo, Background Paper for ch. 5, *World Development Report 1987*, World Bank, Washington DC.

Griffin, K. (1989), *Alternative Strategies for Economic Development*, MacMillan, London.

Hoffman, K. (1988), 'Technological Advance and Organizational Innovation in the Engineering Industry: A New Perspective on the Problems and Possibilities for Developing Countries', Report Submitted to the World Bank, Sussex Research Associates, Brighton.

Karunasekara, M. V. D. J. (1984), *Export Taxes on Primary Products: A Policy Instrument in International Development*, Commonwealth Economic Paper no. 19, Commonwealth Secretariat, London.

Keesing, D. B. (1979), 'Trade Policy for Developing Countries', World Bank Staff Working Paper no. 353.

Kravis, I. B. (1970), 'Trade as a Handmaiden of Growth: Similarities between the Nineteenth and Twentieth Centuries, *Economic Journal*, 80 (Dec.): 850–72.

Krueger, A. O. (1974), 'The Political Economy of the Rent-seeking Society', *American Economic Review*, 64/3 (June): 291–303.

—— (1978), *Foreign Trade Regimes and Economic Development: Liberalization Attempts and Consequences*, Ballinger Press for NBER, Cambridge, Mass.

—— (1984), 'Trade Policies in Developing Countries', in R. W. Jones and P. B. Kenen (eds.), *Handbook of International Economics*, vol. i, North-Holland, Amsterdam.

Krugman, P. (ed.), (1986), *Strategic Trade Policy and the New International Economics*, MIT Press, Cambridge, Mass.

Lazear, E. (1981), 'Agency, Earnings Profiles, Productivity, and Hours Restrictions', *American Economic Review*, 71: 606–20.

Lewis, W. A. (1980), 'The Slowing Down of the Engine of Growth', The Nobel Lecture, *American Economic Review*, 70/4: 555–64.

Lipsey, R. (1957), 'The Theory of Customs Unions: Trade Diversion and Welfare', *Economica*, 24: 40–6.

—— and Lancaster, K. (1956–7), 'The General Theory of Second Best', *Review of Economic Studies*, 6 (Dec.): 11–32.

Little, I. M. D. (1982), *Economic Development: Theory, Policy and International Relations*, Basic Books, New York.

—— Scitovsky, T., Little, I. M. D., and Scott, M. F. G. (1970), *Industry and Trade in Some Developing Countries: A Comparative Study*, Oxford University Press, New York, London, Oxford.

Luedde-Neurath, R. (1986), *Import Controls and Export Oriented Development: A Reassessment of the South Korean Case*, Westview Press, Boulder, Colo., and London.

MacBean, A. (1988), 'Uruguay and the Developing Countries', Draft Paper presented to the Annual Conference of the International Economics Study Group, Isle of Thorns; mimeo, University of Lancaster, Lancaster.

Michaely, M. (1977), *Theory of Commercial Policy: Trade and Protection*, Philip Allan, Oxford.

—— (1986), 'The Timing and Sequencing of Trade Policy Reform', in A. M. Choksi and D. Papageorgiou (eds.), *Economic Liberalization in Developing Countries*, Basil Blackwell, Oxford.

Murray, R. *et al.* (1987), 'Cyprus Industrial Strategy: Report of the UNDP/UNIDO Mission', IDS, University of Sussex, Brighton.

Narsey, W. (1987), 'A Re-interpretation of the History and Theory of Colonial Monetary Systems', Unpublished D.Phil. thesis, University of Sussex.

Neary, P. (1988), 'Export Subsidies and National Welfare', *Austrian Economic Papers*, Empirica 2: 243–61.

North, O. (1981), *Structure and Change in Economic History*, Norton, New York.

Olsen, M. (1982), *The Rise and Decline of Nations*. Yale University Press, New Haven, Conn., and London.

Pack, H., and Westphal, L. E. (1986), 'Industrial Strategy and Technological Change: Theory versus Reality', *Journal of Development Economics*, 22: 87–128.

Pagano, U. (1985), *Work and Welfare in Economic Theory*, Basil Blackwell, Oxford.

Parsan, E. (1988), 'An Investigation into the Potential for South–South Trade.

Riedel, J. (1984), 'Trade as the Engine of Growth in Developing Countries, revisited', *Economic Journal*, 94/373 (Mar.): 56–73.

—— (1988), 'The Demand for LDC Exports of Manufacturers: Estimates from Hong Kong', *Economic Journal*, 98/389 (Mar.): 138–48.

Roemer, J. E. (1977), 'The Effect of Sphere of Influence and Economic Distance on Composition of Trade in Manufactures', *Review of Economics and Statistics*, 59: 318–27.

—— (1982), *A General Theory of Exploitation and Class*, Harvard University Press, Cambridge, Mass.

Rybcynski, T. M. (1955), 'Factor Endowments and Relative Commodity Prices', *Economica*, 22 (Nov.): 336–41.

Samuelson, P. A. (1969), 'The Way of an Economist', in P. A. Samuelson (ed.), *International Economic Relations: Proceedings of the Third Congress of the International Economic Association*, MacMillan, London.

Sarkar, P., and Singer, H. W. (1988*a*), 'Debt Pressure and the Transfer Burden of the Third World Countries', mimeo, IDS, University of Sussex.

—— —— (1988*b*), 'Manufactured Exports and Terms of Trade Movements of Less Developed Countries with Special Reference to Recent Years (1980–1987)', mimeo, IDS, University of Sussex.

—— —— (1988*c*), 'Manufactured Exports of Developing Countries and their Terms of Trade since 1965', mimeo, IDS, University of Sussex.

Schmitz, H. (1989), 'Flexible Specialisation: A New Paradigm of Small-Scale Industrialisation?' Discussion Paper 261, IDS, University of Sussex: 25–9.

Sheehan, J. (1987), *Patterns of Development in Latin America: Poverty, Repression and Economic Strategy*, Princeton University Press, Princeton, NJ.

Sideri, S. (1970), *Trade and Power: Informal Colonialism in Anglo-Portuguese Relations*, Rotterdam University Press, Rotterdam.

Singer, H. W. (1988*a*), 'World Development Report 1987 on the Blessings of "Outward Orientation": A Necessary Correction', *Journal of Development Studies*, 24/2 (Jan.): 232–6.

—— (1988*b*), 'Industrialisation and World Trade: Ten Years after the Brandt Report', Paper prepared for the International Symposium 'The Crisis of the Global System: The World Ten Years after the Brandt Report, Crisis Management for the Nineties'.

—— and Gray, P. (1988), 'Trade Policy and Growth of Developing Countries: Some New Data', *World Development*, 16/3; 395–403.

Smith, A. (1986), 'The Infant Industry Argument and the Reform of Trade Policy', background study for the *World Development Report*, World Bank, 1987, mimeo, University of Sussex.

Srinivasan, T. N. (1986), 'Neoclassical Political Economy, the State and Economic Development', Paper no. 375, Economic Growth Centre, Yale University.

—— (1989), 'International Aspects: Introduction to Part 5', in H. Chenery and T. N. Srinivasan (eds.), *Handbook of Development Economics*, North-Holland, Amsterdam.

Stewart, F. (1984), 'Recent Theories of International Trade: Some Implications for the South', in H. Kierskowski (ed.), *Monopolistic Competition and International Trade*, Oxford University Press, Oxford.

—— (1987), 'Back to Keynesianism', *World Policy Journal* (Summer): 467–83.

Syrquin, M., and Chenery, H. B. (1989), 'Patterns of Development 1950 to 1983', World Bank Discussion Paper no. 41.

Taylor, L. (1986), 'Trade and Growth', *Review of Black Political Economy*, 14/4: 17–36.

Toye, J. (1987), *Dilemmas of Development*, Blackwell, Oxford.

Wade, R. (1991, forthcoming), *Governing the Market: Economic Theory and Role of Government in East Asian Industrialization*, Princeton University Press, Princeton, NJ.

White, G. M., (1984), 'Developmental States and Socialist Industrialisation in the Third World, *Journal of Development Studies*, 21/1 (Oct.): 97–120.

—— (ed.) (1988), *Development States in East Asia*, MacMillan, London.

Williamson, O. E. (1975), *Markets and Hierarchies: Analysis and Anti-Trust Implications*, The Free Press, New York.

—— (1985), *The Economic Institutions of Capitalism: Firms, Markets and Rational Contracting*, The Free Press, New York.

Wood, A. (1991), 'How Much Does Trade in the South Affect Workers in the North?', *World Bank Research Observer*, 6/1 (Jan.).

World Bank (1983), *World Development Report*, Oxford University Press, New York.

—— (1987), *World Development Report*, Oxford University Press, New York.

4
Neo-liberalism, Gender, and the Limits of the Market

NAILA KABEER and JOHN HUMPHREY

1. Introduction

The neo-liberal paradigm is a relatively recent offshoot of the broader and older intellectual tradition of economic liberalism. Several paradigms coexist within this tradition, sharing common methodological foundations, but differing in their enforced assumptions, derived results, and consequent policy prescriptions. In the context of this book, these differences bear on the status and significance accorded to states and markets in achieving economic development in the Third World. As the introduction points out, both the 'trammelled markets' approach of earlier political economists as well as the weight given to market imperfections in neo-classical analysis permit considerable scope for state intervention in the development process. Neo-liberal economists, on the other hand, favour the free market solution. They rest their case on empirical documentation of the high efficiency costs of bureaucratic intervention, including unproductive 'rent-seeking' activities on the part of individuals, groups, and states.

The economists who advocate the *laissez-faire* route to development in the Third World (Lal, Krueger, *et al.*) pay scant attention to the place of women in their vision of this process. Such an omission suggests either that they believe their analysis applies without modification to women or that they believe it is completely irrelevant to women (Jagger 1983). Our analysis of the logic of neo-liberalism leads us to believe that their silence is associated with the former position. In other words, the logic of neo-liberalism may recognize gender differences and indeed gender inequalities, but would still recommend the market route to dealing with these phenomena.

This chapter presents an account of the logic by which neo-liberalism arrives at this position. It also offers a twofold critique of the paradigm, based on (*a*) the robustness of its fundamental assumptions in capturing the realities of women's lives, and (*b*) the effectiveness of its prescriptions in assisting agencies concerned with integrating gender issues into development policy. The chapter first outlines the methodological foundations of neo-liberalism and its implications for maximizing the social good. It examines these implications in the context of WID (Women in Development) policies of agencies like the World Bank and USAID and points to the contradictions encountered by them in their attempts to implement market-orientated solutions. Such contradictions help to highlight the inherent limitations of neo-liberalism in the field of gender and development policy. The paper then evaluates the neo-liberal view of gender relations in households and markets in the light of empirical data from different Third World countries. It concludes with an assessment of the free market as a mechanism for achieving the twin goals of equity and efficiency in the development process.

2. Individualism, Rationality, and Self-interest: The Building Blocks of the Neo-liberal Paradigm

Hayek remains a major influence on neo-liberal thinkers today and we will rely on his eloquent exposition of the basic principles of liberal theory to elucidate the neo-liberal case for the market. These principles—the a priori assumptions of economic liberalism—are individualism, self-interest, and rationality. From these principles are derived a particular view of individual behaviour which is then aggregated to build up a theory of society and the social order; in the process what sets out to be a positivist analysis of individuals and society—a description of what is—is transformed into a normative vision—i.e. private property and free enterprise are essential to ensure that individual decisions taken for private benefit can add up to the greatest general good (Brett 1985).

Individualism or the notion that the individual exists prior to, and separate from, society is, in Hayek's view, diametrically opposed to the 'collectivist' vision of society as a *sui generis* entity, independent of the individuals who make it up. Society is seen instead as the product of 'individual action directed towards other people and guided by their expected behaviour' (Hayek 1949: 6). Social institutions and collectivities can ultimately be traced to the unforeseen and unintended effects of human action, rather than human design. No individual or group has the foresight or information to improve on what each person acting individually can achieve through spontaneous association. In fact, organizations only have virtue when they do not arise out of human design.

The second assumption is that individual behaviour is guided by self-interest. Self-interest arises because the human needs which any single individual can effectively care for are those of a narrow circle of family and friends of which he—or indeed she—is the centre. No individual or group of individuals can know or care about the effects of their actions outside of this immediate and limited sphere. Therefore, they cannot take on the responsibility for defining the needs and interests of those outside this sphere nor should they seek to inhibit others from pursuing their own self-defined interests. To privilege any group over others in defining the social interest is to attribute to them undue omniscience as well as the undue power to thwart the liberty of others.

Finally, individuals are assumed to behave rationally. The assumption of rationality is fully cognizant of differences in individual tendencies to indolence, irrationality, improvidence, but suggests that in the face of unlimited wants and scarce means, institutional arrangements which reward individual effort will lead to adaptation to scarcity and efficient use of available resources. The institutional arrangements which best achieve this condition are private property and the free market; private property because it clearly delineates the sphere of individual choice and responsibility, giving exclusive rights to what is owned (labour, property, capital); and the free market because greater efficiencies are achieved through division of labour, specialization, and exchange. In an increasingly complex society, an impersonal pricing mechanism which embodies 'formal equality of rules' provides the optimal framework within which such exchange can take place.

A role for the state is accepted within classic liberalism, but limited to guaranteeing this 'formal equality of rules' and to remedying deficiencies of the market. Government intervention becomes undesirable if it transgresses these limits; it leads to a configuration of outcomes which are inferior to those achieved through market forces. It may be responsible, for instance, for a divergence between individual effort and remuneration, arbitrary redistribution of the burden of market failures or for a distortion of price signals, leading to long-term persistence of the very market failure it was designed to remove.

On these methodological foundations, neo-liberal thinkers have constructed a theoretical framework which explains and justifies their case for private property and the free market at every level of society, from individuals to the global economy. It rests on the claim that liberty and efficiency are inextricably connected; that free exchange and trade will maximize the welfare of all parties concerned because it allows each to specialize in their areas of comparative advantage. In other words, the principles which work for the individual work for the global economy, which, after all, simply represents the aggregate of individual units. Within this general liberal framework, different paradigms are to be distinguished by the degree to which they can accommodate modifications to these basic assumptions, the significance they attach to market failures, and the role they ascribe to the state. The hallmarks of neo-liberalism are its restricted interpretation, its vigorous critique of policy-induced failures, and its consequent espousal of market forces (despite their imperfections) and a minimalist role for the state.

3. Neo-liberalism, Women, and the Family

The above exposition raises a number of key issues for our argument. They concern the interpretation of social difference and inequality contained within the neo-liberal paradigm. While neo-liberalism recognizes that differences between individuals in terms of their endowments and preferences may lead to inequalities, it judges it to be an acceptable and necessary price for individual liberty. If individuals or groups, through their greater intelligence, conscientiousness, or efforts can secure for themselves 'material or moral standards different from those of the rest of the population' (Hayek 1949: 31), they must be free to do so. In Hayek's words: 'We must face the fact that the preservation of individual freedom is incompatible with a full satisfaction of our views of distributive justice' (Hayek 1949: 22). The market may reproduce social inequalities, but as long as coercive or exclusionary means are not employed in this process, it will still produce the best possible set of outcomes.

Thus the paradigm is not against spontaneous and natural collectivities, only coercive and artificially created ones. Neo-liberalism affirms the value of 'natural' forms of collectivities such as the family and linguistic or religious communities as representing spontaneous associations of individuals in pursuit of their own self-interests. Concealed within this position, of course, is a notion of the family as an 'unproblematic unity' dedicated to the collective interests of members related by ties of blood and marriage. The family—and therefore women's position within it—falls outside the realm of public concern because it is, more than any other, a spontaneous association where individuals pursue their private lives and personal interests.

Most economists are content with this view of family and household matters as outside the domain of economics. The main exception is contained in the 'new' household economics pioneered by Becker and others as one branch of neo-classical micro-economic theory. The primary contribution made by these economists is to extend the logic of the choice-theoretic approach to household behaviour. The formation of households and the division of labour within it is explained as the product of individuals making rational choices, each guided by the goal of maximizing their lifetime utility function.

People are seen as uniting in marriage because of their mutual desire for children. The household division of labour then emerges out of the biologically determined comparative advantage women have in bearing and suckling children. It is this 'natural' comparative advantage and the efficiencies to be gained from specialization that account for the role women choose to occupy, both within the household as well as in the market. Thus, marriage can be conceptualized as a two-person firm (Becker 1974), where women become responsible for domestic labour because their earning power is diminished by their childcare responsibilities while men become the bread-winners because they can reap the advantages of uninterrupted labour market participation. The net welfare of the couple is thus higher than if each had chosen to engage in both domestic and market activities. Since women choose to bear children, they must accept the lower earnings that go with intermittent labour force participation. Gender differentials within the market-place are seen as the consequence of rational individual choice.

4. Women in Development: The Early Years

The silence of the dominant neo-liberal theorists on gender signifies their belief that, despite its acknowledged inadequacies, the market represents the key to resolving the problems of gender and development. The influence of this position has become evident in WID policy documents. As Buvinic (1983) has noted, official WID agencies tend to reproduce the shifts and trends discernible in mainstream development discourses. Each major shift in development thinking has carried its own implications for the location of women within the overall policy framework. Early development policy related to women primarily as mothers or would-be mothers; welfare programmes were devised which made women the primary targets of family planning and maternal and child health care and nutritional services. Welfare-orientated strategies still prevail in much of the Third World, but their scope has been widened to include, for instance, various small-scale income-generating opportunities, frequently in the handicraft sector. They have also been supplemented by other forms of assistance in line with subsequent shifts in development thinking.

The World Bank's assault on poverty, spearheaded by McNamara in 1973, made the target group approach a major plank of the Bank's policy for the rest of the seventies. In their attempts to target poverty subgroups, policy-makers became aware that women, particularly those heading house-holds, bore a disproportionate share of the world's poverty. Women were thus made specific targets of poverty-alleviation strategies. The basic needs approach, first formulated by the ILO, also created a space for women in development policy, because it helped to highlight their important role in providing for their family's basic needs (Palmer 1977, Buvinic 1983).

However, while this new visibility may have resulted in greater benefits being channelled towards women by development agencies, it was offered on very specific and non-threatening terms. Anti-poverty strategies, for women as well as men, focused on issues of deprivation while the basic needs approach emphasized women as providers of family welfare. Either way, the emphasis was on the better distribution of benefits and services to poor women within a predetermined framework of economic and social opportu-nities. A more redistributionist approach, motivated by equity considerations, would entail a restructuring of this framework and would encompass all women rather than focusing on poor women alone. The implications of a redistributionist approach would have been far reaching; it would have called into question the gender stereotypes, recruitment practices, and employment conditions entrenched within the implementing agencies themselves. As Buvinic concludes, 'The continued survival of welfare-orientated programmes for women can be traced to the fact that they are technically simple and politically safe to implement' (25).

5. Women, Development, and Neo-liberalism

By the 1980s, the ascendancy of neo-liberalism within the donor community presented a new challenge to WID practitioners. The renewed emphasis on economic efficiency and market forces ran directly counter to the welfare-based interventions which hitherto constituted the core of WID policy. The neo-liberal message was that such welfare provisions would emerge 'naturally' through the market mechanism (provided they were backed by effective demand). Similarly, price incentives would be sufficient to attract underutilized female labour into market production, if that was what the economy required. State delivery of services and income-generating opportunities merely supplanted—and often suppressed—the efficient operation of market forces in meeting women's needs.

WID practitioners responded to the winds of change by adopting the discourse of economic rationality, without entirely jettisoning their commitment to welfare interventions. If their earlier arguments were concerned with issues of distribution and equity, then their current approach foregrounded efficiency considerations: gender has to be 'factored into the development equation' if returns to programme interventions are to be maximized (Horenstein 1985). The new style of advocacy is to be found in the policy and position papers brought out by the WID sections of influential organizations such as the World Bank and USAID.

The USAID document *Women in Development Aid Policy* (1982) is exemplary in this respect. Its message is that 'improving women's status raised the equity issues', while 'assisting the total development effort' raised issues of efficiency. It declares unequivocally, 'The experience of the past 10 years tells us that the key issue underlying the women in development concept is an economic one: *misunderstanding of gender differences, leading to inadequate planning and designing of projects, results in diminished returns on investment*' (emphasis in original). It cites the example of women in African farming who are estimated to do 60–80 per cent of all agricultural work, and yet are rarely targeted for training, extension, research, technology, or improved inputs.

Implicit in this discourse of efficiency is a model of human rationality which echoes that of Hayek. Pointing to the fact that 'gender-role differences' associate women and men with different productive tasks, the USAID paper argues that there will be a difference in responses to development incentives depending on the extent to which different genders perceive they have a stake in the outcome of particular interventions. 'Knowledge of these gender-role patterns will assist project planners to maximise the chance of project success. Incentives for change which are specifically adapted to gender roles, and are therefore based on a proper assessment of the stake the population feels in the outcome of the project, is critical to success.'

Aside from factoring gender into the project cycle, USAID attaches considerable weight to improving women's access to the market and suggests measures which would help dismantle barriers to women's greater participation in both formal and informal sectors. In the formal sector, it recommends breaking down women's segregation in low-productivity occupations by designing projects which 'expand employment opportunities in sectors where women have not traditionally worked and in those newer areas of the economy where gender-specific work roles are not yet entrenched'. It also emphasizes technical, industrial, and management skills programmes to prepare women for entry into profitable skilled and white collar occupations. In the informal sector, the agency's advice is the provision of credit and technical assistance through various financial intermediaries.

A position paper brought out by the World Bank at the start of the decade echoes many of the above themes. It too makes a strong case for integrating women into development on grounds of economic efficiency: 'If women continue to be left out of the mainstream of development and deprived of opportunities to realise their full potential, serious inefficiencies in the use of resources will persist' (World Bank 1979: 1). At the same time, it deals sympathetically with the double work load that most women face, their lack of power within the trade unions, and their consequent disadvantages in the labour market and notes inequalities in the distribution of resources within the household. More recently, the Bank's WID Unit has launched a 'Safe Motherhood' initiative on the basis that high rates of maternal morbidity and mortality prevailing in many low-income countries represent 'a loss of productivity' for the family, for the economy, and for the development effort itself (Herz and Measham 1987). They call for better primary health care for mothers and children, for improved technologies to reduce the arduousness of women's physical labour, and for 'a variety of measures [which] can build women's self-esteem'.

Despite the stress on market rationality and market-led development, therefore, it would appear that 'neo-liberal' WID policy cannot be reduced to simply 'getting prices right'. The language of efficiency is used to advocate a wide-ranging set of interventions which go well beyond those envisaged by most neo-liberal thinkers. This tension between an agency's overall commitment to *laissez-faire* principles and its acceptance of non-market intervention in specific areas is not unique to the WID sphere of development policy. It is evident also in the area of population control. The Bank, for instance, strongly backs state action to bring down fertility rates on two grounds. The first is the existence of 'externalities', i.e. divergences between private and social calculus of high fertility. The second is the absence of market mechanisms capable of meeting the 'substantial unmet need' for family planning services in many Third World Countries (World Bank 1984). Population policy is declared the province of government because governments are seen here as 'custodians of society', capable of transcending the individual and short-term interests of their constituents. In view of the broad range of interventions recommended to achieve population control, the Bank's policy in this area represents an undeniable departure from the principles of the free market, and an unequivocal tilt towards state intervention in family relations, an area which the neo-liberal orthodoxy would uphold as the private sphere *par excellence*.

A reasonable interpretation of this apparent contradiction between the promotion of market solutions as a general response to development problems and acceptance of state intervention in specific spheres of policy is that while market forces are indeed given primacy, it is also recognized that certain social objectives cannot be achieved through the market. Thus in promoting women's market participation, both the Bank and USAID acknowledge the need for greater rather than fewer interventions to compensate for the apparent failure of the market forces to overcome gender discrimination.

To conclude this section, it is clear that WID programmes, in both their pre- and post-neo-liberal phases, have helped to place women firmly on the development agenda. At the same time, the WID response to the challenge of neo-liberal doctrines throws into sharp relief both the limitations of WID policies as well as the inadequacies of the neo-liberal paradigm itself. In treating women as economic agents in the development process, neo-liberal WID has shifted from the earlier, narrow focus on women as recipients or providers of welfare and taken seriously the findings of recent research demonstrating women's essential contribution to production. However, the prevailing notion of development appears primarily efficiency-orientated, notwithstanding WID's professed concern with equity, and has serious limitations as far as addressing gender subordination is concerned. As Moser points out, women might be essential to the success of total development efforts, but development does not necessarily improve conditions for women (1989).

The basic problem is that while WID agencies recognize gender symmetries in access to crucial resources such as land, credit, training, and employment opportunities, their explanations do not extend beyond 'cultural norms' and 'the division of labour'. The full measure of these constraints on women's life chances is not appreciated. In spite of repeated references to gender roles and gender differences, the larger issue of gender subordination is never confronted. The assumption that drawing women into the market will somehow empower them underestimates the resilience of what Toye has called 'the stable structures of oppression' (1987: 19) that persist, regardless of the state of market forces in a society.

We pointed out that the World Bank identified one set of 'failures' to justify the case for state intervention in population policy. In the rest of the paper, we will point to the existence of 'family failures' as well as forms of market and state failures not encompassed by the neo-liberal paradigm as the basis of our critique of *laissez-faire* development. We will point out that these 'failures' do not represent aberrations in an otherwise adequate paradigm of gender difference, but are phenomena which are excluded by the methodological individualism of neo-liberalism. They are the product of the social norms, practices, and institutions which govern the relations between women and men, define women as a subordinate gender, and lead to the structural reproduction of gender disadvantage in all spheres of the social system.

6. Some Problems with the Neo-liberal Concept of the Family

The model of the family-household which appears in much of liberal economic thinking bears the imprint of its cultural origins. Becker's household, for instance, is a clearly bounded, economically unified entity, based on a Eurocentric commonsense view of the nuclear family: breadwinning male, dependent housewife, together with their offspring. Such a model is patently inadequate to deal with the shifting, flexible structures, the plurality of family and household composition, domestic relations, and residential arrangements which characterize domestic groupings in different parts of the world (Evans 1988, Moore 1988, Kandiyoti 1988). Within the Caribbean region, for instance, family forms include 'nuclear' families, matrifocal families, extended families, single-parent families, and female-headed households (Ellis 1986). Studies from Sub-Saharan Africa show the coexistence of separate purses and parallel economies within the conjugal unit; Whitehead illustrates the complexity of household organization among the Kusasi in Ghana by describing the ideal-typical household composition: 'a male head, his junior brother, both of whom are married with two wives each, an unmarried adult male (brother or son) and able-bodied daughter or daughters, a woman given in pawn and one or more "mothers"' (1981: 95). As a tool with which to analyse domestic arrangements in the highly differentiated societies of the Third World, the paradigm's limitations become glaringly obvious. This ability to impose commonsense views on the analysis of household behaviour, regardless of cultural context, stems of course from a fundamental axiom of neo-liberalism which holds that, at an important level, individuals can be analysed on the basis of certain universal principles.

Putting the problem of conceptualizing households to one side, there are other axioms embedded in neo-liberalism which reveal its political bias. The assumption that individuals are motivated by self-interest and rationality is used to explain their market behaviour. Indeed, it is essential to the model's ability to predict a determinate equilibrium outcome. The same degree of rationality is not claimed for the household. It is seen rather as a site of altruistic behaviour. This dichotomy has of course the convenience that it excludes the necessity or desirability of state intervention in both spheres. Within the market-place, the uncoordinated activities of a multitude of individuals can still be relied on to produce 'Pareto-optimal' outcomes, provided they are all motivated by the pursuit of their own self-interest and by market signals which are not distorted by bureaucrats or trade unions. Within the household, the mutual altruism characterizing relations between family members can be trusted to maximize collective and individual welfare. Attempts by the state to intervene in this process would constitute an infringement of rights and liberties in the most private sphere of its citizens' lives.

Neo-liberal household members thus appear to suffer from a 'Jekyll and Hyde' syndrome. They are motivated by self-interest and competitiveness in the market-place, but inspired by altriusm and benevolence once the sacred threshold of the household has been crossed. Even in Becker's model, where decisions concerning household production, particularly the allocation of household labour between competing uses of time, are made in accordance with economically rational principles, the distribution of household resources is trusted to the 'benevolent dictator' who heads the household and effects the optimal welfare of its members. The familial character of household relations, the ideologies of mutual caring and support which most neo-liberals would attribute to it, render the logic of the market irrelevant to the issue of intra-household distribution.

How possible is it to accommodate conceptually this 'paradoxical . . . juxtaposition of naked self-interest that presumably motivates efficient allocation of market resources and a perfect altruism which presumably motivates equitable allocation of family resources' (Folbre 1986)? To what extent does the empirical literature support the characterization of household behaviour as mutually altruistic and concerned with maximizing the joint welfare of household members? And finally, even if these assumptions are empirically and conceptually acceptable, can the resulting outcomes be regarded as compatible with the objectives of development? We will deal with these issues in the following section on 'family failures'.

7. Family Failures

7.1. Distribution of essential resources

There is now a considerable amount of research by both feminist and other scholars which seriously undermines the neo-liberal vision of family life. It points instead to a rather more complex set of needs, interests, and allocative mechanisms than that captured by the neo-liberal notion of the family as a freely chosen, mutually beneficial collectivity of individuals. In the South Asian context, considerable research has been undertaken into intra-household distribution of resources in response to observed female disadvantage in a number of indicators of physical well-being. These included lower female life expectancy at birth, high rates of maternal mortality as well as marked gender differentials in infant and child mortality. Detailed studies from Bangladesh and India suggest that sex differentials in mortality rates may be linked to the asymmetrical distribution of critical resources, particularly food and health care, between household members (Sen and Sengupta 1983, Chen *et al.* 1981, Kabeer 1989).

At an aggregated level, gender disadvantage shows up in the highly masculine sex ratios which characterize the northern region of the Indian sub-continent. There is a general consensus that these sex ratios are indicators of social rather than biological disadvantage (Harriss and Watson 1987) and as such provide information on the value attached by a society to the needs and well-being of its members. There is also empirical evidence from other parts of the Third World of gender inequalities in food distribution (see Sen 1987 for references), although detailed quantitative data is harder to find. However, the regional pattern of sex ratios (Momsen and Townsend 1987) and sex differentials in mortality rates (Sen 1987) suggests that South Asia, the Middle East, and Northern Africa are areas where the implications of gender discrimination are more severe for women's physical well-being than, for instances, Sub-Saharan Africa and South-East Asia.

7.2. Non-traded family production

A second form of 'family failure' overlooked within the neo-liberal model relates to a particular category of 'non-tradables'—human resources—which are essentially produced and reproduced within the family-based household. The reproduction of human resources goes beyond the act of procreation, it encompasses tasks and activities associated with 'childcare', the care of the sick and elderly as well as those activities which allow members of the household to remain fed and healthy on a daily basis, cooking, washing, cleaning, gathering water and fuel, etc. While the gender division of labour may vary historically and cross-culturally, women tend to be generally assigned primary responsibility for reproductive work in most parts of the world.

The neo-liberal assumption that, if price incentives are right, women will respond to market opportunities in economically rational ways implicitly assumes a substitutability of family labour between the production of material resources and the reproduction of human resources, which does not in fact correspond to empirical reality. These are not equivalent activities, governed by the same set of decision rules, despite the fact that women's time may go into both. While some aspects of reproductive work may be transferred to the market, it is in general far less responsive to economic signals than productive work. This point is clearly made in Elson's critique of structural adjustment programmes, which take for granted that women's unpaid labour will continue regardless of how development resources are reallocated, and will be enough to make up for cutbacks in social services aimed at family welfare. As she says,

the process of reproduction and maintenance of human resources is different from the production of any other kind of resource. It does not respond to economic signals in the same way . . . if the demand for labour falls, if unemployment rises and wages fall, mothers do not 'scrap' their children or leave them to rot untended. Human resources have an intrinsic, not merely instrumental, value. (1989: 58)

Whether economic need or market incentives lead to greater female involvement in market-orientated production, and whether a fall in family income or male unemployment leads to greater demands on women's time, there is a limit to how far the responsibility for reproductive activities can be devolved to other substitute figures, particularly among the poor. Men will not perform domestic labour, generally speaking, even if the price of women's labour rises.

The unequal terms embodied in the gender division of household labour is the basis of 'women's double load' referred to in the World Bank position paper cited earlier. It appears empirically in the longer hours of work documented for women in studies from different parts of the world, some of which are summarized in Goldschmidt-Clermont (1982) and Dixon-Mueller (1985). The impact of change on the gender division of labour often appears to be accommodated at women's expense. The World Bank notes 'A study of the impact of improved rural water supplies on women in Kenya found that when water was made more accessible, women received less assistance from other family members in fetching it' (1979: 21). A study by Folbre (1984) in the Philippines shows that women coped with increased market participation by cutting down on leisure time rather than on domestic labour, while unemployed men increased their leisure time rather than time spent in household work. Folbre's study makes the point that women accommodate increased market participation by cutting down on their leisure time rather than on domestic work; men's involvement in the market does not involve such a trade-off.

7.3. Externalities in human capital formation

The final form of family 'failure' dealt with here concerns human capital formation, specifically in relation to education and skill acquisition. It is a form of externality which arises because of the divergence between those who make decisions within the family and those who bear its consequences. Decisions to invest in education take place very early in an individual's life before she or he is in a position to exercise any choice about their longer-term labour market participation. Such decisions are taken by parents on behalf of their children and if anybody's utility is being maximized it is the parents' or at least the parents' perception of children's utility. Later choices concerning higher education or work experience are closely shaped by these prior decisions and early forms of disadvantage can be cumulative. If this discontinuity in the decision-making process underlying human capital formation is juxtaposed with the strong son-preference expressed in many cultures, then 'family failure' in this context takes on a gender dimension. Daughters are penalized more than sons in the labour market because of decisions taken by parents. There is ample empirical evidence on gender-differentials in literacy, enrolment rates, and educational qualifications (UNDP 1990) to show the widespread nature of this form of family failure. It places a large question mark over both the equity and the efficiency of decisions taken within the family and the ability of market forces to override the consequences of family failures.

8. Alternative Explanations of Family Failures

How are we to judge these different categories of 'family failures'? Up to a point, of course, asymmetry within the family can be explained within the neo-classical paradigm as a matter of individual tastes and preferences. Women eat less, pay less attention to their own health, work longer hours, and invest less in female children because they choose to. Tastes and preferences do not enter into neo-classical household models. They are taken as given, stable, and randomly distributed so that generally speaking 'inexplicable behaviour due to tastes is believed to be either trivial or idiosyncratic' (Amsden 1980: 13). It is therefore perfectly feasible that some members will choose (for altruistic reasons) to deprive themselves of necessary food, medical attention, and leisure time in favour of other members. However, when (*a*) the subordination of personal needs in favour of the well-being of others appears systematically as the property of one social category of individuals (women) while the beneficiaries of such preferences appear systematically to belong to another social category (men) and (*b*) the consequences are life-threatening levels of nutrition and health for the former, then it becomes increasingly absurd to attribute such 'inexplicable behaviour' to 'trivial' or 'idiosyncratic' differences in tastes.

The individual experiences and cultural influences which shape a person's tastes and preferences may be external to the market (a point we will return to later), but they must be treated as endogenous to any model of intra-household distribution—as the New Household Economics purports to be—if they systematically privilege men in the access to consumption resources within the household to the extent of diminishing women's chances of survival. If women acquiesce to such asymmetry in household distribution, then the model must disaggregate the gender basis of rational choice to account for the observed association between male/self-interest and female/altruism in distributional outcomes. If, on the other hand, such asymmetry is imposed (by the community, the family, or the individual male) the model has to be reformulated to take account of the more oppressive aspects of gender divisions within the household. Either way, if the health and well-being of women is to be part of the development agenda, even if it is solely in their capacities as reproducers and nurturers of the future labour force, such household outcomes cannot be regarded as allocationally efficient, let alone allocationally equitable.

9. Gender in the Labour Market

In the previous sections, some aspects of household relations which lead to systematic disadvantage for women have been outlined. In this section, we will consider the imperfections arising from the impact of gender relations within labour markets. Within the neo-liberal paradigm, there is a selective recognition of market failures. Imperfections in labour markets arising from the attempts by trade unions to monopolize labour supply, for example, have received a lot of attention from some governments influenced by the paradigm. The problems raised by natural monopolies (water, for example) are also recognized, although not always acted upon with the same zeal. However, the neo-liberals lay greatest stress on policy-induced imperfections, relegating other forms of imperfections to a very secondary position.

The impact of gender relations within the market itself is to a large extent masked by the attribution of observed differences in the fortunes of women and men to either biological difference or household arrangements. A large amount of women's supposed disadvantage in the labour market would be the result of rational choices to specialize in domestic labour. The interventions of WID in markets would be limited to, first, making sure that development projects recognized existing sexual divisions of labour and design their interventions so as to make them efficient. Secondly, in those cases where externalities result in households making decisions about labour allocation which create inefficiencies or undesirable outcomes for the wider economy (of the sort stressed by the World Bank's policy on population) prices could be altered and schemes promoted to change patterns of male and female participation.

This perspective assumes that the market is relatively open to women. The way to improve the position of women lies in persuading women to take advantage of the opportunities available. For example, the USAID document cited above argues that the utilization of female labour resources is inefficient because established role models for women restrict them from taking full advantage of market opportunities. It suggests promoting the entry of women into new occupations as a reasonable and viable policy (USAID 1982). Collier makes the same suggestion (1987: 8), and he argues that increased participation in the market will remedy the material disadvantage which is at the root of women's oppression (1987: 12–14).

This perspective overestimates the openness of the market, particularly in terms of women's access to the better opportunities within it. Job segregation and sex-typing shows little sign of declining, and in many areas of work, jobs continue to be strongly segregated along sex lines. Access to specific segments of labour markets is highly restricted for men and women, and the areas open to women are characterized by relatively low wages and limited opportunities for advancement. If such patterns persist, women's incorporation into the market will not reduce their disadvantage in work and employment or undermine their disadvantage in the household.

The experience of women in the market, and in labour markets in particular, requires an explanation which is based on the operation of gender relations within the market itself. Certain gender stereotypes relating to work are seen across a wide range of societies. For example, the association of male work with greater short-term physical effort, exposure to risk, and co-operation between workers is found not only in the metalworking factories of Sydney, Paris, and São Paulo (Game and Pringle 1983, Guilbert 1966, Humphrey 1987) but also among the Baruya of New Guinea (Godelier 1982: 37). In almost any workplace situation, the norms of conduct, expectations of performance, and the suitability of particular persons will be heavily influenced by gender considerations. Managers have very clear stereotypes of the kinds of work for which men and women are most suited, and workers themselves have very clear understandings of the work they are most suited to and would prefer to do.

If this gendering of the workplace were just a way of recognizing either biological difference or the different skills and aptitudes men and women acquire as a result of the domestic division of labour, then one could see gender as a kind of short-hand for evaluating potential performance and fitting people to jobs. The fact that populations of women and men display a wide range of overlap of abilities could be accommodated by the notion of statistical discrimination. However, the evaluations of the suitability of men and women for certain types of work involves more than this. First, many studies have shown that decision-makers quite often have erroneous views about the average characteristics of men and women. The people responsible for formulating and implementing recruitment and training policies tend to be male, and they frequently compare women unfavourably to men, even when the available evidence shows that such comparisons are unfounded. Second, the distinctions between women and men are quite often based on characteristics which are not relevant to the occupations they perform. When Chiplin and Sloane state that 'in the industrial case one must recognise that natural endowments differ between the sexes' (1980: 291), a number of questions are left begging. Why are men and women with the same endowments not chosen for the same jobs? Why do maleness and femaleness override other differences? Are endowments only natural, and how does acquisition vary according to sex? Are endowments a cause of segregation or merely a basis on which to justify it? Like so many labour market theorists, Chiplin and Sloane assume that the market works and then impute the endowments which explain the differences observed between men and women. Third, different attributes are themselves valued according to the gender of the person possessing them. The valuation of attributes in sex-specific terms was evident in company responses to the Equal Pay Act in the United Kingdom. The sexual division of labour was redefined so as to minimize comparisons and challenges to job evaluation criteria, rather than use the Act to treat male and female labour more equitably and efficiently (Snell 1979: 44–5).

Gender divides women and men into two distinct and opposite groups. It also assigns them distinct statuses. As Scott argues:

A status . . . implies a hierarchical positional structure with juridical implications (rights and obligations), normative control and the exercise of power . . . The specificity of gender statuses is that (a) identities are ascribed and unambiguous, which means that they intervene in all social situations, including work; (b) they are underpinned by institutions outside the economy as well as within it, which means that gender relationships in the workplace are partly defined by 'external' structures; and (c) gender refers to one of the most intimate of personal identities, i.e. sexuality. These identities are protected by strong sexual taboos against sex-role reversal ambiguity, and in jobs that have become sex-typed these taboos make for resistance to desegregation. (1987: 5, 11)

Scott argues further that in Western societies, 'gender involves at least three elements: power, a domestic division of labour and sexuality. For women, the power aspect implies subordination, dependence, auxiliarity and deference. The domestic division of labour implies care of the young, the old and the sick, education of the young, food production and housework. Sexuality implies beautification, passivity and seducibility. These aspects of gender have positional implications in all social situations, including the workplace' (1987: 8–9). These aspects of gender are not only seen in developed societies. In Brazil and the Philippines, for example, beautification among women workers in industry is encouraged by the staging of beauty contests. The sexual division of labour in industry and services in these countries is very similar in many respects to that found in Europe. Even in countries where gender relations take on a different form, the world of work tends to reflect this form rather than not contain a gender aspect at all. Gender has positional and relational implications and involves a hierarchy. This has consequences for both the valuation of work and segregation.

The attribution of masculinity and femininity to jobs is also an attribution of comparative value. Analyses of job evaluation schemes, for example, show a systematic overvaluation of male traits, while women's work is often defined negatively, in terms of the absence of the masculine qualities which give it value. Gender stereotyping of jobs, therefore, involves the valuation of the work done by men and women, as well as the identification of masculine and feminine aspects of work and the unambiguous allocation of individuals of each sex as suitable for certain types of work.

Market forces fail to break down these valuations because they are protected by segregation. The barriers to mixing of jobs and the entry of men into female jobs (and vice versa) are very strong, and even when men do perform the same tasks as women, their work is often combined into different occupations. Guilbert (1966) describes a wide variety of mechanisms used in the metalworking industry to distinguish male occupations from female when the basic job content was similar. In other circumstances, promotion lines for men are radically differentiated from those available to women. For these reasons, the introduction of women into male occupations tends not to have the demonstration effect suggested by Collier (1987: 9). Instead, men respond by using one of three strategies:

(*a*) moving out of the job *en masse*;
(*b*) trying to force women out of the occupation;
(*c*) redefining the occupation so that a new line of segregation between men and women is drawn within the occupation.

This line might be either horizontal—access to higher grade work is confined largely or entirely to men—or vertical, where men do some jobs and women others. In research on industry in Brazil, the former process was seen in quality control jobs, where women shared lower grade posts with men but were denied access to higher positions. The latter was seen in the entry of women into metalstamping, where women were seen as being suitable for small presses, while the larger ones were reserved for men (Humphrey 1987).

The sexual division of labour and the segregation of women and men at work prevents the differential valuation of male and female labour from being undermined by comparison and substitution. At the same time, it prevents women from gaining access to jobs which really are more productive and are paid higher wages. This sheds fresh light on the question of women's access to the labour market. The neo-classical approach to discrimination emphasizes the 'pure' case, where decision-makers gain utility from discriminating against women and therefore explicitly choose a suboptimal utilization of labour. In theory, these practices should be eliminated by competition, which will drive out inefficient firms (Lloyd and Niemi 1979: 198). However, Arrow has argued that once discriminatory practices arise, they may persist because there are large fixed costs—replacing trained personnel, for example. Arrow suggests that wage differences will persist, alongside tendencies to segregation (quoted in Lloyd and Niemi 1979: 199).

This line of argument can be taken much further. Once wage differences exist, and once segregation exists, a number of factors reinforce them. First, segregation itself impedes comparisons between the worth of female and male labour. Second, patterns of labour use come to determine patterns of labour supply, so that workers of one sex no longer have either the interest or the qualifications for performing work done by the other. Third, individuals who take up jobs normally performed by the other sex are often harassed or marginalized so that the personal costs of transgressing sex boundaries become high. These costs will tend to be imposed by both sexes. Fourth, valuations of female and male labour assessments of its capabilities become institutionalized in labour market practices and structures. Job-grading processes and recruitment policies are two examples. These structures reinforce segregation and devaluation of female labour, providing spurious justifications for differential treatment. Finally, it should be noted that managers also reinforce these processes. In part, they make their decisions within the framework of an existing sexual division of labour. In response to a question about whether jobs performed by women could or should be performed by men, or vice versa, one production manager in a Brazilian pharmaceuticals plant gave an answer in terms of whether the men and women in the plant were doing jobs that were appropriately feminine and masculine (Humphrey 1987: 92–3). In other words, he considered the issue in terms of reinforcing the sexual division of labour, not breaking it down. His attitude was far from untypical. In addition to this, managers also reinforce segregation and devaluation of women in order to take advantage of the wage differentials existing in the labour market. Integrating men and women involves either (*a*) discriminatory wages or (*b*) levelling up women's wages or (*c*) cutting male rates. It is more profitable for managements to retain segregation and feminize wholesale where appropriate.

With this level of segregation and the persistence of differential valuation of labour by sex, the issue of access takes on a new form. Neo-classical theory views discrimination as an exception, and once women have access to the labour market they should be treated according to the endowments they possess. Disadvantage arises from lack of access to the labour market, and improved access will improve women's position. If, however, segregation and devaluation are pervasive, then women will only have access to some parts of the labour market—generally those offering poor wages and conditions. Even when improved access to certain jobs is obtained, new lines of segregation may be drawn and the jobs devalued. If the pay and conditions of jobs vary according to the sex of the persons performing them, then even improved access to better jobs may be no long-term guarantee of less disadvantage.

There is little doubt that women's labour can be mobilized by increased job opportunities and rising wage rates. Women are responsive to price. However, drawing women into the labour market will not, by itself, break down segregation or reduce women's disadvantage. In the 1970s, a massive entry of women into industrial employment in Brazil produced a marginal shift in the boundary-line between male and female jobs but certainly did not break down segregation or reverse the tendency for women to be concentrated into low wage jobs (Humphrey 1987: 38–51). Improving women's position in the market involves much more than reducing state-inspired distortions or making interventions which will compensate to some degree for family failures. While increasing women's access to training and education is important, the USAID's own evaluation of its programmes shows how important it is for employers to be encouraged to employ the female labour being produced by training programmes for women (1985: 35). Perhaps significantly, the employer approached in this case was the government, and it is clear that in the private sector and for blue-collar jobs, segregation is much stronger. If reducing women's disadvantage in the labour market is to be an aim of policy—an aim justifiable on the grounds of both equity and efficiency—then much more, and more effective, state intervention in the areas of equal pay and sex discrimination would be required. With gender bias so pervasive, markets cannot be expected to work efficiently on their own.

10. Gender, Markets, and Households

Neo-liberal policies appear to offer women a chance to enter the market and raise their social status. Without doubt, women would greatly appreciate opportunities to gain self-sustaining improvements in their welfare. They would benefit from better access to farming, self-employment, or wage labour. However, neo-liberal policies cannot deliver on the promise of improvement because of their macro-economic priorities, their analysis of household relations, and their attitude to state intervention. Although neo-liberal WID promises a better deal for women, in practice it is more likely to lead to a deterioration in women's position. The limits of neo-liberalism in practice point to the shortcomings of the neo-liberal paradigm and the contradictions of neo-liberal WID.

The first contradiction of neo-liberal WID concerns the relation between production and reproduction. The neo-liberal paradigm (NLP) and neo-liberal WID seek to attract women into the market, but this is hardly compatible with the emphasis placed on women's reproductive role. The NLP favours reductions in state expenditure of health, education, and social services, and it looks to private provision to compensate for cuts. However, in certain contexts, particularly among the poor in the Third World, access to market provision of these services is either non-existent or extremely limited, so that it is women's unpaid labour which generally offsets reductions in state expenditures. As Elson notes, in the context of adjustment programmes, 'Women's unpaid labour is implicitly regarded as elastic—able to stretch so as to make up any shortfall in other resources available for reproduction and maintenance of human resources' (1989: 4). Unless market access is helped by labour-saving elsewhere (less work required for family sickness or food processing, for example), then women will find it difficult to respond to market signals. They will either not respond at all, or they will increase their total burden of work, or they will be obliged to neglect their reproductive activities. Far from helping women out in this dilemma, the NLP makes it worse. If women are to be drawn into the market, they need more help with reproduction, not less. By stressing efficiency, WID policies tend to go along with economic models which marginalize reproductive activities and place no economic value on them. They also tend to overlook the equity implication of these policies.

The second major contradiction of the NLP concerns the need for conditions for women's equality in the market. Women are being encouraged to enter the market at the same time as cutbacks in state employment restrict one of the few areas of work, where women have a chance of securing higher-wage jobs, and the shift to export agriculture and cash crops places an emphasis on forms of production which have been dominated by men (Elson 1989: 18–20). In these circumstances, women's access to the market will be more difficult, not less. They will be forced into low-income and insecure work and their disadvantage in the labour market will be reinforced, not overcome. In these adverse circumstances, positive action to promote women's integration into the market is required, and yet neo-liberal WID can only advocate half-measures.

In conclusion, it should be noted that in pointing to the limitations of neo-liberal prescriptions, we are not necessarily advocating state intervention as the panacea for ensuring women's interests are met in the development process. Indeed, the emergence of WID as an identifiable concern in development policy is, to an important extent, attributable to the systematic documentation by early WID scholars of the state's failure to take account of women's separate needs and interests in its development interventions

While neo-liberal economists have targeted their criticisms on state corruption, inefficiency, and rent-seeking, WID studies have demonstrated how state policies have created or reproduced gender inequalities in land rights, labour use in agriculture, public sector employment, access to education and family law. If the subordination of women is entrenched within the structures of society, it is hardly surprising that the agencies of the state do not transcend this reality.

This identification of the role of the state in reinforcing women's subordination is important. It cautions against an uncritical reliance on state intervention in achieving gender equity. At the same time, the World Bank is correct in recognizing the significance of the state as 'custodians of society', able to represent broader interests than other institutions and agencies. The key issue is how to use the power of the state to act in women's interests, rather than against them. This would require analysis of the relevance of national and international machineries for defining development agendas, of the politics of policy-making and implementation, and of the role of grass-roots women's organizations in identifying and representing women's interests. The problem with the neo-liberal solution is that it nowhere recognizes the nature of the resistance that the promotion of women in the development process is likely to encounter—in the household, in the market-place, and within the state apparatus. Our analysis of gender relations suggests that there are often conflicts of interest between women and men and their resolution is a political issue. This is the final contradiction of the neo-liberal paradigm. The successful promotion of efficiency and equality of opportunity in societies with structured inequalities and relations of hierarchy will either require extensive social engineering or else lead to major social upheaval. To promote the market fully, neo-liberal policy-makers would need to transform the social relations which they refuse to recognize.

References

Amsden, A. (ed.) (1980), *The Economics of Women and Work*, Penguin, Harmondsworth.

Becker, G. (1974), 'A Theory of Marriage' in T. W. Schultz (ed.), *Economics of the Family*, University of Chicago Press, Chicago.

Brett, E. (1985), 'The Pure Theory of Market Society', mimeo.

Buvinic, M. (1983), 'Women's Issues in Third World Poverty: A Policy Analysis' in M. Buvinic, M. Lycette, and W. McGreevey, *Women and Poverty in the Third World*, Johns Hopkins University Press, Baltimore, Md.

—— and Youssef, N. (1978), 'Women-Headed Households: The Ignored Factor in Development Policy', *Report submitted to the Office of Women in Development*,

Agency for International Development: International Centre for Research on Women, Washington, DC.

Chen, L., Huq, E., and d'Souza, S. (1981), 'Sex Bias in the Family Allocation of Food and Health Care in Rural Bangladesh', *Population and Development Review*, 7/1: 55–70.

Chiplin, B., and Sloane, P. J. (1980), 'Sexual Discrimination in the Labour Market', in A. H. Amsden (ed.), *The Economics of Women and Work*, Penguin, Harmondsworth, 283–321.

Collier, P. (1987), 'Women in Development: Defining the Issues', mimeo, Institute of Economics and Statistics, Oxford.

Das Gupta, B. (1977), 'Village Society and Labour Use', Oxford University Press, Delhi.

Dixon-Mueller, R. (1985), 'Women's Work in Third World Agriculture', *Women, Work and Development* 9, ILO, Geneva.

Ellis, P. (1986), *Women of the Caribbean*, Zed Press, London.

Elson, D. (1989), 'The Impact of Structural Adjustment on Women: The Concepts and Issues', in B. Onimode (ed.), *The IMF, The World Bank and the African Debt*, Zed Books, London.

Evans, A. (1988), 'Gender Issues in Rural Household Economics' IDS Discussion Paper 254.

Folbre, N. (1984), 'Household Production in the Philippines: A Non-neoclassical Approach' in *Economic Development and Cultural Change*, 32/2: 303–30.

—— (1986), 'Hearts and Spades: Paradigms of Household Economics', *World Development* 14/2: 245–55.

Game, A., and Pringle, R. (1983), *Gender at Work*, Sydney, George Allen & Unwin, London.

Godelier, M. (1982), *La Production des grandes hommes*, Fayard, Paris.

Goldschmidt-Clermont, L. (1982), 'Unpaid Work in the Household: A Review of Economic Evaluation Methods', *Women, Work and Development* 1, ILO, Geneva.

Guilbert, M. (1966), *Les Fonctions des femmes dans l'industrie*, Mouton, The Hague.

Harriss, B., and Watson, E. (1987), 'The Sex Ratio in South Asia', in Momsen and Townsend 1987.

Hayek, F. A. (1949), *Individualism and Economic Order*, Routledge, London.

Herz, B., and Measham, A. R. (1987), *The Safe Motherhood Initiative: Proposals for Action*, The World Bank, Washington DC.

Horenstein, N. R. (1985), 'Factoring Gender into the Development Equation', *Horizons*, 4/3 (USAID, Washington, DC). 26–7.

Humphrey, J. (1987), *Gender and Work in the Third World*, Tavistock, London.

Jagger, A. (1983), *Feminist Politics and Human Nature*, Harvester Press, Brighton.

Kabeer, N. (1989), 'Monitoring Poverty as if Gender Mattered: A Methodology for Rural Bangladesh', IDS Discussion Paper 255.

Kandiyoti, D. (1988), 'Bargaining with Patriarchy', *Gender and Society*, 2/3.

Lloyd, C., and Niemi, B. (1979), *The Economics of Sex Differentials*, Columbia University Press, New York.

Momsen, J. H., and Townsend, J. (1987), *Geography of Gender in the Third World*, Hutchinson, London.

Moore, H. S., (1988), *Feminism and Anthropology*, Polity Press, Oxford.

Moser, C. (1989), 'Gender Planning in the Third World: Meeting Practical and Strategic Gender Needs', *World Development* 17/11.

Palmer, I. (1977), 'Rural Women and the Basic Needs Approach to Development', *International Labour Review*, 115/1: 97–107.

Scott, A. (1987), 'Locating the Invisible Connections: Capitalism, Patriarchy and Job Segregation by Sex', Paper presented to Social Science History Association Conference, New Orleans.

Sen, A. (1985), 'Women, Technology and Sexual Divisions', *Trade and Development*, Study prepared for UNCTAD/INSTRAW, United Nations, New York.

—— (1987), *Gender and Cooperative Conflicts*, World Institute of Development Economics Research, Helsinki.

—— and Sengupta, S. (1983), 'Malnutrition of Rural Children and the Sex Bias', *Economic and Political Weekly*, 18/19–21: 855–63.

Snell, M. (1979), 'The Equal Pay and Sex Discrimination Acts: Their Impact in the Workplace', *Feminist Review*, 1.

Toye, J. (1987), *Dilemmas of Development*, Basil Blackwell, Oxford.

UNDP (1990), *Human Development Report, 1990*, Oxford University Press, Oxford.

USAID Bureau for Programme and Policy Coordination (1982), *Aid Policy Paper: Women in Development*, USAID Bureau for Programme and Policy Coordination.

USAID (1985), *Women in Development: AID's Experience, 1973–1985*, vol. i, Synthesis Paper, USAID office.

Whitehead, A. (1981), 'I'm Hungry, Mum: The Politics of Domestic Budgeting', in Kate Young, Carol Wolkowitz, and Roslyn McCullagh, *Of Marriage and the Market*, CSE Books, London.

World Bank (1979), 'Recognizing the "Invisible" Woman in Development: the World Bank Experience', Washington, DC.

—— (1984), *World Development Report*, Washington, DC.

5
International Financial Markets: A Case of Market Failure

STEPHANY GRIFFITH-JONES

1. Introduction

The issue of the appropriate form, mechanism, and extent of external funding of development has become crucial for Third World countries, especially in the 1980s. This paper shows the limitations of private lending to developing countries, and argues that the experience of the last two decades (as well as earlier experience) shows that private financial markets provide an important example of market failures; for this reason, the regulation of these markets, and their partial replacement by public flows in cases where they break down or work imperfectly, is necessary.

The argument that private financial markets are inefficient as intermediators of savings has been made in the past by writers such as W. Bagehot (1873) and T. Veblen (1904) and more recently by H. Minsky (1982) and C. Kindleberger (1978). These writers point to the tendency of private financial markets to be characterized by successive periods of overlending and underlending, often resulting in financial crisis. However, their analysis is relevant to the operation of financial markets in general, rather than to the specific and difficult issues related to international private lending to developing countries, as illustrated by overlending in the seventies and debt crises in the eighties; it is on this specific area which this chapter will focus.[1] In its final part, the chapter describes and evaluates the specific form of public intervention that has occurred in the 1980s to handle Third World private debt crises, and suggests lessons for future policy.

International financial markets underwent a major process of privatization and deregulation in the 1960s and 1970s. This rapid expansion of private flows, mainly via the Euro-markets, was greatly welcomed by orthodox analysts. Thus, McKinnon concluded that 'lack of (government) restrictions

I am very grateful for very insightful and detailed comments by Christopher Colclough and Charles Harvey. I also wish to thank other IDS colleagues, who commented so helpfully on an earlier draft of this paper, when it was presented at Stafford House in December 1988; these include E. Brett, M. Faber, M. Lipton, H. Singer, and A. Wood.

created a model of efficiency in international banking' (McKinnon 1977). Similarly, Duffy and Giddy argued that 'The Euro-markets facilitate market allocation and reduce the role of government allocation . . . undoubtedly, no other force can, on its own, contribute in such an important way to the efficient international allocation of credit as the Euro-markets have done' (Duffy and Giddy 1978).

During the 1970s the share of developing countries' funding provided by private sources rapidly increased and the share of international lending channelled by international banks to developing countries grew rapidly. This 'privatisation' of a large proportion of development funding was strongly welcomed by orthodox analysts as representing the optimal way of financing the development of Third World countries.

This trend was also encouraged by the International Monetary Fund as a convenient mechanism for recycling funds from the surplus countries to oil-importing developing countries, whose deficits had been sharply increased as a result of large rises in the price of oil and of the slow-down in industrial economies. For example, J. J. Polak, a senior official at the IMF, enthusiastically welcomed the new trend: 'The development of international bank credit available to a wide range of countries, including many developing countries, has *reduced the difference* between the U.S. and many other countries, as regards their ability to finance balance of payments deficits. At present, it is not only the U.S. that can finance deficits by issuing liabilities expressed in U.S. dollars—most other countries can do the same, by using the credit facilities of the (private) world banking system' (Polak 1980). As late as July 1982 (only one month before widespread debt crises broke out) the IMF Occasional Paper on Capital Markets (IMF 1982), though expressing some concern about the continuity of bank lending, still concluded that, 'over the medium-term the rate of growth of international bank assets (on loans to LDCs) can be expected to remain high . . . The efficiency of the markets in allocating capital internationally is underpinned by basic commercial principles; these should remain the key stone of banks' decisions'. The voices of critics urging caution in the unrestricted use of private agents for recycling funds to developing countries, a greater role for public flows, and public supervision of private flows were drowned by the enthusiasm of the supporters of the free market (US Congress 1979, Balogh 1980, Griffith-Jones 1980).

The onset of widespread debt crises in the eighties, their pervasive negative effect on development in highly indebted developing countries, as well as the threat they posed to the solvency of international banks eventually led to a reassessment of the virtues of private markets as the optimal mechanism to fund developing countries. Thus, the events of the 1980s led to a strengthening of the position of those criticizing the unrestricted use of the free market.[2] Even so, a hard core of defenders of private financial markets remained. In spite of its serious theoretical and empirical flaws (which we discuss below), this position still has a great influence on the thinking of the major industrial governments.

For example, in the official report of the industrial countries (G-10) submitted to the powerful Interim Committee of the IMF in September 1985 it is argued that: 'improvements in the provision of international liquidity need not be sought through fundamental changes in the system . . . for the foreseeable future, financial markets must be expected to continue to supply the bulk of international liquidity' (IMF 1985). Furthermore, some of the deputies (including the US representative) go further in the report to argue that 'the difficulties encountered by a number of countries (to obtain sufficient international liquidity) are primarily an indication *of their lack of creditworthiness* and are not related to a general shortage of liquidity'. According to these deputies, the creation of official international liquidity (via SDR allocations) is '*not the appropriate tool for providing finance* to countries whose access to international credit markets has been jeopardized' and suggests that 'they might result in *delaying necessary adjustment*' (emphasis added).

The position of industrial governments has become somewhat more flexible since that declaration was made, particularly as regards concessionary official flows to low-income countries in Sub-Saharan Africa. They still believe, however, that the almost exclusive provision of international private liquidity to different categories of LDCs remains a feasible and desirable option; this leads to problematic policy conclusions, from a developmental perspective, such as that SDR issues are unnecessary. Equally, it means that international liquidity for developing countries will be either provided by private financial institutions or under high conditionality lending by the public international financial institutions (IFIs). Then the premiss that international liquidity should basically be market created, has far broader implications: in particular that macro-economic policies and, most seriously, development strategies should be heavily conditioned by the requirements of private bankers and IFIs. This situation gives tremendous power and influence over development to the markets and IFIs.

In the next section we will briefly examine historical evidence in order to assess the effects of private international financial flows on growth and development. We will stress those negative effects on development which have either been ignored or insufficiently treated in the orthodox literature; we shall also discuss the negative effects of excessive private international lending on the creditors themselves.

The final section of the paper suggests three broad sets of policy implications. These will cover the scale and regulation of future private lending, the role of international official funding and liquidity creation, and the future management of debt crises.

We shall argue that industrial governments should play a larger role in the future, both to regulate private financial flows to developing countries and to channel public flows towards them; somewhat paradoxically, however, we shall argue that 'the markets' should be allowed to play a larger (albeit different) role in finding a solution to the debt problem than they have till now.

2. The Effects of Development Funding from Private Sources (1970s)

One of the important issues facing the international economy, which particularly affects developing countries, relates to the appropriate levels and mechanisms for international financial intermediation. The issue arises, both nationally and internationally, mainly because those economic agents that save are not the same ones which invest. Internationally, if financial intermediation between net savers and net investors is not adequately performed, the effect will be to depress the level of output and income, particularly in countries with low net savings and possibly also in the world economy as a whole.

As regards developing countries, most authors agree that economic development normally requires some long-term external capital and short-term balance of payments assistance to help fund both long-term and short-term current account deficits. It is important to stress in the context of our evaluation that specific conditions need to be met so that such external funds contribute to development. Raul Prebisch (1979) attempted to specify these conditions as follows:

(*a*) the net volume of financial inflows should be appropriate to development needs;

(*b*) the outflows generated for payments of profits and interest must still allow for future net inflows; for this reason Prebisch added that the financial terms of such flows (in relation to maturities, grace period, and level of interest rate) should not be too onerous;

(*c*) the net external financial inflows should be used for investments which will contribute to an increase in exports and/or a substitution of imports.[3]

In the discussions preceding and during Bretton Woods, it was proposed by Keynes that a very large public international institution, which he called the International Clearing Union, should channel a large proportion of flows from surplus to deficit countries. However Keynes's detailed proposals were not accepted and the institutions emerging from Bretton Woods—the IMF and the World Bank—were both smaller and less powerful than those he had envisaged.

Furthermore, the relative size of these institutions decreased in the following decades, particularly in the case of the IMF; thus, the ratio of IMF quotas to total world imports has systematically declined, from about 16 per cent in the late 1940s, to 12 per cent in 1960, to only around 5 per cent by the end of 1983, after the eighth (and most recent) General Review of quotas.

In the 1970s, the dramatically increased size of the problem of financing non-oil developing countries' current account deficits, (which according to IMF figures, grew from US $11.3 bn. in 1973 to US $107.7 bn. in 1981), together with the limited response made by the public international financial system, implied that public institutions were able to make only a relatively marginal contribution to deficit countries' funding. It has not been sufficiently stressed in the relevant literature that in the 1973–82 period, the IMF, through all its facilities, financed a mere 3.1 per cent of the current account deficits of non-oil developing countries.[4] Furthermore, during the 1970s, there was an almost total lack of public control or even supervision with respect to the process of expansion of private lending.[5]

In 1973, around 38 per cent of disbursed public and publicly guaranteed external debt of all developing countries was owed to private creditors; by 1982, that percentage had risen to 55; for Latin America and the Caribbean alone, the figures were 58 and 77 per cent. Furthermore, the share of financial market (increasingly bank) credits *vis-à-vis* supplier credits increased from 65 to 91 per cent for all LDCs in that period. The resulting rapid increase in the share of bank credit occurred in the context of a very rapid increase in the total outstanding debt of developing countries.

It is not the main purpose of this paper to attempt to explain why banks engaged in such massive lending and why bank supervisors allowed it. However, it is useful for the analysis to treat this matter briefly. The behaviour of banks and of supervisors can be explained both at macro and micro levels. At the macro-economic level, it is clear that in the early seventies, rapidly growing liquidity in the Euro-markets (due to steep increases in deposits from oil-exporting countries as well as other sources) implied that international banks' deposits were growing rapidly. At this time, however, credit demand from their traditional clients was slowing down due to the recession in industrial countries, and demand for increased funding was growing in developing countries.

However, the very rapid increase in banks' lending to developing countries, leading to a very high share of banks' total assets and capital represented by their exposure to some developing countries, needs also to be explained in terms of micro-economic behaviour. An interesting approach to explain banks' behaviour (and that of bank supervisors) stresses 'disaster myopia' (Guttentag and Herring 1985). This approach is especially relevant in the context of this book, challenging, as it does, the conventional assumptions of rational expectations theory, which assumes that market discipline will ensure that successful decision-makers form expectations correctly; those who make systematic errors incur losses and go bankrupt. But this hypothesis has much less relevance for expectations concerning low-probability hazards

—those which occur so rarely that they can be disregarded without cost for long periods. Guttentag and Herring (1985) argue that as the length of time since the last major incidence of default lengthened (and as in the post-war era, the repayment on country loans was relatively good in relation to other lending), bank decision-makers believed that the probability of a range of countries defaulting was very low, and, effectively, zero.

This 'disaster myopia' on the part of the banks seems to have been accelerated by the high mobility of decision-making staff, who were thus personally able to avoid the possible negative effects of overlending on *future* non-payment, but whose career benefited in the short term as personal promotion was often linked to maximizing credit growth.[6] This behaviour arose largely from the very nature of the product 'transaction' involved, where the moment of selling 'the product' does not, by definition, coincide with the moment of payment. Extreme decentralization of operations, geared towards attempting to maximize speed in credit decisions, also contributed to institutional 'dysaster myopia'. Alexander (1984) has even reported that 'some bankers were so frightened of losing market shares that they even allowed their secretaries, during the banker's lunch-break, to promise US $5 million or US $10 million, as part of any package for Brazil or Mexico over US $1 billion'.

This tendency to neglect low-probability hazards can, however, produce large or even crippling losses, in a context of decision-making under uncertainty about the future. In this specific sense, it undermines the standard assumptions of rational expectations theory. 'Disaster myopia', linked to the perception that the existence of sophisticated economic management and of IFIs reduced risks of country default, seems also to have led supervisory authorities in creditor countries to be lax in the supervision and control of private bank lending. Furthermore, the fashionable belief that markets know best, further discouraged supervisors from attempting to regulate and control private bank lending.

Other factors that explained overlending to LDCs in the 1970s include the fact that banks had access to imperfect information about the borrowing countries and even about the total level of their debt; this was particularly the case for smaller, less internationally orientated banks. This often led to smaller banks relying on information provided by larger banks (thus basing their decisions largely on the prestige of the leading banks in the loan-making process). As a result, decisions of one firm were no longer independent of those by other firms, breaking a key condition for efficient resource allocation. By consequence many decisions on loans (and their prices) were not taken purely on the basis of independent profit/risk analysis, but partly based on 'herd behaviour'—the wish by all to participate in what was generally seen as profitable expansion. Furthermore, it has been argued (Devlin 1986) that the comparison between the profit from, and risks associated with, a particular loan is only one element in the decision to lend;

the possibility of capturing other business—such as obtaining deposits from the borrower, or even deposits from the exporters of the borrowing countries—seems to have further encouraged bank lending.

It should be stressed that the 1970s were by no means the first period in economic history in which bank lending (or other form of private flows) has had a 'euphoric' overexpansion. This has happened usually in times of upward movement in the business cycle, and has often been followed by overcontraction, at times of slow-down in economic activity; Kindleberger (1978) analyses the pattern of boom-bust lending, and illustrates it with historical examples, going back as far as the South-Sea Bubble; in a more recent work, Marichal (1988) describes in some detail the four great lending boom/debt crises that have occurred in Latin America before that of the 1970s and 1980s. These occurred in the mid-1820s, in the mid-1870s, in the early 1890s, and—as is well known, in the early 1930s.

This evidence suggests that private bankers, regulators as well as government officials in developing countries, suffered in the 1970s not only from disaster myopia, but also from an ignorance of history!

3. The Effects of Private Bank Lending in the 1970s and 1980s

Initially, for several of those developing country governments that borrowed heavily in the 1970s, private international credit provided a welcome, easily obtainable, apparently cheap, and low-conditional source of external savings to help adjust to major external shocks without sacrificing growth. The fact that growth was sustained in a large part of the developing world contributed somewhat to sustaining growth in the world economy as a whole.

There is a tendency, in some of the simplistic Latin American literature, to argue that the long-term impact of private international lending was purely negative, particularly once the international economic environment deteriorated in the 1980s. Although this is broadly true (see below) a few countries that relied heavily on private capital in the 1970s were able to sustain development in the 1980s. Thus, the scale and use of private external funds by the developing countries influenced how they affected development. It would seem that the lower the relative size of the external debt in relation to exports, the higher the proportion of the private loans that remained in the domestic economy (and did not leave as capital flight), the higher the proportion of those flows that were devoted to funding investment and the higher the proportion of that investment devoted to the increased production of tradables, the more likely were positive effects on future development and manageable debt repayments (Griffith-Jones and Harvey 1986). In this sense, it seems that the Asian countries demonstrate this more positive pattern, and have had a more favourable growth experience in the 1980s than the Latin American ones.[7] As an illustration, two extreme cases can be mentioned. On one hand, South Korea is an example of a country which borrowed relatively little (in relation to its exports), had very little capital flight, and devoted a high proportion of what it borrowed to investment in tradables, particularly in industrial exports; at the other extreme, Venezuela provides an example of a country where the size of the increase in the external debt to private creditors coincided with the size of the increase in assets held abroad by the private sector (Alvarez 1988).

Although it is clear that the nature of economic policies influences the effect which international borrowing had on individual economies' development, the neo-liberal argument that debt crises 'are primarily due to mistaken policies' (Lal 1988: 3) seems too strong. It totally ignores initial structural differences amongst economies and their politics. Equally it is very narrowly based, focusing only upon trade and exchange rate policies, rather than upon the influence, also, of terms of trade, of war, of climate, and of history in determining outcomes.

For the majority of developing countries which borrowed heavily in the Euro-markets in the 1970s, development has not been sustained in the 1980s, and indeed their development record seems relatively poorer than that of other developing countries.

These negative long-term effects can be attributed mainly to the following features:

1. The modality of the variable interest rate, in the context of loans with relatively short-term maturity, was particularly unsuited to fund long-term development; it was designed by actors in the private market, with the objective of passing on to the borrower the risk of interest rate fluctuation; this was undesirable from a development perspective, as the variability of interest payments added an important additional element of uncertainty to developing countries' attempts to predict and plan their balance of payments flows. This, inevitably, would have disruptive effects both on short-term macro-economic management and long-term development if interest rates rose. This they did in the early 1980s in nominal and real terms. At a more micro-economic level, variable interest rates make it impossible to decide whether the allocation of borrowed funds to any particular use was rational, because economic agents were unable to predict the whole cost of individual projects. Furthermore, even for the private lenders this mechanism was counter-productive, as the interest rate risk was translated into credit risk, with far more threatening effects on their stability than a pure interest rate risk could have had. Thus, the variable interest rate, which was designed to reduce an important category of risk, in fact increased risks arising from unfavourable changes affecting many borrowers simultaneously such as the impact of the world recession. Private actors on the whole, are unable to foresee such risks, or to cope with them (without resorting to governments) when they occur.

This critique is not against private flows in general, but against the modality which private flows adopted in the 1970s (which, incidentally, was different to the long-term, fixed interests bonds which characterized private flows in the nineteenth century). LDC governments did not have much choice in the matter. Private capital markets were not willing to lend through bond instruments in the seventies (and were even less willing to do so ten years later). If bond finance were to have been provided by the markets to LDCs, some form of guarantee from industrial governments in intermediation would probably have been essential.

2. The second problem, applicable to all private flows to developing countries is their instability and their pro-cyclical nature. As the early 1980s illustrated particularly clearly, interest rates, terms of trade, and the supply of lending can interact perversely; as the international environmental deteriorates (together with both the current and perceived prospects of repayment by developing countries) private lenders become unwilling to make new loans, thus making the ultimate inability to pay far more likely.

For the developing world as a whole, rapidly increasing interest rates and counter-cyclical reduction in new private lending have implied that net resource transfers have become negative or 'perverse' since 1985 (see table 5.1). According to World Bank estimates, for the heavily indebted countries, net resource transfers from those economies to their creditors in 1985/7 amounted to $74 billion, equivalent to about 3 per cent of their total GDP.

Undoubtedly, negative resource transfers are a major constraint on developing countries' growth in the eighties. Together with the sharp deterioration in terms of trade that occurred in the eighties, it has contributed to an interruption of growth and development in large parts of the developing world, particularly in Latin America and Africa. This is because an important part of export revenues cannot be used to purchase imports, and an important part of domestic savings cannot be channelled to investment, being absorbed, instead, by debt service.

3. The large private lending for developing countries followed by sharp decreases in financial flows was particularly damaging because most countries had adopted development strategies and macro-economic policies that assumed a permanent large private net transfer. Thus, patterns of consumption and production became more import intensive in the 1970s; furthermore overvalued exchange rates and large budget deficits were feasible and were even encouraged by massive private inflows. Though misguided economic policies are naturally the responsibility of national governments, the 'facilitating' availability of private international liquidity played an important role in encouraging such distorting policies. As net resource transfers were drastically reversed, the recessionary cost of adjustment was greater, precisely because the pattern of development had been so import intensive, and because—in most countries—adjustment was mainly market determined (little use being made of selective policies, such as import controls). Similarly the overvalued exchange rates compatible with large trade deficits had to be

Stephany Griffith-Jones

TABLE 5.1. *Net transfers of public and publicly guaranteed debt (US$ billion)*[a]

	1985		1986		1987	
	Total	Private creditors	Total	Private creditors	Total	Private creditors
All developing countries	−12.7	−18.2	−19.1	−23.6	−28.5	−29.4
Latin America and Caribbean	−14.0	−16.1	−15.6	−17.5	−12.7	−12.5
Africa, South of Sahara	−1.6	−3.0	1.7	−0.7	2.5	−0.4
East Asia	3.4	2.5	−2.2	−1.3	−10.7	−9.8
Europe and Mediterranean	−3.1	−1.5	−5.1	−4.0	−9.1	−6.0
North Africa and Middle East	0.5	−0.4	0.2	0.0	−1.2	−1.1
South Asia	2.2	0.2	1.9	0.0	2.8	0.4
Highly indebted countries[b]	−18.0	−18.7	−18.6	−19.4	−15.2	−14.2

[a] The net transfer figures are far higher if private non-guaranteed debt was included.
[b] The highly indebted countries, as defined by the World Bank, are: Argentina, Bolivia, Brazil, Chile, Colombia, Costa Rica, Ivory Coast, Ecuador, Jamaica, Mexico, Morocco, Nigeria, Peru, Philippines, Uruguay, Venezuela, and Yugoslavia.

Source: World Bank, *World Debt Tables* 1988–9, Washington, DC.

rapidly and drastically reduced so as to accommodate the need for large trade surpluses; these massive real and even larger nominal devaluations contributed to sharp acceleration of inflation in most of the heavily indebted countries, and particularly those in Latin America.

We have focused, so far, on the effects which private flows had on the development of heavily indebted countries. Two other aspects need to be stressed in this context. First, the 'privatization' of financial flows in the seventies led to a very high concentration of external flows to the upper- and middle-income developing countries. It has been estimated that low-income countries obtained less than 3 per cent of total net private lending to oil-importing developing countries, while the share of their access to other flows (e.g. aid) more dominant in the sixties was higher. So the shift to private flows worsened the distribution of access to external finance among developing countries during the seventies; though this trend may have led to slower growth in the seventies, it may have helped some (e.g. India) sustain growth better in the eighties. There is, however, evidence that debt crisis management in the eighties has implied an increase in the share of public flows going to highly indebted mainly middle-income developing countries, thus leaving again a lower share of flows (in this case public ones) available for low-income countries. It thus has been argued that low-income countries have become the lenders of last resort, as their reduced access to public flows allows greater public flows to highly indebted countries, which in turn allow them to service their debts to private banks.[8]

Second, the high exposure of most of the international banks to developing countries, combined with the risk of widespread defaults by them, has undoubtedly posed a threat to the stability of the international banking system. Though the threat significantly receded, its existence has weakened the international banks. Nevertheless, the LDC debt continues to pose a serious threat particularly to some US banks.

In the absence of intervention by industrial country government during the early 1980s, bankruptcy of some major international banks, disruption to world trade, and an even higher cost to development would probably have resulted.

Thus, industrial governments have, since the early eighties, recognized in their actions (albeit partially and implicitly) that stable external financial flows to fund development and stability of the banking system are 'public goods' that cannot be provided by private market agents acting individually; particularly in times of international recession, private actors are on their own incapable of dealing with the systemic risks and crises that arise. The cost of market failure is high because of its potential systemic effect, which could drastically reduce lending to all countries and enterprises, thus further reducing their level of activity. For this reason, the provision of stable financial flows to LDCs and a stable international banking system are public goods, bringing benefits which the market, acting unassisted, finds it difficult or impossible to provide.

4. Some Features of Government Intervention

The actions taken by governments in the 1982–7 period have been both too limited and biased towards preserving only one of the 'public goods' under threat from the LDC debt crisis—the stability of the international banks. Insufficient attention has been given to the other 'public good' under threat, that of providing stable and positive net financial flows to developing countries to help sustain development.

Government intervention in debt crises has not been limited to action by industrial nations. Indeed, one of the most paradoxical effects of the debt crisis is that some developing country governments have assumed—or been forced to assume under pressure from the international banks—the role of borrowers of last resort (or guarantors of last resort). Indeed, even debtor governments like that of Chile strongly committed, as it was, to the operation of market forces, granted (ex-post) guarantees, on international loans previously made by international private banks to private national companies. As Ffrench-Davies (1988) shows, the Chilean government granted an ex-post guarantee to the debt of the private financial sector; Chilean private debt with public guarantee grew from a mere US $69 million in 1981 to US $2.612 million in 1986 (about 10 per cent of the total external debt). Furthermore, there was a more indirect mechanism of 'nationalization' of the external debt in Chile, which also often applied in the other heavily indebted countries. Here, the public sector contracted loans from private creditors to service not only its own debt but also that of the private sector. As a result of these trends, the share of public and publicly guaranteed financial debt in the total Chilean external debt rose from 35.8 per cent in 1981 to 75.9 per cent in 1986.

An asymmetry thus arose in debtor and creditor government actions, as regards private capital flows. While industrial governments did not make explicit provision for an international lender of last resort facility to protect their banks from insolvency, governments of the borrowing nations either provided explicit or implicit guarantees to their private nationals to facilitate their borrowing internationally. The existence of an implicit borrower of last resort in debtor nations during the seventies must have encouraged over-lending to the private sector in developing countries in the 'boom' years; lack of international lender of last resort facilities implied that in the eighties new international private lending was not effectively sustained. Thus, the asymmetrical actions of lender and debtor governments could be said to have accentuated, rather than moderated, the pro-cyclical nature of private flows. Furthermore, when acting as borrowers of last resort, LDC governments were to an important extent showing themselves more concerned with the stability of international banks than with their own economic growth.

A further feature of the intervention of industrial governments (IG) and the public IFIs is that it was based on the assumption that debt crises would be temporary. Based on the very influential analysis by Cline (1983), and that of others, the debt crisis was diagnosed by IGs and IFIs as a 'liquidity' crisis and not a 'solvency' crisis; this implied recognizing that the markets had discontinuities related largely to international events, such as recession. But it also depended on the notions that they were temporary and could be easily overcome by short-term action on the part of IGs and IFIs, together with drastic adjustment policy being applied in debtor developing economies themselves. The probability that new voluntary international private lending might not recover for a long period and that therefore negative net transfers could continue was not faced. If the latter assumption is correct, and if the development of debtor nations is as important a policy objective as preserving the stability of the private banks, the type of government intervention required is far more comprehensive and radical than that implied by the 'liquidity' diagnosis.

A fiction has been created that markets still exist to provide private international lending to the highly indebted developing world; in fact net new lending has declined (and has even in certain years been negative). Furthermore it has been involuntary (obtained by pressure from industrial governments and central banks, as well as from some of the most heavily exposed commercial banks). Equally, it has often had direct or indirect guarantees from IFIs (implying again a 'disguised' role for governments). In fact, a market for private lending to heavily indebted countries does not exist any more, and will not do so again unless major changes occur in the world economy.

Paradoxically the fictitious promise of new private lending (a market in the future) increases the incentive to continue servicing the debt not at its market value but at its far higher face value! Thus, the elaborate machinery of debt crisis management (in which industrial governments and, to a lesser extent, debtor governments have played such a large role) is *de facto* artificially preserving the value of the debt (and of debt servicing) at a level well above its market value.

Finally, the type of new lending which has been encouraged or channelled by governments is on the whole inappropriate to meet the needs of long-term development of the debtor nations.

(a) It is *insufficient*, as it results in large negative net resource transfer (see table 5.1).

(b) It consists mainly of (i) involuntary private lending, still at variable (and currently fairly high) interest rates and (ii) highly conditional public flows from IFIs, with somewhat more appropriate financial terms (e.g. maturity and interest rates), but with very controversial and pervasive policy conditionality.

(c) Practically no use has been made by governments of existing instruments to provide low-conditional or unconditional counter-cyclical liquidity via the IMF: since the debt crisis arose, conditionality associates with the Compensatory Financing Facility has been tightened and there have been no new issues of SDRs (Special Drawing Rights).

To summarize, the governments' interventions in the debt crises have been asymmetrical by preserving far more carefully the stability of international banks than the sustained growth of debtor economies; it is noteworthy that many debtor governments have had a similar bias, by granting ex-post guarantees to previously unguaranteed borrowing by private debtors. The key issue since 1982 has not been whether governments should intervene or not to manage the debt crisis but to what extent, via which mechanisms and (particularly) in whose favour they should intervene.

5. Conclusions and Policy Implications for Future Debt Crisis Management

Since 1982, public flows to developing countries and government intervention have been used to defend not only the stability of the international private capital markets but also the profitability of private international banks, by helping to maintain a fictitious face value of their assets in the Third World. This public intervention was successful in terms of achieving the main objectives of creditor countries and institutions.

The main challenge has now become to restore growth and development in the indebted LDC countries. To meet this new objective, a set of different actions is required. As before, this will require both government and market action focused not on generating new private lending, but upon debt and debt service reduction.

Market mechanisms (e.g. the secondary market in debt) will be increasingly influenced by governments defending the development prospects of LDC economies. At the risk of simplifying, one could argue that markets should become the servants of development objectives, rather than that development objectives be subordinated to the needs of the market.

At the time of writing some action along these lines has been taken, but it has been timid and patchy: Bolivia and Mexico have taken the most important initiatives for debt buy backs, with several countries pursuing exit bond options. The major Latin American governments, meeting in Acapulco late in 1987, signalled their preference for solutions that would allow debtor governments to 'capture the market discount' on the value of the debt. Important industrial governments (such as the Japanese and French ones) in 1988 produced schemes that would move in a similar direction. A major change occurred in March 1989, when the US Treasury announced its support for measures—including actions to be taken by governments and IFIs—to reduce debt and debt service burdens.[9]

New flows: suggested guide-lines for the future

Private flows

An important lesson from recent debt crises is that if international private flows represent a very large proportion of developing countries' GDP or (particularly) exports, their long-term impact on borrowers and lenders may well become negative. This conclusion is particularly true in the case of variable interest medium-term sovereign bank lending, which is especially ill suited to funding long-term development. It would, however, seem that there is now enough historical evidence to show that very large inflows of foreign private savings under any mechanism can be harmful to the long-term interests of both private lenders and developing country borrowers. This is especially so in the context of unpredictable and large changes in key international variables, including the ability and willingness of foreign banks and/or investors to continue to promote sustained flows for long periods.

It can be concluded that for the medium-term future (once the debt crisis is resolved) it will be better for developing countries to err on the side of excessive prudence, realizing that low private external borrowing, particularly in relation to exports, is desirable from the point of view of long-term development. Not only will such a policy make developing countries less vulnerable to unanticipated changes in the international environment, it will also hopefully encourage a style of development that is more reliant on domestic savings and less reliant on import-intensive patterns of production and consumption. Furthermore, distortions in macro-economic policies—such as the large overvaluations of exchange rates that characterized many of the Latin American countries in the late seventies—would become less pervasive and less likely.

To ensure that future private lending to developing countries is not allowed to become excessive, there is need for far greater regulation and supervision of private flows by industrial governments than happened in the seventies. In parallel, developing country governments need to exert more self-discipline and greater control on private agents to curb excessive borrowing. Furthermore, contrary to current fashionable views, historical evidence reviewed here and elsewhere indicates the benefits of some controls by LDC governments on capital outflows, so as to avoid international borrowing being used as a source of capital flight.

A final issue regarding future private flows is that of selecting appropriate mechanisms and agents for development finance. Clearly some lending by banks will be required, particularly for specific production or commercial purposes, especially relating to trade and project finance. The relative share (within private flows) of direct, portfolio, and quasi-equity investment needs to be increased; such flows have the virtue of allowing greater correspondence between countries' and companies' repayment obligations and their capacity to pay; thus the risk variability of the income stream is shared by the foreign investor or lender and the LDC borrower.

Public flows

Given the discontinuities and market failures in the system of private international financial intermediation (some of which are short term and others more pervasive) there is a need for an explicit recognition of the desirability of public financial flows, in particular in three areas where the market mechanism cannot operate appropriately. These are, first, the funding of low-income countries' development, on concessionary terms; second, counter-cyclical funding; and third, the public role in creating international liquidity.

There is little debate about the merits of the first point, and we shall not elaborate upon them here. However, as regards public counter-cyclical funding and the public role for the creation of international liquidity, there is at present far more debate. The rationale for counter-cyclical flows seems clear. Because of the inevitability of business cycles, and their unexpected and disruptive impact on growth and on financial institutions, public counter-cyclical liquidity and credit mechanisms are desirable both to counteract the effect of the trade cycle and the pro-cyclical nature of private flows.

Based on this concept, in the early 1960s the IMF created the Compensatory Financing Facility, to compensate for the instability in countries' export earnings caused by external factors; this facility has been broadened to include (in 1988) international interest rates. However, the maximum size of the CFF credit drawing is not just determined by the externally conditioned export shortfall or interest rate excess, but by a certain proportion of the country's quota. As a result, the size of countries' access to CFF lending is limited, and its positive counter-cyclical effect—on the country and the world economy—is restricted. A second problem, which has emerged in the eighties, is that CFF lending is increasingly linked to highly conditional (upper credit tranche) lending by the IMF in contrast with its previously low-conditional character.

To improve the role of the CFF in providing counter-cyclical funding, its size needs to be increased (or even better de-linked completely from countries' quotas) and its conditionality should either be lowered to previous (pre-1983) levels, or even perhaps eliminated completely. In order to provide enhanced liquidity for the international economy, we believe that SDRs should again be used. Such a proposal, now controversial, would *not* have been so in the late 1960s or early 1970s. The decision to create Special Drawing Rights was originally seen as a major step in the history of the international monetary system. It gave the International Monetary Fund the power to increase the stock of international reserves through a simple book-keeping device.

The role for the SDR has changed since its original creation. On the one hand, developing countries have—particularly in the last decade—had a growing need for but a declining availability of international liquidity. The debt crisis has made developing countries' governments more conscious of the need to hold higher average reserve levels to insulate themselves against severe adverse shocks. High levels of debt and the dramatic decline of private lending by international banks to developing countries in the 1980s has implied that private lenders have for many developing countries made negative contributions to their balance of payments. To defend their reserve levels, developing countries have therefore been forced to improve their trade position dramatically, either by expanding exports or—more frequently

—by reducing imports. Such measures have been extremely costly in terms of growth and development. Therefore, in the eighties, the unsatisfied demand for international liquidity by a large proportion of developing countries dramatically increased, as did the cost of those countries' economies and peoples of the fact that this demand was not met by international creation of liquidity via the IMF.

A major asymmetry has emerged in the international financial system. For practically all industrial countries, the supply of international reserves has become extremely elastic; the total stock of their reserves is basically demand determined. Industrial governments—by having access to very large and integrated private international capital markets—can borrow as much as they wish from private financial institutions. As a result, industrial countries' needs for officially created reserves seem at least temporarily to have entirely disappeared. The relevant distinction is no longer between reserve currency countries and the rest of the world (as it was during the gold standard years or the Bretton Woods era) but between creditworthy countries and those that are not.

Opposition to any issue of SDRs since 1981 has arisen from some large industrial governments. This opposition seems to be based increasingly on the argument given above (for example in the quoted Report of Deputies of the Group of Ten) that 'the difficulties encountered by a number of countries are primarily an indication of their lack of creditworthiness and are not related to a general shortage of liquidity'. The implication is that SDR allocations are not the solution for those who are 'uncreditworthy'; those who are not in the state of grace of creditworthiness must make extreme efforts—via adjustment of their economies—to attain it.

This argument is weak, as we have seen from the historical evidence above. The Managing Director of the IMF gave a lucid summary of its inaccuracy:

The argument that the international financial institutions and the markets are able to provide adequate exchange reserves to heavily indebted countries . . . is far from being confirmed by our day-to-day experience. Since 1981–82, impressive adjustment, equivalent to 8 percentage points of G.D.P., has been achieved on average by the heavily indebted middle-income countries, but still leaves a situation of perhaps greater vulnerability for these countries in their adjustment efforts, because of the general withdrawal of commercial banks from voluntary lending (to developing countries). This is a structural change in the international financial system which makes it more difficult for many countries to finance reserve additions (Camdessus 1988).

Recent events have shown that even if countries are willing to make major sacrifices to make adjustment and substantially improve their trade balance, the private capital markets may not respond with an increase in their supply of lending to them, for a number of reasons largely or completely beyond the control of the developing countries themselves. There is here a clear case of market discontinuity and a need for action by the IMF which contributes to the 'public good' of sustaining the provision of liquidity to LDCs. The lending activities of the World Bank also need to be strongly informed by the need for public institutions to fill gaps and compensate for the discontinuities and limitations of private international financial markets.

Notes

1. For an interesting contribution in this field, see R. Devlin 1986.
2. It is interesting to point out that in another major international financial market—trading foreign exchange of developed countries and determining exchange rates amongst them—a similar disillusion with purely free market operation has occurred in the mid-eighties; a gradual, but clear, move has resulted towards more managed (by governments) exchange rates, via greater agreement between governments on desirable exchange rate reference zones and by greater intervention by these governments to influence movements of exchange rates in desired directions.
3. As we shall see in section 3, the experience of the 1980s adds other conditions that need to be met, such as that the financial terms should be either fixed (as regards interest rates) or related to indicators of capacity to repay (such as the country's main exports' prices).
4. Data based on IMF, *World Economic Outlook*, several issues.
5. See Griffith-Jones and Lipton (1984) for a fairly brief discussion of this point. A very detailed analysis of the extent to which bank supervision lagged behind the internationalization of bank lending can be found in Dale 1982.
6. Based on personal experience and interviews with bankers; see, also Devlin 1986.
7. For a useful review of the evidence, see Hughes and Singh 1991 (forthcoming).
8. I thank Michael Lipton for very valuable comments on this issue.
9. The Brady Plan is based on the assumption that industrial governments and international financial institutions should support debt/debt service reduction. This is an important step forward, in the context of our analysis here. However, doubts remain whether debt/debt service reduction will be sufficient to contribute to the restoration of development in different highly indebted countries.

References

Alexander, C. (1984), 'Jumbo Loans, Jumbo Risks', *Time*, 3 Dec.
Alvarez, A. (1988), 'Economic Crises and Foreign Debt Management in Venezuela', in Griffith-Jones 1988.
Bagehot, W. (1873), *Lombard Street: A Description of the Money Market*, J. Murray, 1917 reprint editions, London.

Balogh, T. (1980), 'General Equilibrium, the International Monetary System and the Oil Price Crisis', Proceedings of the Second World Scientific Banking Meeting, Dubrovnik, May.

Camdessus, M. (1988), 'Chairman's Summing Up at the Conclusion of the Discussions on the Question of SDR Allocations', 23 Mar., IMF mimeo.

Cline, W. (1983), *International Debt and the Stability of the World Economy*, Policy Analysis in International Economics 4, Institute for International Economics, Washington DC.

Dale, E. (1982), *Bank Supervision around the World*, Group of Thirty, New York.

Devlin, R. (1986), 'La estructura y comportamiento de la banca internacional en los años setenta y su impacto en la crisis de América Latina', *Estudios CIEPLAN* 19 (June): 87–102.

Duffy, G., and Giddy, I. (1978), *The International Money Market*, Prentice-Hall, Englewood Cliffs, NJ.

Ffrench-Davis, R. (1988), 'The Foreign Debt Crisis and Adjustment in Chile', in S. Griffith-Jones 1988.

Griffith-Jones, S. (1980), 'The Growth of Multinational Banking, the Euro-currency Market and the Effects on Developing Countries', *Journal of Development Studies* 16/2 (Jan.): 204–23.

—— (ed.) (1988), *Managing World Debt*, Wheatsheaf, Brighton, and St Martin's Press, New York.

—— and Harvey, C. (eds.) (1986), *World Prices and Development*, Gower, Aldershot.

Guttentag, J., and Herring, R. (1985), 'Commercial Bank Lending to Developing Countries: From Overlending to Underlending to Structural Reform' in G. Smith and J. Cuddington (eds.), *International Debt and the Developing Countries*, World Bank, Washington DC.

Hughes, A., and Singh, A. (1991, forthcoming), 'The World Economic Slow-down and the Asian and Latin American Economics: A Comparative Analysis', in *No Panacea: The Limits of Economic Liberalization*, forthcoming Oxford University Press, Oxford.

International Monetary Fund (1982), 'International Capital Markets, Development and Prospects', Occasional Paper no. 14 (July), Washington DC.

—— (1985), Report of the Deputies of the G-10, 'The Functioning and Improvement of the International Monetary System', Appendix 1 in IMF Occasional Paper no. 50 (Feb.), 'Strengthening the International Monetary System', Washington DC.

Kindleberger, C. (1978), *Manias, Panics and Crashes: A History of Financial Crisis*, Macmillan, Basingstoke and New York.

Lal, D. (1988), 'After the Debt Crisis: Modes of Development for the Longer Term in Latin America', Discussion Paper 88–04, University College, London.

McKinnon, R. (1977), *The Euro-currency Market*, Essay on International Finance no. 125, Princeton University, NJ.

Marichal, C. (1988), *Historia de la deuda externa de América Latina*, Alianza Editorial, Madrid.

Minsky, H. (1982), *Can 'It' Happen Again?* M. E. Sharp Inc., New York.

Polak, J. J. (1980), 'Hope for Substitution Account', *IMF Survey* (27 Oct.), Washington DC.

Prebisch, R. (1979), 'La cooperación internacional en el desarrollo latinoamericano', in *Problemas económicos y sociales de América Latina*, Mundo, Mexico.

US Congress (1979), Senate Committee for External Relations, International Debt, the Banks and US Foreign Policy prepared by K. Lissakers, 95th Congress 1st session, Washington DC.

Veblen, T. (1904), *The Theories of Business Enterprise*, Charles Scribner, New York.

6

Recovery from Macro-economic Disaster in Sub-Saharan Africa

CHARLES HARVEY

1. Introduction

This chapter concerns a sample of seven countries in Sub-Saharan Africa, from among those whose economies have suffered from prolonged macro-economic disaster, and whose governments have eventually abandoned previous policies in an attempt to recover. The chapter tries to identify why two of the seven, Ghana and Nigeria, persisted with the policy changes, fulfilled some of the more difficult commitments made to the IMF,[1] and showed signs of macro-economic recovery; while the others, Sierra Leone, Somalia, Tanzania, Uganda, and Zambia, did not.

Each of the seven sample countries undertook, or said that they would undertake, a major policy reversal, abandoning not just previous economic policies but also in some cases a whole political ideology. The change of policy included in all cases a non-marginal devaluation. Governments also promised action concerning some or all of: a reduction in the budget deficit, a sharp rise in interest rates, a reduction in exchange controls, making import licences freely available, the privatization of agricultural marketing, the reduction or ending of subsidies on basic food and or petrol, forcing parastatals to eliminate their deficits or close down or privatize—in short, the neo-liberal package. In every case, these changes were made as part of an agreement with the IMF and the World Bank.

The chapter's starting point is that recovery requires persistence by the government with the new set of policies (Colclough and Green 1988). Persistence is necessary for a number of reasons, ranging from the length of time it takes to implement some parts of an IMF programme, to the need to create confidence among producers of tradables that the new policies will continue. These points are elaborated in section 2.

A draft of this chapter was presented to the IDS Retreat Conference in December 1988. The present version benefited greatly from comments from colleagues at the conference, especially the discussant Reginald Green, who also provided lengthy written comments. Christopher Colclough, David Evans, Hubert Schmitz, Hans Singer, and Adrian Wood also provided written comments.

It is not enough, though, to attribute government persistence to varying amounts of 'political will'. The paper looks in some detail at what happened in each of the sample countries, and argues that some at least of the factors which induce some governments to persist with policy reforms, and others to abandon them, can be identified (section 3).

This has important policy implications. Failure to recover from macro-economic disaster by implementing an IMF programme is very costly, not just in the prolongation of economic misery. Devaluation which does not result in recovery leaves a country in the same disastrous economic position as before, but with a higher rate of inflation. In addition, governments and producers then believe that IMF reform packages do not work. As a result, governments are unwilling to try again, and if they do, producers are even less likely to respond because they have seen the previous programme abandoned.

If it is predictable that a reform programme will fail, it may therefore be better in some circumstances to delay its implementation until the political conditions for success are present. That is directly contrary to the conventional wisdom that it is always better to act sooner rather than later in implementing an IMF programme.

From the sample of countries discussed, there appear to be other, more technical, factors which consistently affected the likelihood of reforms being successful. The most notable are the response of government revenue to devaluation, the timing of the removal of protection for local producers, and the importance of non-conditional foreign exchange inflows. They are less important than the political conditions for persistence, and part of their influence is political anyway; but they do appear to have some independent impact on success and failure (section 4).

Success is relative. There is much criticism, for example, of the nature of Ghana's recovery. This paper takes the position that recovery, of whatever sort, is not possible without growth in output; and that growth in output is not possible if the government does not persist with the new policies. Whether the distribution of the gains from recovery is acceptable is a separate question not tackled in this paper.

The paper does not try to identify the causes of the economic problems faced by these seven countries. There is a vigourous debate as to whether economic decline was caused primarily by bad management (World Bank 1981) or bad luck (such as falling terms of trade and drought). Whatever the causes, the decline of the seven sample economies was a fact to which all their governments eventually reacted by agreeing a new set of economic policies with the IMF.

The World Bank recently reported that GDP in Sub-Saharan Africa showed strong signs of growth from 1985 to 1988, and that 'strongly reforming' countries, all of them with reform programmes agreed with and supported by the Bank and the IMF, did markedly better than 'weakly reforming' countries (World Bank and UNDP 1989). That would appear to provide strong support for the implementation of Bank/Fund policy packages.[2]

But some countries which are classified by the Bank as 'weak reformers' have abandoned Bank/Fund programmes or failed to implement them fully. So the World Bank's claim begs the question as to why some governments are strong reformers, and why some strong reformers become weak reformers. All it shows is the point at which this paper starts, namely that strong reformers (persistent governments) are more likely to recover.[3]

The countries covered in this paper are not typical of Sub-Saharan Africa as a whole: the worse the economic decline, and the longer it lasts, the harder it is to recover. So the experience of the sample is likely to be worse than the average. But it is important to study the experience of this group of countries precisely because their economies were (and in some cases still are) in such a bad state. There are others in the same position; and the number of such countries trying to implement Bank/Fund reforms continues to grow, as does the number of countries making the attempt for the second and third time.

2. The Need for Government Commitment to Policy Reversal

Delay in supply response

The bad news comes immediately, from the impact of devaluation on prices. Even producers of tradables, who should gain eventually, face increased input and credit costs immediately, as well as the same increases in consumer prices as everyone else. The potential increase in their income is delayed, and only occurs if the increased domestic cost of foreign exchange really is passed on to them and they are able to take advantage of it.[4]

The good news, on the other hand, comes later, some of it much later. The response of most producers of tradables is bound to take some time: a few months for manufacturers, a year for producers of annual crops, several years for some tree crops. A few producers with spare capacity may be able to increase output and or exports immediately. For example, coal and sugar were exported from Zambia to neighbouring countries, early in the foreign exchange auction period, because coal and sugar producers had spare capacity, as did the railways, and because such basic products did not require the build-up of new marketing expertise. But most producers of tradables need time to acquire and put to use the necessary resources for increased production, and even more time to develop new export markets. Delay may also occur if infrastructure is run down, and if government is dependent on the capital inflows released by an IMF agreement to start rehabilitation.

First, then, governments need to be able to sustain the new package of policies for as long as it takes for a supply response to occur.

Redistribution against the politically influential

An effective devaluation reduces the income and power of the politically influential—urban wage earners and those who dispense access to foreign exchange and import licences—and increases the income, eventually, of the politically weak—scattered rural producers. Not only do the losers lose before the gainers gain, but the losers are also more certain to be worse off than the gainers are to be better off.

Second, therefore, governments must somehow survive the opposition of politically powerful groups during the initial period when almost no other group has increased its income. And when some groups' incomes do eventually increase, the gainers are politically weak and disorganized.

Producer confidence

Third, producers of tradables will not respond at all unless they believe that the new set of relative prices is going to last long enough for investment in increased production, if only of working capital, to be profitable. Governments must give the clear impression, therefore, that they are sufficiently committed to the new policies for them to be sustained.

Reluctant submission to the IMF, followed by persistent public criticism of the new policies while they are being implemented, will reduce or entirely prevent the supply response of many producers. They will expect old policies to be re-established; and their expectations may be self-fulfilling. That is, their failure to respond will of itself make it more likely that the programme will be abandoned before any benefits accrue.

Even the most determined and therefore publicly convincing government will not persuade all producers immediately that the new system will continue. Producer confidence will increase over time as the government persists; but this requires the government to be even more determined, since it extends the period during which unpopular policies must be continued, without much to show in the way of increased production and exports.

The timing of new policy measures

Fourth, it is almost always impossible for a government to implement all parts of a new policy package immediately. Some new policies take longer, by their nature. Thus while devaluation, for example, is often resisted, it is a relatively easy change to make, and can be made instantly once the decision has been made. The same argument applies to increases in interest rates. On the other hand, cutting government spending, or, even more difficult, reducing the number of government employees, closing parastatals, or removing subsidies on food and petrol, are bound to take some time. This gives time for those worst affected, who are also the most influential politically, to organize their opposition.

Even a fully determined government, therefore, will have to persist with a series of very unpopular actions, during a period when it is already unpopular with many people because of the effects of devaluation. That is, it is not possible to get all the politically unpopular actions out of the way at once. A less than fully determined government may devalue while delaying (sometimes indefinitely) the necessary complementary action. This is a recipe for failure, since doing nothing to reduce a budget deficit will drive up the cost of foreign exchange if the exchange rate is flexible, and will drive up the real exchange rate if it is not.

The combination of devaluation and promises of action can yield short-term benefits: for example, the first drawdown on an IMF credit, and Paris and London Club debt reschedulings. But if it leads to later failure of the programme, the result may be to leave the country with higher inflation, no recovery of output or exports, and an increased reluctance to try again.

Delays in the receipt of increased aid

Fifth, donors have increasingly made their aid conditional on an IMF agreement, and both Paris and London Club debt rescheduling is normally impossible without a Fund agreement.[5] In theory, increased aid should provide some immediate economic and political relief to governments until a supply response has time to emerge. In each of the seven sample countries, the expected or promised increases in aid disbursement, which were conditional on government implementing a policy reversal, were commonly delayed for six to twelve months. This increased yet further the need for sustained political commitment to the programme.

Both sides were responsible for delays. The bureaucratic procedures of the donors were not speeded up to accommodate urgent post-devaluation needs. And recipient governments were not able to handle the administration required, partly because of the run-down state of their own public sectors. In particular, low real salaries meant that civil servants simply could not afford to spend very much of their time at their government jobs.

In addition, large numbers of the most highly educated citizens were working abroad because of the low level of public salaries, or because of opposition to the government in power. Both factors were especially important in Ghana and Tanzania. And some governments could not raise the counter-part domestic funds where that was required for the release of donor finance.

It was entirely predictable that governments suffering from years of economic (and in some cases political) crisis would not be able to administer aid inflows efficiently, especially if aid commitments increased suddenly. It was equally predictable that aid donors would not suddenly prove able to speed up their bureaucratic procedures. What was so damaging was that plans were drawn up that ignored these obvious points. Instead, they were premised on rapid increases in aid disbursements, even though programmes were clearly endangered if the increases were delayed, and delay was itself predictable.

One of the advantages of foreign exchange auctions was that some donors released aid for them without the usual delays. Auction finance should not have required the donors' normal lengthy project appraisal procedures. But even in those countries where foreign exchange auctions were introduced, there were delays in the release of aid money by donors.[6] Partly this was because even auction support money was tied up in various ways, usually to sectors; donors were not willing to forego all conditionality in supporting auctions, even though the rationale of auctions was to allow pricing to determine priorities. And partly it was because not all aid moneys were put into supporting the auction.

Delays in aid disbursement were reported in Zambia, Uganda, Ghana, Tanzania, and Sierra Leone. Somalia was a special case. Its foreign exchange auction was a bit of a sideshow, handling less than $50 m. a year compared to $300 m. in unofficial remittances and $240 m. a year of aid flows, mostly from Italy and the USA and apparently available (as noted below) irrespective of macro-economic policy.

3. Government Commitment to Reform:
Summaries of Country Experience

This section provides brief summaries of what seem to be the key factors affecting the government commitment to reform programmes, in each of the seven sample countries.

Ghana

Ghana had a new government (Rawlings's second) on the last day of 1981. The new government was deeply opposed ideologically to an IMF agreement, so it spent a significant period searching for an alternative set of policies and finance. At the end of that time, the government had become thoroughly convinced of two crucial points: that the economy could not recover without large flows of finance from abroad, and that large enough flows were not available from the socialist block of countries.

President Rawlings and a few key officials were so convinced of these two points that the government set about devising a set of appropriate policy changes. These were intended to be so orthodox, in IMF terms, that the IMF would have no choice but to agree to them. An agreement with the IMF was indeed reached, in direct contradiction to the government's earlier beliefs.

The government devalued, from C2.75 to C30 to the US dollar, some twenty-two months after coming to power. The government also began to adopt politically difficult supporting policies—including, for example, large reductions in the number of employees of the Cocoa Marketing Board.[7]

Many of the original supporters of Rawlings's second coup eventually left the government, and there were some nine unsuccessful coup attempts over the next few years, from the right as well as from the left.[8] But those who were convinced of the necessity of the new policies were the ones who remained in power, and the programme was sustained despite a dreadful first year when there was little to show for it. Thereafter, there was a steady improvement in some key indicators, including output and exports.

Although there was plenty to criticize in what happened, it can be argued that the recovery in macro-economic indicators was a minimum prerequisite for further progress.[9] Moreover, by 1988 the Ghana government was in a position to extract ever increasing amounts of aid from donors, because of its position as an apparently successful example of the implementation of IMF and World Bank policies.

Nigeria

Nigeria also had a new government prior to the major change of policy in 1986. And, like Ghana, the regime of President Babangida was in office for more than a year before it reversed previous economic policies. But the circumstances were quite different from those of Ghana. President Babangida came to power already personally convinced of the need for an IMF programme in Nigeria. Before trying to reach an IMF agreement, however, the government organized a national debate, in 1985, on the whole question. The debate was extremely lively, and resulted in a clear majority of public opinion against borrowing from the IMF.

What the government did, in these unexpected circumstances, was to introduce its own series of measures, which amounted to a full IMF-style programme, but without actually borrowing any money from the IMF. Indeed, it could be argued that the programme was tougher than might have been required by the IMF, because of the absence of IMF credit. It included, for example, an exceptionally tight credit squeeze and the closure of agricultural marketing boards, which meant that some 10,000 people lost their jobs.[10] Such actions were politically possible because they could be presented as the government's own chosen policies, and because the programme did not include an IMF loan.

It was extremely perverse that the government ended up with all the policies that would have been part of IMF conditionality, the bad news, without an inflow of IMF money, the good news.[11] On the other hand, it was reported that the World Bank increased its lending to compensate for the absence of IMF loans;[12] and the IMF did give its formal approval to the programme so that Nigeria could reschedule its official and private foreign debts at the Paris and London Clubs respectively. Debt rescheduling had genuine importance in Nigeria (see section 5.4 below).

Sierra Leone

Sierra Leone had a less radical change of government in November 1985. President Stevens handed over to President Momoh, who was confirmed in office by an election at which he was the agreed and only candidate. This gave President Momoh rather less of a mandate for change than if there had been a more radical change of government, particularly as Stevens remained as Chairman of the only political party. But Momoh made himself popular by attacking corruption, and in particular by getting rid of some of the Lebanese businessmen who were widely regarded as having been at the heart of the corruption under Stevens.[13] The balance of these factors seems to have been against Momoh's government implementing radical policy changes: the pattern was to appoint commissions and committees rather than to act,[14] and to raise some key prices (rice and petrol) but not to end price controls and subsidies.

The political power of the Sierra Leone government to introduce and sustain new economic policies may not, though, have been the main explanation of what happened in Sierra Leone. Even if the government had been very much more committed to a new set of policies, the extreme difficulty of increasing government revenue, and therefore of reducing the budget deficit, despite a series of large devaluations, made the restoration of macro-economic balance extraordinarily difficult (see section 5.1 below).

Somalia

Somalia was deeply affected by the war against Ethiopia in the Ogaden, and by the continuing armed resistance of exiled opposition groups. For a number of reasons, the government was able to give political and military objectives priority, while the economy was relatively neglected. First, by shifting from an alliance with the USSR to one with the USA, the government was able to secure a flow of military aid, and to a lesser extent economic aid, apparently irrespective of whether it was currently pursuing an IMF programme or not. Second, Italian aid was also large and largely unaffected by economic policy. Somalia was Italy's third largest recipient of aid, and it seemed that Italy was determined to maintain its influence there, by maintaining its aid programme.

Third, a large flow of remittances from migrant Somali workers in the Gulf states, nearly all of which reached households in Somalia by informal means, enabled a certain level of welfare to be maintained regardless of what was happening in the formal sector of the economy. The government made several attempts to channel these remittances through the banking system, for example by trying to reduce the gap between the official and unofficial exchange rates. But the banks were not capable of delivering the money to households in remote parts of the country, many of them nomadic (this factor also affected the response of government revenue to devaluation, see section 5.1 below).

There were some periods when IMF programmes seemed to be working, to the point where the IMF was holding Somalia up as an example of success. But improvement never went beyond exchange rate policy and some other financial indicators; nothing was done, for example, despite government promises, about the large number of loss-making parastatals. The official rate of inflation stuck at around 30 or 40 per cent, apart from one year at 90 per cent; exports declined;[15] imports grew; and the economy became increasingly dependent on aid. In the three years 1984–6, exports were only 20 per cent of imports, compared with 82 per cent in 1970–2 and 37 per cent in 1979–81. The Somali government appeared to be an example of one whose objectives were mainly concerned with various armed opposition groups and with security *vis-à-vis* its neighbours; so long as aid was available for the pursuit of those objectives, the state of the economy was of secondary importance.

Tanzania

Tanzania seems to be in an intermediate category. As in Sierra Leone, there was a change of President, but former President Nyerere remained as Party Chairman. Reluctance to abandon old policies was very strong. There had been twenty or more years of popular commitment to the ideology represented by the old set of policies, of which Nyerere was both the architect and the principal spokesman. And Nyerere continued to be very influential after he gave up the presidency.

On the other hand, a lengthy debate on whether to reach an agreement with the IMF did take place, together with a three-year unsuccessful experiment with alternative policies: the Structural Adjustment Programme from 1983 to 1986 *without* IMF support was widely seen as a failure, weakening the case of those advocating non-IMF policies. Moreover, Nyerere himself began to shift his ground in 1986: in various public speeches he expressed doubts about the one-party state, about the use of parastatals to achieve social objectives, and about the fairness of the state trading system in the setting of prices and in the distribution of goods.

But public commitment to the IMF programme when it was finally agreed (in August 1986) was ambiguous at best. Nyerere even claimed the agreement as a victory, on the grounds that the government had not agreed to all the IMF's demands. And he continued to attack the IMF's international role in subsequent speeches while grudgingly supporting its programme in Tanzania.

Although this was consistent in so far as the Tanzanian programme was regarded as being different from what the IMF had originally wanted, it conveyed an ambivalent public message.

Given the circumstances, there was a remarkable lack of public protest, perhaps because the majority of Tanzanians depended on the parallel market before and after the IMF programme was agreed, and were thus little affected by changes in formal sector prices. A cabinet reshuffle in March 1987 strengthened the anti-IMF faction, as (probably) did Nyerere's re-election as Party Chairman in November 1987.[16] These were signals to producers of lack of government commitment to the programme.

The failure to do much about reducing the size and cost of the public sector was also crucial. Parastatal deficits were one of the main causes of macro-economic imbalance. But reducing the public sector would have meant attacking the positions of many party leaders; and the government made a public commitment not to make party members redundant in any parastatal redundancy programme.

Perhaps surprisingly in these circumstances, the programme was not abandoned; and the IMF continued its lending[17] despite lack of progress in reforming the parastatal sector. Meanwhile, some increase in output was reported, although the increases were rather small and may have been partly the recording in official statistics of what had previously been parallel market activity. The indications were, therefore, that the Tanzanian programme would not be fully implemented. And the available export statistics showed no recovery, without which little could be achieved: the value of officially recorded exports in US dollar terms halved from 1981 to 1986, when it was only paying for about a third of imports.

Uganda

Uganda went through more than one attempt at recovery by means of an IMF programme. The one discussed here was in May 1987, some sixteen months after the government of President Museveni took office. His government's commitment was to socialism and self-reliance. It regarded the recovery under Obote's second regime as having been based on a large inflow of funds spent on consumer goods, resulting in an increase in foreign debt for which there was nothing to show. Meanwhile, however, the IMF, the World Bank, and other donors were withholding aid, without which recovery appeared increasingly impossible. Grants recovered in 1986, but were still only half their level of 1981, in current dollars. The IMF agreement of May 1987 was regarded by the government as very much the invention of the IMF.

Perhaps surprisingly, in these circumstances, the government succeeded in eliminating the budget deficit in the first few months after the May 1987 devaluation. The government actually repaid a small amount to the banking system in the second half of the year, compared with a 60 per cent increase in credit to the government in the previous six months. This was greatly helped by the one-off receipt of a 30 per cent tax on currency exchange.

Unfortunately, credit to the private sector increased rapidly, with severe inflationary effects. Coffee producers received higher prices after the devaluation, and this induced a 50 per cent increase in the volume of coffee bought by the Marketing Board. So there was a sudden and large increase in the spending power of farmers. There was the normal delay in receiving foreign exchange and ordering imports, and the government compounded this factor by spending only 17 per cent of official foreign exchange on consumer imports.

Most consumer demand had therefore to be satisfied in the parallel market for goods and foreign exchange. Within seven or eight months the cost of unofficial foreign exchange rose from a small 17 per cent premium after the May 1987 devaluation, to be three or four times the official rate. The rate of inflation accelerated to the point where the new Uganda shilling was again grossly overvalued by the end of 1987.

This re-established all the earlier incentives to avoid official markets, and confirmed the government in its distrust of IMF policy recommendations. A second large devaluation was implemented in 1988, but was much further from approaching the unofficial rate than in 1987. Meanwhile, action on the unmanageable size of the public sector was postponed by commissioning further studies; and people employed in the public sector were paid so little that they were unable to devote much time to their jobs. It would have been very difficult, therefore, for the government to work out its own preferred policy changes, even if it had wanted to do so.

Zambia

Zambia embarked on an IMF programme in October 1985 without a change of government. There had been a number of previous agreements with the IMF, but this was the most radical, involving a foreign exchange auction and, as a result, a much greater devaluation than on previous occasions. The government also promised to reduce basic food subsidies and to liberalize agricultural marketing.

The change of policy was made without any great debate on the issue. Indeed, it was reported that a meeting of the Cabinet and Central Committee, presented with the idea of another IMF programme at short notice, voted overwhelmingly against it. This vote was overruled by the President, who was supported only by the Ministers of Finance and Agriculture.

After the initial rapid increase in the domestic cost of foreign exchange, the auction-determined exchange rate showed signs of stability. But there was a steady stream of speeches against the economic changes, with only very occasional public support, from the President. In April 1986, only six months into the programme, the Minister of Finance and the governor of the Bank of Zambia, who were known to be strong supporters of the new policies, were replaced by people known to be hostile.

The new central bank governor interfered with the working of the auction in a way that destroyed confidence in it. At one stage, the Bank of Zambia actually sold foreign exchange that it did not have, making successful bidders wait up to three weeks before receiving their allocations. Meanwhile, rather little progress had been made with other liberalizing changes, for example in agricultural marketing and pricing, or with reducing the budget deficit. This was partly because an increase in food prices was badly handled and resulted in food riots; but it was also partly because there was never a real political commitment to make a success of the programme. For example, no significant progress was made in reducing public sector employment.

The cost of foreign exchange accelerated upwards, and the programme was finally abandoned for good after about eighteen months, amid an orgy of anti-IMF speeches.

4. Government Commitment to Change: Common Factors

Of the seven countries covered, only Ghana and Nigeria could be described as having a high degree of government commitment to their neo-liberal reforms. Sierra Leone and Tanzania had varying degrees of partial commitment. Somalia, Uganda, and Zambia had very low degrees of commitment. What is interesting, since the proposition that a high degree of government commitment is necessary to make the reforms work successfully appears to have an element of truism about it, is what circumstances led some governments to be relatively highly committed, and why it can be argued that this was not enough to ensure success in Sierra Leone and Tanzania.

4.1. Change of government and internal debate

Two possible factors, a prior change of government and the internal preparation of policy changes, are summarized in table 6.1.

A change of government may make it easier to reverse past policies. But the new government probably then needs a significant period of time before embracing the neo-liberal policy package, to convince itself and its wider support that there is no viable alternative. It is unusual for new governments to acquire office with new economic policies fully prepared; indeed, some of the governments in the sample took office with a general policy stance exactly opposite to the neo-liberal package, for example Ghana and Uganda.

A change of leader rather than of government eases the possibility of policy changes, as compared with no change at all. But continuity also

TABLE 6.1. *Degree of government commitment to neo-liberal package*

Commitment	Country	New government	Were policies internally prepared?	Has the programme been successful?
High	Ghana	22 months before	Yes	Yes
High	Nigeria	15 months before	Yes[a]	Yes, so far
Some	S. Leone	New President[b] 7 months before	Not really[c]	No
Some[d]	Tanzania	New President[b] 10 months before	Not really[c]	Hardly at all
None	Somalia	No	No	Yes at first, later no
None	Uganda	13 months before	No	No
None	Zambia	No	No	No

[a] It could be argued that the policies were simply those of the IMF, but that they were presented as being those of the government.
[b] Former President remained as Chairman of the ruling party.
[c] Some evidence of an internal debate; reforms not implemented because of that debate, but in order to get short-term gains from aid inflows and debt rescheduling.
[d] This commitment was to a distinctly Tanzanian policy package; it is possible that the packages of policies to which the IMF and the Tanzanian government believed they were agreeing were in fact different.

imposes constraints, especially when the former leader remains as chairman of the ruling party as was the case in both Sierra Leone and Tanzania. It is reported that the new President in Sierra Leone was personally committed to an agreement with the IMF, in a way that the new President of Tanzania was not. The very much greater ideological commitment of the Tanzanian government to the set of policies pursued under former President Nyerere, and his immense personal standing, also imposed much more severe contraints on President Mwinyi of Tanzania than on President Momoh of Sierra Leone. While both had to cope with the vested interests of the former presidents' remaining supporters in the government, former President Stevens was somewhat discredited in popular opinion by the corruption associated with his government.

It is clearly possible, although much harder, for an existing government with the same leader to decide to make a radical change of policy. But it seems to be essential for any government, new or long established, to have a prolonged internal debate that leaves key people convinced of the need for change. As part of that debate, government officials need to do extended work on the policy changes rather than to accept IMF and World Bank proposals, however technically competent.

The process of working on the rationale for policy changes forces governments to research the state of the economy in some depth. As a result, those with the power to make decisions and stick to them are more thoroughly convinced of the need for the new policies agreed. In addition, doing the analysis enables the government to set the agenda; and this in turn gives advantages in negotiation. The winning of some negotiating points is likely to increase commitment to the changes.

Government commitment is also likely to be greater if new policies can be presented as the government's own ideas and decisions. If such a process does not take place, the new set of policies emanates from outside and not from within the government, and is thus regarded as an alien imposition. It then becomes more likely that the more difficult parts of the package will be promised but not implemented, or that the whole programme will be abandoned quite quickly.

5. Other Factors Affecting Success

5.1. Reduction of budget deficits

Devaluation plus a continuing large budget deficit financed by the banking system is a formula for a worsening spiral of inflation and devaluation.[18] Moreover, budget deficits need to be reduced very fast, because at rapid rates of inflation even a few months' delay can eliminate the benefits of a devaluation; and devaluation itself increases inflation unless inflationary forces are sharply reduced.

Cutting government spending normally requires time, especially where one of the main targets is the reduction of parastatal deficits by sacking employees, by management reforms, or by closure. Even where the government is, for the sort of reasons discussed in the last section, determined to make the necessary changes, they require time. Thus Ghana, for example, which did set about reducing the number of people employed by the Cocoa Marketing Board, only started the process in 1985, and progress was spread over a number of years thereafter. The sudden closure of agricultural marketing boards in Nigeria in 1986 seems to have been an exception to this rule. The imposition of new taxes, or improvement in the efficiency of collecting old ones, also requires time.

Early success in reducing budget deficits depends, therefore, to a large extent on the short-term response of existing sources of revenue to devaluation, or to be more precise, on the government's ability to tax increases in the domestic value of foreign transactions.

The issue depends a great deal on how easily and cheaply exports and imports can be smuggled to avoid taxation. Higher producer prices for exporters can attract more of the export trade into official channels, and have the same effect on imports as a result. But if smuggling is easy, attempts to tax foreign trade heavily will drive it back into unofficial channels—unless the government can at the same time increase its physical control over smuggling. Because the illegality of smuggling has some cost, some taxation is possible; but the cost of illegality sets an upper limit.

Much depends on the structure of the export trade, since large corporations are easier to control and tax than small-scale producers, on the nature of the product, and on the geography and politics of international borders. Nigeria and Zambia were in the best position to control smuggling of their main exports, potentially. There was virtually no smuggling of Nigerian oil or of Zambian copper, which constituted more than 90 per cent of their respective exports. But the revenue gain in Zambia, or reduction in copper company losses financed by the central bank, was offset by the government's inability to control increases in its spending, notably on food subsidies.

At the other extreme were Sierra Leone and Somalia, Sierra Leone's most important exports, alluvial diamonds, are dug from swamps by small-scale operators using minimal equipment. It is impossible for the Sierra Leone government to control this activity; and diamonds are exceptionally easy to smuggle. Smuggling was made even easier in the 1980s because of declining real wages for government employees, which made bribery of border officials cheap and easy.[19] Attempts to tax exports, not only of diamonds but of other exports and many imports, simply resulted in increased smuggling in these circumstances. For example, the government actually reduced taxes on beer and cigarettes in 1987, at a time of immense pressure on the budget, in an attempt to reduce smuggling.

The position in Somalia was different, but with similar results. The largest source of foreign exchange in Somalia by the mid-1980s was migrant labour remittances. As noted already, the formal banking system was quite incapable of handling these remittances, because the majority of the households to which they were being sent were nomads (60 per cent of the Somali population is nomadic). The informal trading system handled this problem cheaply and efficiently. At times, the gap between the parallel and the official exchange rate gave an added incentive not to remit by official channels; but even when the gap was reduced (the government tried to reduce it for this reason), remittances continued to use the informal system. Since there was also inward smuggling of imports, the response of government revenue to devaluation was small.[20]

At the time of its 1987 devaluation, the Uganda government increased producer prices to coffee growers significantly, although by less than the increases in the cost of foreign exchange (182 per cent compared with 329 per cent). But the government also increased physical control of the countryside, which made smuggling more difficult. This combination was enough to recapture for official channels much of the coffee export trade—official coffee buying increased by 50 per cent. A large part of the increased Coffee Marketing Board profits were paid to the government, so that government revenue did increase significantly for a period. But the gap between the parallel and official exchange rates increased again after devaluation, for the reasons explained above; the incentive to smuggle grew; and, as in Sierra Leone, the low pay of government officials made smuggling easy and cheap.[21]

Ghana and Tanzania appeared to be intermediate cases. Smuggling of cocoa out of Ghana occurred but was estimated to amount to only 25 per cent or so of the crop; and it was possible (as in Uganda) to improve physical control over illegal trade. In the event, the real value of tax revenue in Ghana with respect to devaluation (and improved administration) proved very elastic, increasing by a multiple of four from 1983 to 1986; this, together with grant aid, enabled the real value of government spending to rise two and a half times, while the budget deficit was eliminated. The level of government spending had earlier sunk to very low levels; nevertheless, Ghana's ability to revive some government services was an important part of the relative success of its economic recovery.

Smuggling must also have played a role in Tanzania, because of the large scale of imports financed by unofficial foreign exchange. This limited the impact of devaluation on tax revenue. But smuggling was reduced from 1984 onwards, grants increased, and government borrowing from the banking system fell by 30 per cent in real terms from 1984 to 1987, indicating that the budget balance was improved. On the other hand, the government was slow to tackle all the problems of the large number of parastatals (over 100), partly because so many prominent party members were employed in them.

The reduction of smuggling was not wholly beneficial. In several countries (for example Sierra Leone, Somalia, Tanzania, Uganda) unofficial foreign exchange was the main source of imported consumer goods. Reducing the budget deficit reduced inflationary pressure; but where the increase in official inflows of foreign exchange was not used to satisfy consumer demand, the parallel exchange rate depreciated and inflation increased, thereby wiping out the benefits of recapturing trade for the official sector. More generally, the transfer of foreign exchange earnings, from producers to the government by reducing smuggling, was a net gain only if governments could be expected to make better use of the money than producers, or if inflation really was reduced and the resulting economic gains were greater than the loss to producers of no longer getting border price equivalents for their output.

5.2. The removal of protection

It seems, from the experience of Zambia during the foreign exchange auction period, that removing protection from local industry by trade liberalization can be a major political mistake. At the same time as the auction was introduced, the government allowed imports for which no official foreign exchange was provided; importers could use their own foreign exchange without any questions being asked as to how they acquired it. The result was a flood of imported consumer goods, many of them luxuries not previously available for some years, and many displacing Zambian production which had developed during the years of extreme foreign exchange shortages.

This flow of consumer imports discredited the whole IMF programme and was a powerful weapon in the hands of the IMF's opponents. People of all persuasions were shocked, and some producers were put out of business or suffered heavy losses. The government's statistics, showing that a small proportion of auction proceeds went to consumer imports, carried very little weight because of the amount of 'no foreign exchange' imports visibly available. These factors seemed to have weighed more heavily than the benefit of increased availability of imported goods.

Something similar happened in Tanzania; moreover, some bank credit may have been used to buy foreign exchange for luxury imports, in turn worsening the credit squeeze affecting local industry. And in Uganda in 1987 and 1988, the government clearly believed that the aid provided to the previous foreign exchange auction had been 'wasted' because it had largely been spent on imported consumer goods. This was the reason given for devoting most of official foreign exchange after the May 1987 devaluation to industrial inputs (after paying for oil and debt service), with the inflationary consequences already described.

Consumer imports were less of an issue in Somalia and Sierra Leone, probably because their parallel markets were so well developed that the additional foreign exchange made available following an IMF agreement made little difference. A wide range of consumer goods was available before and after the change of policy.

Nor was this argument used in Nigeria. What did happen was that the more import intensive manufacturers were increasingly unable to make a profit, and the government (very unusually) was reported to be willing to let such businesses fail.

5.3. Shifts in income and power caused by IMF programmes

Devaluation shifts relative prices in favour of producers of tradables and against producers of non-tradables—provided of course that the higher domestic price of foreign exchange is reflected in domestic prices, especially producer prices paid to farmers, and that wages are not immediately raised to offset the rise in prices. The obvious political problem for governments devaluing is that urban wage earners tend to be articulate and organized, while rural producers tend to be inarticulate and disorganized.

If, in addition to devaluation, governments go through with other elements of the neo-liberal package such as elimination of exchange controls and import licensing, reductions in civil service employment and abolition of marketing boards (more politely described as the liberalization of agricultural marketing), formal sector wage earners are further affected for the worse. And those who previously made decisions as to who got access to foreign exchange, import licences, and public sector jobs lose power and, if corrupt, income.[22]

This latter point probably explains why some governments did not go through with large parts of the neo-liberal package. Zambia, for example, undertook to reduce the number of people employed in the civil service, but did very little. Uganda used a classic technique to put off the reduction of its civil service by holding out that more information was needed; the government then failed to publish the census of public employment when it was completed and did nothing to reduce public employment. The Museveni government did not even stop hiring into the civil service; its desire to create a government of all, or nearly all, the people was more important, as was also reflected by a government with over sixty Cabinet ministers. Similar points could be made about Sierra Leone, Somalia, and Tanzania: stated intentions to do something about the civil service and the parastatal sector were continuously put off until a later date which never came.

The two most committed governments, Nigeria and Ghana, did make some progress in reducing employment in the public sector. Nigeria closed its agricultural marketing boards, as already noted; the government also reduced the number of civil servants, for example by 11,000 in the first half of 1985—to the point where there were doubts expressed as to whether new government policies could be implemented. Ghana gradually reduced the swollen number of people employed by the Cocoa Marketing Board (more than 100,000 initially). Although the first cuts were of 'ghost workers', non-existent employees whose salary was being collected by someone else, real cuts were also implemented.

In both cases, there were political repercussions, including one coup attempt in Nigeria, and nine coup attempts in Ghana. In virtually every case the coups were attempted by urban groups who perceived themselves (correctly) as having lost power, influence, and income as a result of the changes in economic policy; the rhetoric of abandoned left-wing principles in some of the Ghana coup attempts may also have been genuine.

The interesting question is not why there were nine coup attempts in Ghana, but why there was only one in Nigeria. Part of the explanation is trivial: Ghana introduced new policies several years before Nigeria. But its number of coup attempts per annum was two, compared to 0.5 for Nigeria.

Nigeria made much less of an ideological U-turn than Ghana. Perhaps more significantly, large numbers of Nigerian urban bureaucrats were reported to be investing in agriculture. In other words, Nigerians who lost income from the shift in relative prices took advantage of the newly created profit opportunities in the tradable goods sector. The abolition of marketing boards, which ensured that farmers really did get something close to border price equivalents, was a necessary condition for this investment to occur. The infrastructure required for rural investment to be profitable was also very much less run down in Nigeria than in Ghana.

The more general point seems to be that governments which persist with implementation of the less popular parts of an IMF policy package need to provide some way of compensating the losers or allowing them to gain from the new system. If not, they must be able to survive severe political opposition, including coup attempts. None of the sample countries did much to articulate the political support of those who stood to gain from the changes.

5.4. The relevance of debt forgiveness

On paper, the debt service obligations of the seven countries were overwhelming, well over 50 per cent of export earnings at most times and occasionally over 100 per cent. It was clear, though, that in the majority of cases debt service had become in one sense a semantic problem, rather than a real one. Both governments and creditors knew that the debt service could not be paid; but various formalities had to be gone through to satisfy formal regulations. Thus debt service was formally paid out of export earnings, and aid used to finance imports; but in most cases the numbers could equally well have been presented as showing that aid paid for debt service and exports for imports.

It was not the same thing, though, as if the debt had been unconditionally cancelled, for at least three reasons: as aid was ostensibly financing imports, it carried all the usual project and sector level conditions as to what it could be used for and where it could be spent; maintenance of the overall quantity of aid was conditional on macro-economic policy changes; and debt rescheduling negotiations were themselves costly, especially because they used much valuable time of senior officials.

The situation was rather different in the case of Nigeria, because a much higher proportion of Nigeria's debt was to commercial banks, and because Nigeria's oil made it seem possible that at some time in the future Nigeria might actually be able to service its debts. For much the same reasons, it was conceivable that Nigeria might be able to borrow commercially at some point in the future. As a result, the Nigerian government had to take debt rescheduling seriously; and had, therefore, to reach an agreement with the IMF because that was insisted on by the Paris and London Clubs, even though the government had kept to its undertaking not to borrow from the IMF.

5.5. Sustainable low-level equilibrium: smuggling and unconditional aid

More than one sample country appeared to be in a sustainable low-level equilibrium, even though their IMF programmes were not working successfully or had broken down (in some cases more than once). There were two main reasons for this: the availability of consumer goods through parallel markets, and the availability to governments of aid that was not conditional on having an agreement with the IMF.

Some economies had significant sources of foreign exchange, either from smuggled exports or from other informal sources. These maintained a supply of consumer goods, which in turn provided some sort of safety valve for the population when reduced aid inflows, the drying up of other foreign credit, and falling official export proceeds would otherwise have caused severe shortages.

Some aid also continued to flow irrespective of macro-economic policy. Periodic IMF agreements provided additional capital inflows; periodic breakdowns of those agreements cut off only some of the aid, and none of the informal foreign exchange earnings through parallel markets.

As a result, the governments of Sierra Leone (smuggled diamonds), Somalia (migrant remittances), Tanzania (a range of agricultural and other exports), and Uganda (smuggled coffee, rents, remittances[23]) could manage for long periods without IMF agreements. Ordinary people could get imported goods through parallel markets, and governments could survive on flows of non-conditional aid (at minimal levels, except in Somalia which got military and economic aid for strategic reasons).

Of the remaining countries in the sample, Ghana had the one sustained and serious IMF programme, in the sense that much more of the neo-liberal programme was actually implemented rather than just promised. Nigeria showed signs of doing the same, although the Nigerian programme was much more recent than Ghana's so that it is too early to put it in the same category.[24] The odd one out was Zambia.

Zambia's copper was not smuggled in significant quantities, if at all. There was some supply of foreign exchange to the parallel market, mainly from smuggled emeralds, but also possibly from illegal drug trading, expatriate rents, and migrant remittances. There was also a legal outlet for these sources of foreign income, in the form of shops with scarce goods available only for payment in foreign exchange. Overall, though, these sources of foreign exchange were smaller than in the 'low-level equilibrium' countries, and the volume of imported goods available through the parallel market was therefore also smaller. Zambia's abandonment of the foreign exchange auction system in 1987, the failure of the government's alternative policies to generate growth in exports, and its refusal to try and reach other agreement with the IMF, seemed likely to be unsustainable for very long, although the rise in the copper price in 1988 gave Zambia's own post-IMF programme a longer life.[25]

5.6. Reducing the size of the civil service

A particular and crucial example of IMF conditionality, where governments promise but do not implement, concerns the size and salaries of the public sector. It is possible to restrain government spending as part of a policy to balance the budget, by paying civil servants less and less in real terms, and by providing less and less of the matching resources needed for them to do their jobs. This does not increase natural wastage: few civil servants resign their jobs, even when their salaries reach absurdly low levels.

While this may achieve financial targets, it is grossly inefficient. Civil servants have to seek other sources of income, which means that they cannot do their government jobs full time. All government services deteriorate badly as a result.

Meanwhile, large numbers of the most educated are very inefficiently deployed, at a cost to the government which is much higher than their salaries, because it supplies them with offices, telephones, transport, housing, and other resources, which are extensively used to pursue their private sector interests. Such a system also encourages rent-seeking (a polite word for corruption) and therefore additional resistance to reductions in government controls.

It is difficult to see how economies can develop over the long term, even those which persist with IMF reforms, while such large numbers of skilled people are so inefficiently employed. Yet the IMF continues to accept assurances that public sector employment will be reduced when it very patently will not, or not by nearly enough to enable the government to pay wages high enough to allow civil servants to do their civil service jobs full time.

Until this problem is tackled, instead of being ignored, other parts of the neo-liberal package will not have the predicted results either: for example, aid necessary for a supply response will not be disbursed in time. More generally, making the right economic policy decisions is virtually impossible if economic information and analysis are not produced, and if those at the top do not have time to consider the little that is produced.

It is simply not credible that most governments will make large numbers of employees compulsorily redundant, at the same time that they are expected to pursue policies that make them very unpopular with the urban wage-earning class as a whole. The same governments cannot afford to provide redundancy payments large enough to cause a significant voluntary reduction in employment, and if they did it would be very inflationary.

If this problem is to be tackled seriously, it requires donor finance.[26]

Alternatively, governments must find some other form of redundancy compensation, for example offering civil servants their government houses as a form of non-inflationary redundancy payment. Civil servants are obviously reluctant to leave government service if by doing so they would have nowhere to live. Transferring houses to civil servants would also reduce government spending on maintenance, and make possible a start on ending the costly practice of providing official housing for public sector employees. Retraining and provision of employment is less of a problem, since by definition civil servants already have other jobs or other sources of income.

6. Some Policy Conclusions

6.1. The need to analyse levels of commitment

Others have noted that in all IMF programmes, a high degree of government commitment is necessary (e.g. Nelson 1984). The degree of government commitment required is significantly greater where economies have suffered a prolonged period of stagnation or decline. Recovery in such cases takes longer, because of the physical state of the economy, and because it takes longer to convince producers that the reforms will be sustained. Moreover, implementing such programmes *without* adequate commitment makes economic conditions worse not better, and makes it harder to implement a successful programme in the future.

There is a particular responsibility, therefore, to avoid trying to implement reform programmes with a high probability of failure. This paper has argued that the probability should be assessed, and that there appear to be some useful indicators to assist the analysis of each individual case.

If a government has not prepared its own proposals for policy changes, and so has not done the work necessary to understand fully the state of the economy and what needs to be done:

- the agenda will be one put forward by the IMF;
- the government will negotiate from weakness;
- it will not be fully committed to the changes;
- it will not inspire confidence among producers that the new policies will be sustained;
- increased production (of tradable goods and services) will be delayed further than is in any case normal;
- failure to follow through with the more difficult and unpopular bits of the reforms programme will be inevitable;
- and as a result the programme will be abandoned before any benefits accrue.

This suggests that it may be better in some cases to delay the implementation of IMF programmes, which goes against the conventional wisdom. In most cases it remains true that policy changes to cope with an economic downturn should be undertaken as soon as possible. Where an economy has been growing at a reasonable rate, and has not suffered prolonged stagnation and import strangulation, delay makes it more difficult to recover. In such cases the conventional wisdom is correct. But the longer the period of stagnation or decline, the greater the political difficulty of sustaining a reform programme, and the greater the risk of the programme being abandoned. It is all the more important, therefore, to analyse the degree of government commitment and avoid predictable programme failure which would leave the economy even worse off than before.

6.2. Spelling out the consequences of reform

It is not generally the job of economic advisers to give political advice, least of all if they represent the IMF and the World Bank. As quasi-diplomatic institutions, they, and the other donors who associate themselves with the IMF's macro-conditionality, are sensitive to accusations of political interference. But if economic analysis can show who is likely to lose and gain from a change in policies, then it *is* irresponsible not to supply that analysis.

The IMF normally wants to implement a programme as soon as possible. It may feel that its advice will not be taken, if it points out to governments that powerful urban groups will be disadvantaged and that weak rural ones will gain, as well as the other high political costs of sustained reform. So it may be tempted to play down the difficulties of implementation. The IMF may also feel it has to believe the assurances of member governments, even when it is predictable that they will not be fulfilled. There is also some evidence of overoptimistic IMF predictions, of export prices as well as of supply response.

But encouraging governments to adopt IMF programmes on the basis of false expectations is counter-productive. It would be better to delay policy changes until the political conditions are right. This is more likely if donors spell out the full cost of programme implementation. Governments would then be fully aware of the political difficulties ahead, and would not agree to politically unrealistic reforms. They might also plan how to cope with opposition from the losers and how to articulate support from the gainers.

6.3. Second-best policy packages

It is possible to identify with some confidence the conditions in which governments will make promises to the IMF, in order to unlock some immediate inflows of capital, but will implement only some of them. If, as IMF economists themselves argue, the success of a policy package depends on the whole package being implemented, then it is possible, even likely, that a country will be worse off as a result of a partial implementation. A 'second-best' policy package may then be preferable. It is possible that devaluation without follow-through on other policy changes is better than no change at all. But analysis of these suboptimal choices is never done. Economists should be able to pick out quite easily those parts of a reform package which are least likely to be implemented (Harvey 1986).

The point here is not to argue about whether the IMF package would necessarily be best if it were indeed all to be implemented. The point is that if it is predictable that parts of the package will not be implemented, and that the package therefore will not work, then the IMF economists themselves might prefer a different set of policies, 'second-best' within their own paradigm.

6.4. New forms of conditionality

The donor institutions are of course aware of likely default on agreements, especially in those countries which have defaulted frequently in the past. Their reaction has not been to wait, but rather to require that some conditions are met before an agreement is reached, rather than afterwards. This is understandable, since quasi-diplomatic institutions cannot say explicitly that they do not believe government assurances as a reason for postponing agreement. And their internal institutional pressure is to reach an agreement if at all possible. But prior conditionality may make success even harder to achieve, because the good news of increased production of tradable goods is delayed even longer from the time when politically unpopular actions are first undertaken.

The argument of this chapter is that it would be better if the IMF could develop an understanding of the probable delays in policy implementation and supply response to their programmes, and that this is readily available from past experience. It would increase the number of successful recoveries and reduce the number of failures with their cumulative worsening of the chances of success at a later date.

Notes

1. IMF programmes and IMF conditionality are used as shorthand in this paper for the programmes and conditionality imposed by foreign donors, usually led by the IMF and the World Bank working together.
2. But note that a World Bank survey in 1988 reported that countries in Sub-Saharan Africa with adjustment loans showed no significant improvement over those without (World Bank 1988: 31).

3. Note also that others record very varied results of policy changes: '. . . similar IMF/World Bank packages generate a spectrum of results . . . the outcomes of orthodox packages ranged from moderately successful to disastrous. Fewer heterodox programmes have been tried. They avoided endings as painful as those in the Southern Cone and Mexico, but produced no famous victories' (Taylor 1988: 147). There were relatively few heterodox programmes in Africa.

4. It was very striking in Zambia during the foreign exchange auction period that the Agricultural Finance Company would only complain of the increased costs faced by farmers and seemed wholly unaware that their clients' profitability had been sharply increased by the devaluation of the Kwacha.

5. Arrears to the Fund itself prevent agreement being reached. This Catch 22 can be got round by commercial banks providing a bridging loan, as was the case for example in Sierra Leone and Nigeria, both in 1986. The loan was then used to repay arrears to the Fund, enabling a new agreement to be reached.

6. For example, in Zambia, where donor delays had not been expected by the IMF and the World Bank, who could do nothing about it (Kydd 1988).

7. The first reductions were relatively easy, consisting of non-existent employees whose pay was being collected by others ('ghost workers'); but later reductions removed real people from employment.

8. Some coup attempts were less serious than others: one was by press conference only, the perpetrators being picked up by the police in a few hours.

9. By no means all indicators were favourable. For example, small-scale industry, which had not declined in line with the rest of the economy, did not enjoy the same growth as medium- and large-scale industry after 1983 (Schmitz 1989).

10. This action may have reduced marketing costs and government subsidies, but it created a problem: the quality of Nigeria's cocoa exports fell sharply, converting a premium of $80/ton over the world price into a discount of $100/ton, and requiring renewed government intervention to impose quality control.

11. The terms of IMF credits, at that time, were arguably too severe; so only the initial inflow would have been good news, not necessarily the whole loan package. The introduction of softer IMF terms, SAF and ESAF, is a response to this point.

12. World Bank project lending rose from $0.2 bn. in 1985/6 to over $1.0 bn. in 1986/7; the World Bank also funded the foreign exchange auction, EIU 1986(4).

13. Unfortunately, the gap left by the departure of the most prominent Lebanese, Jamil, was quickly filled by Liat, an Israeli company run by Russian emigrants, with potentially embarassing South African connections. Liat's manager, Kalman-ovitch was in due course arrested in London for forgery in the USA, and later arrested in Israel for spying for the USSR.

14. For example, a Presidential Economic Advisory Council at State House, and a committee to investigate parastatals.

15. Exports of cattle were badly hit by a ban on imports by Saudi Arabia; but the other main export, bananas, also declined to half the volume of the 1970s.

16. Some argue that Nyerere's re-election was positive for the IMF programme, because of his (reluctant) support for it, and his personal prestige.

17. There was one breakdown, the last tranche of a standby was not drawn, but lending resumed later.

18. Budget deficits are not the only source of inflation; expanded credit to the

private sector can also cause inflation, as explained above for the case of Uganda in 1987.

19. *After* a 90% wage rise in 1987, the lowest paid were estimated to be getting only $100 to $160 *a year*.

20. The response of domestic prices to devaluation was also small, showing how much of the economy was outside the formal system of prices.

21. More than $100 m. a year of imports were licensed without access to official sources of foreign exchange; some (probably a large part) of this must have been financed by smuggled exports.

22. Interestingly, it was reported that the prospect of a reduction in corruption was one of the key reasons why President Kaunda of Zambia was persuaded to introduce a foreign exchange auction in 1985.

23. Uganda caused concern to the ANC for having so many of its citizens working on expatriate contracts in the South African 'homelands'.

24. The Nigerian programme was showing signs of breakdown in 1988, partly because it had become politically impossible to increase the heavily subsidized petrol price; the cost of the subsidy was endangering the budget and future IMF agreements.

25. Zambia's copper is due to be exhausted within 15 or 20 years, making it urgent for non-copper exports to be made profitable over a sustained period. The current programme does not do this. So the high copper price is delaying this necessary policy change.

26. It is reported that a start has been made along these lines in Ghana.

References

Colclough, C. and Green, R. H. (1988), 'Do Stabilisation Policies Stabilise?', *IDS Bulletin* 19/1 (Jan.): 1–5.

Economic Intelligence Unit (various years), *Quarterly Reports* for Ghana, Nigeria, Sierra Leone, Somalia, Tanzania, Uganda, Zambia.

Harvey, C. (1986), 'On the Art of Giving Economic Advice: Tactics, Access, Damage Limitation, Packaging, Confessed Ignorance and Timing', *Public Administration and Development*, 6/4: 445–54.

—— (1987), *Successful Macroeconomic Adjustment in Three Developing Countries: Botswana, Malawi and Papua New Guinea*, Economic Development Institute, World Bank.

Kydd, J. (1988), 'Coffee after Copper? Structural Adjustment, Liberalization, and Agriculture in Zambia', *Journal of Modern African Studies* 26/2: 227–51.

Mohamed Said Samantar (1987), 'The Franco-valuta System and the Foreign Exchange Auction System', Conference paper, Lusaka.

Nelson, J. (1984), 'The Political Economy of Stabilisation: Commitment, Capacity and Public Response', *World Development* 12/10: 983–1006.

Quirk, J., Christensen, B. V., Kyung-Mohuh, and Sosaki, T. (1987), 'Floating Exchange Rates in Developing Countries: Experience with Auction and Interbank Markets', IMF Occasional Paper no. 53.

Sanderson, M. (1987), 'Why Zambia's Auction Failed', Conference paper, Lusaka.

Schmitz, H. (1989), 'Flexible Specialisation: A New Paradigm of Small-Scale Industrialisation?', IDS Discussion Paper no. 261, University of Sussex.

Taylor, L. (1988), *Varieties of Stabilisation Experience: Towards Sensible Macroeconomics in the Third World*, Clarendon Press, Oxford.

Toye, J. (1989), 'Ghana's Economic Reforms and World Bank Policy-conditioned Lending', mimeo, IDS.

World Bank (1981), *Accelerated Development in Sub-Saharan Africa: An Agenda for Action*, World Bank, Washington, DC.

—— (1988), *Adjustment Lending: An Evaluation of Ten Years of Experience*, World Bank, Washington, DC.

—— and UNDP (1989), *Africa's Adjustment and Growth in the 1980's*, World Bank, Washington, DC.

7
Industrialization in Botswana: How Getting the Prices Right Helped the Wrong People

RAPHAEL KAPLINSKY

1. Introduction

This chapter comprises an assessment of one of the major instruments of Botswana's recent industrial policy in the light of the more general appraisal of the neo-liberal paradigm (NLP) undertaken in this book.[1] It begins with a brief statement of the major industrial policy implications of NLP theory and contrasts these with perspectives on the enabling state which are emerging from neo-structuralist and neo-Schumpeterian analyses. Thereafter, Botswana's manufacturing performance is overviewed as a prelude to a more detailed investigation into the performance of the Financial Assistance Policy (FAP), the major instrument of recent industrial policy. Finally, the successes and failures of the FAP, and of wider industrial policy in Botswana, are considered in the light of NLP assertions on optimal industrial policy.

It is possible to draw five perspectives on industrial policy out of the NLP.[2]

(a) Whilst market failure may be prevalent in LDCs, and may have deleterious implications for industrial development, state failure tends to be more pronounced and has an even more adverse impact on industrial performance. Consequently, state intervention ought to be confined to ensuring that markets operate efficiently and to the provision of appropriate public goods.

(b) In so far as industry is to be provided with support (which is, strictly speaking, only justifiable in cases of genuine infant industries), subsidies are more preferable than protection. Price signals are always better than quantitative controls which lead to rent-seeking behaviour.

(c) Infant industries should be nurtured within a strict time frame, and without excessive support.[3]

I am especially grateful to Christopher Colclough for his detailed comments on an earlier draft. Charles Harvey and Michael Hubbard also provided helpful comments.

(*d*) The choice of technology is determined by relative factor prices. When factors are priced at their opportunity costs, markets will be cleared.

(*e*) Long-run industrial and technological capability will be maximized through a succession of short-run allocative decisions based upon competitive market prices.

Discussion of the suitability of this agenda of NLP industrial policy is not confined to the LDCs and is also a source of debate in the industrially advanced countries (IACs). The opponents of the NLP argue that, with very few exceptions, all successfully industrializing economies have seen active state interventions. These have occurred in a variety of forms and have directly negated the principles of policy formulation sketched out above. Moreover, in addition to the significant role played by the state historically, there are reasons why the enabling state will remain an important feature of future industrial policy. This is because of the following main policy issues emerging in industrial development (all of which, as will be argued later, have a bearing on industrial policy in Botswana).

1. After a long period of relative stability in the 'ideal type' of industrial organization, in many sectors the mass production of standardized goods is giving way to 'flexible specialization', in which increasingly differentiated goods are produced in smaller batches. Reorientating production in this way is a complex task, involving changes in work practices, changes in the relationship between firms, and the adoption of new flexible automation technologies.[4] Left to market forces alone, this process of adjustment is slow and uneven. Hence in many countries the state has come to play a key enabling role in promoting the development of these new organizational structures and the adoption of new technologies. This often occurs (as in Japan and Korea), on a sectoral basis. These state interventions may be implemented through the subnational regional state, the national state, or the supranational regional state (for example, the EEC).

2. Economies of scale have become an increasingly important component of industrial production, especially since the mid-nineteenth century. But following the introduction of new flexible automation technologies and the adoption of new organizational structures, optimum plant- and product-scale is beginning to decrease in many sectors. At the same time, as many indirect costs of production such as research and marketing (which have historically underwritten increases in firm-scale economies) have continued to grow, many large firms have become too bureaucratic to adjust flexibly to rapidly changing markets. Thus amalgams of small firms have been particularly successful. The state has been seen to play a crucial role in these restructurings along the dimensions of scale, especially in promoting collaboration between small firms.[5]

3. As the scientific content in modern technology has increased, there has

been a tendency for research and development to become more specialized. In addition, the restructuring of organization mentioned above has tended to require particular skills which are often buried in the bureaucracies of existing producers. Hence an independent productive services sector (comprising design houses, management consultants, advertising agencies, and so on) is becoming an increasingly prominent component of modern industrial competitiveness. The market mechanism seems to have provided inadequate signals to stimulate both the demand for, and the supply of, these productive services and hence a variety of policy initiatives have been instituted to encourage their incorporation in production.

4. These various elements of industrial restructuring have proved difficult to absorb, and technical progress has consequently become uneven globally. This has led to some countries (notably the USA, the UK, and Japan and West Germany) developing sustained balance of payments deficits and surpluses respectively and this has come to be associated with the regrowth of protectionism. In addition, the transition from mass production to flexible specialization in many sectors has also led to increasingly complex marketing strategies. Many individual firms have either found it difficult to adjust to these new competitive pressures or have found themselves excluded from major markets. This has increasingly led to various forms of state involvement such as the roles played by the local state in Italy in assisting small firms with market intelligence and product promotion.

As a consequence of these factors—both those based upon historical performance and those attempting to grapple with the industrial challenges of the future—many observers have come to question the appropriateness of NLP prescriptions for industrial development. In Botswana, though, many of the tenets of the NLP have had an important influence on policy. Consequently it is of interest to determine their efficacy, particularly in the light of contemporary challenges in industrial development and the specific opportunities open to Botswana. But before this analysis is pursued, it is first necessary to provide a brief background of recent economic and industrial growth in Botswana.

2. Botswana: A Brief Background with Particular Emphasis on its Industrial Development[6]

Given Botswana's poor resource endowment, a significant proportion of the male population had traditionally been forced to work as migrant labour in South Africa. As independence approached in 1966, Botswana emerged as one of the world's poorest economies, almost entirely dependent on remittances from migrant labour and on cattle production. The distribution of cattle ownership was markedly unequal. Moreover, the country was subject to frequent droughts with over a fifth of the population dependent on famine relief in 1966, rising to over a half in the severe drought of the early 1980s.

Few could have anticipated the vigour of the next two decades of post-independence development. Suddenly the Botswana economy seemed to emerge from its struggle with subsistence, achieving during a period of declining global economic performance one of the highest compound growth rates of any economy in the world. The source of this growth was the discovery and exploitation of primary commodities. In the early 1970s, the exploitation of copper and nickel played an important role in relieving the foreign exchange constraint and in promoting infrastructural development. This was followed shortly afterwards by a rapid build-up of diamond production. The consequence was a significant growth in per capita incomes and consumption and a boom in the construction and service sectors. The severe drought of the early 1980s, though punitive for thousands of rural households, had little macro-economic impact on overall output growth.

As the decade of the 1990s opens, the Botswana economy is favourably poised for sustained growth, although there is naturally concern about what might continue to fuel growth in the future. Whilst skilled labour is in short supply, there is a surplus of unskilled labour and unemployment is becoming a major policy concern.[7] There is little experience by Botswana in the trade sector, and only the embryonic signs of a class of indigenous industrialists. The revenue provided to the state from the mineral sector[8] has allowed for a series of initiatives to encourage small-scale production with appropriate technologies, of which the most significant is the Financial Assistance Policy which is the subject of this paper. The major cloud on the horizon, however, is that the growing political instability in South Africa may spill over into Botswana with potentially tragic consequences.

Located at the meeting point of independent Africa and South Africa, Botswana has hitherto managed an unusual degree of coexistence with both blocks. Together with its lukewarm reception to South African freedom fighters, its free-enterprise policy agenda has enabled it to establish a *modus vivendi* with South Africa. Moreover, as a bastion of capitalism in a potentially socialist Southern Africa, the Western powers have also tacitly acted as guarantor of independence. Consequently Botswana has unique preferential access to four distinct markets: the Southern African Customs Union (South Africa, Swaziland, and Lesotho), its independent neighbours (Zimbabwe, Zambia, and Malawi, and through them with the Preferential Trade Area for Eastern and Southern Africa), the EEC (through ACP), and the US (through GSP). As we shall see below, this provides a range of important opportunities for the industrial sector.

Between 1960 and 1982, Botswana's GDP growth rate (12.8 per cent p.a.) was almost twice as high as that of any other African country. There were a number of sources of this growth. First, reflecting Botswana's geo-strategic importance, there has been a relatively large inflow of aid which, at $128 per capita p.a. in 1988, was the highest in Africa. However, little of this growth can be attributed to the agricultural sector, which was gripped by drought through much of this period. Indeed the volume of agricultural production actually fell at an annual rate of 2 per cent between 1970 and 1984, and the share of GDP contributed by agriculture fell—mainly because of the dynamism of other sectors of the economy—from 34 per cent in 1965 to 6 per cent in 1985. The discovery and exploitation of copper and nickel and (especially) diamonds has had the most significant impact on Botswana's economic progress and the share of the minerals sector in GDP rose from 7 to 41 per cent between 1965 and 1985.

Manufacturing growth has also been important, although beginning from a tiny base. Between 1965 and 1980 it grew at 12.5 per cent p.a., and although this fell sharply to 5.8 per cent p.a. between 1980 and 1985, it still exceeded the average of 3.5 per cent p.a. for SSA. But growth in this sector has lagged behind that of minerals so that the share of manufacturing in GDP fell between 1965 and 1985, from 12 to 8 per cent.[9] Lewis and Sharpley calculate that excluding meat processing (which was uncharacteristically export-orientated), 55 per cent of growth was directed to new domestic demand, 38 per cent substituted for goods previously imported and only 8 per cent was destined for export markets.

This economic performance might sound like a confirmation of the NLP. After all, here is a country which, in the midst of economic decline in SSA, saw a remarkable rise in GDP and a sustained increase in manufacturing value added. This occurred in the context of macro-economic and industrial policies which explicitly favoured private rather than state ownership and which concentrated government intervention on short-run subsidies and price adjustments. In the face of these achievements it might seem churlish to question the extent of this 'success'. But the fact is that there are a variety of reasons to suggest that this manufacturing progress could have been better. Moreover, evidence will also be presented to suggest that much of the progress which did occur was the result of factors other than those which the policy-makers believed were influencing industrialists. Before considering this evidence, it is first necessary to outline both the Industrial Policy and the Financial Assistance Policy (FAP) which together form the basis of policy towards Botswana's industrial sector.

3. The Policy Framework

Two sets of policies directly impinge upon the progress of the manufacturing sector in Botswana. The Industrial Strategy sets out the general parameters within which industry operates while the Financial Assistance Policy is the major instrument through which industry has been assisted.

3.1. The Industrial Development Policy (IDP)

The IDP was published in 1984. It was designed to promote the government's major planning objectives which were to further economic growth and independence, to diversify the economy away from minerals and cattle and to achieve these objectives in the context of 'social justice'. The explicit aims of the IDP were to create productive employment for citizens, to train citizens for jobs with higher productivity, to increase the GDP accruing in Botswana and to citizens, to diversify the economy and to promote industrialization in rural areas. The heavy emphasis on citizenship as a theme of industrial policy arises from the particular dependence of the economy on non-citizens—it was calculated in 1980 that about 10 per cent of gross national income accrued to non-citizens in the form of employee compensation, with as much again accruing as operating surplus of expatriate-owned enterprises outside the mining sector.[10]

Anxious to minimize the role of the state in industrialization, three basic principles were enunciated. The first was the 'Government's belief that a free enterprise, market-oriented system for this sector is both efficient in producing goods and services and economical in the use of scarce administrative capacity'. Second, the sectoral emphasis was to be the utilization of the country's natural resources and the establishment of linkages with the major sectors of the economy (mining, government, and agriculture). And, third, recognizing the divide between citizens and non-citizens, assistance to the large-scale sector would predominantly take the form of incentives whereas the small-scale sector would be additionally assisted with extension services.

Three incentives were offered—local preference purchasing, protection (limited partly through government design and partly through the terms of the Southern African Customs Union) and financial. However, only the first and (especially) the third of these were effectively utilized. Moreover, the government would only make one of these three facilities available to a single enterprise at any one time. In addition to these incentives, the government committed itself to the provision of infrastructure (priced at opportunity cost),[11] limited state ownership through parastatals (where no private investor was in prospect), and the promotion of foreign investment. Finally, it was believed that the two major obstacles to investment by citizens were the lack of equity capital and the absence of long-term financing.

3.2. The Financial Assistance Policy (FAP)

FAP was the major instrument chosen to implement these general principles of industrial policy. Its focus lay with the creation of productive employment, that is, the creation of jobs with no output traded off. The numeraire for assessing 'productive' was effectively the border price of imports and exports, since the scheme was limited to the production of goods which either substituted for imported items or could be exported. Large-scale mining and cattle production—the areas of historical comparative advantage —were excluded from the FAP. The only service inputs which were included were 'linking industries' which provided a marketing function to 'productive' enterprises, and relevant repair and maintenance.

The FAP scheme made a clear distinction between small-scale enterprise (SSE) and medium- and large-scale enterprise (MLE). The scheme for SSE was initially limited to those enterprises with a capital investment of P10,000 (subsequently raised to P20,000)[12] and was confined to citizen owners. The MLE category was also subdivided between medium- and large-scale enterprises and was open to non-citizens as well.

The SSE scheme provided a grant to those enterprises which had a reasonable expectation of future financial viability at market prices. The grants were primarily for capital equipment (excluding motorized transport), although some leeway was provided to cover raw material (but not working capital) costs. The value of the grants were computed as the lesser of either P2,000 per job created or 40 per cent of the investment costs with a further 10 per cent for female-headed firms and an additional percentage (on a sliding scale of 10–30 per cent) to encourage location in distant rural areas. Thus a male-headed small urban firm would receive a maximum grant of P4,000 (subsequently raised to P8,000) if he created two (subsequently four) additional jobs, whereas a female-headed enterprise in the far west of the country would receive P8,000 (subsequently P16,000) if a minimum of four (subsequently eight) new jobs were created.

This SSE scheme was predominantly seen as a sop to growing political pressure by citizens for participation in industry. It was thus designed to be a once-and-for-all grant (although there existed a loose infrastructure for extension services) and to be simple to execute and administer. By contrast the scheme for MLEs was considerably more subtle.[13] It consisted of two alternative grants.

Automatic financial assistance (AFA)

Subject to the enterprises obtaining a manufacturing licence (involving a judgement by the Ministry of Commerce and Industry of profitable market opportunities), three types of financial assistance became unconditionally available to new enterprises. The first was a *tax holiday* (100 per cent in years 1 and 2, 75 per cent in year 3, 50 per cent in year 4, and 25 per cent in year 5).[14] Second, an *unskilled labour grant* was provided (covering only citizens, and defined as below a specified wage-rate), reimbursing 80 per cent of wages in years 1 and 2, 60 per cent in year 3, 40 per cent in year 4, and 20 per cent in year 5. And, third, a *training grant* was made available to citizen employees covering 50 per cent of off-site costs in approved institutions for 5 years.

Case-by-case financial assistance (CFA)

The CFA grant was offered to both new and expanded enterprises, subject to a series of constraining limits (discussed below). Both the *unskilled labour grant* and the *training grants* available for AFA were extended to CFA firms. But in addition they were also open to two additional grants. The first was a *capital grant*, with a maximum of P1;000 for each projected job (subject to maxima, depending upon location).[15] The second was a *sales augmentation grant* of 8 per cent of sales revenue in years 1 and 2, 5 per cent in year 3, 4 per cent in year 4, and 2 per cent in year 5.

Two overall limits were set on these CFA grants, relating to the benefit accruing to Botswana and to Botswana citizens. For each project an economic return had to be computed over a five-year period, shadow-pricing unskilled labour at 50 per cent of wage costs, all imported and exportable inputs and outputs at 110 per cent of market prices, excluding training costs and financial transfers and deducting foreign capital inflows and financial outflows. Only those projects with an economic rate of return of at least 6 per cent would be funded. The second overall limit for CFA was that the total assistance provided should be the lesser of 50 per cent of the value-added accruing to Botswana citizens over 5 years or a percentage of unskilled wages plus training costs over five years.[16]

All this sounds horrendously complicated, especially in a country in which administrative capacity is weak. But, procedurally, a cost–benefit analysis was programmed into the Ministry of Finance and Development Planning's microcomputer and data were entered—based upon the submission of individual firms—which had received prior evaluation by the relevant Ministry. This program automatically calculated both the firm's private internal rate of return, the economic rate of return as outlined above, and the effect of the constraining limits on grant allocation.

4. The Industrial Development Policy in Practice: An Evaluation of the FAP[17]

The evaluation of the FAP can be conveniently divided into two major categories—a discussion of the overall pattern of loan commitments and disbursements, and an investigation of its performance at the firm level.

4.1. The overall pattern of loan commitments and disbursements

There are a number of features of the overall pattern of grant distribution which have a bearing on subsequent analysis:

1. By the end of 1987, there had been a total of 1,926 grant commitments. Of these, 718 were to SSEs, 284 to CFA, 70 to AFA, and the balance to agriculture. A significant number of these commitments were made in the very early years of the scheme.

2. It was projected that 14,941 additional jobs would be created from these grant commitments, equivalent to an average of 2,500 per year. In reality, many fewer were created—about 50 per cent of the projected total for SSEs, 31 per cent of CFA grants, and 63 per cent for AFA. In total, therefore, about 4,500 additional jobs were said to have been created under the aegis of the FAP over five years. This contrasts with total additional employment in the 'formal sector' of 5,500 jobs in the same period.[18]

3. These grants involved a commitment of over P55 m., of which P19 m. was disbursed by the end of 1987. Of these disbursements, nearly half went on labour subsidies, and approximately 15 per cent to each of capital grants to SSEs, capital grants to CFA enterprises and sales augmentation. Grants to training and counselling were minuscule. A significant part of these disbursements—over a third—could not be fully justified in terms of FAP rules. This was due to various forms of fraudulent claims, including the provision of capital grants on projected jobs which never materialized.

4. Of funds disbursed, the cost per workplace created was P14,690 for CFA grants, P2,064 for AFA, and P1,608 for SSEs.

5. About 60 per cent of CFA grants went to citizen-owned enterprises. This proportion remained fairly stable over the first five years of the scheme, was concentrated in lower technology sectors, and predominantly involved non-indigenous citizens of European or Asian origin. None of the AFA grants went to citizen-owned enterprises. The SSEs were wholly owned by citizens, almost all of whom were indigenous.

6. Only in the SSE sector was there evidence of a wide regional distribution of grants. There was also little evidence of an increase in female-headed enterprises.

4.2. Performance at the firm level

In itself these aggregate figures are not very illuminating and in gauging the success of the IDP and the FAP it is necessary to determine how behaviour changed at the firm level. The discussion which follows distinguishes two sets of issues. The first divides FAP recipients into four distinct groups and discusses the evolution of each of them in the context of FAP. The second addresses the functioning of the FAP scheme itself and its relationship to the overall problems of industrial development in Botswana.

Categories of FAP recipients

(i) The small-scale sector

The setting for small enterprise development outside the towns was not promising. The rural population has traditionally earned meagre incomes from crop and cattle production. Migrant labour in the South African mines occupied many males of working age, but it provided little opportunity for the growth of entrepreneurship or for the acquisition of industrial skills. The pool of small-scale entrepreneurs is therefore shallow and rural incomes are low. Moreover, incorporation within the Southern African Customs Union provides little protection from large scale South African industry.

The pressure emanating from this sector for the introduction of a scheme such as FAP has nevertheless been one of the most significant political developments in Botswana in recent years and the demand for FAP grants, when they became available, was very substantial. The effective freeing of the capital constraint on these small enterprises unleashed a flood of enterprises, more than half of which were knitting and sewing, mostly providing school uniforms.

Yet in the absence of a national capability to provide effective marketing surveys, overcapacity was rapidly reached; this was exacerbated by competition from South African suppliers. Moreover, despite the relatively simple tasks involved in these small-scale sectors, the technological and managerial capability of most of these small entrepreneurs was pathetically inadequate for the task at hand. Their rate of failure has thus been significant.

The 1984 evaluation of these SSEs identified a variety of explanations for this failure rate. The major problems were due to poor entrepreneurial background, poorly functioning markets, excessive competition, and the absence of technological capability. The 1984 evaluation thus concluded that from the policy perspective, what these enterprises needed most was extension services and effective marketing surveys.

Four years later, little had changed except that these same problems had got worse. When in early 1988 the National Institute of Research sent enumerators to visit FAP small-scale projects which they were assured were in existence, only 73 per cent could be located after four visits and few could be classified as either thriving or engaging in full-time production. The 1988 FAP Evaluation Team aimed to interview grantees still in operation but was only able to locate around half of all the sample. Of the ones which they were able to interview (which must be deemed to be the relatively 'successful'), less than two-thirds had created any additional employment over five years. With the exception of a few cement-block manufacturers (where the technology is simple, markets are assured, and producers are protected by the high transport-to-value ratio of their product), most were in a parlous state. They encountered a variety of problems of which the following were most significant—absence of an identified, competitive market segment (38 per cent); poor management skills (34 per cent); shortage of working capital (31 per cent) (which can easily be seen as an expression of general problems); inability to obtain inputs at a price to enable competition with imports (24 per cent); shortage of work-space at affordable rents (21 per cent); inadequately skilled work-force (14 per cent); and problems with technology (10 per cent).

(ii) The 'free riders'

In their analysis of Botswana's manufacturing growth over the period 1973/4–1984/5, Lewis and Sharpley distinguish between the growth of domestic demand, import substitution, and exports.[19] Overall they estimate that excluding meat processing (which was uncharacteristically export-orientated), 55 per cent of growth was directed to new domestic demand, 38 per cent substituted for goods previously imported, and only 8 per cent was destined for export markets. Two sectors stand out in terms of output growth—meat and meat products and beverages. Within this most of the meat products represented an increase in export markets (since Botswana gained access to EEC markets within this period), whilst the surge in beverage growth represented a process of once-and-for-all import substitution. Another sector of significant growth was in textiles; this reflected a combination of import substitution (mainly preferential purchasing of uniforms by government and schools), the growth of export markets (see below) and a growth in real incomes. Finally, there is a miscellaneous category which was heavily influenced by the growth of tobacco production and the transport-support sector (petrol, servicing, etc.), reflecting a twin process of import substitution and growing incomes.

These data put the growth of Botswana's manufacturing production in perspective. It was very lumpy. It occurred in the context of an economy beset with drought (and thus experiencing a fall in rural agricultural incomes) but benefiting from consecutive booms in mineral production, first of copper and nickel, and then of diamonds. Growth in GDP in these circumstances was concentrated in the form of cash incomes, most accruing in urban areas. In addition, in common with many African economies the poor state of the manufacturing sector at independence left considerable scope for what has come to be called 'the easy stages' of import substitution. Thus, with the exception of textiles, the sectors displaying rapid growth over this period were largely either 'pulled' by the success of the mineral sector or filled the spaces left by colonial neglect. Textile growth can be explained by a combination of export opportunities and the expansion of the schooling system.

This analysis suggests that much of this manufacturing growth would have occurred with or without the existence of FAP. Both the 1984 and 1988 appraisals identified significant 'free riding', that is, entrepreneurs who would anyway have gone ahead with their investments. By obtaining financial support aimed to provide scope for the marginal cases, they merely increased their profitability. Such a consequence is inherent in any automatic programme of assistance—indeed it is a form of rent—but what is surprising is the extent to which this phenomenon has prevailed within FAP. Of nineteen MLE enterprises questioned in depth during the 1984 survey, only two would not have invested anyway—both were owned by indigenous citizens and were marginal, given their low level of technological and managerial capability. Of the thirty-eight MLEs visited in the 1988 survey, few could be identified as representing businesses which would not otherwise have been established had it not been for FAP.

Thus the major 'success' of the FAP scheme for MLEs must be sought in its ability to change the origin of its entrepreneurship. But as we noted earlier, not a single one of the AFA firms were owned by citizens; the proportion of citizen owners in the CFA scheme remained static—most of these were immigrants who had been granted local citizenship. Moreover, the proportion of citizen ownership was least in those sectors where the technological content was highest. In other words, the support to manufacturing through the provision of finance and the effective functioning of markets can be judged to have had little effect on either the pace or the character of manufacturing growth. (As we shall see later, it also had little net effect on employment growth). For the medium and large enterprise sector, its dominant expression was to be found in 'free riding'.

(iii) The 'Francistown factor'

A third major category of FAP-funded enterprises has its origins in the wider geopolitical environment within which Botswana is located. This reflects the continuation of white domination in South Africa, the legacy of white domination and subsequent independence in Zimbabwe (formerly Rhodesia), the growing pressure for sanctions against South Africa and support for frontline states such as Botswana, and the trend towards regional economic integration with SSA. All of these affect the desirability of locating production within Botswana.

Botswana has unique access to a variety of markets. Its incorporation within SACU provides the opportunity for Zimbabwean firms to penetrate South Africa by part-processing in Botswana; similarly South African enterprises can utilize Botswana as a base for obtaining quota-free access to Zimbabwe.[20] The prospect of sanctions against South African producers in both the EEC and the US is increasingly leading South African firms to consider utilizing foreign production sites; moreover, Botswana firms not only face lower tariffs in these large markets, but also have access to import quotas under schemes such as the multi-fibres agreement. And, most importantly, all of this market access has built-in provisions for minimum domestic value-added so that to the extent that Botswana is utilized as a production-conduit, there will necessarily be spin-offs in terms of local value-added.

So far, only the 'Zimbabwe factor' has yet had a significant impact upon Botswana's manufacturing sector, and most of this has been concentrated in Francistown, the largest town adjacent to the Zimbabwe border. The 1984 appraisal estimated that around 10 per cent of the MLE jobs created under FAP were within Zimbabwean-owned firms,[21] who invested in Botswana for a variety of reasons. First, a significant number of white and 'coloured' entrepreneurs who are disenchanted with independence have migrated to Botswana, which not only has an absence of exchange controls, but through the FAP scheme also provides some free finance for new or expanded businesses; moreover, the legacy of colonial neglect provides ample opportunity for new businesses. A variety of examples can be found—bakeries, upholstery and furniture, building materials—most of which are in the small-business, low-technology end of the spectrum. A second factor associated with Zimbabwe arises from the possibilities which integrated production provide for transfer-pricing. Zimbabwe has rigorous exchange controls and Botswana has none, so the attractions are manifest. Third, the foreign exchange constraint in Zimbabwe has led to severe restrictions on imports, even of capital and intermediate goods. There are a number of Botswana enterprises whose rationale is to be found in the manufacture of these quota-free inputs for Zimbabwean affiliates. And, finally, there is admission to SACU in which Zimbabwean firms, by under-taking part-processing in Botswana, have managed to obtain preferential access to the South African market.

(iv) Large-scale agricultural enterprises

The major departure from the NLP principles which underlie the FAP scheme has been the support given in recent years to large-scale irrigated farming. Originally excluded from FAP, and not really being within the orbit of manufacturing, the prolonged drought and the depths of food self-insufficiency have led to a price support scheme which directly undermines the resource-allocating role of market forces and which renders cereal production profitable. This has accounted for 29 per cent of total employment created under the CFA component of the FAP scheme, and for 21 per cent of total grant disbursements. Yet there remain doubts not only over the long-term viability of this cereal production, but also over the veracity of the employment 'created'; much of this is temporary (tree stumping) and/or seasonal in nature.

A related agricultural phenomenon has emerged which raises doubts over the period of 'infancy' acknowledged within the FAP scheme. This concerns enterprises involved in tree-crop production, where the gestation period involved is frequently in excess of the FAP's five years (the latter part of which is anyway of relative insignificance). These farms—many of which (such as citrus) are potentially competitive with imports—find it difficult to compete with already sunk investments by South African competitors. Market prices, even those subsidized temporarily by the FAP scheme, do not allow Botswana to realize potential comparative advantage in these areas.

The functioning of FAP and industrial development

There are a number of more detailed characteristics of the FAP scheme which have an impact upon the progress of the industrial sector in Botswana.

(i) Changing factor choice

At the heart of FAP lies the creation of productive employment. This was designed to occur through two separate, but linked processes, namely the stimulation of new enterprises (which because of the labour subsidy were more likely to be profitable in sectors which were inherently labour intensive in nature) and the encouragement of labour-intensive technical choice. This latter outcome was promoted through the temporary correction of market forces by subsidizing unskilled wages, on a declining basis over a period of five years.

The effects of this labour subsidy on the choice of technology have been marginal. Of the nineteen MLEs investigated during the 1984 appraisal of FAP, only one enterprise was identified in which the subsidization of labour led to the choice of a more labour-intensive technology (in packing). Even in this enterprise the owner planned to mechanize this subprocess as the labour subsidy ran out, and indeed had done so by the time he was revisited in 1988. In two other cases the 1984 appraisal identified firms which were utilizing their FAP grants to mechanize activities which were previously undertaken in a labour-intensive mode. The 1988 appraisal found a slightly higher incidence of an adjustment in technology choice (that is, five out of thirty-eight enterprises visited), but once again the majority of the entrepreneurs planned to mechanize these subprocesses in the future when the labour subsidy expired.

(ii) Technocratic decision-makers vs. pro-active planners

The FAP scheme was designed effectively to run on 'auto-pilot', being easy to administer, requiring little discretionary decision-making, and embodying transparent rules. There were two reasons for this approach. The first was that it reflected a shortage of skilled evaluators. But perhaps more importantly, the progenitors of the scheme were fearful of creating rent-seeking behaviour —hence the insistence on transparency and, with the exception of the very large-scale scheme, provided for automatic access to grants. The instrument utilized to calculate available grants was a computerized social cost–benefit analysis.[22] 'Evaluating staff'—either in line ministries or in the Ministry of Finance and Development Planning—entered data provided by grant applicants and read off the results. In isolated cases where interviews with applicants suggested a lack of entrepreneurial capability or bad faith, grants were refused or scaled down. Although this procedure was 'unconstitutional', this was never legally tested.

As we have seen, this system of evaluation has been associated with a significant degree of free riding, for which there are a number of potential explanations. One possibility, discussed above, is that there is a large area of entrepreneurial rent between the marginal and the average and best-practice applicants; FAP was designed to help citizen entrepreneurs at the margin, and hence the free riding has been inevitable. But a second possibility is that this system of technocratic evaluation is conceptually flawed and naïvely assumes the efficacy of technocratic decision-making procedures.

There is much to this latter explanation. For example, soon after the FAP scheme was introduced, a number of the largest accounting firms managed to 'borrow' or replicate the cost–benefit program on their own computers. Prospective applicants then began their journey by consulting these firms who manipulated the data until the target 6 per cent economic rate of return criterion was met and the limiting constraints on the total grants were minimized. Such procedures make a nonsense of a technocratic and reactive approach to industrial policy. Unless the line ministries have access to sectoral expertise enabling them to judge the validity of claims on prospective sales, labour utilization, input availability and cost, and so on, the system lends itself either to a series of 'unforced errors' or fraudulent application. Once again, at issue here is the fundamental role implied for the state in the process of industrial development.

(iii) Promoting technological capabilities and indigenous citizen entrepreneurship

The IDP firmly commits policy towards promoting citizen development. This latter perspective finds expression within FAP in a number of forms— the small-scale scheme is confined to citizens, the extent of the grant is limited in part by the value-added accruing to citizens, etc.

The problem is that not all citizens are indigenous to Botswana and many are fairly recent immigrants from Asia, South Africa, Zimbabwe, and the

UK. Whilst the FAP scheme makes no distinction between the origins of citizen applicants, the political pressure for the programme as a whole almost exclusively emanates from the indigenous community. Moreover, there has been a perceptible increase in the pressure for assistance to indigenous citizens and, indeed, the experience of the FAP scheme has been such as to justify this orientation. For the phenomenon of free riding has its origins in the margin of entrepreneurial capabilities between indigenous citizens at the one extreme and non-indigenous citizens and foreign investors at the other.

Eschewing moral issues, this is an issue of considerable policy importance. There is no doubt that these political pressures will increase further and that industrial policy will have to bend to accommodate them. But the FAP assumes that the provision of finance will enable entrepreneurs to buy services on the market which will enable them to move significantly towards competitiveness. Yet it ignores the reality of entrepreneurial and technological development, which is that these capabilities are generally cumulative in nature and not easily purchased on the market.

An illumination of this can be found in a brief case-study of the largest indigenous citizen-owned business in Botswana. Founded and managed by a woman, it utilized FAP finance to expand from a small tailoring business to employ around 100 people, manufacturing garments for schools and government. Yet the provision of this finance alone has proved disastrous, since the owner lacked the experience and technological capabilities to command such a relatively large enterprise. The result has been a growth in corporate and personal debt and at various times bankruptcy has loomed. Most recently the enterprise was saved by technical expertise provided by the Swedish Development Agency which effectively substituted for help which could, under a different policy regime, be expected to emanate from government. Briefly, the situation was one in which the system utilized for cutting patterns from sheet cloth was suboptimal—wastage was around 20 per cent (in a context where, even in efficiently run factories, material costs are around 50 per cent of ex-factory prices). The Swedes provided access to a computer-aided design and grading system which provided a new set of patterns which reduced material wastage to 5 per cent.[23] Without access to this type of expertise, there would be no hope of this enterprise, or any of the other similarly sized local firms continuing to survive in a competitive environment. But only one Botswana firm—owned by a non-citizen and exporting garments to Zimbabwe—has been able to identify and purchase this computerized equipment and even then there must be doubts about whether it can utilize this effectively without external technical assistance.

This brief case-study shows that the problems of promoting indigenous citizen entrepreneurship do not lend themselves to market solutions. Various forms of practical assistance are required in building both managerial and technological expertise; moreover, this is a task which is bound to take longer than the five years' infancy implicit in the FAP scheme.

But whilst the problems of indigenous citizens are particularly acute, they are not unique. The general level of technological and managerial expertise in Botswana is weak. The 1988 appraisal of 39 FAP-funded MLEs identified the following most general problems: shortage of suitably skilled work-force (33 per cent); shortage of working capital (a surrogate for general problems of competitiveness) (31 per cent); shortage of appropriately priced inputs to allow for competitive production with imported final products (27 per cent);[24] and absence of a clearly defined market niche (27 per cent).

Once again, market solutions offer little hope of addressing these problems since the very absence of these technological capabilities is in itself a source of ignorance about what should be bought in the market-place.[25] Finally, in the case of the key productive-service sector there is also a chicken-and-egg problem in that the absence of demand has failed to draw forth a supply response to meet these needs.

(iv) Coping with economies of scale

There are various problems facing a small and relatively poor economy such as Botswana—the domestic market frequently appears to be too small to allow local enterprises to realize scale economies in production; when this does occur it might allow for only a single producer and may hence involve the pervasive growth of monopolies; and enterprises may be too small to finance important indirect production costs such as marketing and R&D. On the other hand, smallness is not without its own advantages, not the least of which is that it facilitates (but does not necessitate) flexibility in orientation and undermines bureaucratic structures of managerial control and makes competition possible.

Thus the policy challenge facing Botswana is to minimize the costs and to maximize the benefits of smallness. Indeed, the transition from large-scale inflexible production to smaller-scale flexible production noted in the introductory section offers significant opportunities to Botswana and other small countries. Two sets of reorientation are immediately apparent. The first concerns the necessity of re-educating the business community away from its fixation with large-scale production. A good case in point in Botswana relates to the production of claybricks where current proposals to build a very large-scale factory will exclude the prospects for a number of smaller-scale plants.[26] The second is to provide some mechanism whereby Botswana firms, which are small by international comparison, can find some way of sharing indirect costs of production. Here the case of the garments industry is particularly apparent. Botswana possesses significant opportunities in a number of markets, but to take advantage of this will require access to computer-aided design and grading equipment (costing in excess of $200,000), market intelligence on future patterns, and marketing itself. The Italian garments industry has shown that all of these indirect inputs in production, as well as the shared utilization of computerized equipment, can be done on a common basis, but that these common services require the stimulus and co-ordination of an effective state mechanism.[27]

So far—with the exception of government-provided accommodation and technical support in the industrial estate schemes[28]—the Botswana government has left it to the market to provide a stimulus for this sharing of common facilities and services. The same is true of the provision of productive services where, aside from accounting and legal services, precious few of these productive inputs have yet emerged.

(v) Skill creation and the labour market

The IDP recognized that one of the primary constraints limiting industrial development in Botswana was a shortage of adequately trained workers. Consequently a training grant was built into FAP, covering half of the costs of off-the-job training for citizens in institutions licensed by the Ministry of Education. Yet of the P18.9 m. disbursed between 1982 and 1987, a mere P81,787 was allocated under this heading. Given the severe skill constraint in the economy, this element of financial assistance has clearly not served its purpose.

In searching for an explanation it is once again clear that the market is an imperfect mechanism for transmitting the allocation of resources towards dynamic comparative advantage. In part this is because the decision-takers themselves are not aware of their own limitations, a point which can be illustrated by the extent to which 'worker efficiency' was said to vary amongst a sample of the largest employers in Francistown. Six enterprises were visited whose managers had operating experience in Zimbabwe/South Africa/elsewhere. They were asked to rate the performance of their work-force, and responded as follows: 60 per cent of Zimbabwe and 30 per cent of South Africa (textiles); 25–30 per cent of Zimbabwe (furniture); 90 per cent of Zimbabwe, 75 per cent of South Africa, and 50 per cent of Germany (textiles); 50 per cent of Zimbabwe (textiles); 80 per cent of Zimbabwe (bakery); and 100 per cent of Zimbabwe (ceramics).

All of these enterprises were foreign owned and managed. All utilized a common pool of labour and three were in the same sector. Yet it is striking that there is such a high variation in their estimation of relative 'worker efficiency'. Indeed what this reflects most of all is in fact a variation in 'management efficiency'. The absence of indigenous supervisory skills was also mentioned by other firms, only one of which had made a conscious attempt to train its work-force. It had also made recourse to the market for this training and after a considerable search it identified the Institute of Development Management (a parastatal) to run a supervisory course. Three months after the contract was signed and ten days before the course was due to start, no word had been received so the course was cancelled.

Thus, what emerges from the experiences of these various firms is an absence both of the demand for relevant training (reflected in part by low worker productivity) and of the supply. Allowing market forces to correct this structural imbalance clearly holds little prospect of success.

5. The FAP and the Neo-liberal Paradigm

There are distinct prospects for expanding the manufacturing sector in Botswana particularly in production for foreign markets. One source of optimism is Botswana's unique access to a variety of markets; this provides particular incentives for South African and Zimbabwean firms establishing affiliates in Botswana in order to take advantage of this market access. Another positive feature lies in its attractiveness to 'exiles' from both its southern and northern neighbours. And, of course, as long as the mining sector continues to grow and the easy stages of import substitution remain unfilled, there is also the possibility of expanding production for the domestic market.

But to take advantage of these opportunities Botswana has to be able to overcome some of its disadvantages, of which its remoteness, its small population and labour force, its poorly developed supplier industries (including productive services), its lack of infrastructure, and its low technological development are most apparent. The question raised in this paper is whether the policy prescriptions implicit in the NLP lend themselves to the development of policies which enable these opportunities to be grasped. More specifically, what role does the FAP play in furthering growth and structural change in Botswana's manufacturing sector?

In discussing these issues it is helpful briefly to consider the extent to which Botswana's recent industrial policy has reflected or diverged from the framework set out by the NLP. In the following respects it can be regarded as being in harmony with the NLP.

- Primacy was given to private sector development and wherever possible, state ownership was avoided.
- Public infrastructural goods were provided at opportunity cost and were not subsidized.
- Attempts were made to correct for market failure by subsidizing labour and penalizing the use of foreign exchange.
- Protectionism was largely avoided, so where support was given, it was provided in the form of subsidies rather than tariffs.[29]
- Quantitative controls were not employed and price signals were used in preference.

- Support to the private sector was provided on a temporary basis in order to discourage inefficiency and permanent infancy.
- Border prices were utilized as the basis for assessing social welfare.

Nevertheless there were also some key areas in which industrial policy diverged from the NLP.

- Some state ownership did exist, especially in meat processing. It is significant that this was the major sector of manufacturing growth, especially of exports.
- Local ownership was favoured, largely through confining the SSE scheme to citizens. In addition, the constraints on overall grant provision were based on domestic value-added accruing to citizens.
- Female-headed entrepreneurs were favoured in the SSE scheme, as was regional decentralization in the whole programme.
- A tax holiday was provided in the AFA grants to MLEs.
- Preferential purchasing was made available through a sales augmentation scheme.

But despite these areas of divergence from the NLP, by comparison with industrial policies implemented in other countries (including many industrially advanced countries) Botswana's policy framework can be considered to be a relatively faithful reflection of the NLP ideology. So how can it be judged?

At an overall level, the performance of the manufacturing sector was very good. But it would seem that this was due to massive income growth arising from the expansion of the minerals sector, import substitution, and the overall attractiveness of Botswana in the context of regional instability and the *dirigiste* policies adopted in neighbouring countries. More specifically, the success of Botswana's industrial policy in changing the choice of technology appears to have been limited. Because of the price inelasticity of demand for labour, the degree of rent ('free riding') inherent in the system was consequently high. In addition, because the MLE scheme was open to all-comers, potential productive opportunities have been blocked for emergent indigenous citizens, storing up political tension for the future and potentially blocking the accretion of indigenous technological capability in the future.[30] In both the small-scale and larger-scale sectors, the provision of finance tackled the wrong sort of market failure—the FAP scheme intervened in capital markets, rather than technology and productive services markets. Consequently, the rapid diffusion of new SSEs was associated with a high degree of entrepreneurial failure and some significant immiserization in rural areas, and many MLEs operated with high degrees of X-inefficiency. The period of infancy recognized by FAP (five years) was too short for indigenous citizens to develop the requisite technological capabilities, and too short for the gestation periods involved in tree-cropping agriculture. And, consequent upon these various shortcomings of the FAP policy, significant industrial opportunities appear to have been neglected, especially in production for foreign markets.[31]

The question is whether these undesirable consequences of industrial policy could have been avoided, and if so, how? Broadly speaking, two alternative approaches can be envisaged. On the one hand, minor changes could be made to bring Botswana's industrial policy even more closely in line with the NLP schema. Primarily, attempts could be made to redress market failure. If this proved to be impossible, then the subsidization of wages could be extended beyond five years. (This labour subsidy—targeted at market failure—is distinct from the infant industry argument and there is no theoretical reason why it should have been temporally limited). The favouring of indigenous citizenship could be phased out, tax holidays could be removed, preferential purchasing abolished, and more rigorous attempts made to privatize the few enterprises where state ownership existed.

Yet in view of the problems faced by Botswana's industrial sector (catalogued in earlier sections), it is dubious whether these steps would have had the desired effect. The transition to more flexible 'niching' strategies, which is a key component of contemporary external competitiveness, especially in garments production, seems to be beyond the reach of existing entrepreneurs and there are no market-based institutions providing this form of stimulus to local industry. Similarly, the sharing of overhead costs which would allow smaller-scale Botswana enterprises to maximize the benefits of smallness by sharing design and marketing and by taking advantage of new flexible technologies almost certainly requires state co-ordination. Moreover, the long-run accretion of technological capability does not seem likely to arise from providing conditions for greater short-run profitability. And, based both on Botswana's own experience and that of other countries, the positive role to be played by the productive services sector in the development of the manufacturing sector is unlikely to emerge from the play of market forces.

For these and other reasons, it would therefore seem that for Botswana to grasp its market opportunities, some form of strategic capability is required in the state. But some forms of state intervention may create more harm than good. It has to be appropriately focused since in a small economy such as Botswana, and one with such a severe skill constraint, some form of sectoral targeting will be essential. State policy also needs to be geared to the challenges of the modern world, rather than to the inflexible dogma of earlier *dirigisme*. But what is clear is that left to market forces alone, there will be little prospect of Botswana exploiting the industrial potential which its geographic position rather tantalizingly provides.

Notes

1. Technically, 'industry' includes utilities, construction, and mining and quarrying in addition to manufacturing. However, the analysis in this chapter is largely confined to manufacturing and productive services.
2. These five issues are identified in so far as they inform the discussion of Botswana's industrial policy—they do not comprise the complete terrain of NLP industrial policy. For a fuller treatment of these issues see the introductory chapter by Colclough and Manor. For a statement of the NLP perspective on industrial policy see Balassa and Associates 1982, Lal 1983 and Little 1982.
3. Balassa argues for a maximum support of 20% effective protection for five to eight years declining to no more than 10% thereafter. See Balassa and Associates 1982: 69.
4. There is an extensive literature on this transition. For a broad outline of the major issues see Freeman, Clark, and Soete 1982, Hoffman and Kaplinsky 1988, Piore and Sabel 1984, and the bibliographical references cited in these sources.
5. This has become an especially important phenomenon in parts of Italy. See Piore and Sabel 1984 and Brusco 1982.
6. A variety of sources have been utilized in this section. See Colclough and McCarthy 1980, Ghai 1987, Lewis, Harvey, and Sharpley 1990, *World Development Report* 1987.
7. There is some debate about the best way to cope with this problem of unemployment. One solution being canvassed is to lower real wages in the belief that this will clear the labour market. Of course this policy proposal is precisely what could be expected to emanate from the NLP. But, as we see in discussion of the functioning of FAP, there is no evidence that a lowering of real wages will have this desired policy effect.
8. Botswana has followed a cautious fiscal and monetary policy and currently has deposits in foreign banks of around $2.5 bn.
9. The share of the service sector—almost entirely made up of traditional labour-intensive services and those provided by the state—remained static during this period of two decades.
10. See Colclough and Olsen 1983: 52, 87, and 95.
11. This principle was particularly germane to the supply of water in the context of pervasive drought as the government was reluctant to promote the development of water-intensive operations.
12. The March 1989 value of a Pula was 2.00 to the $US and 3.49 to the £UK.
13. Large-scale enterprises (initially with an investment cost exceeding P750,000) were eligible for the AFA (automatic financial assistance) scheme if they were new projects. In the case of CFA (case-by-case financial assistance) they would not only have to show the 6% economic rate of return, but a full 20-year discounted cash flow analysis should be conducted to ensure the project's long-run viability. In other words, much more discretion was built into assistance for these large-scale projects. This differential was appropriate, given the much larger potential costs to the public purse.
14. For enterprises outside peri-urban areas, the rates were marginally higher.

15. Not more than 40% of total fixed investment in urban areas, on a sliding scale to a maximum of 70% in the far west of the country.
16. These percentages were regionally determined, ranging from 80% for the capital city to 120% for the far west of the country.
17. The performance of FAP has been evaluated twice, once in 1984 (Isaksen *et al.* 1984) and subsequently in 1988 (Smith *et al.* 1988). These two evaluations were undertaken by teams working with the co-operation of the Botswana government. On both occasions a significant number of small and medium-sized enterprises were visited. Interviews were also conducted with government officials and key participants in the private sector (including business services). Access was also freely given by the government to its data bases and evaluation records on applications for FAP grants.
18. The informal sector is defined in official statistics as comprising firms employing more than 10 people.
19. See Lewis, Harvey, and Sharpley 1990.
20. Except in a few sectors which have become the source of some trade friction between Botswana and Zimbabwe; yet the heavy trade surplus in Zimbabwe's favour provides some incentive for it to keep its markets similarly open to Botswana-based firms.
21. The 1988 appraisal did not directly address these issues.
22. The original scheme was designed to run on an Apple IIe, but as computer power increased, the central ministry converted to IBM-compatible format. This meant that data-bases between various ministries were wholly incompatible. Coupled with the absence of effective training, the implementing staff were unable to 'mine' these data bases, either to generate an overview on the extent of loan commitments and disbursements or to analyse the trends of applications.
23. Probably almost as important, the Swedes also provided assistance with the layout of the plant and production scheduling. In addition, both the owner-entrepreneur and some of her key staff were provided with training in Sweden.
24. One recent and especially troubling source of competition emanates from Zimbabwe, where two *dirigiste* policy initiatives have led to sharp price reductions. The first is an export subsidy; the second, and perhaps even more important innovation, is to allow Zimbabwean firms to keep a percentage of their export revenues to import intermediate inputs and capital goods.
25. Some years ago Vaitsos made the same point succinctly—'In the formulation of the demand for information, as in all other markets, a prospective buyer needs information about the properties of the item he intends to purchase so as to be able to make appropriate decisions. Yet, in the case of technology, what is needed is information about information which could effectively be one and the same thing. Thus, the prospective buyer is confronted with a structural weakness intrinsic to his position as purchaser with resulting imperfections in the corresponding market operations' (Vaitsos 1974: 87).
26. See Kaplinsky 1990.
27. In Italy, however, it is the district state which is important. Nevertheless, in many cases the resources commanded by these district-level authorities are larger than those available to the central government in Botswana.
28. These have been pitched at the upgrading of informal sector enterprises—such as tailoring, furniture manufacture, and elementary metal-working—and have

not ventured into sectorally shared facilities or more technologically complex industries and services. Even in the traditional sectors, the sorts of inputs provided are often basic and offer none of the help required to penetrate foreign markets (for example, design intelligence or common marketing in garments).

29. The avoidance of protectionism was partly conditioned by Botswana's membership of the SACU.
30. Open-door policies can block the development of indigenous technological capability. For an illustration of this see Evans and Tigres' comparison between the Brazilian and Korean computer industries (Evans and Tigre 1989).
31. See Lewis, Harvey, and Sharpley 1990 for corroboration of this judgement.

References

Balassa, B. (1981), 'The Process of Industrial Development and Alternative Development Strategies', in id., *The Newly Industrializing Countries in the World Economy*, Pergamon Press, Oxford.
—— and Associates (1982), *Development Strategies in Semi-Industrial Countries*, Johns Hopkins University Press, Baltimore, Md.
Bauer, P. T. (1984), *Reality and Rhetoric: Studies in the Economics of Development*, Weidenfeld & Nicolson, London.
Brusco, S. (1982), 'The Emilian Model: Productive Decentralisation and Social Integration', *Cambridge Journal of Economics*, 6/2: 167–84.
Colclough, C., and McCarthy, S. (1980), *The Political Economy of Botswana: A Study of Growth and Distribution*, Oxford University Press, Oxford.
—— and Olsen, P. (1983), *Review of Incomes Policy in Botswana: 1972–83*, Ministry of Finance and Development Planning, Gaborone.
Evans, D. E., and Alizadeh, P. (1984), 'Trade, Industrialisation and the Visible Hand', *Journal of Development Studies*, 21/1 (Oct.): 22–46.
Evans, P., and Tigre, P. B. (1989), 'Going beyond Clones in Brazil and Korea: A Comparative Analysis of NIC Strategies in the Computer Industry', *World Development*, 17/1: 1751–68.
Freeman, C., Clark, J., and Soete, L. (1982), *Unemployment and Technical Innovation: A Study of Long Waves and Economic Development*, Frances Pinter, London.
Ghai, D. (1987), 'Successes and Failures in Growth in Sub-Saharan Africa: 1960–82', in L. Emmerij (ed.), *Development Policies and the Crisis of the 1980s*, OECD Development Centre, Paris.
Hoffman, K., and Kaplinsky, R. (1988), *Driving Force: The Global Restructuring of Technology, Labor, and Investment in the Automobile and Components Industries*, Westview Press, Boulder, Colo.
Isaksen, J., Kaplinsky R., and Odel, M. (1984), *Report on Evaluation of FAP*, Chr. Michelsen Institute, Bergen.
Kaplinsky, R., (1990), *The Economics of Small: Appropriate Technology in a Changing World*, Intermediate Technology Press, London.
Lal, D. (1983), *The Poverty of 'Development Economics'*, Hobart Paperback No. 16, Institute of Economic Affairs, London.

Lewis, S., Harvey, C., and Sharpley, J. (1990), 'Botswana', in R. Riddell (ed.), *Industrialisation in Sub-Saharan Africa*, James Curry, London.

Little, I. M. D. (1982), *Economic Development: Theory, Policy and International Relations*, Basic Books, New York.

Piore, M. J. and Sabel, C. F. (1984), *The Second Industrial Divide*, Basic Books, New York.

Republic of Botswana (1984) *Industrial Development Policy*, Government Paper No. 2 of 1984, Gaborone.

—— (1985), *National Development Plan 1985–91*, Ministry of Finance and Development Planning, Gaborone.

Smith, C., Kaplinsky, R., Menz, J., and Selabe, B. (1988), *Evaluation of the Financial Assistance Policy: FAP and its Role in Botswana Business Development*, Massachusetts.

Toye, J. (1985), 'Dirigisme and Development Economics', *Cambridge Journal of Economics*, 9/1 (Mar.): 1–14.

—— (1987a), *Dilemmas of Development*, Basil Blackwell, Oxford.

—— (1987b), 'Development Theory and the Experience of Development', in L. Emmerij (ed.), *Development Policies and the Crisis of the 1980s*, OECD Development Centre, Paris.

Vaitsos, C. V. (1974), *Intercountry Income Distribution and Transnational Enterprises*, Clarendon Press, Oxford.

8
Learning to Raise Infants:
A Case-study in Industrial Policy

HUBERT SCHMITZ and TOM HEWITT

1. Introduction

This chapter examines a recent case where an interventionist policy was pursued: the creation by the Brazilian government of a market reserve for national computer firms. In the context of this book, the case is particularly interesting because the policy has been heavily contested by a political opposition which has made frequent use of neo-liberal arguments. The chapter proceeds as follows: sections 3 and 4 give a brief overview of the policy regime and of the political setting which gave rise to the policy. Sections 5 to 11 contain the assessment; we try to answer the questions which neo-liberals would ask about the effectiveness of intervention but also raise some essential issues which they would tend to ignore. The purpose of section 2 is to set the case study in the context of the current industrialization debate.

2. Critical Issues in the Industrialization Debate

The debate on industrialization has always pivoted around two interrelated issues:

- state versus market;
- self-reliance versus integration into the world economy.

In the 1980s LDCs have come under unprecedented pressure to integrate into the world economy and reduce state intervention. This pressure comes both from academic and institutional sources, including advice and actions from the international finance institutions. In neo-liberal circles such policies are justified by reference to the history of industrialization in LDCs over the last four decades. It is argued that protectionist policies in pursuit of import

This paper has benefited from critical comments of many colleagues, in particular José Cassiolato, Christopher Colclough, David Evans, John Humphrey, Raphie Kaplinsky, Robin Murray, and Jörg Meyer-Stamer.

substitution have not worked (except in their early stages) and export-orientated industrialization under liberal policies has been so successful that LDCs in general should follow this route (Balassa 1981, Krueger 1981).

In an earlier survey of industrialization strategies (Schmitz 1984), we concluded that import substitution has indeed led to (static) inefficiency and foreign exchange problems, but that from a dynamic perspective (learning and externalities) many existing analyses of protection are unsatisfactory—for both conceptual and empirical reasons. Second, we concluded that the alleged superiority of export orientation is not so much due to the adoption of more 'rational' market-orientated policies, as to a favourable combination of historical factors and substantial state intervention.

The latter point has since been developed and documented clearly. Luedde-Neurath (1986), for example, has shown that South Korea's export success was neither preceded nor accompanied by significant across-the-board import liberalization and that market forces were not given a free reign to allocate resources. Instead there was a targeted two-pronged import policy: liberal towards inputs for export manufacturing and highly restrictive towards the domestic market by making access to the (protected and hence profitable) domestic market conditional upon satisfactory export performance. The overall conclusion was that the Korean import regime was highly managed.

In the wake of this and other empirical studies, agreement is emerging that the East Asian industrialization experiences (with the exception of the city states) are showpieces of hands-on rather than hands-off industrial policy (White 1988). Many neo-liberal economists, however, remain unconvinced. A currently pervasive attitude in the profession is that most LDC governments are not capable of pursuing strategic industrial policies.

Of course, scepticism about the difficulties of successful state intervention is justifiable, given that many industrial failures have been policy-induced. As stressed in the introduction to this book, neo-liberals have contributed a great deal to the critical analysis of state intervention, particularly with their work on policies of protection. However, sight is often lost of the fact that governments need to *learn* how to promote industrial development. Moreover, aphorisms such as 'imperfect markets are better than imperfect states' seem to introduce an unwarranted passivism—if not defeatism—into the debate on industrial policy.

In what follows we present a case-study of active industrial policy: the promotion of national firms in the Brazilian computer industry. The chances of this selective state intervention succeeding seemed very unlikely at the time because it occurred in a period of increasing internationalization of the Brazilian economy and when the technological frontier in computer design and production was advancing rapidly.

3. Policy Regime

Until the late 1970s, Brazil's computer industry was in the hands of foreign firms which either imported finished products or carried out the final assembly of goods locally. By the mid-1980s, this situation had changed almost out of all recognition. By 1986, the number of firms operating in the nationally owned computer and peripherals market increased to 310 from 4 in 1977. Employment in these firms grew from just 4,000 in 1979 to over 40,000 in 1986. Total sales of national firms were in the region of US$1,520 million, accounting for 51 per cent of the computer market (Piragibe 1987).

This rapid growth resulted from the creation of a reserved market. Foreign corporations were not excluded from the Brazilian computer market. Rather, they were limited to specific market segments. Other segments were reserved for Brazilian private capital.

The principal tool of policy has been the creation of a reserved market for mini- and microcomputers and their peripherals. This policy is carried out by the Special Secretariat for Informatics (SEI) which is a specialized government agency working under the Ministry for Science and Technology.[1] The main policy instruments used by SEI are quantitative import restrictions and the concession of manufacturing licences to national firms. Foreign firms are limited to the production of mainframe computers. They are also controlled by SEI to the extent that the granting and withholding of import licences can force these firms to have increasing indices of nationally produced inputs in their final products and also to show positive export balances (Piragibe 1985).

These policies have their origin in the Commission for the Co-ordination of Electronic Processing Activities (CAPRE) which was created in 1972 and had a regulatory role over information technology. Control over computer imports began in 1975, at which time a number of complementary policy measures were also set in motion.[2]

At the same time, government concern and recognition that the computer industry was to be a key area of local development prompted the creation in 1974 of the state firm Computadores e Sistemas Brasileiros (COBRA) to develop and manufacture 'national' computers. COBRA produced two minicomputers under licence, one for military and one for civilian use. With the experience obtained, the firm was then able to produce the first almost wholly Brazilian-designed minicomputers in collaboration with the Universities of São Paulo (hardware) and Rio de Janeiro (software).

COBRA was conceived as being a 'national champion' for the local computer industry and as a training ground for technical and engineering labour (Tigre 1983: 66).[3] COBRA, however, ran into difficulties as a commercial enterprise. This contributed to a decision against further state involvement in production (although the state retained control over the areas in which firms could operate). Thus, minicomputer production, then peripherals and, subsequently, microcomputer production was put to tender in 1977 for national firms.[4] This was the beginning of the market reserve.

Just as the preference for private national enterprise in computer production was influenced by the experiences of COBRA, the emergence of SEI was a result of the experiences of CAPRE. CAPRE moved from being an 'administrative and pedestrian' body (Evans 1986) to one which established the market reserve for mini- and microcomputers. In 1979 it became transformed into SEI with a wider mandate. The protected market for national firms under SEI's guidance gradually spread to other areas such as superminicomputers, automation equipment, microelectronic components, digital instruments, and others.[5] In 1984, the market reserve and complementary measures were enshrined in the 'Informatics Law'.[6]

4. The National Alliance

The passing of the Informatics Law was the result of an intense political struggle. It is through understanding the origin of the policy for the computer industry that we can make sense of its present political sustainability in the face of internal and external opposition. CAPRE and COBRA were the result of a particular alliance of political forces. It included the military, technologists, and economists. The glue was nationalism. At the time, this proved a strong enough link to resist pressures for an open door policy.

It was an unlikely alliance because it occurred at a time when the Brazilian economy was in a phase of internationalization. In this developmental coalition there was, first, a small caucus of highly skilled engineers trained in technology institutes and universities in the US and in Brazil whom Evans (1986: 792) has called 'frustrated nationalist technicians'. They were neither satisfied with working as salespeople for foreign computer manufacturers nor did they want to remain in universities. Their ambition was to find a commercial outlet (and, therefore, real test) for their prototype computer designs.

These engineers found political and financial support from three groups in the state apparatus. In the national development bank (BNDE) there was a group of economists who were keen to promote a national capital goods industry. The federal data processing agency, SERPRO, had been doing their own hardware and software development to suit their particular needs and supported the creation of a national industry which could supply equipment to their specifications. Finally, the navy was keen to see the development of a national computer technology to supply its frigates and thus avoid technological dependency in what was considered to be a strategic and sensitive military area (ibid. 793).

The convergence of these forces produced a particular breed of nationalism based on a combination of security, developmental, pecuniary, and techno-logical considerations (Evans 1985). The presence of private national capital was minimal in the initial decision-making process. With the installation and then rapid expansion of the industry, national capital played an increasingly important role and as a consequence has become a more powerful pressure group. In particular, the national banking sector now has a strong presence in the computer industry.

Nationalism is still a strong cohesive force but internal and external pressures to change computer policy have been growing.[7] The opposition comes primarily from two groups: the excluded foreign computer firms who are backed by their governments and from the user firms who demand quicker access to the latest international technology. The outcome of these conflicts will be determined not just by ideological factors but also by the record of the industry to date.

The latter will be examined in the sections which follow through the neo-liberal eye. While neo-liberals are not against infant industry protection in principle, they would neither favour the use of quantitative controls, nor give preferential status to national firms.

5. Growth and Competition

The computer industry was responsible for 40 per cent of the US$8 billion total sales of electronic equipment in Brazil in 1986. This represents the largest electronics market segment in Brazil (superseding that of consumer electronics and telecommunications). Within computer production, it is the national firms which have undergone the fastest growth in output of 300 per cent from 1981 to 1986. Indeed, by 1986, national firms had passed a watershed by attaining 51 per cent of the total computer and peripherals market (Piragibe 1987).

Although impressive, rapid growth on its own is not a sufficient indicator of success. In our assessment we proceed as follows. First, we examine the questions which neo-liberals would ask about intervention in the computer industry. This is not merely an academic exercise since there has been powerful opposition to the policy using neo-liberal arguments. Accordingly, we examine the issues of internal competition, lack of international competi-tiveness, detrimental effects on users, opportunity costs, and intrinsic problems of state intervention. We then examine the questions to which neo-liberals assign less importance, in particular the process of learning in both industry and government.

The widespread disillusion with protectionist policy is in many cases not the result of protection *per se* but of monopoly positions built up behind protective barriers.[8] An undoubtedly positive feature of the reserved market for small computers and peripherals is that there is *fierce internal competition*.

The number of national firms increased from 4 in 1977 to 310 firms in 1986 (excluding software houses[9]). The number of foreign-owned computer firms increased from 4 to 37 in the same period. However, IBM still held more than 50 per cent of the mainframe market in 1986.

The large number of firms operating in the lower end of the computer and peripherals market has meant that there is considerable competition between firms in most product groups, particularly the general purpose computer systems market.[10] Developments in the computer industry since 1986 show that internal competition is forcing producers to become more competitive despite protective barriers. There are now signs that the growth of the national computer industry is slowing down for the first time in its (short) history. Even during the recession of 1981–3, the national industry grew at annual rates of 30 to 35 per cent, but by 1988 growth had slowed down to 10 per cent. Competition has increased further and what was once perceived as a huge market, now appears more limited. The need to become more internationally competitive is now perceived as a priority within and outside the industry.

6. International Competitiveness

International competitiveness can be measured in terms of the cost, quality, and technological up-to-dateness of Brazilian products relative to international standards. That is, in terms of export performance or, in the absence of exports, in terms of the comparison of Brazilian and international prices and quality.

Although there are no studies on the competitive strength of foreign computer firms in Brazil in terms of product prices, these firms seem internationally competitive.[11] For example, for the US$163 million exports of computer equipment from Brazil in 1987, IBM alone accounted for 81 per cent (SEI 1989).

The key question in this chapter is the level of international competitiveness of the *national* computer industry, that is, the subsector which enjoys protection. First, the price comparison. Two of the nationally produced microcomputers were analysed by Tigre and Perine (1984): the Apple II and the TRS80. Both microcomputers were introduced into the US market in the late 1970s and into the Brazilian market in the early 1980s. That is, by the standards of the product cycle in electronics, they were not the most up to date by the time of their introduction in Brazil.

Nevertheless, between 1982 and 1984 Brazilian producers did manage to reduce the domestic/US price ratio of the Apple II from 2.2 to 1.0 and to reduce that of the TRS80 from 2.79 to 1.18. These reductions take into account the fact that prices in the US were also falling in this period. In addition, Brazilian firms were able to keep pace with the incremental product innovations which were being introduced in the US, such as expanded memory and faster processing.

The cost of whole systems—microcomputers plus peripherals—however, does not show such a good performance. In other words it has proved more difficult to reduce the price of peripherals. Piragibe's (1984) study shows that Brazilian-produced serial printers underwent very small price reductions in two years and remained between 2 and 3 times the US price in 1984. This is explained partly by the higher import content of printers compared to microcomputers and by the duties to be paid on such imports.

Since these two studies were undertaken, the IBM Personal Computer (PC) has become the *de facto* international standard in small systems. Copies of this equipment and its peripherals now form the bulk of micro-computer production in Brazil (as well as in South Korea and USA).

According to a survey carried out in 1985, a PC compatible system produced in Brazil at the end of that year cost 2.5 times the original IBM system in the US. Of this, peripherals accounted for 52 per cent of the cost in Brazil and for 32 per cent of the cost in the US (*Info* August 1985: 24). In the course of 1985, the price of a PC compatible produced in Brazil fell by 62 per cent, while the price of a PC compatible printer fell only 7 per cent (*Info* January 1986: 16). However, prices were also falling in the US. The price of the IBM-PC fell by 31 per cent in 1985, which was probably caused by competition from PC compatibles which—internationally—fell in price by the same amount (*Info* April 1986: 34).[12] The price reduction of printers internationally was much steeper, at 35 per cent, compared to the small reductions achieved in Brazil (ibid.).

More recently (April 1989), Brazilian producers have narrowed the price gap in peripherals. For matrix printers the domestic/US price ratio fell to 2.0 and for monitors (12 inch) to 1.8. However, in micro computers differentials in April 1989 were only slightly lower than in earlier years. The domestic/US price ratio for IBM-XT compatibles was 2.1 and for IBM-AT compatibles it was 1.8 (Corsepius and Schipke 1989). It is important to note that these price comparisons are problematic since they do not take into account the differences in import duties on components. For example, components assembled in the Far East and reimported to the US are exempt from import duties. In contrast, Brazilian firms have to pay import duties for imported parts and components, which raise their actual costs by between 30 and 85 per cent (Tigre 1985). While import duties do stimulate the achievement of higher indices of nationalization, they also give a certain inflexibility in product price reductions.

The above evidence nevertheless indicates that Brazil's computer industry is high cost in international terms. A critical issue is whether the price gap decreases over time. This appears to be occurring but not in a linear way. There are several cases of Brazilian firms almost catching up, but then international competitors make a new leap forward and a new round of catching up begins.

Brazilian firms have been able to keep reasonably close to technological changes and product updates. Initially, the output of the industry was not sufficiently different from what was available internationally to enable exports of niche market products. This situation is now changing and the export of Brazilian designed systems is beginning. National firms are exporting locally designed banking automation systems to Europe and Latin America (Tigre 1988, Botelho 1987). While such exports are small compared to those of foreign computer producers, there seems to be a future for Brazilian exports in some niche markets where independent design strategies are a real possibility. To a great extent, this will depend on the continued development of technological capability by national firms. This process would also be aided by a more selective approach to import duties on intermediate components which Brazil does not yet have the capacity to produce competitively (Evans and Tigre 1989*b*, Perez 1985: iv).[13]

In sum, as a general rule goods produced by Brazilian firms are more expensive than their international competitors but there are repeated examples of this gap diminishing significantly. The beginnings of exports in niche markets augurs well for the future viability of the national industry.

7. Implications for Users

In spite of the advances made by the national computer industry, opponents claim that the informatics law dooms the user firms to obsolescent and expensive equipment and undermines the broader competitiveness of Brazilian industry in the world market (for example, Campos 1985, Moad 1988).

In examining such claims, three points need to be made. First, the diffusion of computers made by national firms has been rapid by any standards. The average annual growth rate of the Brazilian microcomputer market between 1984 and 1987 was the highest in the capitalist world at 74 per cent.[14] This exceptionally fast growth does not in itself answer the case made by the opposition, but it gives some testimony to the quality and relative cost performance of the national firms. Second, the difference between Brazil and, say, US prices does not measure the cost to the Brazilian user. There is little concrete evidence to suggest that the import prices of computer products into developing countries reflect world market prices. The same applies to internal production by foreign corporations. Their LDC subsidiaries often sell at above world market prices and/or produce equipment that is less up to date or of lower quality than that produced for other markets. For example, the prices which IBM tends to charge in the Brazilian market are significantly higher than in the US market. A case in point is the IBM 4341 system which was in 1984 between 2.4 (according to IBM) and 3.02 (according to the association of national computer producers) times as expensive in Brazil (Frischtak 1986: 29). Third, higher prices or less up-to-date equipment does not necessarily mean a loss of competitiveness. Four years ago (a long time in the history of this young industry!) a Brazilian researcher concluded that 'there is little evidence that the technological gap creates a serious productivity bottleneck for their users' (Erber 1985: 303).

Does this remain true? In answering this question one may have to distinguish between those user firms which incorporate computers into their own *products* and those which use them in order to automate their production *processes*. The former are likely to suffer more than the latter. For example, the competitiveness of Brazilian producers of CNC (computer numerically controlled) machine tools seems to be hampered by the higher price of national computer controls[15] but hard information is not yet available. User firms that need the new technologies in order to automate their own production processes also complain, but one must question whether the market reserve threatens their competitiveness. It is often forgotten that free access to international technology does not mean efficient use of that technology; especially when very advanced equipment is imported, maintenance and repair tends to be a major problem. In fact, the indirect evidence that is available strengthens the position of the defenders of infant industry protection. For example, a recent study based on a comparison of a British and Brazilian car plant argues against the 'technological imperative' (Silva 1988). It shows that the Brazilian plant is less automated than its British equivalent but has not as a result lost out in competitiveness, either in price or quality of output.[16]

A similar conclusion can be drawn from Brazil's macro-economic record. In spite of the world economic recession, Brazilian industry stepped up its exports during the 1980s. This does not suggest that the industry suffered from outdated or overpriced technology. It could even be argued that user firms benefit from the establishment of a national computer industry. The international literature emphasizes that the successful use of electronically controlled equipment depends on the close relationship between suppliers and users (Sayer and Morgan 1987). The high percentage of skilled personnel in national firms (see section 9 below) provides a capability of adjusting equipment to local conditions. Probably the heightened internal competition will force national firms to put this capability to use.

None of this is to deny that some user firms encounter problems in their attempt to modernize as a result of the government policy. In many cases these are unavoidable learning costs which result from infant industry protection. Of course, this learning argument can be abused. However, the political opposition to the market reserve policy is so strong that this is unlikely to happen. 'There is a limit to the differences between local and international products, beyond which the combined pressure of customers and excluded competitors becomes irresistible' (Erber 1985: 306).

8. Opportunity Costs

The case of the opposition is driven by an interest group which feels it is losing out because of the market reserve. Its arguments are largely identical with the neo-liberal agenda. In one respect, however, the latter would go beyond the former. A neo-liberal enquiry would include the question of opportunity costs. Could labour and capital not have been employed more productively elsewhere in the economy?

By 1987, the national computer industry employed over 40,000 people. The case that there is a social opportunity cost to this labour could only be made if there was full employment. This assumption does not hold in Brazil. The opportunity cost argument would even be difficult to uphold for highly trained personnel. Although the national computer industry has attracted some highly educated people from other productive sectors, there is little doubt that the industry has made a substantial net addition to 'human capital' (see section 9).

There is a similar answer in the case of the opportunity cost of capital. One of Brazil's major problems in the 1970s and 1980s was that capital flowed into financial operations rather than manufacturing. Profits in short-term financial markets were easier and higher than in industry.[17] Particularly noteworthy was the high profitability in the banking sector arising from short-term financial and speculative operations.[18] Unlike in Japan and South Korea, Brazilian bankers were rarely strategic promoters of industry. The only major exception is the computer industry. Banks are not only major users of computers,[19] but also invest heavily in their production (Fioravanti 1989). National banks own and/or control six of the ten largest national computer firms (SEI 1986). Thus, far from drawing capital away from more productive uses, the computer industry attracted capital which otherwise would have probably stayed in short-term financial and/or speculative operations.

9. Learning and Externalities

From a neo-liberal perspective, one might ask whether the build-up of the computer industry could not have been achieved more successfully if foreign capital had been granted entry into these subsectors. That is, if there had been no market reserve for national firms.

Ultimately, this counterfactual is impossible to answer. But we can suggest some of the likely trajectories of the industry. This can be done by way of a comparison with other subsectors of the electronics industry where the market reserve has not applied, namely the foreign-owned mainframe producers and the consumer electronics industry, most of which is foreign owned.

The Brazilian electronics market amounted to sales of US$8 billion in 1986. Foreign computer firms accounted for approximately 20 per cent of these sales[20] and consumer electronics firms for a further 36 per cent. Neither of these market segments is subject to such rigorous control over imported inputs, although they have to abide by a generalized 'law of similars'.[21] In comparison with national computer firms, they rely to a greater extent on import know-how. This is reflected in their labour force composition.

Piragibe *et al.* (1983) show that foreign computer firms employ 3 per cent of their work-force in R&D; by contrast, in national firms R&D accounts for 14.3 per cent. Our own research (Hewitt 1988) tends to confirm these findings: while a representative sample of national computer firms employ 12.5 per cent of their labour force in R&D, the share in foreign computer firms is only 3.7 per cent.[22] There is even lower incidence of R&D employment in the largely foreign-owned consumer electronics sector: 1.9 per cent of the labour force.[23] The relative R&D intensity of national firms finds further confirmation in a recent survey (SEI 1989: 25) which shows the activities engaged in by employees who have completed higher education. R&D accounts for 25.3 per cent in national and 5.7 per cent in foreign computer firms. In contrast, the latter firms employ 36.1 per cent of such personnel in marketing, compared with 19.7 per cent in national firms.

The relatively high percentage of skilled engineering and technical labour engaged in R&D of national computer firms is striking. This build-up in human expertise in electronics has occurred as a result of the market reserve which has forced these firms to develop and accumulate their own technological expertise since they have had no parents to turn to.[24] The above data cannot prove the case, but it nevertheless suggests that such a fostering of talent and human resources would not have occurred if foreign firms had been allowed to enter this industry.[25]

While it is, then, beyond doubt that the national computer firms employ more of their available professional human resources in R&D than foreign firms, neo-liberals would query the usefulness of this. Some, indeed, have dismissed electronics R&D in Brazil as simply 'reinventing the wheel' and a waste of valuable resources (Ayres and Guanães 1985: 58). Contrary to this view, we argue that building up an R&D capacity is a cumulative process which passess through various stages, and that what is occurring has to be viewed in a dynamic, longer-term sense.

Since neo-liberals tend to see long-run growth arising out of the pursuit of short-run efficiency (see introduction to this book) they tend to ignore the benefits of cumulative learning. In what follows, its significance for the

Brazilian computer industry is examined. The stages in the learning process which can be distinguished in accordance with Tigre (1986) are: imitation, modification, redesign, and innovation.[26] The labour requirements for these activities differ. For example, imitation requires mainly manufacturing and organizational skills, but, with the progression towards innovation, a design capability becomes increasingly important.

Most national computer firms are engaged in imitation and modification of existing products. Indeed, since the major international microcomputer manufacturers have been able to establish *de facto* world standards in hardware and software, national firms have relied heavily on reverse engineering to develop a capacity for *creative imitation*. This requires not only copying and understanding[27] but also adaptations to local needs and available inputs. The complexity of this task should not be underestimated. Furthermore, the educational returns for the engineers and technicians involved in the process are substantial.

The *redesign* of existing products may be viewed as a form of 'minor innovation'. It appears that those firms which have, in the past, engaged in creative imitation are in a much stronger position to redesign products to enter niche markets. This, for example, is so for firms which have developed specialized applications for microcomputer hardware and software.

Innovation represents the highest level of R&D activity. In the general purpose computer market, innovation is a tall order for all but the few leading firms in the world.[28] By contrast, creative imitation has been an effective way for Brazilian firms to enter the microcomputer market and to create a local technological capability.

The growth of the industry, of its competitiveness and of its skill base, all indicate a degree of success which can, in good measure, be attributed to timely policy intervention. Intervention has given the industry time to learn (which includes making mistakes) and to build up a local technological capability. It is not clear how a policy based on short-run efficiency would have produced longer-term learning on the scale that has taken place in Brazil.

The process of learning has repercussions for the whole economy in the form of external economies. Judging from the experience of other sectors of electronics, computer products and know-how would, if left to the market to provide, have been imported. Instead, a capability was generated locally. Its benefits now stretch beyond the computer industry itself. Given the increasing use of electronics throughout the economy, the computer industry has a similar role to that normally attributed to the capital goods industry (Hoffman 1985: 266). It has become an important general source of innovation and skills which are applied in other sectors.

In practice, externalities are difficult to measure. But the results of an assessment of the success of infant industries will often depend upon the ways in which externalities are considered in the analysis.[29] Whilst we have only indirect indications from our case-study, we nevertheless conclude that externalities are greater under the present protected regime than they would have been in its absence. As shown before, national firms invest a higher percentage of their resources in R&D than the foreign owned subsectors do. Equally significant is the fact that there is a high loss of R&D engineers and technicians by national firms (Hewitt 1988: 126). This drift of engineers from firm to firm, lured by greater remuneration and/or new professional challenges, may be damaging to individual firms, but it contributes to the technological capability of the computer industry as a whole and strengthens that of user firms.[30]

10. Intrinsic Problems of Government Interference

In assessing the policy regime adopted in Brazil, we have so far concentrated on developments in industry. We now turn to the government itself and to its performance.

The widely observable poor record of governments in pursuing protectionist policies has contributed a great deal to the influence of neo-liberalism. It has strengthened the thesis that there are 'intrinsic problems of government interference' such as bureaucratic delays or corruption (Little, Scitovsky, and Scott 1970). In this and the next section we argue that first this is only partially applicable to the protection of the Brazilian computer industry. Second, and more positively, a learning process within the government is observable, which would tend to escape the neo-liberal eye.

Let us begin with the question of administrative delays. All imports of electronic hardware and software have to be approved item by item by SEI (unless they are smuggled into the country). Both producers and users of new technology often have to wait between six and twelve months to have their application dealt with. Such delays are excessive and have brought the agency and the informatics policy into disrepute. The pressure of its critics, however, has recently forced SEI to speed up the processing of import requests.

As regards the question of corruption (a form of rent-seeking within government), SEI has a remarkable record. Our discussions with government officials and critics of SEI suggest that bribery within this organization is unheard of.[31] Of course, one can never be totally sure that there are no clandestine deals; but it is noteworthy that the opponents of the informatics policy have not been able to come up with a single case of corruption. Since the policy was so fiercely contested, the agency and its officials could ill afford to be seen to be involved in corrupt practices.

11. Learning in Government

Certainly, this case of protectionist policy does not conform to the following neo-liberal expectations: protection provides opportunities for both public and private actors to engage in rent-seeking; once established, these interest groups try to ensure the continuation of protection; if policy modifications are made, these are influenced by rent-seeking rather than developmental objectives. In contrast, we have observed a more positive trend: government agencies are learning and adjusting their policies in order to find an appropriate balance between, on the one hand, the domestic accumulation of capital, skills, and know-how, and on the other, the international competitiveness of producers and users.

However, anti-statism is so deeply ingrained in neo-liberal thinking that government learning has little room in its agenda. In our case-study, such learning is an essential part of the assessment.[32] There are several examples of it, none of which are spectacular but need to be recorded. First, government learned early on not to engage directly in the production of computers, in view of the difficulties encountered by the state firm, COBRA.[33] Instead, government concentrated on what it is better equipped to do, namely, controlling the quantity and prices of imports. We have recorded above how in this particular case protection helped to build up a national capacity in computer production.

Second, in spite of the achievements made, government agencies in charge of information technology are caught up in the same race as the national firms. Neither can rest on their laurels. The political opposition to the market reserve and the fast technological developments in the world market do not allow them to do so. The 1984 informatics law itself sets a deadline of 1992 for the end of the protection.[34] In anticipation of that date, some members of the nationalist coalition have already indicated that the market reserve policy needs to be revised. The former chairman of the Special Secretariat for Informatics (SEI), Edison Dytz, has suggested that the phase of stimulating the creation of new national firms is over.

We need to launch a second phase, encouraging the association among firms, universities and research centres with well defined technological goals. After some time of supporting producers and researchers, we would have to assess what we have obtained and then select the most successful areas for continued support. Those areas in which our support has not lead to adequate local capability will have to be supplied from abroad, even if this means the elimination of some national firms. (*Globo*, 7 June 1987; quoted from Bastos 1989)

Similarly, Veiga da Rocha, Chairman of SEI from 1987 to 1989, announced that where protection 'only results in higher product prices and no significant technological advance is made, there is no reason for keeping imports out'.[35]

The implication is that for some items which are now in the market reserve the government might liberalize imports ahead of schedule, even if some national firms were to die as a result.

In our view this is not a retreat from the nationalist position. On the contrary, it strengthens it and makes it more viable. It is the clearest indication that the government is learning along with the national industry and its political opponents.[36] This learning argument is worth spinning out because there is more to it than the trivial point that one learns from mistakes. It is true that errors were made in the raising of Brazilian electronic infants, but the foster parents have also learnt from the successes. More importantly, the acquired knowledge and experience can be put to use because many of the infants have grown. Let us explain.

First, choices now exist because a national capability for producing computers has been created. The capacity to innovate still lags behind that of international competitors, but these latter firms can now be brought to the negotiating table. For selected product and process innovations it is important to have at least the option of collaborating with foreign electronics firms; in some cases it is the best way of finding a balance between strengthening local technological capability and achieving international competitiveness. This possibility now exists but did so less before.

In the late 1970s, for example, foreign computer firms were unwilling to make any concessions to Brazilian firms. The large foreign firms (IBM, Burroughs, DEC, Data General) refused to transfer technology for mini-computers without majority ownership (Piragibe 1985: 142).[37] By 1985 they had reconsidered this position and had begun to forge links with national firms. For example, IBM embarked on a joint venture with a nationally owned data processing company in order to commercialize its software, while other large North American firms granted licensing agreements for national firms to manufacture super minicomputers (Tigre 1986, Meyer-Stamer 1988). It should be stressed that these collaborative strategies by foreign electronics firms were a response to the policies adopted by the Brazilian government. Foreign firms which are unwilling to be excluded from the fastest growing market segments have been forced to co-operate with Brazilian capital.

Second, the government itself has learnt alongside its industry.[38] Even though SEI has rightly been criticized for slowness in administering import controls (see above), the government has had a small cadre of officials who (1) keep abreast of national and international developments in the electronics industry, (2) are capable of participating in technical debates about the benefits of the market reserve, and (3) recognize the need for greater flexibility and selectivity in the application of policy to different segments of the market. To understand such government learning and the need for more selectivity, we need briefly to look back. In 1984, the informatics laws extended the market reserve. The following areas were added: semiconductors, automation equipment, super minicomputers, process control, and instrumentation. SEI took on more than it could deal with. With hindsight, a more differentiated treatment would have been desirable. But that is a technocratic point to make. The preparation of the informatics law ignited ideological warfare between nationalist and internationalist forces. The issue received extraordinary attention in public debate and the media. Eventually a bout of nationalist fever saw the law through Congress. It was not a time for careful picking and selecting.[39]

It would, however, be wrong to see the reason for the ambitious scope of the informatics law in nationalist zeal alone. It was also influenced by the arguments of electronics experts. They emphasized the interdependence of the various electronics subsectors. The buzz word was synergy. While Japan has demonstrated that the technological and economic benefits which arise from having an 'electronics complex' are real, fascination with synergy clouds the reality of most countries.

The present Brazilian reality has led government agencies to move towards a more pragmatic position. There is a recognition that (1) it is less necessary to maintain the protection for all subsectors covered by the law; (2) it is more important to concentrate on selected subsectors and to complement import controls with more support for research and training.[40]

The informatics law has only been in operation for five years and some subsectors have only enjoyed protection from competition since then. It could be argued that for them a change in policy is premature, that they need more time. Perhaps. The fact is that the government agencies are under enormous pressure to re-examine the application of the law. This brings us to the final point in this section: the (involuntary) contribution which the political opposition made to learning in government.

The opposition has been both external and internal. In the initial years, it came mainly from the foreign computer firms operating within the country. Since then, the opposition has grown considerably.[41] External pressure has come from the American Electronics Association, the US Computer and Business Equipment Manufacturers Association, and the US government which has threatened a series of sanctions against Brazilian exports and has taken the Brazilian case to GATT. Growing internal opposition has come from users and industrialists (e.g. the industrial employers association, FIESP) who have become dissatisfied with high product prices and administrative delays. Foreign electronics firms have maintained their opposition and have, in some cases, managed to obtain support from the Brazilian judiciary in the interpretation of the informatics law. Apart from helping to keep the nationalist alliance together, this unrelenting pressure has forced the government to review its policies, to become more selective, and to improve implementation by speeding up the processing of import requests.

In summary, the protectionist policy kept out the competition from the world market. Without state protection, most Brazilian infants would never have seen the light of day, let alone grown. While the international competitive pressure was not felt directly it was mediated through political pressure from internal and external opponents. The latter gave local producers and government little option but to adopt and learn quickly. The benefits of these pressures have thus been substantial.

It could be argued that neither industry nor government learned quickly enough. This is a matter of judgement. Nevertheless, one outcome which is undeniable is that Brazil now has choices which would not have existed without the market reserve. These are choices about the degree of openness to imports and of collaboration with foreign firms. The latter are now prepared to negotiate where previously they were not. What is more, they have to negotiate with Brazilian partners who know what they are after. In both industry and government a familiarity with complex technology and markets has been established. This is a necessary condition for successful negotiation.

Neo-liberals rightly force us to investigate the problems which arise in the execution of government policies. However, what tends to escape their analysis are the equally important questions of learning in government, and the conditions under which it occurs. If the frame of mind does not even allow for such learning to take place, there is indeed little alternative to believing in the wisdom of the market.

12. Conclusion

The record of the computer industry and of its regulation by government reveals both strengths and weaknesses. Indeed, a final assessment of this case of infant industry protection is not yet possible. The market reserve has operated for little more than a decade and the bulk of national computer firms is even younger. Is this sufficient time to grow up and achieve international competitiveness? Bell *et al.* (1984), in their review of infant industry experiences, emphasize that there is no agreement on what duration of infancy is acceptable. Neo-liberals generally tend to be impatient in this respect. For example, Balassa (1975, Balassa and Associates 1982) prescribes that protection for infant industries should be lifted after five to eight years. Bell *et al.* (1984) point out that there is often a large discrepancy between this expectation and the time that appears to be needed to become internationally competitive.[42]

While available data do not allow a rigorous quantitative analysis, we have tried in this paper to make an interim assessment. We have shown that a verdict based only upon a comparison of domestic costs of production with the costs of equivalent imported products would be negative. This is not because the infants have been unable to reduce costs but because the technological frontier in this industry has been moving very quickly. Nevertheless, we have also shown that:

- an export capacity in the nationally owned segment is beginning to emerge, particularly in specialized markets;
- there are substantial external economies arising from the learning efforts of national firms;
- without the market reserve, the creation of jobs, skills, and know-how would have been lower than in fact occurred;
- foreign firms are now willing to transfer technology on terms which they had previously refused.[43]

If these points are sufficient to justify a positive assessment of this experience—as we believe they are—what general lessons can we draw for other countries? Clearly there is a need for caution in advocating that other LDCs follow the same route because of the size of Brazil's internal market and its relatively advanced stage of industrialization. However, in the 1970s, few would have thought that the Brazilian computer industry could have achieved as much.[44]

The case-study has shown that opportunities for successful state intervention arise even under adverse political and technological circumstances. A rapidly expanding infant industry, in which national firms compete fiercely behind a temporary protective barrier, is growing up. This growth has been facilitated by government agencies which have pursued a sectoral strategy, and have themselves been positively affected by the experience of the infant industry and by its adversaries. State efficiency is thereby increasing. There are, then, some short-run costs, but it seems likely that they will be more than outweighed by benefits over the longer run. Taking a more dynamic perspective than typical neo-liberals, then, it seems that selective state intervention along the above lines can work.

It is worth reiterating that most neo-liberals are not against infant industry protection in principle, but they would insist that such protection be pursued by using price measures rather than quantitative restrictions. One cannot tell what would have occurred if tariffs or subsidies had been the main instrument. However, we do know that the combination of quantitative and administrative measures produced, in this case, a range of *national* benefits which the price instrument could not deliver. The latter would have stimulated production within the country, but by foreign rather than national capital. Many benefits would thereby have been lost.

To conclude, this paper does not present a clear-cut success story of protection. An examination through the short-run lens reveals deficiencies. Taking the longer view, what impresses is the enormous learning which both infants and fostering parents underwent. It is a lesson in national industrial development and politics which is still underway. In our view it conveys a message of optimism[45] for active industrial policy which contrasts with the neo-liberal gloom on state intervention.

Notes

1. Initially, computer policy came under the National Security Council. With the abolition of the Ministry of Science and Technology in October 1988, SEI became formally subordinated to the President's Office.
2. These have been amply documented in a number of texts, for example, Piragibe (1985 and 1988), Tapia (1984), Tigre (1983).
3. See Helena (1984) for a detailed account of the formation and development of COBRA.
4. The *national ownership* of the computer firms has a strict definition: they are corporations established in Brazil, under permanent, exclusive, and unconditional direct and indirect control (over managerial decision-making power, technological development, and stock ownership) of individuals resident in Brazil or of domestic public entities (Frischtak 1986: 8).
5. It is this wide range of activities related to data processing through machines which is termed 'informatics' in Brazil, and not just the computer industry itself.
6. For details see Piragibe (1988) and Meyer-Stamer (1988).
7. For a detailed account, see Bastos (1989).
8. Monopoly is attributable often to foreign capital (e.g. the cathode ray tube production in Brazil) which can then afford to market products which, elsewhere, have become obsolete.
9. In 1986, there were an estimated 1,200 software 'producers' and 15,000 data processing centres in Brazil (*Dados e Idéias* August 1986: 8).
10. For example, in 1985 there were an estimated 37 different firms producing copies of the IBM-PC family of computers alone (*Informática Hoje* 15 Oct. 1985).
11. Since the cost of inputs has a bearing on competitiveness, it is worth mentioning that, for most of the 1980s, imported inputs accounted for approximately 20% of total sales of foreign computer firms. Inputs used for export production can, however, be imported duty free under the BEFIEX scheme.
12. The price of PC compatibles, mostly from Asia, fell 70% in the three years to 1985 (*Info* April 1986).
13. Particularly components which rely on precision engineering such as drive and printer mechanisms and those inputs whose cost depends on third parties (such as fine chemicals essential for locally produced printed circuit boards).
14. Estimated by the Office of Computers and Business Equipment, US Department of Commerce. Cited in Cassiolato (1989).
15. According to verbal communication from researchers of the University of São Paulo.
16. In this respect it is worth referring also to comparisons between Japanese and Western car makers. They show that in the early 1980s Japanese firms often had a lower degree of automation than their European and North American rivals and that Japan's competitive advantage stemmed above all from their superior organizational structure (Kaplinsky 1988). Similarly, Bessant and Haywood (1986) and Hoffman (1988) show that the benefits of advanced flexible manufacturing systems come more from organizational than technological innovation (even though the two cannot be strictly separated).
17. See e.g. *Gazeta Mercantil*, 4 Oct. 1978.

18. See e.g. *Gazeta Mercantil*, Balanço Anual, Various years.
19. Approximately 30% of the national industry's output is used by the financial sector (SEI 1986: 34).
20. IBM accounted for more than half of this ratio.
21. Imports are only allowed if equivalent locally made products are not available.
22. The share of engineers and technicians in the labour force of national and foreign computer firms is very similar, namely 22.7 and 20.6% respectively (Hewitt 1988: table 4.5). However, engineers in the latter firms are more often involved in marketing, management, and administration.
23. For a detailed account of occupational and skill composition in the various subsectors of the Brazilian electronics industry, see Hewitt (1988).
24. In absolute terms, 4,900 professionals were employed in R&D by national firms (in 1986) and their R&D expenditure reached US$154.1 million which amounted to 10.1% of total sales (Piragibe 1987).
25. Apart from the example of the consumer electronics industry which has experienced two decades of the free market without showing any signs of a build-up of technological capabilities, the case of the Argentinian electronics industry is illustrative. What was once a burgeoning sector under national control is now virtually non-existent due, it seems, to the opening up of the sector to uncontrolled imports of electronics goods (Tigre 1988).
26. Bell *et al.* (1984: 34) employ a similar schema: replicative copying, minor improvements and modifications, formalized overall redesign, and innovation through R&D.
27. Having know-how *and* know-why in Lall's terminology (Lall 1982).
28. Frischtak (1986: 22) argues that 'The Brazilian market does not seem to be sufficiently large to support firms which, in isolation, would have the financial means to conduct R&D in the scale and depth necessary to introduce major innovations.'
29. Recovering the costs of coming down the learning curve (as in Bell *et al.* 1984), even if infants become internationally competitive, can probably only be achieved by including externalities in the calculation.
30. As Bell (1982: 132) has pointed out: 'Perhaps the most important intra-industry externality is the direct acquisition of labour-embodied change-capacity that has been accumulated through expenditure by other firms . . . the inter-firm movement of experienced managers, engineers and technicians will carry not only knowledge and skill about how to effect change, but also information about what changes to effect—detailed information about specific changes that have been implemented or attempted in other situations.'
31. This is not true, of course, for Brazil as a whole.
32. This emphasis on learning in government must not hide the existence of interministerial conflict. This has arisen mainly because the formulation and execution of policy for one subsector of the electronics complex, namely telecommmunications, lies with the Ministry of Communication.
33. For details see section 3 above. The government is currently examining whether COBRA should be privatized.
34. The informatics law is open to different interpretations with regard to the duration of the market reserve for national firms and for protection from imports. Article 9 states explicitly that the adoption of restrictive measures in

favour of *national* firms is temporary, without setting a time limit. Article 8 stipulates that SEI's mandate to control imports ceases 8 years after the introduction of the law, that is, 1992. The latter could be interpreted to mean that CACEX would take over this function from SEI. (CACEX is the government agency in charge of administering foreign trade regulations for most other sectors.)

35. *Jornal do Brasil*, 24 Oct. 1988.
36. For a different interpretation, see Fleury (1987: 31) who emphasizes the 'bureaucratization of the Brazilian informatics policy formulation process'.
37. As a result national firms were forced to seek and obtain licences from smaller firms such as Sycor, Logabax, Nixdorf, and Fujitsu.
38. National industrialists joined forces in ABICOMP, a sectoral association which is active in lobbying and producing information. The joint learning was helped by the fact that the government itself has a sectoral focus and a specialized administration for this industry.
39. This is based on direct observation. We were in the country at the time and participated in a number of open seminars and public debates.
40. This is a lesson also learnt in other Latin American countries, for example, Venezuela. See Perez 1985.
41. For a detailed account, see Bastos 1989.
42. For example, the textiles industry took two or three decades to mature in Japan and four decades in South Korea. The Japanese car industry took anything between three and six decades to mature. By contrast, the South Korean steel industry appears to have matured in two years (Bell *et al.* 1984: 23, 25).
43. We should add a factor which has not been examined in this paper: the expatriation of profits. Between 1974 and 1983, foreign computer firms sent profits home from Brazil of almost two times the value of their total direct investment (Botelho 1987: 44). While there are no comparable data for national firms, their retention of profits and dividends was almost certainly higher.
44. One dimension which could not be pursued in this paper was a comparison with countries such as Argentina, Mexico, India, or South Korea. Lack of space did not permit this. However, brief mention should be made of a recent comparison between Brazil and South Korea, the most advanced Third World computer producer. Evans and Tigre (1989*a*, 1989*b*) show that, overall, Brazil had a larger computer industry than South Korea in 1986 and, more significantly, that Brazil has progressed further in designing and producing 'non-commodity' computers which can be exported to specialized markets. On the other hand, they show that South Korea is more competitive in the production of 'commodity computers' (PC clones).
45. If this optimism needs dampening, it is not because of the performance of the computer industry or related government agencies. On the eve of the 1990s, the greatest danger comes from the general crisis of the Brazilian economy which has its roots in both internal policy failures but also in failures of international capital markets.

References

Ayres, R. V. and Guanães, V. (1985), 'Automation and Competitiveness of Multi-nationals in Brazil', Paper prepared for UNDP/ILO Project Bra/82/024, Brasília, (June).

Balassa, B. (1975), 'Reforming the System of Incentives in Developing Countries', *World Development*, 3/6: 365–82.

—— (1981), 'The Process of Industrial Development and Alternative Development Strategies', in id., *The Newly Industrializing Countries in the World Economy*, Pergamon Press, Oxford.

—— and Associates (1982), *Development Strategies in Semi-Industrial Economies*, Johns Hopkins University Press, Baltimore, Md. (for the World Bank).

Bastos, M. J. (1989), 'State Policies and Private Interests: The Struggle over Information Technology Policy in Brazil', mimeo, Brasília.

Bell, M. (1982), 'Technical Change in Infant Industries: A Review of the Empirical Evidence', mimeo, Science Policy Research Unit, Brighton.

—— Ross-Larson, B., and Westphal, L. E. (1984), 'Assessing the Performance of Infant Industries', World Bank Staff Working Paper no. 666, Washington, DC.

Bessant, J., and Haywood, B. (1986), 'The Introduction of Flexible Manufacturing Systems as an Example of Computer Integrated Manufacturing', *Operations Management Review*, Spring (Part 1), Summer (Part 2), Autumn (Part 3).

Botelho, A. J. J. (1987), 'Brazil's Independent Computer Strategy', in *Technology Review*, 90/4 (May–June): 37–45.

Campos, R. (1985), *Além do Cotidiano*, Record, São Paulo.

Cassiolato, J. E. (1989), 'Some Notes on the Need for High Tech Policies in Latin America with Special Reference to Brazil', mimeo, University of Sussex.

Corsepius, U., and Schipke, A. (1989), 'Die Computerindustrie in Schwellenländern—der Fall Brasilien', *Die Weltwirtschaft*, Institut für Weltwirtschaft, Kiel University, no. 1.

Erber, F. S. (1985), 'The Development of the "Electronics Complex" and Government Policies in Brazil', *World Development*, 13/3: 293–309.

Evans, P. (1985), 'Varieties of Nationalism: The Politics of the Brazilian Computer Industry', Paper presented at the MIT Symposium on 'The Computer Question in Brazil', Cambridge, Mass., Apr.

—— (1986), 'State, Capital and the Transformation of Dependence: The Brazilian Computer Case', in *World Development*, 14/7: 791–808.

——and Tigre, P. B. (1989a), 'Going beyond Clones in Brazil and Korea: A Comparative Analysis of NIC Strategies in the Computer Industry', *World Development*, 17/11: 1751–68.

—— —— (1989b), 'Paths to Participation in "Hi-Tech" Industry: A Comparative Analysis of Computers in Brazil and Korea', *Asian Perspective*, 13/1: 5–35.

Fioravanti, C. (1989), 'Os donos da reserva', *Istoé Senhor* (10 May).

Fleury, A. (1987), 'An Institutional Analysis of Policy-making in Brazil: The Case of Microelectronics', Paper prepared for the United Nations University, New Technologies Centre Feasibility Study, mimeo, University of São Paulo, Feb.

Frischtak, C. (1986) 'The Informatics Sector in Brazil: Policies, Institutions and the

Performance of the Computer Industry', mimeo, Industrial Strategy and Policy Division, World Bank (Mar.).

Helena, S. (1984), *Rastro de Cobra*, Editora Prensa, Rio de Janeiro.

Hewitt, T. (1988), 'Employment and Skills in the Electronics Industry: The Case of Brazil', D.Phil Thesis, University of Sussex.

Hoffman, K. (1985), 'Microelectronics, International Competition and Development Strategies: The Unavoidable Issues—Editor's Introduction', *World Development*, 13/3: 263–72.

—— (1988), 'Technological Advance and Organizational Innovation in the Engineering Industry: A New Perspective on the Problems and Possibilities for Developing Countries', Report submitted to the World Bank, Sussex Research Associates, Brighton.

Kaplinsky, R. (1988), 'Industrial Restructuring in LDCs: The Role of Information Technology', Paper prepared for Conference on Technology Policy in the Americas, Stanford University (Dec.).

Krueger, A. O. (1981), 'Export-led Industrial Growth Reconsidered', in W. Hong and L. B. Krause (eds.), *Trade and Growth of the Advanced Developed Countries in the Pacific Basin*, Korea Development Institute, Seoul.

Lall, S. (1982), 'Technological Learning in the Third World: Some Implications of Technology Exports', in F. Stewart and J. James (eds.), *The Economics of New Technology in Developing Countries*, Frances Pinter, London.

Little, I., Scitovsky, T., and Scott, M. F. G. (1970), *Industry and Trade in Some Developing Countries: A Comparative Analysis*, Oxford University Press, Oxford, London, New York.

Luedde-Neurath, R. (1986), *Import Controls and Export Oriented Development: A Reassessment of the South Korean Case*, Westview Press, Boulder, Colo., and London.

Meyer-Stamer, J. (1988), *Informatik in Brasilien*, Institut für Iberoamerika-Kunde, Hamburg.

Moad, J. (1988), 'The Plight of the Brazilian User', Special Report, *Datamation* (1 Nov.).

Pérez, C. (1985), 'Hacia una estrategia de desarollo integral del sector electrónico en Venezuela', Proyecto CONDIBIECA – ONUDI VEN 80/003, July, mimeo.

Piragibe, C. (1984), 'Competitividade dos equipamentos periféricos fabricados no Brasil: impressoras', Texto para Discussão no. 61, Instituto de Economia Industrial, Universidade Federal do Rio de Janeiro (Dec.).

—— (1985), *Indústria de Informática: Desenvolvimento Brasileiro e Mundial*, Editora Campus, Rio de Janeiro.

—— (1987), 'Policies towards the Electronics Complex in Brazil', Textos em política científica e tecnológica no. 28, CNPq, Brasília.

—— (1988), 'Políticas para a indústria electrônica nos novos países industrializados: lições para o Brasil?', in H. Schmitz and R. Quadros Carvalho 1988.

—— Penna, M. V., and Tigre, P. B. (1983), *Recursos humanos na indústria brasileira de equipamentos de processamento de dados*, Research Report, Instituto de Economia Industrial, UFRJ, Rio de Janeiro.

Sayer, A. and Morgan, K. (1987), 'High Technology Industry and the International Division of Labour: The Case of Electronics', in M. J. Breheny and R. McQuaid (eds.), *The Development of High Technology Industries: An International Survey*, Croom Helm, London.

Schmitz, H. (1984), 'Industrialisation Strategies in Less Developed Countries: Some Lessons of Historical Experience', *Journal of Development Studies*, 21/1: 1–21.

—— and Quadros Carvalho, R. (eds.) (1988), *Automação, competitividade e trabalho: a experiência internacional*, Editora Hucitec, São Paulo.

SEI (1986), *Panorama da indústria nacional: computadores e periféricos*, mimeo, Secretaria Especial de Informática, Boletim Informativo, Brasília.

—— (1989), *Panorama do setor de informática*, Secretaria Especial de Informática, Séries Estatísticas, 2/1, Brasília.

Silva, E. B. (1988), *Labour and Technology in the Car Industry: Ford Strategies in Britain and Brazil*, Ph.D. Thesis, University of London.

Tapia, J. G. B. (1984), 'A política nacional de informática: 1970–1984', Núcleo de política científica e tecnológica, University of Campinas (UNICAMP), mimeo (Nov.).

Tigre, P. B. (1983), *Technology and Competition in the Brazilian Computer Industry*, Frances Pinter, London.

—— (1985), 'Estrutura de custos e formação de preços na indústria brasileira de computadores', Estudo preparado para a Secretaria Especial de Informática, Instituto de Economia Industrial, Federal University of Rio de Janeiro.

—— (1986), 'Perspectivas da indústria brasileira de computadores na Segunda Metade dos Anos 80', mimeo, Instituto de Economia Industrial, Federal University of Rio de Janeiro (IEI/UFRJ).

—— (1988), 'How Does Latin America Fit High Technology?', Paper prepared for the International Symposium: Technology Policy in the Americas, Stanford (1–3 Dec.).

—— and Perine, L. (1984), 'Competitividade dos microcomputadores nacionais', Texto para discussão no. 60, Instituto de Economia Industrial, Federal University of Rio de Janeiro (Nov.).

White, G. (ed.) (1988), *Developmental States in East Asia*, Macmillan, London.

9
Who Should Learn to Pay? An Assessment of Neo-liberal Approaches to Education Policy

CHRISTOPHER COLCLOUGH

Public provision of education has traditionally been judged necessary to the promotion—or protection—of a number of commonly held equity and efficiency objectives. The following arguments typically underpin the case: first, the benefits of education accrue not only to its direct recipients, but also to society at large; the presence of such 'externalities' encourage smaller expenditures on education, in the absence of state provision, than would be desirable. Second, the private purchase of schooling, and especially of higher education, would be beyond the means of many poor families, even where their children were able and diligent enough to gain access. Substantial equity and efficiency costs would follow—especially so in poorer countries and in those with highly unequal distributions of personal income. Efficient credit markets do not provide an effective solution, owing to the existence of strong imperfections outside such markets which reduce participation, particularly by very poor people, in them. Third, since education helps to determine future individual incomes, market allocation would strengthen existing inequalities, by giving privileged access and higher future incomes to the richer groups. For these and other reasons, there has seemed to be a strong case for educational provision remaining an important arena for state action. Market allocation seems to conflict with some important social goals, and would probably result in the level of educational investment remaining suboptimal.

A recently influential group of writers deny this case. They charge that public provision of education is itself largely responsible for existing inequities and inefficiencies associated with schooling in developing countries. Much of the research on which these conclusions are based has been sponsored by the World Bank. By this route, its results have formed part of the agenda for

The author wishes to acknowledge helpful comments on an earlier draft from David Evans, Martin Godfrey, Charles Harvey, Raphie Kaplinsky, Colin Lacey, Keith Lewin, James Manor, and Peter Ngomba.

policy reforms which northern governments and institutions have encouraged their aid recipients to adopt.[1] This body of work can properly be described 'neo-liberal', for two main reasons. First, its authors advocate a substantially greater role for the price system in allocating educational services than have most earlier writers. Second, they advocate a much reduced role for the state as provider and organizer of educational services. These writings—hereafter collectively referred to as 'Edlib'—thus provide an illustration of the more general neo-liberal case, as applied to education. Strong parallels with the neo-liberal analysis of health and other economic sectors will be noticeable.[2]

This paper examines the Edlib case. It argues that the aims of its proposed reforms are laudable: most analysts share with it the objectives of achieving a more productive and equitable allocation of public resources in the education sector, together with the generation of additional resources for educational investment. It will be shown, however, that the instruments proposed by Edlib to achieve those ends are more problematic. In particular, the central section of the paper will show that recent changes to the economic circumstances of Sub-Saharan African states invalidate some of the assumptions made by Edlib and, in turn, undermine the viability of reform strategies based upon introducing user fees at secondary and tertiary levels. It will be argued that alternative strategies should be sought.

1. Diagnosis and Strategy

There are two major sets of problems which Edlib attempts to address. The first is quantitative: at present education systems throughout the Third World are underexpanded in the senses that large numbers of people are still precluded from access even to primary schooling and that, even where not, returns to further investment in schooling seem to remain strong. Nevertheless, governments—particularly those in SSA—are hard pressed to maintain expansion at rates equal to the growth of population. Thus, relative decline in enrolments is frequent and absolute decline is not unknown. Under existing circumstances, where budgetary revenues are not increasing, and further savings are often sought, resources for expansion seem not to be available from existing government sources.

The second set of problems is more qualitative. Present expenditure patterns are frequently characterized by misallocation in both efficiency and equity terms: primary schooling is the only part of the system which reaches the mass of the people, and appears to be highly beneficial for the poor in terms of private and social benfits. Yet in per capita terms tiny amounts are spent upon the primary system—particularly as compared with tertiary education which caters for only a small and highly privileged fraction of the population. This is because the beneficiaries of higher education are mainly children from upper-income families who themselves will receive further high returns from the educational subsidies diverted toward them by the state.

These circumstances are well known, and there is a large literature which documents them. There is agreement about the need to seek reforms which reduce unit costs, which generate additional resources for education, and which promote greater equity in the access to and use of educational resources. There remains somewhat less agreement about the best ways of achieving these ends.

The strategy proposed by Edlib comprises four important elements.

1. User charges should be introduced at tertiary and, sometimes, at secondary levels (Jimenez 1987: 65–76; Mingat and Tan 1986*b*; World Bank 1986: 17 ff.). These should cover all the living expenses of students where board and lodging is provided and some, or all, of the tuition costs. The costs of these items would thereby be passed from the state to parents, not all of whom have the ability to pay. Thus, scholarships would be needed to provide for bright children of poor parents. This would, it is argued, increase equity, since the minority of families who use tertiary/senior secondary facilities will, where they are rich enough, pay for these services—thereby avoiding subsidies from those who do not use them, many of whom are less well off. Efficiency, also, would be promoted by this reform because, the authors claim, the children of paying parents tend to be more diligent about their studies and more vigilant about the costs of their institutions.

2. Student loans should be introduced at tertiary level for all students (Jimenez 1987: 98–100; Mingat, Tan, and Hoque 1984; World Bank 1986: 24 ff.). This is viewed as additional to, rather than competitive with user charges. Such schemes would be associated with increased equity and efficiency gains mainly because costs would then be met by the direct rather than indirect beneficiaries of tertiary education—the students rather than their parents. Three particular benefits are expected: first, students would be even more diligent and vigilant; second, the future income of students rather than the present income of their parents would finance current educational expenditures, thereby generating dynamic rather than merely static benefits for income distribution.[3] Finally, demand for tertiary study would be a closer reflection of its opportunity costs, and excess demand (relative to 'need' or absorptive capacity of the economy, or some other, similar, idea) would be reduced and eventually eliminated as a result of the equilibration of perceived private costs and benefits at interest rates roughly equal to the social opportunity cost of investible resources.

3. The private provision of schooling at all levels should be encouraged (Jimenez 1987: 102–5; World Bank 1986: 33–7). This view is advanced mainly on efficiency and resource generation grounds. On the one hand this appears to reflect part of the debate about whether private schools are more efficient than public schools. If so, they therefore involve smaller costs per pupil unit. On the other hand they provide additional resources for education

by taking pupils out of the public system, and by generating local resources for education which would not otherwise be made available. Equity problems are viewed to be containable by the use of state grants to equalize the quality of educational provision among different schools (World Bank 1986: 33). Increased competition between private and public schools is judged to be an additional means of achieving greater efficiency.

4. Finally, the savings generated by the above measures should be used to expand and improve the quality of those parts of education which are most socially profitable. This, says Edlib, would usually be primary and junior secondary schooling (Mingat and Tan 1985; Wolff 1984: 27–33; World Bank 1986: 2).

In assessing this programme for reform of educational financing one must ask two important questions. First, is it the case that the package will promote lower educational unit costs, more resources for education, and greater equity of resource use than is typically so with most current structures of educational provision? Second, are there other reforms which are excluded from this package which hold promise of supplementing or even of more efficiently replacing the proposed reforms? These questions reduce to the more general issue of whether Edlib writers are focusing upon the right variables and seeking to influence them in the right directions. These questions will be considered in turn.

2. Cost Reduction

The case that too much public money is spent upon higher education relative to lower levels in developing countries is difficult to deny. Table 9.1 indicates the astonishingly high per pupil expenditures—particularly in Africa—on tertiary provision relative to output per capita, to expenditures on primary and secondary schooling, and to the proportions of the population enrolled at each level. Evidence from some Latin American and Asian countries, furthermore, indicates that the bulk of subsidies at the higher levels of education are received by the higher income families (World Bank 1986: Appendix table 13).

In such circumstances, two broad strategy alternatives are available to try to change this distribution: ways of reducing educational costs could be sought, so that more resources are available for use by the majority, and/or the minority could be required to pay (more) for the resources which they use. Assuming, then, that the main constraint is finance—rather than the physical supplies of teachers, materials, or buildings—either of these reforms could have favourable implications for the availability of resources in primary and secondary schools.

A substantial body of research exists upon the determinants of educational costs (much of it usefully reviewed in Psacharopoulos and Woodhall 1985).

TABLE 9.1. *Public expenditure per student on education and enrolment ratios, major world regions, around 1980*

Region	Public expenditure per student as percentage of per capita GNP			Enrolment ratio (%)			Number of countries reporting
	Primary	Secondary	Higher	Primary	Secondary	Higher	
Anglophone Africa	18	50	920	77	17	1.2	16
Francophone Africa	29	143	804	46	14	2.4	18
South Asia	8	18	119	71	19	4.4	4
East Asia and Pacific	11	20	118	87	43	9.1	6
Latin America	9	26	88	90	44	12.0	19
Middle East and North Africa	2	28	150	82	36	9.4	11
Developing countries	14	41	370	75	23	6.9	74
Developed countries	22	24	49	100	80	21.0	20

Source: World Bank 1986, table 9.

Although many variables are important, those which universally have a dominant impact upon unit recurrent costs are the levels of staff salaries and the staff–student ratio. This is particularly so where materials and maintenance costs have shrunk to an irreducibly small proportion of recurrent budgets—as has happened in much of Africa in recent years. Attempts to reduce costs, therefore, have focused upon salary reform, school size and location, class size, shift teaching, and the introduction of new technologies, all of which have some impact upon these two fundamental variables. Boarding costs are separate and important elements which have received increasing attention in recent years.

Edlib writers have chosen not to focus upon these lines of enquiry. This is in spite of the facts that cost reduction is at the heart of their avowed concern, and, more fundamentally, that important changes have recently been occurring in one of the two central determinants of educational costs: i.e. the absolute and relative levels of earnings of education sector personnel. As shown later in this chapter, this omission raises some fundamental questions about the main policy implications which are derived.

Edlib reforms would, therefore, only affect costs indirectly. For example, the introduction of user charges, which is the centre-piece of such reforms, would have no direct impact upon educational costs. Rather, such charges would shift their incidence from one group to another: in this case, from government (or, indirectly, from the whole tax-paying population) to those who (or whose children) use the service in question. Nevertheless, Edlib argues that the increased exposure of the school system to market forces *will* act to reduce costs. This is on three main grounds: first, consumers would increase pressures upon managers to reduce operating costs, and cause them to seek out the more efficient (or cheaper, which is not necessarily the same thing) institutions; second, students would work harder, because the costs to them of failure would be commensurately greater; thus, the costs per successful student would fall (World Bank 1986: 23). It should be noticed that the case for both of these assertions is mainly a priori. Yet their truth is by no means self-evident. The first implies that the consumers (students or parents) are the best judges of efficiency—even though cheapest, in education, is unlikely to be best. The second does not follow: students might not work harder, since ability and motivation are not necessarily correlated with ability to pay. Indeed if examination standards remained unchanged the changing characteristics of the student population encouraged by the introduction of user charges might actually cause the cost per successful student to rise. The opposite conclusion would only hold if the composition of the student population were completely unchanged by the introduction of user charges. In the light of the sharp changes in relative prices implied by such a reform, this condition cannot be assumed.

The third major way in which Edlib believes these reforms capable of reducing costs derives from its proposals concerning the role of private schools. It is argued that the removal of restrictions on the private sector will increase both the quantity and quality of educational provision, thereby mobilizing resources which otherwise would not be available, and liberating some public resources for use by other children. The improvement of quality is thought to arise not merely from the increased resources made available by those who wish to pay for the education of their children, but also from the efficiency gains arising from exposing the schools to competitive pressures. Although supporting research results are not usually cited, it seems that this position is informed by the public/private schools debate initiated by Coleman's work in the USA (Coleman 1982), concerning which the associated literature is now substantial. However, whatever view of this debate one takes, the relevant evidence on the 'efficiency' of private schooling in developing countries is much more limited.[4] Owing to the very different role of private schooling in rich and poor countries (in the latter group, private schools are much more usually 'second chance' institutions for those who have failed to get a place in public institutions than is the case in industrialized countries) it would probably be invalid to anchor policy conclusions for poor countries upon the results of rich-country-based research.

The proposals for policy change made by Edlib represent, then, a cost-shifting rather than a cost-reducing strategy. Claims to the contrary represent as yet no more than statements of faith. Although the case for expecting some limited cost-reduction is plausible, there is as yet little evidence which demonstrates that this would be so—even in the rather different circumstances of developed market economies.

3. Resource Generation

The main rationale for each of the reforms proposed by Edlib is to generate additional resources for educational investment: user charges, with or without scholarships, loans schemes at tertiary level, and the encouragement of private schools and colleges, are all ways of inducing the better-off members of the population to pay more for the educational services which their children receive.

These proposals obviously make some fairly strong assumptions about society's behavioural response to the increase in the price of education. Specifically, it is assumed that people will choose to pay in sufficient numbers to meet the nation's goals (however defined) and that the changes in the composition of the student population brought about by the change in price would be either positive, or neutral, from the standpoints of equity and quality.

The judgement that people will be prepared to pay, particularly for higher education, is based upon the results of rate of return studies to education from around the world, which have been collated by Psacharopoulos. He has summarized their findings several times over the past fifteen years (Psacharopoulos 1973, 1981, 1985), and has been an energetic proselytizer of their implications. The recent World Bank policy paper on educational financing accords these results central importance. An early table shows that the private rate of return to higher education is 32 per cent in Africa, based upon sixteen 'countries reporting', 18 per cent in Asia, and 23 per cent in Latin America, based upon ten countries each (World Bank 1986, table 3). This becomes the core of the report's rationale for reducing student allowances, and charging for services in higher education. Such charges are deemed justifiable because:

Evidence indicates that people are willing to pay for education. In Africa, private returns to higher education are so high that even after student allowances are reduced or fees imposed, higher education will remain an attractive personal investment. (World Bank 1986: 17)

This rate of return evidence is, however, not substantial enough to support such a strong conclusion, for a number of reasons: first, the evidence includes a startlingly small amount of data which reflect recent or contemporary events. Of the thirty-six countries from Africa, Asia, and Latin America furnishing rate of return evidence, twenty-five included calculations of private rates of return. However, the great majority of these studies refer to the 1960s and 1970s. Assertions about the differences between private and social rates of return in the different continents appear to be based upon only four African country cases using data for 1980 or more recent years, none for Asia and only one (Venezuela 1984) for Latin America. In the African case, the 1980s data comprised Botswana (1983), Lesotho (1980), Malawi (1982), and Somalia (1983). This country sample is hardly typical of Sub-Saharan Africa as a whole, and accounts for less than 4 per cent of the region's population. Moreover, given that the substance of rate of return calculations rests entirely upon differences in relative prices, for such important policy conclusions to be based upon historic information seems, at the least, unwise. Conclusions which presuppose that relative prices have remained unchanged over the past decade are a fragile foundation on which to base changes to current policy. In other economic sectors similarly based economic advice, affecting strategically important variables, would not be taken seriously.

   The datedness of these results would not matter, of course, if rates of return to different levels of education had, in fact, remained stable over time. Although such stability is often asserted, evidence is presented in what follows which suggests that the 1980s have witnessed sharp changes in these values, and particularly so in Sub-Saharan African countries.

   In Table 9.2 the movement of real non-agricultural average wages over the 1970s and 1980s are shown for those developing countries where comparable data are available. It can be seen that between 1971 and 1985/6 there was sharply different performance between different regions. In Asia, real wages rose in the countries shown. This result was particularly influenced by the newly industrializing countries and by China after 1979/80. In Latin America, wages generally fell—although with differences between individual countries: Brazil, Argentina, and Colombia registered significant gains in real wages over the period 1971–84, compared with sharp falls elsewhere. In Sub-Saharan Africa, however, the situation was completely different. Wages fell in almost every country for which data are available, and in some cases (Ghana, Tanzania, Sierra Leone) dramatically so. In the countries shown, real wages fell by a fifth over the 1970s and by a further third between 1979 and 1984. By consequence, wages in Sub-Saharan Africa were typically halved between 1970 and 1985.

What, then, do these circumstances imply for rates of return to education over the period? It should be recalled that private and social returns are proxied on the benefit side by the future net earnings stream associated with a particular level of schooling, net and gross of tax, respectively. Costs, in each case, are taken to comprise net and gross incomes foregone during schooling together with the direct costs incurred in undertaking or providing it. The rate of return is simply the discount rate which equates the stream of costs with the expected benefits in each case.[5] It is clear, then, that the real wage decline in SSA shown in table 9.2 will have resulted in a fall in both the costs and benefits of schooling, measured as indicated above. However, since earnings comprise the entire benefit side, but less than the entire cost side, *ceteris paribus*, benefits will have been reduced more sharply than costs. This implies that rates of return to education will have fallen through the entire range.

Before accepting the validity of this general conclusion, however, two further qualifications must be made. First, the effects of the real wage decline upon rates of return to schooling have been exacerbated by rising levels of unemployment in SSA over the past decade. Open unemployment has particularly affected those countries with the heaviest adjustment burdens —which, in turn, have often been those states having the greatest falls in the real average wage.[6] Thus, the reduction in rates of return arising from real wage decline will have been exacerbated by the reduced probability of school leavers being able to find employment in the formal sector.

Secondly, the changes in direct costs (materials, maintenance, depreciation of buildings and equipment, board, lodging as well as teachers' salaries) will have affected particularly the social rates of return. Because education is generally financed by the state, and because fees charged are seldom a significant part of private costs, private rates of return are influenced on the cost-side much more heavily by opportunity costs (forgone earnings) than by fees, school uniforms, books, and boarding expenses. Thus, although private and social returns will both have fallen as a result of the real wage trends shown in table 9.2, net changes to private rates from this source will

TABLE 9.2. *Average annual growth rates of real non-agricultural wages in developing countries, 1971–1986*

	Period (1970s)	Average annual growth %	Period (1980s)	Average annual growth %
Sub-Saharan Africa				
Burundi	1973–9	−2.4	1979–86	+2.3
Ghana	1971–9	−13.4	1979–83	−18.6
Kenya	1972–9	−1.9	1979–86	−3.3
Malawi	1971–9	−1.9	1979–85	−7.5
Mauritius	1971–9	+5.3	1979–86	−3.6
Sierra Leone	1971–9	−5.3	1979–86	−14.3
Tanzania	1971–9	−3.4	1979–83	−17.3
Zambia	1972–9	−4.7	1979–84	−4.6
Zimbabwe	1971–9	+1.5	1979–84	+0.2
MEAN[a]		(−2.9)		(−7.4)
Asia				
Bangladesh	1976–9	−2.5	1979–84	−0.5
Burma	1971–9	−7.8	1979–83	+1.1
China	1971–9	+2.7	1979–86	+4.4
Fiji	1971–9	+4.8	1979–84	−1.8
Rep. of Korea	1971–9	+10.6	1979–86	+4.1
Singapore	1971–9	+2.2	1979–85	+6.1
Thailand	1971–9	−8.4	1979–84	−2.9
MEAN[a]		(+0.2)		(+1.5)
Latin America				
Argentina	1971–9	−2.7	1979–84	+7.9
Brazil	1971–9	+4.2	1979–84	+1.5
Bolivia	1971–9	−0.5	1979–84	−10.4
Colombia	1971–9	0.0	1979–84	+4.0
Costa Rica	1973–9	+3.8	1979–85	−1.2
Ecuador	1971–9	+4.2	1979–83	−0.9
Guatemala	1971–9	−5.5	1979–83	+9.1
Mexico	1972–9	+1.5	1979–84	−5.0
Paraguay	1971–9	−2.0	1979–84	−0.9
Peru	1971–9	−3.7	1979–86	+0.8
Uruguay	1971–9	−8.0	1979–84	−5.0
Venezuela	1971–9	+2.3	1979–86	−3.3
MEAN[a]		(−0.5)		(−0.3)

[a] Simple unweighted arithmetic averages of the average annual growth rates for the countries in each region.

Sources: Data for 1970s from ILO 1987*a*, table 5.1, p. 99. Data for 1980s mainly calculated from ILO 1987*b*, tables 16 and 23. Otherwise, from ILO 1987*a*.

be influenced primarily by the extent to which direct private costs feature in their calculation. In many countries of SSA where school fees are not charged, such effects will often have been small.

Of great significance, therefore, for the judgement as to what has been happening to private rates of return to education in recent years, is the question as to what has happened to the earnings structure, and in particular to income differentials between workers at different levels of education and training. Here, evidence is more difficult to assemble because few countries collect data on average wages by education. Nevertheless, table 9.3 utilizes data on starting salaries for leavers from different levels of the school/ university system for a number of countries in Sub-Saharan Africa derived from a range of different sources. Taking changes in starting salaries as an efficient proxy for movements in salary scales, the table shows that salary differentials by education in African public service have declined consistently since independence. In several countries that between graduates and secondary leavers was reduced by more than half between 1970 and 1985 (Botswana, Ghana, Tanzania) and the average reduction for the eight countries shown was 42 per cent. During the 1980s—a period which, as we have seen, has been characterized by dramatic downward realignment of the level of real wages—the reduction of differentials in earnings between highly and less educated workers has been particularly sharp. The table shows that differentials were reduced by a third after 1975, and a quarter after 1980, which indicates some acceleration in the rate of decline. Unless private direct costs

TABLE 9.3. *Indices of differentials in starting salaries for university graduates compared with secondary school leavers in African public service, 1970–1988 (or latest year)*[a]

	1970	1975	1980	1985–8	Reductions (%)		
					1970–88	1975–88	1980–88
Botswana	4.08	3.52	3.68	1.92	53	46	48
Gambia	4.45	3.28	3.25	3.15	30	4	3
Ghana	3.49	2.67	1.69	n/a	52	37	n/a
Kenya	4.38	3.88	3.62	3.38	23	13	7
Malawi	2.35	2.35	n/a	1.37	42	42	n/a
Sierra Leone	4.65	4.33	4.00	3.11	34	29	23
Tanzania	4.25	n/a	3.23	1.69	60	48[b]	48
Zambia	2.14	2.14	1.69	1.32	39	39	22
AVERAGE					42	32	25

[a] Graduate starting salaries expressed as a ratio to those of secondary leavers.
[b] 1980 used in absence of data for 1975. The estimate is thus a minimum.

Sources: Salaries Commissions, Recurrent Estimates, Establishment Registers and Circulars for each of the countries and years shown. Sources, notes, and data from which the calculations were made are shown in Colclough 1989.

have been more than proportionately reduced, it follows from the method of calculation that these reductions are minimum estimates for the consequent impact upon private rates of return to higher secondary and tertiary education over the same period. The private rate of return to higher education in Africa, which was reported by Psacharopoulos (1985) to be 32 per cent, was the simple average of the rates of return calculated for ten countries, half of which utilized earnings data collected prior to 1975. Thus, provided that the countries in our own sample are representative of what has happened elsewhere, our results suggest that the rate of return would, by 1985, have fallen by about a third below that reported by Psacharopoulos—i.e. to around 20 per cent. This result confirms that conclusions which are derived from the price levels and economic circumstances holding during the 1970s are an inappropriate basis for design of current economic and financial policy in Africa.

The importance of this verdict is given by the need to predict how African students and their families would react to the introduction of user changes in the ways advocated by Edlib. Existing estimates of price and income elasticities of demand for schooling are not helpful for the purpose of answering this question in current African circumstances. Evidence from nine countries, three of which are from SSA, indicates short-run price and income inelasticity for small changes in each of these variables (Jimenez 1987: table 7-2). But the important issue is how demand will change, not with respect to marginal changes in income, but to substantial reductions in real household incomes (as has happened) and to sharp increases in the price of schooling (as proposed by Edlib).

The above estimates lead us to conclude that substantial increases in the private costs of education arising from the introduction of user fees would now reduce the private rate of return at tertiary levels towards 10 per cent in many countries.[7] At these levels it becomes rational for households to consider alternative, more profitable, uses of private funds and student time. Although its total effects cannot at present be quantified, it is certain that, under these circumstances a large number of individuals would change their minds about the wisdom of embarking upon tertiary studies. We should expect such reassessments to be particularly concentrated amongst those in the lower income groups.

4. Equity

The above analysis implies that even if gross enrolments in tertiary education were unaffected by user charges (i.e. if the impact of recent income changes plus proposed cost increases were to reduce 'excess' rather than 'effective' demand) the composition of the student body would change in ways which reflected ability to pay rather than ability to learn. This would have major implications for any country, but particularly so for many in Africa, where skill shortages—especially in technical and science-based disciplines—remain acute. The question arises, therefore, whether student aid schemes could be designed so as to mitigate the equity and efficiency costs of user charges and increased private sector provision, whilst preserving some of their intended benefits.

The case for increased private funding advanced by Edlib includes the argument that it will be promotive of greater equity by making the rich households pay more for the education they receive. This is premissed, at minimum, on the introduction of scholarships for the bright poor. Evidence from Europe, where this system used to hold, however, suggests that scholarship schemes are inefficient: not all the bright poor are captured, either on 'intelligence' or 'inability to pay' criteria. Second, unless scholarship support were provided on a sliding scale basis (the inverse of taxation where, in this case, most would receive some subsidy) private provision and/or user charges would be regressive at all income levels above the maximum income qualifying for scholarship support. Furthermore, the non-bright poor would be doubly disadvantaged in comparison with the non-bright rich, since the latter groups would continue to have access to schooling under a private system with consequent remedial implications which would be denied those with equal or better abilities who happened to be from poorer households. Finally, any shift to private funding must heighten differentiation within educational levels. Since resource inputs appear to affect cognitive outcomes (Heyneman 1983), both promotion within the system and life-chances thereafter would be a positive function of household income for children of equal ability. It is difficult to advance the case that such a system would be promotive of greater equity, however defined.

At tertiary level, some of these difficulties are countered by Edlib in the advocacy of a student loan scheme, covering both living and tuition costs. The evidence on these from both developing and developed countries is mixed (Jallade 1973, 1974; Woodhall 1983, 1987). Without embarking here upon a full discussion of student loans (such can be found, together with the case for an alternative approach in Colclough 1990) three sets of points are important in the present context. First, there are positive equity benefits to be expected in comparison with fees/scholarships in that ability to meet educational costs is no longer a function of household income. Intergenerational equity is also improved in that the burden shifts from parents to children, the direct beneficiaries of the investment. Nevertheless, the costs of taking out a loan—and therefore its perceived risks—are positive. The poor, being more risk averse, and with higher opportunity costs of participation than the rich, use them least. Even here then, there are equity costs.

Secondly, it is important to notice that loans do not solve a public financing problem in the short run. For example, if loans were typically taken out to cover four years of study, with a twenty-year pay-back period, the government would not recover even 50 per cent of the initial generation of student loans until fourteen years after the start of the scheme. This calculation ignores any continued subsidy elements in higher education provision, default rates, unemployment of loan recipients, non-participation in the labour market owing to family responsibilities, and the costs of collection of loan repayments. This list may often amount to a substantial proportion of potential revenue. Clearly then, loan schemes can provide no solution to the *current* funding problems of higher education, or of the sector more generally.

Finally, it should be noted that although student loans schemes might (slowly) increase resources available for education—in that pay-back is from future rather than present income—this is only so if repayments were treated as additional to the government budget. If, on the other hand, loan repayments were treated as a source of general revenue, they would simply affect who pays for education, rather than the absolute magnitude of resources available. Under these circumstances, student loans become merely a way of reducing the private rate of return to tertiary education rather than a separate and additional source of educational finance.

5. Conclusion

Some aspects of the Edlib critique of existing modes of financing education in developing countries are strong: at present, schooling is too costly to expand coverage to all who need it, resources are inefficiently used and benefits are disproportionately captured by the richer groups in society. However, the reforms advocated by Edlib writers do not seem to provide adequate solutions. We have seen that user charges, student loans, and the encouragement of private schooling primarily represent a cost-shifting rather than a cost-reducing strategy. Additional resources for education could be raised by those means assuming no countervailing reductions in existing public expenditures on education. Nevertheless, we have shown that during the 1980s there have been sharp changes to salary levels and structures which, particularly in Sub-Saharan Africa, will have reduced private rates of return to levels well below those assumed by Edlib. Under these circumstances user fees would sharply reduce demand for higher education. Although this need not always threaten the resource generating objectives of the reform, the composition of the student body would, by consequence, shift even more towards children of richer households with some associated decline in the average quality of those enrolled. User charges in higher education, then, are risky, inequitable, and bring associated efficiency costs as compared with current financing mechanisms. This paper has also argued—contrary to Edlib writers—that solutions are not easily provided by scholarships/loans schemes, since, to the extent that the equity and efficiency costs of user fees are mitigated by these means, so the resource generating aims of such charges are further undermined.

In many ways, a more efficient way of raising additional resources for education, in a manner which is mindful of equity consequences, would seem to be to increase rates of taxation in the context of a progressive tax structure. The desirability of increasing rates of personal income tax is not necessarily implied. This is merely one option amongst many—including the introduction of payroll taxes of various kinds (Colclough 1990). In this general case, however, the rich (parents and non-parents) would pay (more) for the bright progeny of the rich and poor. Distributive costs include the result, therefore, that the rich childless (and those with non-bright children) subsidize both poor and rich parents of bright children. But this may be justifiable in view of the fact that education delivers social as well as private benefits. Moreover, rates of return to education would still be reduced under this scheme, to the extent that higher personal tax rates or lower real earnings (depending upon which tax instruments were used) reduced some of the private financial benefits of education.

Finally, to an important extent the arguments of Edlib reflect a more general ideological position that the role of the state, in Africa and elsewhere, must be reduced, and that private provision is more effective and efficient. However, this paper has indicated important logical and empirical gaps in the application of these ideas to educational policy. The case certainly seems not yet strong enough to proceed in the directions indicated by Edlib without much better data on the actual rates of return to education (particularly in Africa) after the round of currency devaluations which have occurred since 1980, and without more effective mechanisms for avoiding the undesirable equity and efficiency consequences of greater reliance upon user charges and upon the private provision of education.

Notes

1. The results published in the academic press include Jimenez 1987, Mingat and Tan 1985, 1986*a*, 1986*b*, Psacharopoulos 1977. A major Bank policy paper on educational financing was an indirect product of this work (World Bank 1986). A more recent policy document on educational reform in SSA (World Bank 1988*a*) also draws heavily upon these research results, as do parts of the *World Development Report* 1988 (World Bank 1988*b*, particularly ch. 6).
2. See, particularly, Chapter 10 of this volume.
3. Of course, students would not be forced to take out a loan. Its availability, however, would reduce the distortions involved in having to depend upon intra-household transfers.
4. Some evidence is provided in Jimenez *et al.* 1988 and Psacharopoulos 1987*a*. However, that presented in the latter source for Colombia and Tanzania is not

entirely convincing: test score advantages associated with private schooling in these countries are small and not always significant and between two-thirds and three-quarters of the variance of test scores remains unexplained. See Carr-Hill 1987 for a critique.

5. An exposition of the standard methodology for calculating rates of return to education can be found in Psacharopoulos 1981.

6. These two phenomena are frequently closely linked by consequence of the types of stabilization policies introduced at IMF behest. These typically incorporate specific targets for rates of currency depreciation and reductions in government spending and in public sector employment. In the short run these policies tend to reduce both the level of the real wage and the level of employment in the formal sector. (For analysis of these issues see Colclough and Green 1988).

7. It can be shown that a private rate of return of 20% on a three-year undergraduate programme would be reduced to less than 10% if the annual study costs recouped via the introduction of user fees were the equivalent of two-thirds, or more, of the average graduate salary. These conditions are by no means implausible. In the case of Botswana, for example, the annual public costs of undergraduate programmes were, in 1986, equal to 70% of the average annual earnings of graduates in that year. (The relevant data are presented in Colclough 1990, table 1.)

References

Carr-Hill, R. (1987), 'Ideology and Inference: A Comment on the Assessment of Evidence on Private Versus Public Schools', *International Journal of Educational Development*, 7/2: 133–5.

Colclough, C. (1989), 'Wage Differentials and Labour Market Flexibility: Evidence from Africa', mimeo, IDS, Sussex.

—— (1990), 'Raising Additional Resources for Education in Developing Countries: Are Graduate Payroll Taxes Superior to Student Loans?', *International Journal of Educational Development*, 10/2–3: 169–80.

—— and Green, R. (eds.) (1988), *Stabilisation—For Growth or Decay?*, IDS *Bulletin*, 19/1.

Coleman, J. (1982), *High School Achievement: Public, Catholic and Private Schools*, Basic Books, New York.

Heyneman, Stephen P. (1983), 'Improving the Quality of Education', *Finance and Development* (Mar.): 18–21, Washington, DC.

International Labour Office (ILO) (1987a), *World Labour Report*, vol. iii, Oxford.

—— (1987b), *Yearbook of Labour Statistics, 1987*, Geneva.

Jallade, J. P. (1973), 'The Financing of Education: An Examination of Basic Issues', Staff Working Paper no. 157, World Bank, Washington, DC.

—— (1974), 'Student Loans in Developing Countries: An Evaluation of the Colombian Performance', Staff Working Paper no. 182, World Bank, Washington, DC.

Jimenez, E. (1987), *Pricing Policy in the Social Sectors: Cost Recovery for Education and Health in Developing Countries*, Johns Hopkins University Press for the World Bank, Baltimore, Md.

—— Lockheed, M. and Watanawaka, N. (1988), 'The Relative Efficiency of Private and Public Schools: The Case of Thailand', *World Bank Economic Review*, 2/2 (May): 139–64, Washington, DC.

Mingat, A., and Tan, J.-P. (1985), 'Subsidisation of Higher Education Versus Expansion of Primary Enrollments: What Can a Shift of Resources Achieve in Sub-Saharan Africa?', *International Journal of Educational Development*, 5/4: 259–68.

—— —— (1986*a*), 'Who Profits from the Public Funding of Education? A Comparison of World Regions', *Comparative Education Review*, 30/2: 260–70.

—— —— (1986*b*), 'Expanding Education through User Charges: What Can Be Achieved in Malawi and Other LDCs?', *Economics of Education Review*, 5/8: 273–86.

—— —— and Hoque, M. (1984), 'Recovery of Cost of Public Higher Education in LDCs: To what Extent are Loan Schemes an Efficient Instrument?', mimeo, World Bank Education and Training Department, Washington, DC.

Psacharopoulos, G. (1973), *Returns to Education: An International Comparison*, Elsevier, San Francisco.

—— (1977), 'The Perverse Effects of Public Subsidisation of Education', *Comparative Education Review*, 21/1: 69–90.

—— (1981), 'Returns to Education: An Updated International Comparison', *Comparative Education*, 17/3: 321–41.

—— (1985), 'Returns to Education: A Further International Up-date and Implications', *Journal of Human Resources*, 20/4 (Autumn), Madison, Wis., 583–604.

—— (1987*a*), 'Public Versus Private Schools in Developing Countries: Evidence from Colombia and Tanzania', *International Journal of Educational Development*, 7/1: 59–67.

—— (ed.) (1987*b*), *Economics of Education: Research and Studies*, Pergamon, Oxford.

—— and Woodhall, M. (1985), *Education for Development: An Analysis of Investment Choices*, Oxford University Press for the World Bank, Oxford.

Wolff, L. (1984), 'Controlling the Costs of Education in Eastern Africa: A Review of Data, Issues and Policies', World Bank Staff Working Paper no. 702, Washington, DC (mimeo).

Woodhall, M. (1983), 'Student Loans as a Means of Financing Higher Education: Lessons from International Experience', World Bank Staff Working Paper no. 500, Washington, DC.

—— (1987), 'Student Loans', in Psacharopoulos 1987*b*: 445–50.

World Bank (1986), *Financing Education in Developing Countries: An Exploration of Policy Options*, Washington, DC.

—— (1988*a*), *Education in Sub-Saharan Africa: Policies for Adjustment, Revitalisation and Expansion*, Washington, DC.

—— (1988*b*), *World Development Report 1988*, Washington, DC.

10
Managing Health Sector Development: Markets and Institutional Reform

GERALD H. BLOOM

1. Introduction

The World Bank has become the largest single source of international funding for the health sector in developing countries (World Bank 1986). A large number of population, health, and nutrition (PHN) projects have been established around the world. In many cases they provide a framework within which other donors define their support. The Bank has also taken a leadership role in analysing the health sector and providing policy guidelines. For example, a policy study was published on the health sector in 1987 (World Bank 1987). This document, which is heavily influenced by neo-liberal thought, is subtitled 'An Agenda for Reform'. It is to this ambitious claim that this paper will be addressed.

The discussion of policy-related issues is particularly difficult where an international funder is an important source of analysis. It is necessary to distinguish between practice in the field, general policy suggestions, and the theoretical model employed. No systematic evaluations of Bank-funded PHN projects are yet available. So it is not possible to assess their success in fostering appropriate development. On the other hand, many of the policy proposals are well founded and will play a part, in some form, in many countries. However, the argument put forward in this paper is that the neo-liberal model is not appropriate to the realities of health sector development. A false confidence in partial market solutions can mislead people into reaching quick decisions without taking the realities of a particular health sector into account. There is, in consequence, a risk that policies might be introduced without adequate regard for the available options or the possible conse-quences. The advocacy of the introduction of user charges for out-patient visits as a high priority in most countries could easily lead to this kind of error.

If the neo-liberal approach to the health sector has tended to be rather simplistic, so has the practice of management of health sector development. In many countries this has consisted largely of building facilities, training personnel, establishing pilot primary health care (PHC) projects, and strengthening preventive programmes. There is an increasing sense that more is needed in order to establish and sustain effective services. Attention is shifting away from implementation of investment programmes to the organization of the sector. It is in the context of this questioning of the adequacy of many (frequently donor-funded) PHC programmes that the neo-liberal analysis has found an audience. The concluding sections of the paper will consider some of the issues which must be addressed by those responsible for managing health sector development.

2. The Health Sector Ten Years after Alma Ata

In 1978 the World Health Organization (WHO) and UNICEF published the Alma Ata Declaration (WHO 1978). This document presented the broad outlines of a policy aimed at meeting the health needs of the people: that is, the primary health care approach. It recognized that in order to achieve significant improvements in health status there is a need for appropriate development in a number of sectors. In the health service, priority was to be given to the establishment of a capacity to organize preventive programmes and provide easy access to basic curative care for all. This general approach to health-related development has been widely accepted. Major publications by a number of international organizations have drawn similar conclusions.[1] Ten years later, in 1988, a majority of countries had officially accepted PHC as the basis of national health policy.[2] In many cases, however, the reality does not live up to the policy expectations. There is broad agreement on the problems which exist, some of which are summarized below.

It could be argued that a discussion of health-related policy should consider all those aspects of development which have a bearing on health. However, a narrower view will be taken of the health sector. The focus will be on those activities which are aimed specifically at improving health and are organized within an institutional framework recognized to be part of the health sector. It is not implied that these particular activities are the most important contributors to an improvement in health. Rather, it reflects the fact that the establishment of an effective health service is an important development goal which requires the support of specific policy-orientated analysis.

2.1. Inadequate funds for essential health activities

In many countries there is inadequate funding for 'essential' health services. It is not a simple matter to define a threshold below which they cannot be provided. There are indications, however, that health services are under economic pressure. Personnel have to function in run-down facilities with virtually no equipment and few drugs. In many cases wages and salaries account for as much as 60 to 85 per cent of public health expenditure (EEC 1986). Signs of underfunding have been found in evaluations of particular components of health services. For example, the effectiveness of many PHC projects is hampered by insufficient funds for drugs and transport, lack of supervision, and inadequate back-up from higher levels in the health service. A large proportion of medical equipment does not function due to inadequate provision for operation, maintenance, and depreciation.[3] A recent study has reported that there was a substantial fall in public sector funding for health in a number of countries during the early 1980s. Of those countries for which data were available, 47 per cent of those in Africa, 61 per cent in Latin America, 40 per cent in the Middle East, and 33 per cent in Asia showed a fall in per capita expenditure for health during the early years of the decade (Cornia *et al*. 1987). The case of Zambia provides an especially dramatic illustration of the problem of underfunding. It has been estimated that real per capita expenditure on health in 1985 was only 37 per cent of that which had prevailed in 1970 (Freund 1986). The results have been described in a report by an ILO mission which found that the health services in one province lacked virtually all resources except personnel (ILO 1987).

2.2. Inefficient use of available resources

The pattern of expenditure is often not appropriate to health needs. Sophisticated hospitals are favoured at the expense of PHC. For example, a study of the Zimbabwean health service shortly after Independence found that 44 per cent of all expenditure in publicly funded facilities was by the central hospitals in the two major cities. On the other hand, all PHC and basic hospital care serving the rural population (85 per cent of the total) accounted for only 24 per cent of expenditure (Zimbabwe 1984). The sacrifice of PHC in favour of referral hospitals is inefficient on two grounds. In the first place, initiatives aimed at preventing and treating common conditions can save lives and improve health at considerably lower unit cost than can hospital care. Secondly, access to urban facilities falls sharply with distance, so that rural people make relatively little use of them, although they are most in need of health services.

Relative expenditure on the various inputs to the health sector has not been efficient. Construction of facilities has gone ahead faster than has the capacity, or willingness, to fund the cost of running them.[4] Personnel have been trained and deployed regardless of the availability of complementary inputs. The result is that the cost-effectiveness of the services is low. In a number of countries, the potential impact of a relatively small increase in expenditure on consumable inputs and maintenance could be quite large. There are also problems of operational efficiency. For example, significant savings could be made if drug purchases were limited to the products which have been shown to be cost-effective and if procurement practices were improved. There is also a need for improvement in the management of health services at every level.

2.3. Inequitable access to health resources

There is plentiful evidence of very unequal access to health services. Rural people generally have poorer access than do those in the towns. For example, the study of Zimbabwe, which was quoted above, reports the per capita expenditure on health (in Zimbabwe dollars) to be: $144 on private patients: $31 on urban dwellers; $4 for rural districts; and even less in the more remote areas. In both urban (Harpham 1986) and rural areas it is the poor who have the least access to services. A study in Indonesia, for example, has documented the differential access to health services by the different social classes in both urban and rural areas. In Java, the poorest are most likely to be treated at home by their own family or at a traditional practitioner's house, while the rich tend to be seen by a physician. The difference in access is underlined for the specific case of childbirth. The large majority of rural dwellers and the urban poor are attended by traditional practitioners. Access to modern services rises with income, especially in the urban areas (Chernichovsky and Meesook 1986).

3. The Health Planning Approach

A large number of health sector initiatives have been undertaken in the name of PHC and a corpus of writings has been produced. There is considerable debate about what 'really' constitutes PHC development, and there are many disagreements about what an appropriate policy should be. None the less, much of the discussion shares a common approach to planning. The starting-point is the health needs of the people. The relative roles of health professionals, administrators, and grass-roots political movements in the establishment of needs is one of the major areas of debate. However, there is agreement that the health sector must be assessed in terms of its capacity to meet them. Furthermore, in the case of countries where the level of public health is very low, there is a consensus on the combination of basic services which should be provided. The job of the planner, in these circumstances, is to envisage the distribution of facilities, the mixture of health workers, and the kinds of activities which are required in order to answer the priority health problems more effectively. Quantitative targets can then be established for the medium and longer term. The description of an appropriate health system and the setting of targets to meet 'needs' is the heart of much of PHC policy-making. As was noted in the introduction, however, few countries have succeeded in transforming the health sector into one capable of providing essential services on a sustainable basis.

4. The 'Neo-liberal' Response

In recent years another way of looking at planning in the health sector of developing countries has been gaining influence. The production, distribution, and consumption of health services are viewed as analogous to those of any other commodity. It is argued that, all things being equal, it is best to allow the supply of goods to be guided by prices established in a free market. Many of the problems in the health sector are attributed to inappropriate interference with this process. The major recommendation is that fees should be charged for all services unless a specific market failure can be shown to exist.[5]

From this analytical vantage-point the important policy question is the identification of those activities for which the public sector should seek to complement the market mechanism. The arguments are summarized succinctly in the recent policy study published by the World Bank (World Bank 1987). This document argues that curative care should be regarded as a marketable commodity for which users should pay. On the other hand, public health measures (e.g. disposal of wastes) and preventive programmes (e.g. immunization) may have to be organized and financed collectively. This is because there is no means to ensure that everyone who benefits from these interventions can be induced to pay for them. Further exceptions to the case for full cost-recovery include ignorance about the possible benefits of health care, such as with preventive care for mothers and children, and inability to pay, due to poverty.

These arguments are not new. They represent one side of a long-running debate which has taken place in the UK and North America, between those who advocate a health service financed and provided by the state and those supporting a free market.[6] It is no surprise that the health service which emerges from the application of these principles is very similar to that of the United States—a combination of privately run and financed curative services complemented by public health programmes targeted at certain defined classes of patients.

4.1. Does the market know best?

A number of factors make health care quite unlike a typical commodity, the value of which is best established in the market.[7] In identifying some of its special properties, a number of issues relevant to planning the development of the health sector are raised.

How is the quality of care controlled?

The provision of service of a reasonable quality is an important priority of health development (Roemer and Montoya-Aguilar 1988). Unfortunately, this has not always been achieved. A study of PHC programmes in a number of countries found health personnel working with almost no equipment or drugs. They were frequently demoralized and felt very isolated (UNDP 1983). Problems of quality exist in the private sector as well. A number of programmes, for example, have been devised to improve the care given by traditional birth attendants. There are also many anecdotal reports of private doctors who overprescribe drugs and whose medical practice is inadequate (Roemer 1984).

There is evidence that patients are aware of the existence of different standards of care. A number of studies of the pattern of utilization have found that the poor make greater use of traditional healers and of free public sector clinics, while the better off are more likely to pay for the services of doctors and may also seek care in private hospitals.[8] It could be argued that this reflects different attitudes to health care amongst people of various social classes. There is some evidence to suggest, however, that rural people value modern health care which is perceived to be of adequate quality. One study in Kenya, for example, found that even those who are relatively poor will pay for a better standard of care when they consider that the free service has been ineffective (Mwabu 1986).

The function of a typical commodity is relatively well defined and the person who uses it is capable of judging its quality. Although it may be desirable to regulate standards, it is not necessary to interfere unduly with the production process. Much of the responsibility for assessing value for money can be borne by the consumer. The case of health care is quite different. Health workers, in whatever tradition they work, receive special training on how to approach various situations. They subject patients to risk by recommending the use of toxic chemicals and cutting the body surgically. The consequences of a bad choice of practitioner can be very serious. It may not be possible, however, for a patient to assess the advisability of a particular form of treatment without expert advice. This brings into question the likely efficacy of the market as a mechanism for ensuring that the services provided are of adequate quality.

Almost all societies establish mechanisms to influence health workers. These include training programmes, organizations which certify practitioners and monitor their practice, and a legal system which punishes serious malpractices. Performing surgery and the use of dangerous or addictive drugs may be limited to qualified practitioners. Such prohibitions provide the favoured profession with power, which can be used for sectional interests. There is widespread agreement that the medical profession has had a very large influence on the development of the health sector in most countries. Many argue that this has been one factor behind the disproportionate concentration on the construction of sophisticated hospitals in both developed and developing countries. It could be argued that increased competition would provide the necessary countervailing force to rent-seeking behaviour by doctors. On the other hand, others have pointed to the fact that doctors are expected to take the needs of patients into account in decision-making. An increased tendency to view health care as a commodity to be bought and sold could damage the underlying social consensus and diminish the constraints to self-seeking behaviour by health workers (Titmuss 1970). It would seem, therefore, that neither the market nor the organized medical profession can be depended on to ensure, on their own, the provision of health services which are effective, efficient, and safe. Mechanisms which allow the users to express their interests need to be established. The state has a role to play as do other forms of organizing people to plan, monitor, and struggle for health services.

Who knows how much health care is needed?

Health care is an unusual commodity. Most people prefer to have as little of it as possible. But, when they are ill, they want as much as is needed to get better. Many factors influence the utilization of health services. These include, among other things, cultural attitudes to health care and the availability and cost of services. There is evidence that health practitioners have a significant influence on the kinds of care which are sought. The capacity of doctors to act as 'gatekeepers' to hospitals and as stimulators of the use of referral services indicates that the incentives facing them and the means taken to influence their behaviour can affect the kind of health service which develops. For example, a study which was undertaken in Brazil has shown that the mechanism by which doctors were reimbursed, salary or fee-for-service, influenced the mode of delivery of children. Women who were insured for the use of private doctors had a rate of Caesarean sections well in excess of recommended practice, and much higher than those treated in public hospitals (Barros *et al.* 1986).

It could be argued that health workers have less direct influence on the utilization of out-patient services and that they will be overused if provided free of charge. The introduction of fees would, in these circumstances, eliminate the least valuable interventions and allow health workers to concentrate on the sick. There is some doubt, however, as to the existence of 'excess use' of health services. One important goal of PHC is to make the benefits of modern knowledge about health and health care available to all. The level of popular understanding about the working of the body and of the symptoms which indicate a need for medical treatment is often very low. In such circumstances, it is to be expected that a number of consultations will be for trivial problems while some serious conditions go untreated. Lack of knowledge about when to seek help from the health services is most directly tackled through educational programmes. These can be aimed at both the general population and community health workers. In addition, however, attention should be paid to the existence of barriers to access to services.

The appropriate level of utilization of out-patient services is one where unnecessary visits are minimized while those for treatable and preventible conditions are encouraged. The cost of an unnecessary consultation is relatively low. Inadequate treatment, on the other hand, can generate substantial costs due to expenditure on health care, loss of working time, and disability or death. Thus, the balance should be weighted in favour of encouraging the use of health facilities (assuming that they are providing an adequate standard of service). Many factors, in addition to money costs, act as a disincentive to attendance at a clinic. These include the time lost in travel and waiting and the cost of transport.[9] There is no evidence to show that total utilization of PHC services is too high in most developing countries. On the other hand, some facilities, such as specialized hospital out-patient departments, may be overcrowded if the first level of care is bypassed. In such a case a substantial fee could be charged to those who are not referred. The aim would be to encourage use of the PHC system, not to decrease total levels of utilization.

The dependence of patients on the advice of health workers to establish the amount of health services they need brings into question the appropriateness of the market as a mechanism for allocating resources. There is a considerable risk that people with treatable conditions will be deterred by fees and that ability to pay will become an important criterion in determining the pattern of health services provision.

User charges and access to health services

If user charges are to be used as a mechanism of revenue generation, it is important that they do not constitute a significant barrier to care. The cost of in-patient treatment can represent a very heavy burden on a family. Thus, it is necessary to establish a means for people to insure themselves if recovery of a large proportion of hospital costs is to be reconciled with the provision of access on the basis of need. One exception might be the case of patients using private beds in public facilities, where fees less than full costs would represent a subsidy for privileged access. The implications of insurance for the market model of health sector organization is discussed below.

The question of out-patient fees is less clear. The average cost of health care would represent a relatively small proportion of total income if the mean number of visits per year were 2–3 per person. None the less, a number of studies have demonstrated that poorer households, especially in the rural areas, tend to utilize low cost government health services (as well as traditional healers) even when they are perceived to provide a less effective service (Berman *et al.* 1987). Although fees for PHC services may not represent an impossibly high burden, they may be substantial enough to encourage households to hesitate before seeking care. In this cost/benefit calculation some members of the household may be valued less highly. There is evidence that this is the case for women in some countries (Chen *et al.* 1981). Furthermore, if the cost of health care, in terms of time lost from work and transport expenses, is already substantial, a further cash charge may tip the balance. Those who are already disadvantaged because of their distance from a health facility may find their effective access to services further cut by a cash fee. The net result is that a significant proportion of the population will utilize the health services less than would otherwise be desirable.

Cash payment may be an insurmountable barrier to care for some households. Included among these will be the very poor, who have to struggle to survive. Illness and some of the other characteristics of poverty (illiteracy, malnutrition, and poor environmental conditions) are mutually reinforcing. When a person is sick he or she is less productive and, in addition, other household members may have to divert labour-time and money in order to care for them. Episodes of illness increase the vulnerability of the individual to the impact of other stresses, such as temporary food shortage. In addition, an episode of poor health of a productive member of a household may initiate a ratchet effect whereby loss of production, coupled with the cost of health care, may result in the sale of productive assets. The vulnerability of the household to eventual impoverishment and of its individual members to suffering, debility, and death will be increased.[10] There is evidence that the availability of effective health care at an affordable price is an important contributor to decreases in mortality in a number of countries. It is not only a good in itself, but may be part of a development process aimed at diminishing the vulnerability of the poor.

User charges need not be rejected out of hand as a means of financing health services. A number of countries have demonstrated very impressive improvements in health and health care, while requiring patients to pay directly for some components of their treatment.[11] However, the potential of this mode of revenue generation to create an undesirable barrier to access cannot be ignored. This is especially the case in countries where there are large inequalities of income and wealth. For example, there are great differences between the likely impact of user charges on peasants in the more productive areas of China and on the very poor, who constitute a large proportion of the population in many countries. Of course, if a mechanism for charging only those who are unlikely to be deterred could be established, this problem would be diminished.

Once the potential disadvantages of user charges are recognized, it is clear that the case for introducing them cannot rest on the supposed optimality of the market. The decision has to be made on the basis of an assessment of a number of possible means of raising funds in terms of their likely impact on meeting the priority objectives of the health sector, including access on the basis of need.

Insurance and provision against uncertainty

The example of the ratchet effect illustrates an important property of health care. Although average health expenditure may be low, there will, at any one time, be a small number of people who require substantial resources to deal with a serious illness. The pattern of utilization of health services varies during a person's lifetime. If the cost of care has to be borne when a person is rendered unproductive due to illness it can be financially ruinous. This effect can be prevented if a means is provided for insuring against possible future need.

The introduction of insurance coverage for health care can influence the pattern of services provided. If health facilities and individual health workers are paid on the basis of the quantity of the work they do, they will have an incentive to provide more services. There will be a tendency for the utilization of these services to rise in the absence of regulation. If some services are covered and others are not, a biased pattern of provision may develop, as is illustrated by the case of Canada (Evans 1984). In the 1950s, a scheme was introduced which insured the population for hospital care but left ambulatory patients to seek treatment from private doctors. The response was a sharp rise in total hospital expenditure. A decade later, health care coverage was extended to the full spectrum of preventive and curative services. During the 1970s and early 1980s, a number of measures were introduced to penalize hospitals which exceeded their budgets and to encourage the development of less costly forms of care. As a result the rise in hospital costs in Canada slowed down. A similar expansion in curative care is claimed to have occurred in a number of countries in Latin America, where insurance schemes cover relatively small proportions of the population. In a number of cases sophisticated hospitals for the beneficiaries have expanded, while preventive care has been neglected and the public services can provide only the most basic of care.[12]

It is argued by some that schemes which cover only part of the population can impede the development of appropriate health services. For example, if a social security scheme covers only those in formal employment, or those with politically sensitive jobs, such as in the public service or the army, there may be pressure for the provision of increasingly sophisticated care for the beneficiaries, while the gap with the public sector widens. Others claim that such schemes are an improvement over a disorganized private sector, and can be integrated with the public services, should the political will exist.[13] Almost all analysts agree, however, on the importance of organized interest groups in influencing the development of the health sector. The unregulated working of the market, including the insurance schemes, cannot be counted on to drive the health sector in the desired direction.

The importance of health insurance is accepted in the proposed agenda for reform of the World Bank (World Bank 1987). However, by drawing a stark distinction between tax-based financing and cost-recovery, which is defined to include insurance, a vital point is blurred. When health care is financed through insurance it is necessary that the provision of services be planned, monitored, and regulated. Once this is recognized, the sharp divide between public and private financing of services becomes less clear. The question becomes one of defining the relative roles of the bodies which collect revenue, provide care, and oversee the overall development of the health sector (Maynard 1982). There are a number of different methods for organizing prepayment for health care. These include private sector schemes, compulsory social insurance, community funds, work-related insurance, and tax-based financing of care. In assessing any particular scheme, the likely impact on the pattern of health services which are provided and on the goal of providing care on the basis of need has to be considered. The regulatory mechanisms necessary to ensure that the insurance coverage is integrated into the overall process of health sector development have to be defined.[14]

4.2. Is 'getting prices right' a useful basis for policy formulation?

The question posed in the previous section was: 'Does the market know best?' The answer of the neo-liberals is 'yes', or 'at least it knows better'. At times, however, this seems to derive more from economic theory than from the realities of the health sector itself. For example, a recent book which argues for the need to establish markets for curative care makes no attempt to compare countries with more and less effective health services to establish what role the price mechanism may have had in contributing to successful sectoral development (Jimenez 1987). The examples of Sri Lanka, Cuba, Costa Rica, and China suggest that quite different policies can successfully provide access to appropriate health services (Halstead *et al.* 1985). There would seem to be no reason to assume that an unregulated market will inevitably result in a health sector which provides cost-effective care to those in need. This means, to use the jargon of Welfare Economics, that we are in the realm of the (considerably less than) 'second best', where the likely effect of an intervention cannot be inferred on the basis of whether or not it moves prices closer to market clearing ones. In this situation policy must be based on a solid knowledge of the health sector and an assessment of the likely impact of any particular initiative in meeting policy objectives. The remainder of this paper will address some of the issues which have arisen out of the experience of PHC development and have been raised by the World Bank.

5. Planning and Implementation of Health Sector Reform

The establishment of an effective and sustainable PHC-based service implies a major change in structure and functioning of a complex sector which accounts for between 2 and 5 per cent of the GNP and employs a similar proportion of those in formal employment. The 'anatomy' (infrastructure) of the health sector is changing, in many countries, from one which was based in a relatively small number of facilities situated in the urban centres towards one with activities spread throughout the country. However, in many cases, its 'physiology' (or means of functioning) has not adapted to the needs of the new reality. The health sector includes a number of institutions which differ in the activities they undertake, their administrative practices, their legal relationships with each other, their mode of finance, their policies and priorities, and the population groups which they serve. The process of integrating them into an effective service has to be planned and managed.

The usual approach to planning in the health sector focuses on the preparation of a public sector investment plan. Development is seen as the sum of completed projects. This perspective is inadequate for overseeing a process of structural change. In addition to expansion of infrastructure and growth of the number of skilled personnel, the use made of existing resources has to be redefined and new relationships between the various components (public and private) of the sector have to be established. The management of such a development process requires a different approach to policy formulation and implementation. Strategies must be based on a knowledge of the working of the sector and a definition of the constraints to change. The objectives of policy have to be clearly stated, the tools available for influencing development (construction, planning systems, changes in laws, training programmes, redefining career structures etc.) identified, and the likely outcome of various options assessed. There is a need to establish a management system capable of overseeing such a process of change and of administering an increasingly complex service.

6. Management of Resource Use in the Health Sector

The World Bank agenda for reform includes a triad of interventions; the decentralization of financial management in the public health system, strengthening of non-government providers, and introduction of new sources of revenue, especially users' charges and insurance schemes.[15] These are linked together by the neo-liberal paradigm into a unified package for reforming the system of resource management. Once the theoretical under-pinning is removed it is no longer possible to claim to have a universally applicable model for sectoral development. None the less each element of the package highlights a significant weakness in existing health sectors. The approach to strengthening resource planning and management, however, is not as simple or clear cut as the clarity of the market model would imply.

6.1. Strengthening public sector planning and control of expenditure

Successful implementation of PHC-based development requires the establish-ment of an effective system of planning and controlling the use of resources in the public sector. The approaches to management of resource use which were developed for a small service based in a few urban centres are, in many cases, inappropriate for overseeing a significant change in the pattern of resource allocation. As the system has expanded, the existing mechanisms for monitoring for theft, controlling expenditure, and planning resource allocation have all become increasingly inadequate (Bloom 1988). The need to develop new models for managing the use of resources in the health sector is common to both industrialized and developing countries.[16]

The annual preparation of estimates is the mechanism for short-term planning of health expenditure (Enthoven 1973). The usual approach has been to fund existing services and to add an allowance for expansion. The underlying assumption is that overspending on the previous year's allocation represents an underestimated need. This incremental approach to planning tends to reinforce the existing pattern of health activities. Programmes and facilities which overspend are rewarded and underspenders are penalized. The overspenders are likely to be the sophisticated hospitals which have dynamic leaders and a clientele with rising expectations of service. They have the capacity to identify new ways in which resources could be used and the influence to make their needs known. Those facilities which serve the disadvantaged and are staffed by relatively junior personnel may, on the other hand, be unable to spend their allocation. This tendency may be exacerbated by understaffing and periodic drug shortages which, in turn, induce patients to go directly to urban hospitals or the private sector. The underspending which is interpreted by the planning system as a low need for resources may actually be a sign of serious problems in organizing services.

The development plan frequently consists of little more than a public sector investment programme—a list of construction projects to be under-taken during the plan period. In making decisions about the construction of new facilities, no consideration may have been given to the likely cost of running them or to the alternative uses to which resources could have been put. Development becomes equated with the consequences of investment. There is a need, however, to consider other approaches to the improvement of services. In some countries, basic preventive and curative services are not adequately funded. Once these essential activities have been organized, attention needs to be paid to the quality of services provided by existing facilities and personnel. Capital-led planning cannot provide, on its own, an effective framework for transforming the pattern of health activities.

If the goal is to oversee the development of a very different kind of health sector, mechanisms are required to plan and manage a change in the pattern of resource use.[17] For example, targets can be set for the allocation of resources by geographical area and by function. The use of resources by various levels of the health service—PHC, basic hospitals, referral facilities, and national referral centres—can be expanded at different rates. Mechanisms are required to ensure that programmes and facilities can keep within their budgets. The establishment of a capacity to plan and manage the use of resources to fund PHC-based services is an important goal of institutional development in the public sector.

6.2. Decentralization of decision-making in the public sector

A health service is a rather complex structure consisting of a large number of individual facilities and specialized programmes. In the early stages of establishing a PHC-based service the priority is to build the necessary facilities, train and deploy health workers, establish basic services, and mobilize communities to undertake public health activities. This lends itself to a centralized, command model of administration. As the focus shifts towards establishing sustainable services and raising standards, success becomes increasingly dependent on the capacity of local services to plan and organize their own activities.

There is a consensus on the need to devolve financial responsibility in order to encourage local health services to improve their effectiveness and efficiency. However, some functions can best be undertaken at the national level. For example, the selection and procurement of drugs and equipment requires considerable technical expertise and a knowledge of the world market. There are significant benefits if a standard list of basic inputs can be developed. National-level support is required to inform health workers about the appropriate use which should be made of these technologies. There are similar advantages to organizing a number of preventive pro-grammes at national level. One example is immunization which needs to be supported by a functioning cold chain. Although the work may be undertaken by integrated local services, the overall structure is the responsibilty of a national team. Similarly, there is a need for manuals and guide-lines on how to undertake a number of health sector activities. The balance between central planners and administrators and those implementing programmes is a delicate one. Guide-lines can become rigid directives, and technical support can be transformed into national programmes which duplicate those activities already being organized at district level (Chambers 1988). The relative roles of the national level which provides expertise and technical support and districts and facilities which organize most of the services will continue to be an important issue of institutional development in the years to come.

In the complex, widely dispersed system which is the result of the implementation of PHC policies, the capacity of the centre to monitor and control the activities of individual programmes and facilities is limited. In this situation it is useful to assess the incentives which are facing decision-makers. These may influence behaviour as much as do national policies and ministry directives. For example, the system of resource management can encourage growth of hospital costs in spite of a commitment to PHC. A budgeting system is required which rewards improvements in efficiency and punishes overspending.

Incentives facing individuals also influence behaviour. In many countries, while PHC-based development is the national priority, the jobs with the best pay and highest status for health workers are in specialized hospital work. Furthermore, organized professions may recognize a number of specialities in curative care although similar recognition is not given to expertise in PHC. This further encourages the development of skills which are particularly relevant to the needs of the minority. Earnings in the private sector are frequently much higher than in the public service. Policies towards private practice must aim to minimize these perverse incentives. For example, in a situation of shortage of skilled personnel, it might be desirable to limit the difference in earnings between private and public sector doctors by imposing a licensing fee for the right to practise privately.

6.3. The sectoral approach: the role of the private sector

The previous paragraphs have focused on the complexity of the public health services. In many countries, there are a number of other actors in the health sector. These can be categorized in subsectors (ministry of health, local government, medical missions, private hospitals, social security facilities, etc.), within which the providers of services share a number of characteristics (Mach and Abel Smith 1983). These include legal status, funding mechanism, services provided, and populations served. The simple distinction which is sometimes drawn between public and private sectors is not appropriate for purposes of policy formulation. This is especially the case in countries with substantial inequalities of income, where there is a great difference between those services which it is feasible to provide to all on the basis of need and those to which only the most affluent can hope to gain access. In such circumstances the various non-governmental institutions play quite different roles.

Publicly accessible/publicly plannable

Some private facilities and health workers provide services which are widely accessible. Their services are of a similar character to those of the public sector. For example, medical missions and other non-government organizations are often located in the rural areas or peri-urban slums. Similarly, community health workers are relatively accessible even when they earn their income by charging fees. These services frequently benefit from support from the state, in the form of direct grants, access to low cost drugs, tax concessions, and special dispensations for using expatriate personnel. This makes them amenable to influence from decision-makers in the public health service. In many countries, however, their potential role in support of PHC-based development has not been addressed by policy-makers. They have had little involvement in the planning process. Among the issues which have to be addressed are the cost-effectiveness of the use made of public funds, avoidance of duplication of services, co-ordination of services with the public sector, integration into national programmes, and maintenance of quality of services (Green 1987).

Private sector

Some providers, on the other hand, serve a small proportion of the population. Access is regulated by the ability to pay. The services are of a complexity and cost which cannot be made available to the general population. In the case of these truly private services, the important issues for policy-makers are quite different. There are few grounds for continuation of subsidies from public funds. In pre-independence Zimbabwe, for example, a number of wards in the national referral centre were reserved for private patients who paid only a fraction of the cost. This, along with tax concessions for those covered by medical insurance, represented a considerable subsidy for the services which were enjoyed by a small minority who consumed, none the less, a quarter of all health services. These funds could have been used to support services for those with greater needs. The existence of a dynamic private sector can influence the overall pattern of development of the health sector. The policies of medical schools, statutory licensing bodies, and professional organizations often reflect its interests. The high income and elevated status of private sector specialists provide, in many countries, an incentive for young doctors to aspire to similar careers in curative care. Policies towards the private sector should reflect the need to minimize potential negative impacts on PHC-based development.

Categorization of a provider as private is not a question simply of its legal status. It is a reflection of the kind of services provided and the clients who are served. For example, in some countries it is possible to find hospitals run by a medical mission or by other not-for-profit organizations which provide relatively sophisticated care for the élite. Their fees may be comparable to those of private hospitals. In such a case, it may be appropriate to classify that facility as private on the basis of the kind of services provided and the limited population who have access to it.

Households

A large proportion of health care is provided by household members, especially women. The need to care for a sick family member can compromise the capacity of the household to meet its other needs. Travel to a health facility and the nursing of acutely ill children, for example, require a considerable input of time which could be allocated for other purposes. If local hospitals cannot provide adequate care for the sick, the choice may be between providing nursing care at home and ensuring that someone is present to protect the interests of the hospitalized patient. This may significantly disrupt the household. The role of the health sector in supporting household members who provide health care and in minimizing the loss of productivity which may arise when someone falls ill is poorly understood. This is an area in need of research.

6.4. Financing PHC-based health services

Many discussions of users' charges seek to solve the underfunding of a particular service by mobilizing additional resources directly from those who use it. Thus, charges to users of PHC-based services and other forms of community financing are proposed as a means of funding rural health services. If, however, there is a capacity to manage the pattern of allocation of resources in the health service, there need not be such a direct link between resource generation and availability of funds. At times, the case for users' charges seems to rest on the argument that there is no alternative: if user charges are introduced and, as a result, most people have access to better care, then the result would, on the whole be beneficial. What is not assessed in such a scenario is the other possible approaches to augmenting funding of essential health services.[18]

The need for a financing strategy

Once one looks beyond the narrow approach which links the funding of particular activities to that of cost-recovery, the need to establish a strategy for financing the health sector becomes clear. Such a strategy will include a combination of approaches selected on the basis of their impact on access to PHC-based health services and on the pattern of services which results. Users' charges create barriers to care, especially in societies where there are substantial inequalities; they also encourage providers to concentrate on those activities for which they receive payment. It may be possible to identify other options which conflict less with health development priorities.

In some countries the private sector receives subsidies from the state. These funds could be made available for PHC. It is often the case that urban workers utilize the relatively sophisticated hospitals and clinics much more than do those in the rural areas or the urban slums. It would seem reasonable to focus efforts to recover costs on the users of these services, which frequently account for a large proportion of total expenditure. Charges for in-patient care would have to be based on some form of insurance scheme which requires a greater administrative effort than does an increase in fees for out-patient treatment. In many countries, although the call may be made for an equal level of cost-recovery at all levels of curative care, the immediate result may be increased fees for PHC, while the more sophisticated hospital care continues to be subsidized. Such an arrangement would be directly counter to stated national priorities and would increase the existing bias against the poor. The institution of an insurance scheme to fund the superior care to which a segment of the population has access is an explicit recognition of the existence of more than one tier of health care. There is a danger that existing inequalities could be perpetuated. Measures are required to ensure that the kind of care which is covered is such that it is realistic to expect to be able to extend coverage to an increasing proportion of the population in the foreseeable future. This might include out-patient treatment in urban polyclinics and basic hospital care.

The discussion has focused on potential sources of revenue earmarked for health. However, what is not clear is why direct user charges or compulsory insurance should be able to raise revenue which could not be collected as taxes. Is this a question of political resistance by taxpayers, or one of administrative weakness in the tax collection agencies? Or does this reflect the preferences of international organizations? There is a need to set the establishment, in a number of sectors, of new revenue generation schemes in the broader context of the problem of financing public services. Each system for raising funds imposes administrative costs and new limitations on the capacity to plan the development of the sector. The trend towards establishing a number of earmarked schemes in each sector may answer immediate needs but could prove costly in the long run. The option which needs to be assessed is the feasibility of establishing a sustainable system of public financing based on combinations of progressive revenue generation schemes at national, local, and community levels. In this context, charging fees in the health sector is just one of a number of possible approaches to funding public health services.

There is an international dimension to the health financing problem. Underfunding of essential health services is one of the many consequences for the poor of economic crises and consequent structural adjustment programmes (Cornia *et al.* 1987). In this context, the potential impact of significant users' charges in a service which is not meeting basic needs has to be acknowledged. International donors have become aware of the problem of the resource gap through evaluations of projects which they have funded. The lack of recurrent funding has been identified as a threat to their sustainability. It is increasingly recognized that aid to the health sector has been inappropriately biased towards construction projects. The cost of establishing and maintaining effective health services has been underestimated by many. If previous investments are to yield ongoing benefits, there may be a need for recurrent support during a period of rehabilitation of national economies and of the health sector. This crisis management might usefully be linked to efforts to develop more appropriate mechanisms to manage resource use and to establish a sustainable strategy for funding essential public services. Otherwise it will not be possible to provide access to essential services on the basis of need in the foreseeable future.

6.5. Politics and PHC

A number of explanations have been put forward for the failure adequately to fund 'essential' public health services. One major factor may be that the forces opposing change are more powerful than those supporting it. Where few channels are available for democratic oversight of the working of the health sector, those with access to power determine the pattern of resource use (Brett 1988). One recent review of the experience of several countries which have significantly decreased mortality in spite of low GDP concluded that the existence of organized political movements capable of mobilizing workers and peasants to press their rights has been an essential factor in their success (Caldwell 1986). A number of people benefit from the existing situation. Included among them are those who work in the favoured facilities and those who utilize them. They tend to belong to politically powerful social groups and may successfully oppose policies seen to be against their interests.

The lack of political commitment to PHC on the part of governments has been put forward as an argument for decentralizing revenue collection and resource allocation to the level of the district or the individual facility. It is not possible, however, to predict the impact on access to effective care of such a step without analysing the likely response of the various interest groups involved. For such an initiative to result in improvements in local health services, current levels of funding by national and local governments would have to be sustained. In addition, the districts would have to allocate additional money to PHC. In the absence of adequate political support in the districts such an outcome cannot be guaranteed. The introduction of charges for out-patient services in the rural areas could even result, in some circumstances, in a situation where peasants pay for unimproved services while the urban élite enjoy subsidized hospital care. The attempt to move towards equity in health in a society with substantial and persisting inequalities of income and wealth is a project full of contradictions. Successful PHC-based development is constrained in many countries by a lack of commitment to meeting the needs of the majority. In such a situation, an assessment of the relative roles of competitive markets, state planning and regulation, and alternative forms of organization of groups of people to influence the health service must take political as well as technical considerations into account.

7. Bureaucratic Regulation vs. The Market: An Agenda for Reform?

The neo-liberal analysis presents decision-makers in the health sector with a series of choices:

- central planning vs. decentralization;
- regulation vs. individual choice;
- public vs. private ownership;
- underfunding vs. users' charges.

Such a formulation reflects neither the complexity of the health sector nor the richness of the options available. The health sector consists of a number of systems for raising revenue, of providers with varying relationships with Ministry of Health administrators, and of social groups with differential access to health services. Systems of resource mobilization and management are required to support the development of an appropriate health sector. They need resemble neither a competitive market nor a command economy. The challenge is to develop approaches which provide flexibility for providers of services, as well as recognizing the need for national level planning and administration. On the one hand there is the danger of excessive bureaucracy, inflexibility, and a lack of incentives to encourage the provision of effective and efficient care. On the other hand, there is a risk of a disorganized development of services of questionable quality and unnecessary cost which do not address the needs of a large proportion of the population.

The broad acceptance of PHC as the basis of health sector development, and the consequent expansion in infrastructure and personnel which has taken place, have put the need to establish sustainable services high on the agenda of the health sector. Although the neo-liberal attempt to provide a blueprint for reform is unconvincing, it has contributed to the recognition of the size of the task involved in implementing such policies. The process of structural change in the health sector will take a number of years and must be planned and managed. It requires a political commitment, not just at national level, but in districts and among the population. This commitment has to be expressed in mechanisms capable of influencing the pattern of services provided. The test of any proposed change in the existing system should be whether or not it supports the development of PHC-based health services. The agenda which arises for the health sector out of the experience of the past decade is not a model of how to structure a health service. It consists of a number of issues which have to be addressed by decision-makers and a programme for action-orientated health systems research.

Notes

1. These include: Halstead *et al.* 1985, World Bank 1980, and WHO 1986*a*.
2. WHO 1986*b*, table 6, p. 29.
3. Two broad reviews of a number of PHC projects are American Public Health Association 1982 and UNDP 1983. The report by Bloom and Temple-Bird (1988) focuses on the problem of medical equipment.
4. See Gray 1986 and Heller 1979.
5. See De Ferranti 1985, Jimenez 1987, and World Bank 1987.
6. Many of the issues of this debate are summarized in MacLachlan and Maynard 1982. The basic arguments are also summarized in Cullis and West 1979.
7. The seminal paper on this issue is by Arrow (1963). For a recent discussion see Evans 1984.
8. See Akin *et al.* 1985, Chernichovsky and Meesook 1986, and Heller 1982.
9. See Akin *et al.* 1985, Ayalew 1985, and Dor *et al.* 1987.
10. This concept is discussed in Chambers 1983 and in Corbett 1989. Abel Smith (1987) suggests that this has been an important consequence of user charges in Thailand.
11. China is a prominent example. It should be noted, however, that inequalities in both health status and access to health services persist in that country (Jamison *et al.* 1984).
12. See Abel Smith 1986 and Ugalde 1985.
13. See Midgely 1984, and Roemer and Maeda 1976.
14. See Mills 1983 and Zschock 1982.
15. World Bank 1987 focuses on the health sector and World Bank 1988 takes a broader look at the public sector.
16. See Rodwin 1983 for a comparative study of several industrialized countries and Jones and Prowle 1982 for a discussion of the UK. Some discussions of this issue with regard to developing countries are Segall 1983, World Bank 1988, and WHO 1988.
17. See Bloom 1988 and Segall 1983.
18. See Mach and Abel Smith 1983 and Stevens 1984.

References

Abel Smith, B. (1986), 'Funding Health for All: Is Insurance the Answer?', *World Health Forum*, 7: 3–32.

—— (1987), book review of World Bank, 'Financing Health Services in Developing Countries: The Potential for the Health Sector', *Health Policy and Planning*, 2/4: 355–6.

Akin, J. S., *et al.* (1985), *The Demand for Primary Health Services in the Third World*, Rowman and Allanheld, Totowa, NJ.

American Public Health Association (1982), *Primary Health Care, Progress and Problems*, Washington, DC.

Arrow, K. (1963), 'Uncertainty and the Welfare Economics of Medical Care', *American Economic Review*, 53: 941–73.

Ayalew, S. (1985), 'Time Budget Analysis as a Tool for PHC Planning', *Social Science and Medicine*, 21/8: 865–72.

Barros, F. C., Vaughan, J. P., and Vitora, C. G. (1986), 'Why So Many Caesarean Sections? The Need for Further Policy Change in Brazil', *Health Policy and Planning*, 1: 19–29.

Berman, P., Ormond, B., and Gani, A. (1987), 'Treatment, Use and Expenditure on Curative Care in Rural Indonesia', *Health Policy and Planning*, 2/4: 289–300.

Bloom, G. (1988), 'Planning Health Sector Expenditure in Support of PHC', *Health Policy and Planning*, 3/1: 59–68.

——and Temple-Bird, C. (1988), *Medical Equipment in Sub-Saharan Africa: A Framework for Policy Formulation*, IDS Research Report Rr19.

Brett, E. A. (1988), 'Adjustment and the State: The Problem of Administrative Reform', *IDS Bulletin*, 19/4: 4–12.

Caldwell, J. C. (1986), 'Routes to Low Mortality in Poor Countries', *Population and Development Review*, 12/2: 171–220.

Chambers, R. (1983), *Rural Development: Putting the Last First*, Longman, London and Harlow.

—— (1989), 'Bureaucratic Reversals and Local Diversity', *IDS Bulletin*, 19/4: 50–6.

Chen, L., Huq, E., and D'Souza, S. (1981), 'Sex Bias in the Family Allocation of Food and Health Care in Bangladesh', *Population and Development Review*, 7/1: 55–70.

Chernichovsky, D., and Meesook, O. A. (1986), 'Utilisation of Health Services in Indonesia', *Social Science and Medicine*, 23/6: 611–20.

Corbett, J. E. M. (1989), 'Poverty and Sickness: The High Costs of Ill-Health', *IDS Bulletin*, 20/2: 58–62.

Cornia, G. A., Jolly, A. R., and Stewart, F. (1987), *Adjustment with a Human Face*, Oxford University Press, Oxford.

Cullis, J. G., and West, P. A. (1979), *The Economics of Health*, Martin Robertson, Oxford.

De Ferranti, D. M. (1985), 'Paying for Health Services in Developing Countries: An Overview', World Bank Staff Working Paper 71, World Bank, Washington, DC.

Dor, A., Gertler, P., and Van Der Gag, J. (1987), 'Non-price Rationing and the Choice of Medical Care Providers in Rural Côte d'Ivoire', *Journal of Health Economics*, 6: 291–304.

EEC (1986), *Proposal for Basic Principles derived from an Evaluation of ACP-EEC Health Projects and Programmes*, VIII/EV/1266(86) – EN, Brussels.

Enthoven, A. J. H. (1973), *Accountancy and Economic Development Policy*, North-Holland Publishing Company, Amsterdam.

Evans, R. G. (1984), *Strained Mercy*, Butterworth, Toronto.

Freund, P. (1986), 'Health Care in a Declining Economy: The Case of Zambia', *Social Science and Medicine*, 23/9: 875–88.

Gray, C. S. (1986), 'State-sponsored Primary Health Care in Africa: The Recurrent Cost of Performing Miracles', *Social Science and Medicine*, 22/3: 361–8.

Green, A. (1987), 'The Role of Non-governmental Organisations and the Private Sector in the Provision of Health Care in Developing Countries', *International Journal of Health Planning and Management*, 2/1: 37–58.

Halstead, S. B., Walsh, J. A., and Warren, K. S. (1985), *Good Health at Low Cost*, Proceedings of a Conference held at the Bellagio Conference Centre, Rockefeller Foundation, New York.

Harpham, T. (1986), 'Review Article: Health and the Urban Poor', *Health Policy and Planning*, 1/1: 5–18.

Heller, P. (1979), 'The Underfinancing of Recurrent Development Costs', *Finance and Development* (Mar.): 38–41.

—— (1982), 'A Model of the Demand for Medical and Health Services in Peninsular Malaysia', *Social Science and Medicine*, 16/3: 267–84.

ILO (1987), *World Recession and Global Interdependence*, Geneva.

Jamison, D. T., *et al.* (1984), *China the Health Sector*, World Bank Country Study, Washington, DC.

Jimenez, E. (1987), *Pricing Policy in the Social Sectors*, Johns Hopkins University Press, Baltimore, Md.

Jones, T., and Prowle, M. (1982), *Health Services Finance*, Certified Accountants Educational Trust, London.

Mach, E. P., and Abel Smith, B. (1983), *Planning the Finances of the Health Sector: A Manual for Developing Countries*, WHO, Geneva.

MacLachlan, G., and Maynard, A. (1982), *The Public/Private Mix for Health*, Nuffield Provincial Hospitals Trust, London.

Maynard, A. (1982), 'The Regulation of Public and Private Health Care Markets', in MacLachlan and Maynard 1982: 471–512.

Midgely, J. (1984), *Social Security, Inequality, and the Third World*, John Wiley, Chichester.

Mills, A. (1983), 'Economic Aspects of Health Insurance', in K. Lee and A. Mills (eds.), *The Economics of Health in Developing Countries*, OUP, Oxford, 64–98.

Mwabu, G. (1986), 'Health Care Decisions at the Household Level: Results of a Rural Health Survey in Kenya', *Social Science and Medicine*, 22/3: 315–19.

Rodwin, V. (1983), *The Health Planning Predicament*, University of California Press, Berkeley, Calif.

Roemer, M. I. (1984), 'Private Medical Practice: Obstacle to Health for All', *World Health Forum*, 5: 195–210.

—— and Maeda, N. (1976), 'Does Social Security Support for Medical Care Weaken Public Health Programs?', *International Journal of Health Services*, 6/1: 69–78.

—— and Montoya-Aguilar, C. (1988), *Quality Assessment and Assurance in Primary Health Care*, WHO Offset Publication No. 105, Geneva.

Segall, M. M. (1983), 'Planning and Politics of Resource Allocation for Primary Health Care: Promotion of Meaningful National Policy', *Social Science and Medicine*, 17/24: 1947–60.

Stevens, C. (1984), 'Rationalising Health Sector Expenditure in Less Developed Countries', in National Council for International Health, *Alternative Health Delivery Systems: Can They Serve the Public Interest in Third World Settings?*, Washington, DC.

Titmuss, R. M. (1970), *The Gift Relationship*, George Allen & Unwin, London.

Ugalde, A. (1985), 'The Integration of Health Care Programs into a National Health Service', in C. Mesa-Lago, (ed.), *The Crisis of Social Security and Health Care*, Latin American Monograph and Document Series No. 9, Center for Latin American Studies, University of Pittsburgh, Pa.

UNDP (1983), *Evaluation Study No. 9: Human Resource Development for Primary Health Care*, New York.

WHO (1978), *Primary Health Care*, Geneva.

—— (1986*a*), *Intersectoral Action for Health*, Geneva.

—— (1986*b*), *Evaluation of the Strategy for Health for All by the Year 2000, Seventh Report on the World Health Situation*, Geneva A39/3.

—— (1988), *Economic Support for National Health for All Strategies*, Geneva.

World Bank (1980), *Health Sector Policy Paper*, Washington, DC.

—— (1986), *Review of PHN Lending in the Health Sector*, by A. R. Measham, World Bank, Washington, DC.

—— (1987), *Financing Health Services in Developing Countries: An Agenda for Reform*, World Bank Policy Study, Washington, DC.

—— (1988), *World Development Report 1988*, published for the World Bank by Oxford University Press, Oxford.

Zimbabwe, Republic of (1984), *Planning for Equity in Health*, Government Printer, Harare.

Zschock, D. K. (1982), 'General Review of Problems of Medical Care Delivery under Social Security in Developing Countries', *International Social Security Review*, 35/1: 3–15.

11
Neo-liberalism and the Political Economy of War: Sub-Saharan Africa as a Case-Study of a Vacuum

REGINALD HERBOLD GREEN

To fight the military and the economic fronts of the war separately will assuredly result in losing both.

(David Martin)

The struggle continues. The dream lives.

(Mozambican mobilizing slogans)

1. Introduction: A Vacuum and a Query

Neo-liberal economics has almost nothing to say about the economic consequences and policy implications of war and development economics says very little more. In Sub-Saharan Africa (SSA) this is a remarkably odd state of affairs. In two regions, Southern Africa (the Southern African Development Co-ordination Conference (SADCC) states) and the Horn (Somalia–Ethiopia –Djibouti–Sudan) war is the largest single economic fact and seeking to understand or influence these countries without analysing the economic consequences of war is an example of wilful tunnel vision. The same can be said of the Saouri Democratic Republic, while the political economies of Uganda, Chad, and Zaïre are warped or dominated by the consequences of past civil and/or regional wars and by the very real danger of their rekindling.

This paper is not a study of militarism nor of conflict/disorder in general, but of the economic consequences of war (or of safeguarding against it). Riots, strikes, and small scale localized conflicts fall outside its scope unless directly related to actual or potential civil and/or interstate war. In that sense the food riots on the Zambian copper belt are not part of the topic. However, the activities of the Mshala Gang and border clashes with and raids by South Africa's occupation forces in Namibia are part of it. That is so because real or realistically feared aggression by South Africa has created many of the burdens of a full-scale war. Similarly, economic tactics short of overt violence are covered if they form (as in the case of RSA) part of a 'total strategy' which quite clearly does involve actual or threatened military action.

A problem arises in arriving at an operational definition of neo-liberalism in Sub-Saharan Africa. Economic theory and analysis has always treated SSA as ultra-marginal. With the exception of a limited number of African and foreign specialists little serious attention is paid to the contextual application of economic analysis (or of political economy) to SSA. Thus the *locus classicus* of neo-liberal economics in SSA is the International Financial Institutions: The International Monetary Fund and the World Bank. We should note, however, that the Fund and Bank approaches are in tension and the Bank is very far from monolithic. This interpretation, therefore, has limitations, as indicated below.

The Fund operates on the basis of a monetary, demand driven, short-term model. This does not incorporate, and cannot be directly related to, real output, at least not at a disaggregated level. Therefore the basic Fund goal is adjustment by demand contraction and its principle tools are devaluation and credit constriction. In SSA the Fund is willing to allow for supply expansion through soft external finance, but primarily it sees adjustment as laying the base for subsequent larger external resource inflows, exports, and domestic output rather than as including them as essential components of stabilization *per se*. The economic logic for this is uncertain; its political and economic naïvety is not.

The Bank operates on the basis of a sectoral and macro-economic medium-term supply side model. Its present perception is that in SSA growth is a necessary part of both stabilization and adjustment to provide augmented resources to continue the process; to provide domestic incentives; and to avert massive civil disorder and the general withering of state authority. As a result the Bank has a more varied and articulated set of policy demands (suggestions is too mild) than the Fund. As regards trade liberalization, freeing selected prices (the prices of labour, capital, exports, and imports are normally required to be manipulated—thus the demand is not for *laissez-faire* pricing) and either privatizing or operating public sector agencies as if they were private, it is not so much that the two institutions disagree as that the Bank's approach provides a firmer base for specific proposals than the Fund's and that the Bank's time frame is considerably longer.

These two different models underlying the Fund and Bank approaches lead to inevitable tensions. Reducing trade and budget gaps (as opposed to financing them in sustainable ways) and reducing the constant price levels of total bank credit are not consistent with short-term growth in severely depressed (let alone war-torn) SSA economies. This is independent of whether either of them are neo-liberal. The Fund's model long pre-dates neo-liberalism and the Bank's present variant is now more eclectic than its starting point in the Berg Report (World Bank 1981) would have suggested (or approved).

The last point poses another problem. The Fund has a history of remarkable coherence at any time and over time. This is true even when its Articles, and, probably, its dominant members, would permit more flexibility. That history can be interpreted as unity of purpose and freedom from faddery or as a monolithic continuation of past errors. The Bank is much more varied in approaches and personnel both at any time and over time. This can be pictured as contextual realism, informed by flexibility and a pragmatic reading of the lessons of experience, or as faddism and expediency escaped from a coherent framework but regularly reined in by the lessons of non-success. Nevertheless, it is not unreasonable to argue that from 1980 the Fund and the Bank taken together have been the leading overt heralds, tools, and paymasters of neo-liberalism in SSA.

This said, the supposed SSA governmental conversion to economic neo-liberalism is much more apparent than real. In the first place the basic causes of the selective 'retreat of the state' turn largely on real resource constraints. Second, many pronouncements and some actions are based on two premises: external resources are essential for survival and reconstruction; they will not come in adequate amounts unless selective consolidation of state activity and some pricist policies are followed. Third, orthodox Marxist-Leninist doctrine is very conservative (neo-liberal?) on deficits, both budgetary and external. Equally, 'New Economic Policy' reforms may appear market and foreign investment orientated, yet do not constitute capitalist neo-liberalism. Thus Algeria and Angola are arguably pursuing parallels of Lenin's NEP or Gorbachev's *glasnost/perestroika*, rather than neo-liberal economics—even if in some respects they appear to be to the right of the IMF. Even the present Ghanaian policy could be interpreted as NEP plus F'eldmanite investment maximization with the liberalization of tariffs and exchange rates partly enforced by the size and openness of the economy and partly by the need for substantial net external resource inflows.

2. Government Expenditure and its Scope

Neo-liberalism in principle views government expenditure (with the partial exception of infrastructural investment which is viewed as a base for the private directly productive sector) as a drag on the economy, but —up to some point—a necessary one. In general it views both current public consumption of goods and services and transfer payments (to individuals or, especially, public enterprises) as well beyond that point. The state's expenditure is seen as crowding out the private sector in investment and the household in consumption.

There are, in practice, qualifications of this approach. Education and health (especially the former) are sometimes viewed as investment in labour productivity as, on occasion, is accessible pure water. More particularly the law and order roles are, with very limited exceptions, viewed as irremediably within the proper ambit of the state. Privatization of security and especially of violence is not on the whole a goal of economic neo-liberalism.

In practice neo-liberalism—at the theoretical and often even at the applied level—has little concrete to say about state recurrent spending (other than about subsidies to public and—less vehemently—private enterprises). It does tend to play the mirror image of Oliver Twist, saying 'less' fairly regularly. Here, the World Bank is an exception believing that in many African states public recurrent spending is too low (absolutely and as a proportion of GDP) to provide an adequate foundation for directly productive enterprises or a stable social fabric. The Bank is not entirely consistent on this stance, which appears to represent a significant change in perception from about 1985. It amounts to a more cautious and pragmatic variant of Robert MacNamara's emphasis on the 'elimination of absolute poverty' during the 1970s.

Neo-liberalism is nominally concerned with greater efficiency in, and on occasion, with broader access to, basic public services. (This is of course not a distinguishing characteristic.) The former is frequently used as an argument that expenditure cuts can be consistent with enhanced real services. This is true, albeit not within the time frame of an IMF programme. The latter seems to turn on providing a minimum level of services to all (in practice not even approximately attained in more than a handful of SSA states) with anything further paid for by the user. In general neo-liberalism (except when tax revenue is below 10 per cent of GDP) opposes higher taxes but advocates higher fees. To the argument that the latter—especially in respect of basic health, education, and drinking-water—are regressive, the reply is that in many cases (e.g. university education, expensive hospital treatment) the poor almost never have access at present so that subsidization or free provision is in practice regressive. (Important qualifications to this argument are given in Chapters 9 and 10 of the present volume.)

The problem in evaluating this position on government expenditure both in general and in SSA is that, like the curate's egg, it is good in parts. It finds partial support from a somewhat surprising range of non-neo-liberals. For example, African Ministers of Health and UNICEF appear to agree on fees as a desirable, substantial source of finance for primary health care as set out in the 1987 Bamako Declaration. At a different level of difficulty, the Fund tends to advocate little in detail: it wishes to reduce spending, and has a bias against 'subsidies' (sometimes defined to include financing fixed investment even in profitable public enterprises). Thus, any detailed examination must focus on World Bank prescriptions. Since 1985 these are arguably more Smithian than neo-liberal. A substantial state role is defined and considerable stress is placed on increasing the quantity of resources used to provide services as well as on the efficiency with which they are deployed.

3. Military Spending: Silence and Whispers

As regards military budgets the Fund and the Bank rarely have much to say, either openly or in camera. Since the wish to preserve political neutrality seems not to prevent their intervention on basic health charges, cutting food subsidies on staples, or delaying universal primary education there must be some other explanation. It may be that they view (not by any means wrongly) defence/security spending as the hardest to control or to cut, and judge attacking it to be an inefficient way of reducing overall government spending. Further, the Bank's post-1985 perception that adjustment which rends the fabric of society is not sustainable clearly applies to contexts, processes, and measures leading to civil explosions (as in Zambia). This may be seen to imply the need for caution in cutting the budgets of men with guns lest the result be not fiscal efficiency but a coup. If that is the explanation, however, rather more overt analysis of the constraints involved would be useful to planners and negotiators in both the Bank and SSA governments.

Nevertheless, there have been a number of cases where the Bank has challenged military spending levels—at least three in the context of war. These include Tanzania's border defence operation in Mozambique over 1986–8, the similar but larger Zimbabwean operation from 1983, and the general level of military spending in Morocco. (The Bank almost certainly takes a negative view of military spending in Ethiopia and the Sudan but has not had the scope to express it in the first case and it probably despairs of having any impact if it did so in the second.) It may be coincidental that the three cases cited all relate primarily to spending in respect to a war outside the countries' borders (albeit in two cases clearly a defensive one).

4. War as an Economic Actor: *Terra Incognita*

Neo-liberalism in general and the World Bank more specifically do pay marginal attention to military expenditure, albeit less so than to some other categories. However, they do not analyse war as an important exogenous (whether civil or external) variable with major political and economic content.

The fact is clear enough. World Bank studies on Tanzania allude in passing to the cost of the war pursuant on Amin's 1978 invasion, and those on Zimbabwe to costs of creating a national defence capacity and of defending transport routes in Mozambique. Prior to 1988, studies of Mozambique mention the war there three to five times, have no analysis of its attendant problems, and devote to it perhaps one-quarter of a per cent of the space in the main country report. Later ones, while looking at some consequences in an *ad hoc* manner, still neither analyse coherently nor seek to consider how the causes may constrain remedial action *vis-à-vis* specific symptoms. The recent Angolan studies mention war more frequently and attempt to highlight the burden of defence on the budget but still *en passant*. War is very much 'noises offstage' (like Fortinbras in *Hamlet*), not a lead actor.

One would not realize from this treatment that, in the absence of war Tanzania would probably have had a growth rate of GDP which was higher by 2 or 3 per cent per year from 1979 onwards, or that Zimbabwe would have had a negative domestic government borrowing requirement on combined recurrent and capital accounts. Nor could the casual reader intuit that Mozambique's actual GDP is less than half the level it would probably have achieved had the 1979–81 lull in RSA aggression continued or that the very marked contrast between managerial and technical capability in defence and civil institutions in Angola suggests that a not insignificant portion of administrative capacity in that country is the direct result of war.

Why this reluctance to face the obvious? Treating war as a one-line 'given' without any further articulation or analysis is not typical of the way other major exogenous events—e.g. drought, terms of trade shifts—are treated. Nor is it self-evident that analysing the direct and indirect economic impact of war is inherently 'political' or amounts to 'interference'. (In any event the Bank does not shrink from such 'interference' in other sectoral policies and programmes). One possible explanation is that war economics—even in capitalist economies—tends in large part to be the economics of intervention, rationing other than by price. Modern wars are not run on *laissez-faire* economic bases (albeit budgets sometimes appear to be). Therefore, neo-liberals and the World Bank may feel both a lack of expertise as to war economics and that to admit the magnitude of war impact would reopen the door for state economic interventionism in a fashion which they would find harder to challenge. Finally, in analysing civil wars or conflicts with neighbouring states it is very hard to avoid making normative judgements about the conflicts themselves. Understandably the Bank and the Fund wish to avoid placing themselves in that position.

This is not to say that the Fund and Bank oppose emergency relief programmes following war damage. Their general attitude to them is benevolent. But both view them as somehow extra-economic and at best parallel to stabilization, recovery, structural adjustment, and renewed development. They do not involve themselves in their planning or funding.

nor seek to view survival, rehabilitation, adjustment, and growth as an integrally interlocking continuum.

In fairness neo-liberals and the Bank are not alone. Sectoral and macro-economic studies of war impact and ramification in SSA are few and far between. A handful have emerged in respect to Southern Africa (and to a lesser extent South Africa and Namibia) from the mid-1980s. Even national governments, judging by their budget speeches, economic reviews, and published plans, do not give serious attention to war as a major economic parameter/variable. Since 1985 Mozambique has become something of an exception to this generalization as, less clearly, has Angola. In some cases states do not seem to realize the full economic impact of war (e.g. Tanzania); in others they have tended to view it as beyond economic intervention and therefore not needing detailed applied economic analysis (e.g. Zimbabwe); in some the need to relate the economic and military fronts of war to achieve efficiency on either has been overlooked (e.g. pre-1985 Mozambique). In still others the general principle of preserving security in relation to war activities seems to have come to encompass analysis of its articulated economic impact (e.g. Angola, Ethiopia, Somalia, and probably Morocco); while in a last group the capacity for analysis and the data to analyse are so limited that adding a new 'sector' may be virtually impossible (e.g. Sudan, Uganda, Chad). Perhaps a mix of these factors plus an absence of focused academic or international agency economic concern with the field is the basic explanation in most cases.

Whatever the cause, the result is unsound. For about sixteen countries—Angola, Chad, Egypt, Ethiopia/Eritrea, Malawi, Morocco, Mozambique, Namibia, Somalia, the Sudan, the Saouri Republic, Tanzania, Zambia, Zimbabwe, and arguably the Republic of South Africa and Libya—war (external or civil and including preventative defence against the danger of war) is the largest exogenous economic variable. (Arguably, in the cases of Ethiopia, Morocco, the Sudan and *a fortiori* South Africa, war is substantially endogenous but this is not so economically.) Other states have been similarly affected in the past, notably Mauretania, Nigeria, Burundi, Uganda, and Zaïre. Twenty-one countries out of fifty-three African states is a substantial proportion and they account for the majorities of continental population and GDP.

A closer examination of the economic impact of war in SSA is therefore appropriate on purely economic grounds. Since 1980, it has probably caused losses of GDP and foreign exchange availability for non-military purchases which have been substantially greater than those from drought and comparable to those from declines in terms of trade.

5. Economic Components of War Costs

The most evident and cited aspects of war costs are military expenditure above some minimum 'normal' threshold (say 5 per cent of budget in many cases) and/or their foreign exchange content. Less frequently direct war damage is cited. However, these would appear to be only two of eight components of macro-economic war cost;

- excess military expenditure and especially its foreign exchange content;
- direct war damage;
- non-maintenance or non-replacement of capital stock as a result of limited financial or foreign exchange resources consequential on war costs;
- the multiplier (or divider) impact of the three previous items on non-military GDP especially in the presence of severe budgetary and/or foreign exchange constraints;
- economic spill-over costs (e.g. transport blockages or cost increases and refugee inflows) from wars in adjacent countries;
- the shock impact of a large, sudden leap in war costs (analogous in macro-economic terms to a severe deterioration in the terms of trade or a major drought) on fragile macro-economic systems;
- strategic and policy distraction: during a major war it is not possible to focus government attention on medium-term macro and sectoral economic strategy, and military expenditure is harder to control than any other category;
- priority allocation of skilled, trained personnel (especially managerial and technical) to military institutions significantly limiting the scope and efficiency of the civil sectors.

The relative importance of these cost categories varies widely, as do their levels relative to GDP. Each is significant in some SSA economies and at least the first and fourth are important to most.

The first point presumably does not require illustration nor does the literal military destruction component within the second. However, the damage to roads by military traffic (especially tracked vehicles), the dislocation of production or its transportation, and the opportunity costs of diverting scarce high- and middle-level manpower to war are often passed by. The first two were very significant in Tanzania/Uganda and perhaps to a somewhat lesser extent in Nigeria/Biafra, Ethiopia/Eritrea, and Rhodesia/Zimbabwe. They are at their highest in Mozambique/South Africa and Angola/South Africa. The personnel cost was particularly evident in Rhodesia where all white males were full or part-time soldiers. It is obvious, too, in Angola where the high technological and managerial capacity of many military institutions contrasts sharply with those of the social and non-hydro-carbon economic sectors.

Non-maintenance and non-replacement of fixed assets over 1974–9 (and to a lesser extent 1965–73) by Rhodesia, primarily because of the war and sanctions has imposed very heavy burdens on Zimbabwe. Because the domestic financial constraints were less severe, maintenance and replacement of low import content assets was largely kept up so that the deferred cost manifested itself in an explosive rise of the investment import/Gross Fixed Capital Formation ratio in the four years after independence. The Nacala–Malawi railway provides an even more extreme case. Completed by Portugal at the end of the 1960s (as the liberation war in Mozambique reached a high level of intensity albeit rarely directly disrupting the line) it was nearly non-functional over much of its length by 1980. The reason was that maintenance and replacement was negligible throughout the decade because of both budgetary and foreign exchange constraints imposed by war.

5.1. Spill-over costs: dislocation of people and production

Spill-over costs of adjacent wars have three main aspects—military incursions, transport or other cost-raising dislocations, and refugee flows. Several major examples result from South Africa's systematic destruction—directly and by proxy forces—of Angolan and Mozambican transport routes. For Zimbabwe, Malawi, Zambia, and Zaïre this has resulted in very sharp increases in freight costs (reflected in lower FOB (free on board) prices for exports and higher CIF prices (inclusive of cargo, insurance and freight charges) for imports) because they are forced to use more distant ports—primarily East London and Durban in South Africa. Semi-official cost estimates for Zimbabwe and Malawi each exceed $100 million a year (on some estimates approach $150 million) and the total for Zaïre and Zambia together may be of the same order of magnitude. In the case of Malawi this cost represents about 30 to 50 per cent of export earnings. As a result the macro-economic cost of war is very heavy despite there being a small army and no significant combat. Indeed Malawi arguably could best reduce its war costs by totally forbidding MNR forces from crossing its territory to attack Mozambique and by acting jointly with Mozambique to defend the corridor to its natural ports of Nacala and Beira. Since December 1986, Malawi has taken substantial steps toward such a strategy.

Refugee flows from major wars have been a particularly heavy burden for the Sudan, Somalia, Malawi, and—during the Rhodesia/Zimbabwe independence war—Zambia. War, expulsion of aliens, drought, and economic disaster have driven refugees to a majority of SSA states. In the absence of other significant war costs they do not usually represent a crippling burden at macro-economic level but they represent a major human cost of war.

5.2. The macro-economic implications of shock and distraction

The multiplier effect is a widely used macro-economic tool whose relevance to any autonomous decrease in supply or increase in non-productive demand should require no explanation. However, it has to date very rarely been applied to direct war costs in SSA. Given marginal import/GDP ratios and the dislocative impact of war expenditure on inflation and production generally, and the external balance (or more accurately imbalance) in particular, an estimate of total GDP loss (or at any rate non-defence GDP loss) of the order of three to five times the foreign exchange costs of war does not appear to be an unreasonable starting point.

Shock impact has been little explored in the macro-economic analysis of SSA economies. It has, however, been increasingly seen as significant both in relation to major natural disasters (e.g. Sahel droughts) and sudden, massive negative terms of trade movements. The basic proposition is that, beyond some level, increased resource demands become unmanageable and macro-economic policy deteriorates into an increasingly fragmented series of measures to postpone disaster. War is particularly likely to have this effect, especially as overoptimism about the duration and level of war costs, as well as underestimation of its direct costs, appears to be endemic.

Strategic and policy distraction from macro-economic concerns, once stated, is presumably both self-explanatory and non-controversial. The history of Rhodesian policy as the liberation war grew indicated decreasing ability to pay attention to non-military issues or to contain military spending. The lag in Tanzanian strategic response to the 1978 export price collapse (in contrast to its very rapid response to 1973–4 oil and drought shocks) relates directly to the distraction of the Amin invasion in 1978 and subsequent efforts to provide a security frame within which Ugandans could reconstruct their policy.

5.3. Human costs: lives and misery

Constricted vision and underestimation of costs have also characterized the human price of war. Combat and crossfire civilian deaths are the only regularly mentioned aspect (with the exception of the six Southern African studies alluded to in the source notes to this chapter, and in particular the UNICEF reports). It is possible to identify six main aspects or components of these costs:

- direct military/combatant casualties, including militias and semi-organized forces;
- civilian casualties, including crossfire victims as well as those massacred by terrorist tactics, killed in selective sabotage attacks and falling victim

to unselective over-reaction by government and/or invader or insurrectionist forces;

- victims of increased mortality—especially infants and young children—resulting from destruction or breakdown of health and pure water services as a direct or indirect effect of war;
- victims of starvation resulting from war-caused dislocation of food production or blocking of relief food distribution;
- non-lethal human costs of the dislocation of people, production, and services;
- the multiplier (divider) effect on production, incomes, and access to basic services.

As with macro-economic costs, the absolute and relative significance of these components vary widely but all have been at very high levels in five or more SSA states. Military and combatant casualties are in fact usually a small proportion of war related deaths, under 5 per cent in Angola and Mozambique and 2 per cent in Tanzania. Genuinely accidental crossfire victims are probably an even smaller proportion.

Terrorist tactic victims are much more numerous in some wars—notably Mozambique and Angola/South Africa but also the Ugandan, Chadian, and Sudanese civil wars. Terrorist tactics are here defined as attacks on human or material targets designed to cause fear and dislocation, to wipe out highly valued services (e.g. health posts, schools, shops, local transport) and their staff and/or to use enforced starvation as a political weapon. Their goal is killing the dream of development and undermining perceived legitimacy by reducing both service and security provision. Their direct military or economic impact is totally secondary. In other terminology they are aimed at 'soft targets'. Over-reaction by combatant forces is very common, especially when the area is perceived as basically hostile by the forces in question.

The largest single war-related death toll, especially in the case of combat within a country, is usually increased infant and child mortality. This arises from the destruction of health services, or their increased inaccessibility as a result of combat, and from their deterioration because of war claims on fiscal and foreign exchange resources. For Angola and Mozambique the UNICEF (1987/1989) studies estimate a total of 800,000 war-related infant and young child deaths between 1980 and 1988. This is now equivalent to one every four minutes or, as UNICEF Executive Director James Grant put it, comparable to crashing a fully loaded jumbo jet of under-fives daily. Even in Tanzania where the mortality deterioration (relative to pre-1978 trends) is the result of the divider effect of war-deepened macro-economic malaise, the 1979–88 death toll certainly exceeds 25,000 souls and may be up to 125,000. War-related increases in older child and adult mortality—except for mass starvation —are significant but significantly smaller (and harder to estimate) than for infants and young children because older children and adults (except the aged or already infirm) are less physically vulnerable.

Mass starvation because of destruction of crops, dislocation of farmers, armed intervention to prevent food distribution, and the divider effect on food import capacity have killed several hundred thousand Africans over the past two decades. Unfavourable climatic conditions have often been a catalytic factor. The vast majority of the victims have been Angolans, Mozambicans, Sudanese, Ethiopians/Eritreans/Somalis, Chadians, Biafrans, Nigerians, South Sudanese, and West Nile and Karamojang Ugandans. Except for refugees from Ethiopia in Somalia camps and Ugandan and Ethiopian/Eritrean refugees in the Sudan, all of these cases involve bitter, long duration wars (whether civil or externally generated) within the country experiencing famine.

Dislocation—of up to half the rural populations of Angola, Mozambique, and the Southern Sudan and perhaps over a quarter in Chad and Uganda— has high human costs at the non-lethal level. Refugees from war, as from drought, have usually lost literally everything: home, land, household equipment, tools and seeds, livestock, access to public services. Even if they survive, they are in abject poverty and frequently unable even to begin reconstructing their lives and household incomes without substantial direct and infrastructural support. War makes the resources for adequate levels of such support quite literally unavailable for more than a small minority. Security concerns (of the dislocated human being and/or of the state) may force those dislocated to remain in overcrowded or agriculturally unsuitable areas because there they may have some protection whereas if they returned to their homes they would have none.

Trans-border refugees are an extreme case of dislocation. For example, of over seven million displaced Mozambicans somewhat over one million have fled to Zimbabwe, Malawi, Zambia, Swaziland, and the Republic of South Africa. There are practical differences: they may be in greater danger of expulsion back into the combat zone (e.g. Mozambicans in South Africa); they cannot fully begin rehabilitation of their lives and livelihoods until they are able to return home (as most Zimbabwe refugees in Zambia did after independence) or until they decide, and are allowed, to integrate into the host country (as 100,000 Rwandans and Burundians have in Tanzania); because of the international definition of refugee they may receive more international assistance than refugees (dislocated people) in their own country.

The divider effect of macro-economic war costs can also be documented in human terms. Access to basic services deteriorates (as does their quality), inputs and markets for production shrink as do job opportunities and goods to buy. The percentage of households in absolute poverty rises. These human costs can be very marked even in an economy like Tanzania which has had very little combat within its territory.

6. War in Southern Africa: South Africa's Total Regional Strategy

The regional impact of war in Southern African has been studied more than other cases and is larger than elsewhere in the continent. A subregional perspective is necessary not only on account of its importance, but because the external cause of the wars—South Africa's 'total strategy'—is common and because a substantial amount of military, political, and economic co-ordination in defence against South African strategy has been regionally organized through the Front Line States (Angola, Botswana, Mozambique, Tanzania, Zambia, and Zimbabwe) and their political/economic affiliate the SADCC (FLS members plus Lesotho, Malawi, Swaziland). However, the nature and economic consequences of war in the region are by no means uniform, with fighting occurring mainly in two states. The economic consequences are felt mainly in the same two countries, but are very severe in four more and low in the other three.

South Africa's regional strategy has sought to make the Southern African region safe and profitable for apartheid. Both are security considerations but the possible methods used to pursue them are not identical and are possibly contradictory.

The main instruments of South African military aggression have been:

- direct overt use of RSA armed forces against the victim state—primarily in respect to Angola;
- limited use of RSA armed forces for terror raids against African National Congress personnel (but with wider psycho-military goals) in seven of the states;
- similar long-distance sabotage operations, with or without proxy force involvement—notably Angola, Mozambique, Zimbabwe;
- use of proxy forces organized, trained, supplied, financed, and often supported by key RSA/mercenary personnel—massively in Angola (armed rebels/'UNITA') and Mozambique (armed bandits/'Renamo') and to a lesser extent in Lesotho ('Lesotho Liberation Army'), Zambia ('Mashala Gang'), and Zimbabwe ('Super Zanu');
- manipulation of domestic armed forces to achieve political change—Lesotho;
- threatening to use any or all of these tactics, thereby creating a need for massive defence expenditure to deter or limit the impact of the threatened action.

The first, fourth, and sixth of these measures are the most economically damaging. The first and fourth have been concentrated against Angola and Mozambique where the goals have been destruction of key economic facilities—especially those providing transit traffic routes for the five core landlocked states (Botswana, Malawi, Swaziland, Zambia, and Zimbabwe)

—and mass terrorism to destroy the rural economy, isolate the towns, and create large refugee populations. The sixth by itself is not economically devastating but it has crippled Tanzanian and Zambian efforts at recovery, severely reduced Zimbabwe's growth rate, and slowed the build-up of Botswana's external assets.

The selectivity in the use of large-scale, overt military action creating economic devastation appears to have been deliberate: Botswana, Zambia, and probably Zimbabwe could have been crippled economically just as readily as Angola and Mozambique. Blocking the non-South African routes from the landlocked states to the sea and forcing their attention (and expenditures) towards defence in the face of military threats was seen as sufficient to prevent their acting against South Africa. This strategy was also consistent with expanding captive markets for goods and services as well as creating new transport markets (and leverage over economic policy) by replacing the severed Angolan and Mozambican links.

Through 1986 the combined strategy clearly worked reasonably well from a South African perspective. Trade with the SADCC states (dominated by manufactured exports) grew rapidly. Vulnerability of the landlocked states —despite their individual and regional efforts, especially at alternative transport route rehabilitation—increased. Together with the devastation (economic, social, and military) of Angola and Mozambique, this increased dependence ensured that there was no serious security threat to RSA from within the Southern African region. To this broad pattern of success there were three limitations. The Angolan adventure had grown from a forward defence of Namibia to a much larger, more costly and open-ended venture without halting the deterioration of the economic, political, or even military position of RSA in the occupied territory. Increased transport costs and refugee flows undermined the economy of Malawi. Most important perhaps, the war bill (economic, foreign exchange, budgetary, human, and political) was large and may well have reduced South Africa's economic growth from 1980 by 1 or 2 per cent a year whilst also increasing the growing tendency of external enterprises and governments to distance themselves from it economically.

More recently the strategy has worked much less well. Indeed as 1988 ended it was arguably in ruins. Militarily the Mozambican proxy force has been broken, even though remaining deadly as a terrorist presence, and the military position for South Africa—and potentially for the UNITA proxy force—in Angola had become untenable. Transport rehabilitation was nearing the point at which dependence on RSA routes would become secondary. The region had managed to return to average growth rates in excess of 3 per cent per year. Regional commitment to economic disengagement (and external support for it), far from being broken, had increased and was showing results. The war bill to RSA had continued to rise and the low growth trend of 1981–8 seemed to be an increasing threat to domestic security.

7. War in Southern Africa: The Price of Pretoria

There are three basic ways of estimating war costs. The first is to make up a
list of items. In the case of the SADCC economies these include direct war
damage, extra defence spending, higher transport costs (e.g. Malawi to
Durban or Port Elizabeth as opposed to Nacala or Beira), loss of transport
revenue (on routes damaged or closed by South African and proxy action),
higher energy costs (e.g. South African vs. Cahora Basa power), looting and
smuggling (basically from Southern Angola), destruction of exports from
destabilization preventing production (e.g. in terrorized rural areas) or
transport (e.g. from Moatize colliery), support for domestic displaced
persons and international refugees, trade boycotts, and embargoes (overt or
covert) by South Africa, excess costs of South African goods and refusal to
renegotiate inequitable trading arrangements, loss of existing production
(consequential on war damage), and loss of growth (from diversion of
resources from new investment to military, relief, and reconstruction spending).

SADCC (1985) estimated these costs over 1980–4 as $10,120 million, and
a subsequent revision (Green and Thompson 1988) put them at $12,940
million. Carried through 1986 (UNICEF 1989) they came to $25,120 and
$27,240 million respectively. Through 1988 the total on this basis is of the
order of $44,000–46,940 million on a historic price basis and over $50,000
million, in 1988 prices. Defence spending and lost economic growth are the
dominant heads, with war damage, transport and energy costs, refugee
relief, and existing production losses; also significant are export losses
(including transit traffic) for Mozambique and, outside the petroleum
sector, Angola.

The chief problem with this first approach is that it is likely to produce
double counting, e.g. among loss of exports and production losses. It is also
likely to underestimate the indirect losses from lost growth. While all of the
heads can be roughly estimated none is really subject to precise calculation.
Furthermore, several items (e.g. excess defence spending, loss of output
from new investment) depend on problematic estimates (e.g. non-war basic
defence budgets, and 'normal' incremental capital/output ratios).

A second method is to compute estimated non-war growth rates for gross
domestic product and compare them with actual outturns. In UNICEF (1989)
this produced estimates of $5,500 million for Mozambique and $13,000
million for Angola over 1980–6 in 1986 prices assuming non-war growth
rates of 5 and 8 per cent respectively.

The regional total estimated in the same study, of $25,000–30,000 million
over 1980–6 includes $5,000–8,000 million for the other 7 SADCC states
calculated on a modified list basis. This total is somewhat misleadingly
similar to the 1986 list total of $25,000–28,000 million. The list includes,

while the GDP calculation excludes, loss of capital stock except in so far as it is reflected in current production losses and expenditure with some GDP impact (e.g. refugee relief, military salaries, and local purchases) represents a shift in actual GDP make-up, not a direct loss of GDP. The similarity of the two figures therefore tends to confirm orders of magnitude implying either gaps in the list estimation or assumptions about the growth rates of non-war expenditures in the GDP calculation that are too high.

As of the end of 1988 on a GDP loss basis (the third approach to measurement) war costs were of the order of $60,000 million at 1988 prices or about twice achieved GDP. The impact on regional growth was to reduce it from a probable peacetime rate of 5 to 6 per cent to an actual 2 to 3 per cent, i.e. less than the rate of population growth. In short, in the absence of war waged against it by South Africa the SADCC region would have had far less serious output declines in the early 1980s and far more marked and sustainable recoveries in the mid and late 1980s, even had all other factors remained unchanged.

It must be stressed that the end of South African aggression would not end this stream of losses, it would merely reduce it. Even on the list approach the largest cost component is loss of potential growth. The coming of peace, an ability to cut defence costs and attaining access to lower cost transport routes and import sources could—if backed by rehabilitation support—restore regional growth to a 5 or 6 per cent annual trend rate. But that would not alter the fact that the base income level would be at least $10,000 million lower. Thus an annual loss of $500 to $600 million would continue to accrue indefinitely. Nevertheless this is a different order of magnitude entirely to $10,000 million per year.

7.1. Human cost of war

The economic damage described above itself entails widespread and severe human costs. The standard of living of a majority of the people of the SADCC states is very close to the absolute poverty line. Were current GDP 25 per cent higher and growing at 5 to 6 per cent a year, the numbers in absolute poverty and/or lacking access to basic education, health, and water services would be substantially lower. However, war—as waged by South Africa—has three even more telling consequences: loss of food security, massive displacement of people, and death.

Proxy and regular South African military force attacks have not seriously sought to set up new South African installed governments, with brief exceptions in Angola in 1975 and possibly Mozambique in 1986. Their activities have focused on sabotage aimed at specific (usually transport and power) targets, on mass terrorism designed to destroy governmental authority and rural production, and on smaller, briefer murder raids and kidnappings by RSA's own forces. While financed, supplied, planned, directed, and often led by South Africa the first two aspects have been carried out primarily by South African proxy forces notably the armed bandits of Renamo in Mozambique and UNITA in Angola but also the Lesotho Liberation Army in Lesotho, the so-called Super-Zapu in Zimbabwe, and smaller gangs in Zambia. Renamo has also attempted terror operations in Tanzania, Zambia, and Zimbabwe with limited success, and has sought to coerce the government of Malawi to allow the use of its country by South Africa/Renamo as a transit and resupply base.

The terrorism has aimed at and resulted in keeping rural populations in Mozambique and Angola on the move, unable to settle down and restore production. The results have included massive food shortages resulting from production shortfalls of up to 1,500,000 tonnes of grain a year. The economic consequences of war (exacerbated in the case of Angola by the 1986 petroleum price collapse) have prevented commercial imports being substituted, while food aid to the two states has never exceeded 600,000 tonnes a year and—because of transport sabotage and rural terrorism—has proved very difficult to distribute.

Furthermore about half the populations of Angola and Mozambique— 14,000,000 souls—have been driven out of their homes at least once (usually with virtually total loss of all possessions and often of the lives of some family members). About 1,500,000 are now international refugees, 4,000,000 are registered rural displaced persons with no significant ability to restore their production and incomes, up to 2,000,000 are urban migrants largely in slum or shanty areas with very low incomes, and about 7,000,000, nominally again self-supporting, are unlocatable because of the degree of rural dislocation or are held as slave labour by the armed bandits. It is noteworthy that the armed bandits do not carry out basic service provision or food relief operations (they destroy services, killing, maiming, or driving out personnel as prime targets and steal or destroy food). No one flees to them, rather large numbers cross borders or take refuge in government-controlled urban or less insecure rural areas. That in itself is adequate comment on the Renamo and UNITA claims to be liberation movements with popular bases, rather than what they are—proxy South African terrorist and sabotage forces.

By the end of 1986 UNICEF estimated (probably conservatively) the numbers dead at the hands of South African aggression as 1,000,000 people in Mozambique and Angola (UNICEF 1987). Half were infant and child victims of war-caused malnutrition and of the destruction or running down of health services. Another 200,000 were famine victims and 100,000 older child and adult victims of medical service collapse. The 200,000 estimate for direct civilian and military war victims is shown by an AID (US) estimate of 100,000 for Mozambique alone over 1986–7 to be an underestimate. A conservative re-estimation through 1986 would be at least 325,000 (200,000 in Mozambique and 125,000 in Angola). War-related deaths over 1987–8 can be estimated as of the order of 500,000 (325,000 infants and young children, 50,000–75,000 older health and malnutrition victims, 125,000 war casualties) for a 1980–8 death toll of 1,900,000 human beings now dead who would have been alive in the absence of war.

That figure relates to Angola and Mozambique alone. In the other seven states direct calculation is less easy. In several, but not all cases, war costs have enfeebled the economy and the budget, eroding food security as well as medical and water services. A cautious estimate of these deaths plus those of terror raids and limited proxy terrorism might be 25,000–100,000 over 1980–8 depending primarily on how much war costs have eroded the basic health care systems of Tanzania, Malawi, and Zambia.

As with the economic costs, ending South African aggression can, especially in the short run, only reduce human costs. Rehabilitating health and water services and restoring rural production and livelihoods is a task which will require at least five years of peace and the reversal of the negative infant and child mortality trends and bringing their levels down to those pertaining in other low income SSA countries will take yet longer. However, by the second year of peace the death toll could be halved and by the fifth reduced by perhaps 80 per cent assuming priority attention to food security, mass immunization, and access to pure water and basic health care services.

7.2. Policy implications, domestic, regional, and global

The level of the price of Pretoria to the SADCC region means that it must be seen as of central economic and human concern. It is necessary to take its impact into account in all sectors—especially but not only in Mozambique and Angola—and to relate priorities in resource allocation to its reduction and alleviation.

Increasingly the independent Southern African states have understood and acted on this brutal reality both individually and collectively. National prioritization of food security, rehabilitation and emergency relief, basic health care, restoration of regional transport routes and defence do speak to this as, perhaps slightly less directly (and, to date, less effectively), do attempts to increase intra-regional trade, partially as a substitute for trade with RSA.

The SADCC Programme of Action focuses squarely on the economic side of the price of Pretoria especially in its priorities for transport, power, and telecommunications rehabilitation and expansion to break South Africa's non-military grip on the region. So too do the emphases of SADCC and the PTA (Preferential Trade Area of Eastern and Southern Africa grouping fourteen states including six SADCC members) on bolstering intra-regional trade as a means to re-sourcing imports and re-targeting exports away from RSA.

The Frontline states (FLS) have increasingly co-ordinated regional defence and international diplomatic offensives against South Africa. The solidarity shown in the defence of Mozambique demonstrates the reality of that co-operation. So does the leadership they have taken in calling for effective international action—especially sanctions—against South Africa to hasten the end of its regional policy of total aggression and of apartheid itself.

This external role of the FLS, like the resource mobilization one of SADCC, calls attention to the fact that by themselves the independent Southern African states cannot meet the costs of ending unilateral economic dependence on South Africa, blocking direct and proxy military aggression, sustaining existence and beginning rehabilitation for refugees and displaced persons, restoring growth and development. Poor and beset with most of the other exogenous shocks (including drought, debt, and terms of trade) which have overwhelmed most of SSA since 1980 this is not surprising. They are, with the exception of Botswana, foreign exchange constrained, indeed in several cases import capacity strangled, economies. The annual foreign exchange cost of excess defence spending, higher cost transport routes, lost exports, survival relief, and rehabilitation of direct war damage is—regionally—of the order of three-quarters actual annual export earnings.

7.3. Regional costs: a summary

The total regional cost of South African destabilization and aggression is now running at about $10,000 million annually or of the order of 40 per cent of achieved regional GDP. Over 1980–8 it totalled about $60,000 million in 1988 prices or over twice present annual GDP and about three times gross external resource (grant, soft loan, export credit, and commercial loan) inflows over the same period.

That cost was very unevenly distributed by country with Angola bearing the largest absolute burden—$4,500 million in 1988 and $27,000 to 30,000 million over 1980–8—and Mozambique next with $2,500 to 3,000 million in 1980 and $15,000 million for the period. Between them the two lusophone states bore 70 to 75 per cent of the GDP losses. However, no state escaped a significant loss, $30 million for Lesotho and Swaziland being the lowest in 1988, and $200 million for Swaziland the lowest of the 1980–8 estimates. Over the period, six states had cumulative losses of over $1,000 million.

The current rate of losses also varied sharply as percentage shares of achieved GDP from around 100 per cent of actual GDP for Angola and Mozambique to 10 per cent or less for Botswana, Tanzania, Lesotho, and Swaziland. However, even 5 to 10 per cent of GDP must be seen as significant for a small, poor economy with narrow fiscal, foreign exchange and food security margins at the macro-economic level and with a majority of households with yet narrower margins of abject poverty and a very real danger of premature death. The main elements in the losses were excess defence costs, loss of merchandise exports, excess transport costs on external trade, and loss of transit traffic revenue. Loss of rural production and remittances had a smaller macro-economic impact albeit they were the most burdensome economic factors for poor households especially in Mozambique and Angola.

The losses suggest that in the absence of war the region's annual GDP growth trend would have been of the order of 5 and perhaps 6 per cent as opposed to 3 per cent or less actually achieved over 1980–8. In the cases of Angola and Zimbabwe healthy per capita growth—up to 5 per cent a year—could have been achieved and in the cases of Mozambique, Tanzania, probably Malawi, and perhaps Zambia, GDP growth would have been able to be held at levels equal to or in excess of population growth.

Human costs are harder to summarize quantitatively. The most shocking is that for 'excess mortality'—over 1,900,000 lives lost over 1980–8 as a direct or indirect consequence of South Africa's regional strategy. In Mozambique the total was of the order of 1,100,000 or nearly 8 per cent of estimated 1988 population and in Angola 750,000 or 7.5 per cent. The total for the rest of the region was much lower, perhaps 100,000. The second indicator of human costs is displaced persons and refugees. Over half of the population of Angola and Mozambique—14,000,000 persons—fell into this category. In addition Malawi's land access, food balance, and ecology were hard pressed by the well over 500,000 Mozambicans (almost 7 per cent of Malawi's national population) who had taken refuge there.

These totals are appalling—no milder term will do. They confirm the hypothesis that in Angola, Mozambique, and arguably Malawi and Zimbabwe, the dominant cause of economic unsuccess and human misery in Southern Africa is South African destabilization plus overt and proxy aggressions.

8. War and Neo-liberal Economics: What Linkages?

One direct implication of the neo-liberal economic approach is that, by keeping war outside the framework of economic analysis, it is almost certain to reduce efficiency of resource allocation in a war context. However, as noted earlier, this is by no means unique to that economic paradigm.

A central question is whether neo-liberalism in economics causes or exacerbates (or removes or ameliorates) contexts giving rise to wars. In SSA there is little evidence of correlation—positive or negative. The Chadian, Saourian, and Horn conflicts long pre-date the rise of neo-liberalism or the launching of its African flotilla flagship, the Berg Report. The Southern African conflicts do parallel the rise of neo-liberalism in that they were greatly stepped up from 1981, even though earlier phases date back to the 1960s. However, the driving force for war—South Africa's total regional strategy—is very clearly not a product of neo-liberal economics and to the extent it is economically motivated bears a family relationship to Hjalmar Schacht's 1930s policies in Nazi Germany, not to Chicago School models.

So too with declines in levels of war. Military defeat and lives lost (perhaps reinforced by recession and defence budget burdens) explain South Africa's evacuation of Angola and potential ending of the occupation of Namibia. Military reverses on the Eritrean and Tigrean fronts, not economic policy rethinking and probably not even the continuing economic stagnation, led to Ethiopia's 1988 moves to reduce actual and perceived probable hostilities levels *vis-à-vis* Somalia and Ethiopia. The Sudan's renewed—but very problematic—quest for an end to civil war by negotiation turns on human and social costs and exhaustion rather more than on direct economic condition causes and certainly has no direct link to economic strategy reformulation.

In certain contexts there do seem to be direct links from neo-liberal economic policies and pressures to civil disorder and short-term violence. Zambia's 1986 maize meal price riots and the 1985 Sudanese bread price riots leading to the overthrow of the el Nimeiry regime are examples of this. So also are the 1989 Sudan food price riots which greatly weakened the el Mahdi government. However, neither was a war as defined here. The Zambian case was a brief period of massive (but geographically limited) civil disorder which was rapidly contained and partly defused by policy reversals. The first Sudanese case did lead to a change in government but neither to a northern civil war nor to a solution to the northern–southern civil war; the second has weakened both the political system in the north and the Khartoum government stability needed for a north–south settlement without directly leading either to a change of government, a coup, or sustained intra-northern violence.

Even at the level of civil disorder two problems arise. The same type of measure—for example, food subsidy reduction or abolition—may be accepted in one country but lead to riots in another (*vide* Tanzania 1984 and Zambia 1986). A similar contrast is provided by the massive petroleum price increases which were to be tolerated by Ghanaians over 1983–5 and the riots which broke out over a 3 per cent increase in Nigeria in 1988. The differences seem to turn on general public perceptions of the state, its goals, and its competence, not on the specific measures themselves nor on whether they are taken in the context of war. Furthermore, each of the above initiatives could be justified on grounds other than neo-liberal economics: the Tanzanian reduction on food subsidies was in fact decided and defended on a quite different rationale. The difference in reaction may relate to perceptions of unwelcome external imposition rather than to views on neo-liberal economics or even the merits or the specific changes themselves.

9. Conclusion

Neo-liberalism calls for a small, nightwatchman state but provides little guidance as to priorities, levels, or qualitative improvements in state spending; nor does it treat war as a major macro-economic parameter needing to be disarticulated sectorally and factored into analysis, evaluation, and proposals. This is a major failing in SSA and especially in over a dozen severely war-affected states with populations approaching 250 million. Furthermore, it is exacerbated by failure to co-ordinate economic policy and projects with their military counterparts.

However, there is no very plausible evidence in SSA that neo-liberalism (whether practised or rejected) and war (whether heightened or reduced) have substantial causal or empirical links (in either direction). While severe war costs do tend to force changes in political and economic strategies, the direction is by no means uniformly toward freeing market forces and, in any event, leave the presumptive priority tasks—waging and ending the wars—squarely in the state sector. Massive opening up to the private sector, 'war communism', and a mix of more limited but intensive intervention using more market management and less administrative instruments have each been resorted to in SSA cases of national economic implosion caused by war. Only the last of these seems to be likely to survive the ending of war-imposed economic constraints.

References

Green, R. H., and Thompson, C. (1988), 'Political Economies in Conflict', in D. Martin and P. Johnson, *Destructive Engagement: Southern Africa At War*, Zimbabwe Publishing House, Harare, 1986; updated version Four Walls Eight Windows, New York: 245–80.

Hanlon, J. (1988), *Beggar Your Neighbours*, Catholic Institute for International Relations—James Curry, London.

SADCC (1985), *Overview* (Annex on Costs of South African Aggression) for 1985 Mbabane SADCC, Gaborone.

UNICEF (1987), *Children on the Front Line*, New York.

—— (1989), *Children on the Front Line*, revised and expanded to include Namibia, New York.

United Nations Inter-Agency Task Force Africa Recovery Programme/Economic Commission for Africa (1989), *South African Destabilisation: The Economic Cost of Frontline Resistance to Apartheid*, UN, New York.

World Bank (1981), *Accelerated Development in Sub-Saharan Africa: An Agenda for Action*, Washington, DC.

12

The State and Rural Development: Ideologies and an Agenda for the 1990s

ROBERT CHAMBERS

We have left undone those things which we ought to have done,
And we have done those things which we ought not to have done,
And there is no health in us.

(The Book of Common Prayer)

1. Ideologies and Rural Development

To generalize about the state and rural development in the south is rash. Almost any statement needs qualification. It is difficult to talk in the same breath about, say Angola and the Andaman Islands, Togo and Thailand, India and Iran, or Cyprus and Kampuchea. Nations vary physically, economically, and socially, and are politically diverse. Within national boundaries there are regional differences, and within regions ethnic, social, and economic differences between households and people. Any commentator is also influenced and limited by personal experience, in my case largely in Sub-Saharan Africa and South Asia, on which this paper is based.

These obvious problems have done little to inhibit the search for general policies and their dissemination. National policy-makers need laws and programmes for whole countries. Aid agencies with large budgets, especially the Banks, need packages to promote. Academics need ideologies to dissect and denounce. Institutions and their members need and seek shared values and concepts to sustain solidarity and to support effective activities, especially where they have direct responsibility for policy. And all these need a common language and set of concerns for dialogue and debate, for securing and legitimating flows of funds, and as a framework for thought and action.

I wish to thank Charles Harvey, James Manor, and Hans Singer for comments on an earlier draft. Responsibility for the views expressed and for errors is mine.

Historically, the fashions for ideologies, packages, and programmes in rural development have changed. In part, this reflects changing rural conditions. The community development ethos and programmes of the 1950s, and the stress on agricultural extension and the dissemination of innovations of the 1960s, look dated and wrong now, even naïve, with their stress on cultural obstacles to change, on community self-help construction, and on early adopters and laggards. Yet in the conditions of the time, they fitted better than they do now. The lesson is to see ideology and action in context, not as constants, but as arising from and adapting to, as well as moulding, those conditions. In this view, they are always likely to be out of date, always requiring an imaginative effort to be ahead of current convention. This could support a forced straining for originality, change for its own sake, and new fashions to sustain the market for consultants, advice, technical assistance, and research. What it should support is a continuous effort to see what best to do for the future. There will always be changing perceptions and policies. Given the centralization of power and communications with which we live, we have to generalize; not to do so is to generalize by default. The problem is how to do it better.

It is modestly in that spirit that this paper addresses the question of an agenda for state action in rural development in the 1990s. It approaches this with a historical view of neo-Fabian prescriptions of the 1970s and neo-liberal prescriptions of the 1980s, and then with a contemporary view, from below, of the rural conditions which both these have tended to miss.

1.1. Neo-Fabians in the 1970s: redistribution with growth

If the 1960s saw the zenith of national planning, the 1970s experienced only a slow decline. In a Fabian tradition, government organization was seen as a principal instrument for action against poverty. In many countries national plans had high profiles, and set styles and patterns to be followed also at lower levels, in rural regions and districts. In both decades, in Sub-Saharan Africa (SSA), major and widespread attempts were made to prepare and implement district and even subdistrict plans, with donor-supported integrated rural development projects following close behind. In South Asia, especially India, national programme followed national programme for rural development, to be administered through field bureaucracies. The pervading sense, supported by the best development wisdom of the time, was that government could and should do more.

A good illustration is the volume *Redistribution with Growth* (Chenery *et al.* 1974), a joint study by the Development Research Center of the World Bank and the Institute of Development Studies at the University of Sussex. *Redistribution with Growth* (*RWG*) was inspired by the thinking and experience of ILO missions, notably to Colombia (1970), Sri Lanka (1971), and

Kenya (1972), and especially by Sri Lanka's outstanding achievements in health and education. It was also influenced by India's directly administered rural programmes. Significantly, Kenya, which received and influenced one of the ILO missions, was closer to South Asian than to most African conditions in having a strong rural administration. Not surprisingly, direct administrative action by the state in rural development was taken for granted as a major mode of intervention. If not a Bible of development in the 1970s, *RWG* was at least a revered text, cheap (my copy cost £1.40), accessible, and much prescribed and studied, as the heavily thumbed copies in the IDS library testify. *RWG* is a prospectus composed by humane economists, having a second go after the planning fantasies of the 1960s. The authors had learnt the lesson that rural élites tend to capture the benefits of government programmes. They sought solutions through targeting: there were to be rural target groups, and urban target groups. In targeting the rural poor, asset distribution through land reform was stressed, together with services specially for small farmers, as in the statement that 'A land reform which breaks the power of large farmers and the rural élite will . . . provide a framework within which public goods and services can be directed to the target groups with minimum leakage' (ibid. 135).

To provide these services, new organizations were suggested—'wholly new institutions endowed with ample resources and the best cadres' (ibid. 68). An Agency for Small Farmers would conduct a co-ordinated programme with a package combining credit, crop extension, crop insurance, and input supplies (ibid. 128–90). The faith in direct government action, and the socialist sympathies of the time, are reflected in the opportunities seen in Tanzania:

we would stress that the lack of rigidity in much of tropical Africa makes possible interventionist policies designed to create new forms of rural institutions, such as the ujamaa villages in Tanzania, which can provide for the more efficient use of public infrastructure, agricultural capital, and such government-supplied services as extension, health care, and education. (Ibid. 135)

To reach and help the rural target groups, special institutions and programmes were needed. Economies, planning, and the state were all seen in terms of growth. To do more for the poor, government must grow. The solution to rural poverty was not less government but more.

1.2. Neo-liberals in the 1980s: structural adjustment without a human face

If the 1970s were the decade of equity, the 1980s have been the decade of efficiency. This is not to assert how much or how little either equity or efficiency have been achieved, but to say that these have been prominent in rhetoric and ideology. Efficiency has been linked to neo-liberal prescriptions with freeing markets and slimming government. In the 1980s, especially in SSA, but perhaps excepting Botswana, state organizations have been seen as overgrown, inefficient, corrupt, and costly. The solutions advocated and introduced in structural adjustment packages have included devaluation which raises agricultural incomes from exports, higher domestic prices for agricultural produce, derestricting food grain movement, and deregulation of prices. Government recurrent expenditure has been cut back, and parastatals shrunk or disbanded. Even among those who have opposed structural adjustment for its lack of concern for the poor—its lack of a human face—there has been a degree of acceptance that governments should do less in some respects in order to do better in others.

A classic statement of neo-liberal prescriptions is *Accelerated Development in Sub-Saharan Africa: An Agenda for Action* (*The Berg Report*) (World Bank 1981). This sought more efficient use of scarce resources. In his Foreword, the President of the World Bank said that administrative and managerial capacity were the scarcest resources in all countries. In that context, the report suggested that African governments should examine ways in which public sector organizations could be operated more efficiently and more reliance could be placed on the private sector. In agricultural and rural development, this implied competitive private input supply and marketing, and user charges and cost-recovery for services. The solution to the problems of development was not more government but less.

2. Contrasts and Commonalities

To polarize two schools of thought in this way is to simplify and even caricature; but it provides a basis for asking how they have been applied, what they have in common, and what they miss.

In rural development policy and its application, South Asia, especially India, contrasts with most of SSA in adhering to neo-Fabian approaches. It was, indeed, in India that some of the policies advocated in *RWG* originated, and where attempts to implement them have subsequently been most sustained. To my knowledge, India is alone among developing countries in its persistence with massive administered programmes targeted to individuals or households. These include the Small Farmers Development Agency (1971), Training Rural Youth for Self-Employment (1979), and the Integrated Rural Development Programme (IRDP) (1979), which latter continues on a vast scale all over the country. In a neo-Fabian mode, rural development programmes in India have been standardized, subsidized, packaged, and targeted. That the packages often do not fit and often miss their targets are commonplaces of field observation; but the approaches and programmes are stable. There are several reasons for this: some programmes are protected by misleading evaluation surveys (for a perceptive critique see Drèze 1988);

subsidized programmes play their part in local political patronage; the Indian government, despite a rural population almost twice that of SSA, has had the financial and administrative means to persist with a rural development strategy in which field bureaucracies play a major part; the successes of the green revolution are seen by policy-makers as linked with the transfer of technology through agricultural extension and other services; and India has had the relative freedom from debt and aid dependence to be able to resist donor pressures to change its policies. In consequence, India's field bureaucracies show little sign of being eroded by neo-liberal thinking.

In contrast, many of the countries of SSA, with their declining economies, heavy debts, large government organizations, and weak administrations, have evoked and been subject to the neo-liberal prescriptions of structural adjustment. Both the state and the market have shrunk back. With recurrent budgets squeezed by smaller revenues and the conditions required by the IMF, World Bank, and other donors, existing field bureaucracies have been starved of resources, with the familiar tragedies of agricultural extension staff without tyres for their bicycles, schools without textbooks, clinics without drugs, and teachers and health staff without pay. With economies in decline, basic goods have become scarce and costly. In places it has been NGOs, rather than the market, that have filled the vacuum left by the decline in government services. In India, the state tries to extend its activities to help the poor individually; in much of SSA, the state struggles simply to maintain some contact with them collectively and to sustain basic services.

These contrasts conceal commonalities. The neo-Fabian and neo-liberal prescriptions of *RWG* of the *Berg Report* respectively have in common that both have been elaborated and propagated by economists and in association with the World Bank. The authors of *RWG* were all economists—Chenery, Ahluwalia, Bell, Duloy, and Jolly (though Bell and Jolly at least had rural field experience). Berg was also an economist. It may be no coincidence that while the *Berg Report* criticized the size of government in SSA, the one part to be strengthened was planning—'The appropriate response now is to reinforce the central planning agencies, and to endow them as quickly as possible with the investment evaluation capacities they need' (World Bank 1981: 33). Both ideologies, and both sets of prescriptions, embody a planner's core, centre-outwards, top-down view of rural development. They start with economies, not people; with the macro not the micro; with the view from the office, not the view from the field. And in consequence their prescriptions tend to be uniform, standard, and for universal application.

3. A Counter-ideology of Reversals

Centre-outwards, core-periphery views have their validity and strength; after all, since most power resides in the centre, it is in the centre where

change can most readily be effected. But they also mislead unless complemented, qualified, and offset by the reverse view, from the periphery. This
amounts to a counter-ideology to those generated and diffused from the
cores, whether Marxist, socialist, structuralist, or neo-liberal, and whether
red, pink, blue, or any other hue but certain shades of green. It is a counter-
ideology which takes as its starting-point the conditions and priorities of
rural people, especially the poorer, and the problems and opportunities
which they face; and it leads to a different constellation of prescriptions.

The reversals have been elaborated elsewhere (Chambers 1983, 1987,
1988*b*). The switch or flip of view can be recognized by reflecting on the
normal meanings attributed by professionals to the word 'remote', a word
as profoundly as it is unconsciously urban-biased in élite usage; to a villager
far from town it is the town that is remote. The reversals are of location,
learning, explanation, values, control, authority, and power, to put first the
poor and the periphery.

When related to the role of the state in rural development, reversals
provide an agenda for the 1990s. They point to two key aspects: first, the
changing priorities of poorer rural people; and second, the conditions and
behaviour of the government field staff with whom they interact.

For any urban-based outsider to state the priorities of poor rural people is
yet another core-based act of paternal guesswork. But not to attempt this is
also an act by default. Any statements have to be subject to qualification and
change; and one of the greatest unmet needs in rural development is a
continuous, sensitive exercise to understand the conditions, strategies, and
priorities of the poorer. When this is undertaken (as shown by e.g. Beck
1989, Breman 1985, Corbett 1988, de Waal forthcoming, Heyer 1989, IDS
1989, Jodha 1988, Rahmato 1987), the reality revealed can differ from
beliefs commonly held by outsiders. Using these and other insights from
fieldwork, my best inference is that many of the aspirations of poor rural
people can be captured in the concept of secure and sustainable livelihoods,
with access to basic goods and services, and freedom from fear and hassle.
But priorities change, and differ; as the extended family and patron–client
obligations have weakened, and as costs of services for health and education
have risen, so command over assets to handle contingencies and buy services
have become more important; and with rapid social and political change,
and with more education and better communications, so self-respect has
come to matter more.

For their part, field-level government staff have similar aspirations. They
are often committed to their professional work but lack resources for it.
They want and often badly need to earn more. Promotion is usually out of
the question. Especially in SSA, their salaries have typically declined in real
terms, eroded by inflation. Quite often, they no longer provide even for a
basic livelihood. In Eastern Uganda in 1987 the monthly salary of a nursing
aid would buy one kilo of sugar and two loaves of bread, and it required two

months' salary of a secondary school headmaster to buy a bicycle tyre (Whyte 1987: 8–9).

Faced with the need and desire to increase their earnings, field-level staff who do not resign or manage to move to urban centres have two main strategies:

1. *Moonlighting and daylighting*. Clandestinely or openly, staff undertake economic activities. Farming and other self-employment are common. In part of Uganda in 1987 'agriculture was—for most professionals—the strategy of necessity which allowed them to remain professionals' (ibid. 12). In Burkina Faso it is known, and in Sudan it is widespread, for government field staff to be paid officially approved salary supplements by NGOs to work in the NGOs' programmes. Some activities are moonlighting—illicit and concealed; others, in countries as different as Sudan and Vietnam, are daylighting, carried out openly because they are condoned.

2. *Extracting rents*. The extraction of rents takes several forms:

(a) Subsidies are shared. Subsidized programmes and inputs provide a surplus which can be creamed off. In India, for example, there are standard understandings of percentages for sharing the subsidies for purchasing IRDP milch buffaloes.

(b) Services are sold. This practice takes many forms. In much of West Africa, government rural health services have been *de facto* privatized. There and elsewhere, whatever small amounts of drugs are supplied get sold by staff, operating what are in effect private dispensaries. Parents pay teachers for admitting children. Officials are paid for moving files or providing documents. Irrigation staff are paid for providing water. Examples abound.

(c) Rents are extorted. Frequently, government rules give local-level staff powers which they can use to extract rents. Poor people are blackmailed with threats of persecution or prosecution. Payments are demanded for waiving restrictions. At the field level there are then conflicts of interest between poor people and poorly paid staff. Moreover, the less poor often pay less while the poorer pay more.

The perspectives of poor rural people, and the realities of field administration, are basic to the practical counter-ideology of reversals. This seeks to see things from the point of view of the poorer. In doing this, it is complementary to other ideologies, not an alternative. Macro analysis will always be needed as well as micro. But when generating agenda and assessing policies, core professionals normally neglect what poor people want and need, or assume they know what it is, or treat it as a residual. A balanced view can be gained, offsetting and correcting core-based ideologies and views, by putting first the priorities of those who are poorer and peripheral.

In thinking through what the state should and should not do in the 1990s, three approaches help. The first is to learn lessons from the failures and successes of the past two decades. The second is a stance of eclectic pluralism, open to a mix of ideas. The third is this counter-view, of reversals, starting with the perspectives of the poorer. The prescriptions which follow may fit neo-liberal tendencies in saying what the state should not do, and neo-Fabian tendencies in saying what it should do; but they do not depend on either philosophy. Based on reversals, they stand on their own.

3. What the State Must Do

(Everyone can read this section.)

Three universal functions of the state are fundamental for the rural poor. It must do the following:

1. *Maintain peace and the democratic rule of law.* The appalling suffering and poverty resulting from civil disturbance and war is so obvious that it is easily underestimated. The fear, pain, and anguish; the destruction, theft, or loss of property; the insecurity of tenure; the disincentive to invest; the danger of loss of crops; the weak labour power when adults are fighting, guarding, or killed; the interruptions to education; the disruption of services; the distress, migration and destitution of refugees—any listing of bad effects can start with these and continue with many more. The record of the 1970s and 1980s includes Afghanistan, Angola, Burundi, Chad, Eritrea, Ethiopia, Iran, Iraq, Kampuchea, Laos, Lebanon, Mozambique, Namibia, Palestine, Rhodesia (as it was), Sri Lanka, Sudan, Tibet, Tigre, Uganda, Vietnam, West Iran, and Western Sahara, without even starting on Latin America.

The democratic rule of law is also fundamental. In some radical circles in the 1970s, democracy was seen as a form of Western cultural imperialism, and 'law and order' were dirty words associated with oppressive police action. Law can indeed favour the rich and the exploiters. Where force and intimidation prevail, as in much of Bihar, the poorest suffer. Where laws give power to petty officials, they may abuse it. It is the fairly administered rule of democratic law, and accessible justice for the poor, that matter.

Colin Leys once wrote on the primacy of politics (in Seers and Joy 1971). One can add the primacy of peace, and of fair laws and justice for the poor.

2. *Provide basic infrastructure and services.* Fiscal management of revenues and budgets is again fundamental. Beyond and based on that is the provision and maintenance of basic amenities to serve rural areas like trunk roads, railways, secondary and often primary schools, community and preventive health care, agricultural and veterinary extension, water supplies, weights and measures inspectorates, and in some areas telephones and electricity. Often, these are beyond the power of local communities to command and install or of the market to provide. NGOs, it is true, especially in some of the more afflicted states of SSA such as Sudan, have increasingly complemented

and substituted for the state, and may do so even more in future. But the state remains the logical long-term institution to provide and maintain much of a country's basic infrastructure and services.

3. *Manage the economy.* Managing the economy, both externally and internally, is accepted by all except anarchists to be a legitimate and necessary function of the state, though views differ sharply on what and how much it should do. These issues are the subject of other essays, but three points relating to the rural poor can be noted.

First, the debate on pricing policy for agriculture (see Colclough, introduction to this volume; Harvey 1988) has not generated simple feasible policies applicable world-wide, given the conflicts of interest between poor rural producers and poor urban consumers; but higher prices for agricultural produce have often proved powerful means of enhancing the well-being of most poor rural people.

Second, parastatals for production support and marketing present a spectrum of monopoly and competition, and of performance. At one extreme is inefficient, overgrown, and corrupt monopoly. Some West African marketing boards in the 1960s and 1970s are one example. Another is the introduction of monopoly government organizations in some parts of India to market the minor forest products gathered by tribals. This was designed to bypass contractors who paid little. In effect, though, it merely introduced another stage in marketing with its own costs, with the result that the tribals received even less than before (personal communication from N. C. Saxena). In such conditions, it is common for field staff to gain power which they use to extract rents. Near the other end of the spectrum is the degree of democratic control and efficiency in marketing organizations achieved in Zimbabwe (Thomson 1988). The question has to be asked, case by case, whether in the real, local world, poor rural people will be better or worse off with a parastatal marketing organization. Sometimes, but not always, the best solution may be plural, with a competitive private sector but a government agency providing a floor price.

Third, from the point of view of the rural poor, managing the economy entails much more than just ensuring growth, good prices, and marketing: it also includes providing conditions with access to food and to basic goods at affordable prices, a function which some states in SSA have failed to fulfil.

4. An Agenda for Abstention

(Neo-liberals can read this section.)

The neo-liberal critique of state intervention in the economy has included the size and inefficiency of government bureaucracy and of parastatals, with prescriptions that the state should do less and the market more. A full review of the scope for limiting or reducing state intervention to make things directly better or less bad for the poor would require a book of its own. Here, some illustrations must suffice, proceeding from the more to the less obvious and recognized.

4.1. Forced collective agriculture and villagization

Were it not for continuing attempts to maintain collective agriculture, as in North Korea and Ethiopia, this section would be unnecessary. Only, it seems, with exceptional and voluntary ideological commitment, as with some of the kibbutzim in Israel, can producer co-operatives work at all well; and even the kibbutzim have had problems of sustainability. That the USSR, China, and Vietnam have been reversing collectivization is a recognition of the ultimate force of what most people want. That the USSR is finding the reversal difficult is an indication of the powerful inertia of vested bureaucratic interests once institutions have been established. In SSA, producer co-operatives have been more important in ideological debates than an economic reality (Hedlund 1988: 12), and have performed badly; even ujamaa, the simple and limited form of collectivization attempted in Nyerere's Tanzania and remarked on positively in *RWG*, did not work.

Villagization induced by degrees of force has often been linked with collectivization, as in Ethiopia, North Korea, and Tanzania, and as now (1989) proposed for parts of Zimbabwe. The pros and cons have been the subject of much debate. The official motives are often a desire to control a disgruntled and dispersed peasantry. Against the officially listed advantages of better access to services must be set higher health risks from population concentrations, loss of control over and protection of land, including productive micro-environments, and loss of incentives to invest in more sustainable agriculture. Most important of all, villagization is rarely what people want.

It seems inherent in the contemporary human condition for most rural people to seek a secure and independent land-based livelihood where resources are controlled and commanded by the family and where returns are directly linked to efforts. With secure tenure and rights to land, livestock, and trees, farm families tend to take the long view and invest in sustainable agriculture (Chambers 1987). Without it, they take the short view and environmental degradation often follows. Not only are collectivization of agriculture and forced villagization undesirable as forms of core-based, top-down, ideological and political paternalism, which puts rural people's priorities last; they are also environmentally unsound.

4.2. Shining islands of salvation

Islands of salvation are small projects which receive special support and attention. Most governments deceive themselves and the international community through visits to these privileged entities and through superficial reports and studies. Mick Moore (in this volume) cites the water co-operatives on canal irrigation in Gujarat, supposed by an international authority (Repetto 1986) to buy water wholesale on a volumetric basis. However, almost all evidence of these co-operatives traces back to a single small project, the accessible, heavily subsidized, closely administered, and frequently visited Mohini Water Co-operative Society; and sustained searches by academic sleuths elsewhere in Gujarat have drawn an almost complete blank. The outcome is prescriptions which, as Moore shows, are physically and administratively unfeasible and, worse, which distract attention from the main priorities for the poor—better management of canal main systems to improve supplies to the underprivileged at the tails. Or again, much of the insight and understanding about the progress and feasibility of ujamaa villages in Tanzania in the late 1960s was based on repeated visits to and articles about three special cases—the Ruvuma Development Association, Mbambara, and Upper Kitete. Generalizing from these exceptional examples helped to mislead policy-makers into a disastrous decade of trying to do what poor rural people did not want.

4.3. Borderline big projects

Not all big projects in rural development are bad. Few would wish to argue that the rural poor of Egypt would have been better off if the Aswan dam had not been built. Big infrastructure is sometimes needed, and indivisible. The case for heavy investments in communications and in power can be strong. There may also be a case for some large-scale flood control works, for example in the watersheds that flow into Bangladesh.

That said, the case against big new rural development projects has strengthened. Completing current projects, and maintenance and cost-covering for those completed, are often higher priorities than new construction. Complex projects have also tended to do badly. The World Bank's frank, sober, and sobering evaluation of its experience with rural development from 1965 to 1986 found an uneven record. Area development projects did worst, especially in SSA, leading to the comment that 'That form of area development project which came to be known as "integrated rural development" (that is, a multicompetent project involving two or more agencies) performed so poorly as to raise questions about the utility of that approach in many situations' (World Bank 1988: p. xvi). While irrigation projects outside Africa did better, the position has changed now that many of the best sites have already been exploited. Those that remain tend to require the displacement of larger numbers of people, and they are often poor and politically impotent. The record with resettlement and compensation of oustees (though improving under pressures from the World Bank) is so bad that big projects are still likely to mean many poor losers. And when their livelihoods are given due weight in the calculus of gains and losses, appraisals are liable to be more negative.

4.4. Standard packages for diverse conditions

Normal bureaucracy centralizes, standardizes, and simplifies. In capital cities, programmes are designed for whole countries and orders issued for implementation, regardless of diverse conditions. Targets, too, are set centrally and disaggregated to regions, districts, and subdistricts, where they often make no sense. Agricultural extension, at its near-worst, promotes the same package of practices in different agro-climatic zones. Health services supply the same drugs to clinics regardless of local and seasonal incidence of diseases. Such standardization fails to serve the public, demoralizes staff, and has again and again been found wanting.

4.5. Controls which harm or exclude the poor

Many controls which make sense to central policy-makers in practice harm the rural poor. The administrative reflex is to control and regulate for the common good; but with astonishing frequency, across a wide range of countries, conditions, and domains, such control and regulation hurts the poor. Some examples can make the point:

Movement restrictions hinder work-seeking. For refugees, restrictions on movement imposed by host countries can prevent migration essential for livelihood, and weaken their bargaining power when they do move, since employers can threaten to turn them over to the police. In consequence, their employment is less secure, their wages liable to be lower, and the danger greater of not being paid at all. More generally, freedom of movement for the landless and for poor rainfed farmers can be essential to permit migration to fill in seasonal gaps in work.

Effective nationwide price controls on scarce basic goods hurt the rural poor. Where the controls are effective, as in Zambia in 1980, it does not pay for rural traders to stock goods since they cannot cover transport costs and risks. Goods then stay in towns. Urban people have better access, and rural black markets, if supplied at all, have higher mark-ups (ILO/JASPA 1981). Attempts by a central government to stamp out a black market, as with basic goods like paraffin, sugar, oil, rice, and flour in Darfur in Sudan in 1984, only further push up the black market prices (Diab 1988: 44). The rural poor pay more or get nothing.

Restricted movement of food crops creates local seasonal shortages which the market cannot relieve. In Ethiopia in 1987, where such regulations prevailed, the price of sorghum at Degan market, on the main tarmac road from Addis Ababa to Assab, reportedly rose to three times its price at harvest, the highest prices being at just the time when poor people were having to eat less at fewer meals.

Regulation for minimum distances between tubewells in some parts of India protect the privileged access of those who sink tubes first. The restrictions do not deter the better-off, who have independent sources of credit: they can ignore the rules and go ahead anyway. The restrictions do exclude precisely the poorer, who need institutional credit which requires that the regulations be observed. As so often, the haves have access denied to the have-nots (Tushaar Shah pers. comm.).

Prohibitions on cutting trees on private land, and on their transport and sale deter planting, especially by poorer farmers who cannot handle contractors and the bureaucracy. In many countries, but on the largest scale in India, farmers are either prohibited from cutting trees on their land, or require permission to do so. This means that even if farmers are able to cut, transport, and market their trees, they get less for them. Of twelve cases reported by N. C. Saxena (Chambers, Saxena, and Shah 1989) of sales of trees or tree products in India, the highest receipt by the seller was 43 per cent of the disposal price, while in eight cases it was less than 20 per cent, among which three were less than 10 per cent. Cutting and transit restrictions were a major factor in price formation. Sellers were in a weak bargaining position, having to rely on the contractors who bought their trees to make the necessary side payments to the authorities. Though intended to conserve the environment to benefit all, restrictions on cutting, transport, and sale discriminate against the poorer and weaker, induce them to cut and sell while they can, and discourage them from replanting. Poor people's private trees are savings, but in these conditions they can only cash them on bad terms. To restrict harvest, transit, and sale is like a bank manager refusing withdrawals; not surprisingly this inhibits deposits—tree planting—especially by the poorer. There is probably no measure so easy, quick, and vast in impact, and which would help poorer farmers and the environment more, than the abolition of such rules.

Restrictions such as these—on movement of people, on retail prices for scarce basic goods, on movements of food grains, on sinking tubes for groundwater, and on the harvest, transit, and sale of private trees—are manifestations of the disabling state. Whatever their intentions, in practice such rules impoverish and deprive the rural poor—by loss of opportunities for earning; by denial of access to productive resources; by disincentives for saving; by less to buy and higher prices; and by the hassles, uncertainties, and costs of dealing with rent-seeking officials or those who can pay them off. Those who are less poor and more influential can flout or bypass regulations, while the poorer are excluded, or have to pay. Not always, but all too often, restricted access and imperfect markets penalize poor rural people. Again and again, they want the state off their backs. One of the quickest and easiest ways for the state to help poor rural people on a large scale is to abolish damaging restrictions, to dismantle the disabling state.

For neo-liberals who want the state to wither more than somewhat, these points may warm the heart. They should provide an acceptable and practical agenda. But let them not relax and rejoice too soon. For there is more to come.

5. An Agenda for Action

(Neo-Fabians can read this section.)

5.1. Normal bureaucracy: doing the double

Since field bureaucracies normally centralize, standardize, and simplify, it is commonsense to give them tasks for which these tendencies are strengths. These are of two types.

The first is where a standard receiving environment can be found or created, suitable for a standard input. Immunization for people or livestock is an example, with simple one-off inputs into the closely controlled and predictable environment of the human or animal body. To differing degrees the GOBI (growth charts, oral rehydration, breast feeding, and immunization) programmes promoted by UNICEF lend themselves to simple repetition, and have scored successes in child welfare even in bad economic conditions such as those in Zimbabwe in 1982–4 (Cornia *et al*. 1987: 290). Sometimes, too, uniform environments can be created, as when irrigation and fertilizer modify the farm environment to fit green revolution genotypes.

The second feasible task for normal field bureaucracies is the transfer or supply of technology which is robust and usable in a wide range of conditions. In India, the Technology Missions based in the Prime Minister's office have stressed high quality blackboards and good handpumps. Blackboards and handpumps can be designed and made to work well almost anywhere, given schools and groundwater respectively. It is again the doable that is being done.

5.2. Safety nets

Almost all poor people, including many of the ultra poor or near-destitute, struggle hard, even desperately, to avoid becoming even poorer; but they are vulnerable to contingencies. When bad years and disasters strike, they are further impoverished, whether through sale of assets, new debts, new obligations, or physical disability. Big health care costs are one new threat to the poor who have a sick relative; they can impoverish utterly, reinforcing the case for effective free or cheap treatment. Once impoverished by loss of productive assets, say in a famine, recovery is hard. To help those who have become poorer to claw back to their previous condition is costly and difficult, although there have been successes, as shown by experience with Oxfam-supported restocking programmes for pastoralists in Kenya (Moris 1988). In general, though, it is likely to be much more cost effective, besides more humane, to provide safety nets to help poor people avoid becoming poorer in the first place.

Measures to do this are many. They include: public works and food for work programmes, among which the Maharashtra Employment Guarantee Scheme provides a model in which groups of people can demand work paid at the minimum wage; early interventions to keep food prices down and incomes up at bad times, for example by buying at good prices whatever poor people decide to sell (livestock, jewellery, charcoal, etc.); when famine threatens, food or other relief provided early enough to prevent the poorer having to dispose of their assets, together with clean water and immunization (de Waal 1989); and at all times, effective preventive and curative health services available free or at low cost. Also, wherever the state has the resources and capacity, and social supports are feeble, there is a case for help for the destitute and indigent, as provided for widows in some Indian states.

The weaker the state, the greater the part NGOs can have to play; but in most countries, at most times, it is to the state that the safety net role falls.

5.3. Changing rules

The micro perspective, from below, can reveal scope for gains by the poorer from changing rules. Tushaar Shah's fieldwork on groundwater markets in India, coupled with economic analysis, led to a switch of electricity charging policy in Gujarat, from pro rata to graduated per horsepower rates. This resulted in between 1.5 and 2 million buyers of irrigation water (generally the poorer and smaller farmers) paying 25 and 60 per cent less to sellers (Chambers, Saxena, and Shah 1989). The question is whether this was a unique opportunity, or whether other fieldwork and analysis could reveal other simple changes with similar vast, quick impact. At the very least, micro-level investigation merits attention to search for other potentials.

5.4. Secure rights and information

The poorer people are, the more they need secure rights. To enjoy their rights, they need to know what they are and how to claim them. They also often need organization and solidarity to overcome vested interests. Two aspects can illustrate the potential here.

First, where restrictions are abolished, the changes must be credibly known. In India a forester has told me that although in law no restrictions on movement of certain trees applied, the Forest Department pretended to the public that they did. A first step in the reversal of power needed in such a case is information, and then encouragement, through countervailing organization, and even through changes in the judicial system, for people to claim their rights, resist extortion, and eliminate hassle.

Second, for resource-based livelihoods to be sustainable, rights and access to the resources must be secure. Without secure tenurial rights, groups and families lack the incentive for long-term investment in land, water, pasture, soils, and trees. In practice, it is precisely the more fragile environments— forests, uplands, swamps, wetlands, semi-arid savannahs, and arid pastures —disparate though they are ecologically, where tenure is least secure and least exclusive. Urban-based interests sometimes seek to gain or maintain open access and to deny exclusive tenurial rights to communities or individuals; and this can reinforce the common failure in central places of policy-making to recognize the importance of secure tenure to those who seek their livelihoods in such remote and ecologically vulnerable areas.

Communication of their rights to poor and scattered rural people is perhaps the most promising frontier for the state in rural development in the 1990s. In contrast with earlier decades, it will be easier to inform peripheral people about changes in regulations and rights. The revolution in communications is already reaching the most remote places. Using multiple channels —radio, television, video, newspapers, handbills, noticeboards, meetings —public information and public consultations will be more credible and convincing. It will be harder to mislead the poor at the local level. The benign state cannot be assumed, and communications can be used for many bad purposes. Where, though, there is central desire to inform and empower through credible and correct information, the means to do so will more and more be there. Communications are a corner-stone of an enabling state.

6. Reversals, Diversity, and the Enabling State

The prescriptive paradigm of reversals for rural development is neither neo-Fabian nor neo-liberal. Nor is it just eclectic pluralism. Putting poor rural people first provides starting-points which are at once dispersed, diverse, and complicating. Linear teleology in development thinking has long since fallen from favour (for critiques see e.g. Nettl 1969 and Streeten 1983: 881–3) but linear measures of development along scales (per capita GNP, infant mortality rate, female literacy . . .) persist as universal tools of assessment and comparison. They are needed, but they condition analysts to think in linear terms. In contrast, field-level realities—whether ecosystems, farming systems, or livelihood strategies—are non-linear, adaptive, and differentiating. For some professionals, development is still, consciously or unconsciously, seen as convergent; in the paradigm of reversals, development is decentralized and divergent. While normal bureaucracy and normal markets centralize, standardize, and simplify, it is in contrast by becoming more complex and diverse that ecosystems and livelihood strategies become more stable and more sustainable.

Near the core of this paradigm is decentralized process and choice. One expression of this is farmer participatory research for resource-poor agriculture (Farrington and Martin 1988; Chambers, Pacey, and Thrupp 1989). This is coming to stress not the transfer of technology in the form of packages of practices for the uniform, simple, controlled environments of the irrigated green revolution, but provision of baskets of choices for the more diverse, complex, and risk-prone farming systems of rainfed agriculture. Bureaucratic reversals are implied, with varied local requests passed up from farmers replacing preset technologies passed down to them. Approaches which put farmers' analysis and priorities first complement those which generate and transfer technology. In this mode, the state is not school but cafeteria, and development is decentralized, becoming not simpler but more complex, and not uniform but more diverse.

The paradigm of reversals takes us even further; for it resolves the contradiction between the neo-Fabian thesis that the state should do more and the neo-liberal antithesis that the state should do less. In terms of this paradigm, the state has often done those things which it ought not to have done, and has left undone those things which it ought to have done. The patterns vary and diverge. In much of SSA the state has been so weakened that it has retracted too far, and made errors of omission. In India it has expanded too far, and made errors of commission. The worst mistakes have been rules and restrictions which give field-level staff power to extract rents from the weak. Here a new neo-liberal agenda can liberate the poor by abolishing the regulations used to exploit them. The task is to dismantle the disabling state. In parallel, there is more that the state can and should do.

Here a new neo-Fabian agenda can decentralize while providing safety nets, secure rights, and access to reliable information, and permitting and promoting more independence and choice for the poor. The task is to establish the enabling state. For both these new agendas, the unifying theme is reversals, to put first the diverse priorities of poor people. To understand and support these is equitable (helping people gain what they want), efficient (mobilizing their creative energy), and sustainable (providing incentives for long-term self-reliant investments by the poor). The vision is then of a state which is not only protector and supporter, but also enabler and liberator; and of the 1990s as a decade for equity and efficiency through reversals and diversity.

References

Beck, T. (1989), 'Survival Strategies and Power Amongst the Poorest in a Village in West Bengal, India', *IDS Bulletin*, 20/2 (Apr.): 23–32.

Breman, J. (1985), *Of Peasants, Migrants and Paupers: Rural Labour Circulation and Capitalist Production in West India*, Oxford University Press, Delhi, Bombay, Calcutta, Madras.

Chambers, R. (1983), *Rural Development: Putting the Last First*, Longman, Harlow, and London.

—— (1987), 'Normal Professionalism, New Paradigms and Development', IDS Discussion Paper no. 227, IDS, University of Sussex, Brighton.

—— (1988a), 'Sustainable Livelihoods, Environment and Development: Putting Poor Rural People First', IDS Discussion Paper no. 240, IDS, University of Sussex, Brighton.

—— (1988b), 'Bureaucratic Reversals and Local Diversity', *IDS Bulletin*, 19/4: 50–6.

—— (1988c), 'Farmer-First: a practical paradigm for the third agriculture', typescript, IDS, University of Sussex, Brighton.

—— Pacey, A., and Thrupp, L. A. (eds.) (1989), *Farmer First: Farmer Innovation and Agricultural Research*, Intermediate Technology Publications, London.

—— Saxena, N. C., and Shah, T. (1989), *To the Hands of the Poor: Water and Trees*, Oxford and IBH, New Delhi, and Intermediate Technology Publications, London.

Chenery, H., Ahluwalia, M. S., Bell, C. L. G., Duloy, J. H., and Jolly, R. (1974), *Redistribution with Growth*, Oxford University Press, Oxford and London.

Corbett, J. (1988), 'Famine and Household Coping Strategies', *World Development*, 16/9: 1099–112.

Cornia, G. A., Jolly, R., and Stewart, F. (eds.) (1987), *Adjustment with a Human Face*, i. *Protecting the Vulnerable and Promoting Growth*, Oxford University Press, Oxford.

de Waal, Alex (1989), 'Is Famine Relief Irrelevant to Rural People?, *IDS Bulletin*, 20/2: 63–7.

—— (forthcoming), *Famine That Kills: Darfur, Sudan, 1984–85*, Oxford University Press, Oxford.

Diab, M. (1988), 'Famines and Household Coping Strategies in Sub-Saharan Africa', typescript, final report to IDRC, IDS, University of Sussex, Brighton.

Drèze, J. (1988), 'Social Security in India: A Case Study', Papers for the workshop on Social Security in Developing Countries held at the London School of Economics, July 1988.

Farrington, J., and Martin, A. (1988), *Farmer Participation in Agricultural Research: A Review of Concepts and Practices*, Agricultural Administration Unit Occasional Paper 9, Overseas Development Institute, London.

Harrell-Bond, B. E. (1986), *Imposing Aid: Emergency Assistance to Refugees*, Oxford University Press, Oxford, New York, Nairobi.

Harvey, C. (ed.) (1988), *Agricultural Pricing Policy in Africa: Four Country Case Studies*, Macmillan, London and Basingstoke.

Hedlund, H. (ed.) (1988), *Cooperatives Revisited*, Seminar Proceedings No. 21, Scandinavian Institute of African Studies, Uppsala.

Heyer, J. (1989), 'Landless Agricultural Labourers' Asset Strategies', *IDS Bulletin*, 20/2 (Apr.): 34–40.

IDS (1989), 'Vulnerability: How the Poor Cope', *IDS Bulletin*, 20/2 (Apr.).

ILO/JASPA (1981), *Zambia: Basic Needs in an Economy Under Pressure*, International Labour Organization, Jobs and Skills Programme for Africa, Addis Ababa.

Jodha, N. S. (1988), 'Poverty Debate in India: A Minority View', *Economic and Political Weekly*, special number (Nov.): 2421–8.

Moris, J. R. (1988), 'OXFAM's Kenya Restocking Projects', ODI Pastoral Development Network Paper 26c (Sept.).

Nettl, J. P. (1969), 'Strategies in the Study of Political Development', in Colin Leys (ed.), *Politics and Change in Developing Countries: Studies in Theory and Practice of Development*, Cambridge University Press, Cambridge: 13–34.

Rahmato, D. (1987), 'Peasant Survival Strategies', in Angela Penrose (ed.), *Beyond the Famine: An Examination of the Issues Behind Famine in Ethiopia*, International Institute for Relief and Development, Food for the Hungry International, Geneva (Jan.): 1–26.

Repetto, R. (1986), *Skimming the Water: Rent-Seeking and the Performance of Public Irrigation Systems*, Research Report 4, World Resources Institute, Washington, DC.

Seers, D. and Joy, L. (eds.) (1971), *Development in a Divided World*, Penguin, Harmondsworth.

Streeten, P. (1983), 'Development Dichotomies', *World Development*, 11/10: 875–89.

Thomson, A. M. (1988), 'Zimbabwe', in C. Harvey (ed.), *Agricultural Pricing Policy in Africa: Four Country Case Studies*, Macmillan, London and Basingstoke: 186–219.

Whyte, M. A. (1987), 'Crisis and Recentralization: "Indigenous Development" in Eastern Uganda', Working Paper 1987/1, Centre for African Studies, University of Copenhagen.

World Bank (1981), *Accelerated Development in Sub-Saharan Africa: An Agenda for Action* (The Berg Report), World Bank, Washington, DC.

—— (1988), *Rural Development: World Bank Experience, 1965–86*, World Bank, Washington, DC.

13

Rent-seeking and Market Surrogates: The Case of Irrigation Policy

MICK MOORE

1. Introduction

The neo-liberalism which is currently so influential in much of the world has two relatively distinct bases in social scientific doctrine. There are on the one hand the venerable canons of economic liberalism: the superiority of competition over monopoly; of the private over the public economy; of market-determined over administered prices; of choice and freedom over regulation; of decentralized decision-making over hierarchy; of integration into markets over autarky; and of individual personal responsibility over paternalism. On the other hand one finds the novel school of rent-seeking analysis, only a decade or two old, which complements economic liberalism by providing a political critique of the motives for state involvement in the economy.[1] The meta-hypothesis behind rent-seeking analysis is that a great deal of public involvement in the economy is motivated by the search for (illegitimate) 'rents'[2] on the part of individual actors—citizens, politicians, public officials, enterprises, and corporations. Each seek to use their influence over public agencies to shape public policy to their own material advantage. Import restrictions are expected to be motivated by the interests of existing domestic producers rather than by larger motives of developing indigenous industry. Statutory regulation of labour conditions is anticipated to originate less from altruism than from the attempt by larger and more organized commercial enterprises to use the cover of humanitarianism to drive their smaller competitors out of business.

A close affinity exists between neo-classical economics and rent-seeking analysis both at the level of policy—the preference for the private, competitive, market economy—and at the level of method. Both are founded upon methodological individualism and utilitarianism. In this sense rent-seeking analysis is but one manifestation, albeit a particularly important one, of a

I am indebted to a number of colleagues, especially to Chris Colclough, for comments on an earlier draft of this paper.

major new social scientific paradigm, variously labelled 'rational choice', 'the economics of politics', 'neo-classical political economy', or 'the new political economy'. The unifying feature of the various fields of this paradigm is the attempt to see how far one can explain political phenomena by exploring the assumption that political decisions are the product of the interactions of individual agents each rationally pursuing individual material self-interest.[3] The central methodological postulates of neo-classical economics are thus applied to political analysis.

This is not the place to review the large and rapidly growing literature on the rational choice paradigm or even to list in any detail its strengths and weaknesses. For present purposes it is adequate to mention a few major limitations: it is not an appropriate tool to explain major societal or institutional transformations; and its usefulness depends on careful specification of the institutional and cultural environment and on the formulation of hypotheses about actors' objectives, resources, and constraints which are appropriate to specific circumstances.[4] Similarly, it is not possible here to detail the major doctrinal biases which have given birth to rent-seeking analysis and influenced the way in which it has been used.[5] A tool should not be rejected simply because it can be and has been misused.

It is argued below that, in the context of irrigation policy in the Third World, rent-seeking analysis provides an explanation of the current situation which, at a relatively high level of generality, is consistent with the evidence, convincing, economical, and superior to alternative explanations. The diagnosis is not only to some important degree correct, but the associated prescription—the application of more 'commercial' principles to financing recurrent activities and capital investment—is to some extent viable and convincing. To this degree the paradigm is fruitful. However, it moves rapidly into fallacy. For there are major 'natural' obstacles to the full application of commercial principles to the financing of recurrent irrigation operations in the Third World. In a high proportion of cases it is physically impossible or prohibitively expensive to charge consumers for irrigation water in such a way as to affect the amount of water they use. It is then not feasible to use financial mechanisms to ensure that the scarce resource is used in a socially responsible fashion, and by this means put an end to the abuses of irrigation facilities which result from the existence of rent-taking opportunities. The particular physical features of large-scale irrigation schemes result in strong incentives for both scheme managers and consumers (farmers) to adopt socially irresponsible and economically costly practices of water management.

The impracticability of water pricing does not however exhaust the options for encouraging responsible use of irrigation water. The Taiwanese case is particularly useful in illustrating how *political* mechanisms—hierarchy, concentrated institutional power, bureaucratic allocation of water to the consumer, and a kind of political accountability of management to clients—

may be employed as implicit market surrogates to generate incentives for efficient resource use. These incentives, however, bear on behaviour of the supplier of water (the irrigation management agency) and not (directly) on the demands of the consumer (the farmer). Ironically, irrigation fees are an important component within this nexus of political and institutional controls; however, they operate more as a political and institutional signalling device than as economic resource allocation and signalling mechanisms. The hostility to political and institutional controls on economic life which lies at the heart of neo-liberal doctrine proves misplaced in this case.[6]

2. Rent-seeking Analysis of Irrigation Policy

There has over the past decade been a major expansion in the amount of attention paid to irrigation in the Third World by social scientists, especially by sociologists and anthropologists. This was motivated by a wide range of concerns about the performance of the major investments in irrigation which have been made since World War II. At the most general level it has become conventional wisdom that the returns on these investments have been inadequate. Social scientists in particular have popularized the view that this is in large part because the engineering cadres which dominate almost all aspects of irrigation provision appear more interested, active, and competent in relation to new construction projects than to the maintenance of existing facilities or, even more strikingly, to the management of irrigation water.

It has not been difficult to detect patterns of self-interest in this implicit preference ranking of irrigation activities. In so far as it is plausible to assume that the staff of irrigation establishments are able to siphon off a proportion of the funds they handle, then they are likely to benefit most from engaging in new construction and least in managing irrigation water. Where they have few alternative sources of supplementary incomes, control over irrigation water may nevertheless be used to extract bribes from farmers. Eliciting bribes however requires that farmers be kept in uncertainty about likely irrigation supplies. This may lead to a pattern of water allocation that appears arbitrary and uncontrolled, and certainly is socially and economically suboptimal (Wade 1982*b*). The very absence of control over irrigation water may be to the advantage of minorities of wealthy and influential cultivators whose land is located near the main water source and who consequently are able to use physical position to capture generous supplies of scarce water and deprive other farmers. 'Poor water management' may not be to every farmer's disadvantage (Chambers 1988: chapters 1 and 6).

However, such self-interest explanations of irrigation policy have competed with a wide range of other types of explanation: economic history arguments about lags in the adaptation of irrigation institutions and management practices in the face of rapid changes in the economic environment (Levine

1981); environmental arguments about the effect of differences in the natural environment on the feasibility and desirability of different types of institutions or management practices (Wade 1988); and, most commonly, arguments about institutional deficiencies. Indeed, at the level of practical policy discourse social scientists have tended to focus on *institutional* diagnoses and prescriptions: the reorientation and retraining of engineers to become water managers as well as system builders; internal reforms of irrigation agencies; the separation of engineering construction agencies from agencies responsible for maintenance and operation (or even the separation of maintenance from operational responsibilities); the mobilization of farmer organizations of various kinds to participate in water management; the creation of institutions which oblige engineers to share responsibility with agricultural specialists, farmers, and other parties involved in irrigation; and more training for everyone (Wade 1982*a*).

It was in this context, in which the debate about causes was becoming more complex and in which a growing range of institutions were developing a vested interest in detailed research and debate, that Robert Repetto (1986) stepped in with an application in rent-seeking analysis to the irrigation field which, while generating considerable controversy, appears to provide the essential broad framework upon which one can build detailed and situation-specific diagnoses and prescriptions. His explanation is too general to be complete, but is the base on which more complete explanations should be founded.[7]

There is little or nothing which is original about any single component of Repetto's analysis. The same is true of his central proposition: that public irrigation policy is adversely affected by organized private interests using official position to skew public policy in their favour. The originality and analytic power of Repetto's thesis lie in its comprehensiveness: in the wide range of irrigation-related phenomena which it can claim to explain (at a high level of generality) through pursuing the basic ideas of rent-seeking analysis.

The key actors in Repetto's rent-seeking (and rent-taking) model are: the staff of irrigation engineering agencies aiming to maximize the flow (and 'leakage') of funds they control; foreign aid agencies who need both to spend budgets which are large relative to their own organizational capacities and to please powerful engineering consultancy and construction firms within the donor countries; politicians who wish both to share the engineers' supplementary earnings and to be seen to be providing new public facilities which will benefit as many people as possible; farmers located on irrigable plains who are more easily organized politically than other farmers because they tend to be wealthier, enjoy better communications, and are demographically more concentrated; and, once the irrigation facilities are constructed, the 'top end' farmers near the water source who may be relatively little disadvantaged by 'poor water management' (see above). Repetto argues that these actors constitute a powerful coalition, and it is the pressures of this coalition which in large part explain the shape of Third World[8] irrigation policy and why the net social (as opposed to the private) returns to very large irrigation investments have been small.

At the most general level Repetto points out that this rent-taking activity is dependent upon (and helps explain) the near-complete absence of 'commercial' principles from the financing of irrigation in the Third World. The capital costs of new irrigation construction and most of the recurrent costs of operations and maintenance are provided on a subsidy basis by domestic governments and foreign aid agencies. Irrigation construction agencies and politicians have no incentive to choose projects which will be economically viable; they are not responsible for repaying the capital investment costs. Farmers pay little or nothing for the irrigation water they receive; such fees as are levied frequently fail to cover even recurrent operations and maintenance costs.[9] Irrigation fees, typically levied on a flat per acre rate per year or per crop season, are often paid directly into consolidated government revenues, and the recurrent budgets for irrigation agencies provided independently. Since the irrigation management agencies do not depend financially on fees collected from farmers, they have little incentive to provide farmers with an efficient service. It is this lack of any financial mechanism linking resource use decisions with resource costs that lies at the heart of the rent-seeking diagnosis. Lacking the discipline of financial responsibility for their resource use decisions, various interests compete and coalesce to divert public resources to private ends.

In relation to *investment planning* the consequences of the power of this rent-seeking coalition are:

1. Investment programs are pushed beyond their economic limits and the economic analysis of investment proposals is undermined by optimistically biased predictions of anticipated costs and benefits. At levels of performance currently being realized, few new major public irrigation projects can be economically justified in any of the countries for which data are available.
2. Investment priorities are biased toward large new projects at the expense of improving existing systems, developing dispersed small-scale community-controlled irrigation facilities, and improving rainfed farming methods.
3. The number of projects sanctioned and under way far exceeds the public funds available for implementing them. Available funds are doled out among projects, which prolongs construction periods, inflates construction costs, and delays the realization of benefits. (Repetto 1986: 22)

In relation to project design the pressures, originating in the politician–citizen relationship, are towards inefficient extensive rather than efficient intensive development: the provision of irrigation infrastructure beyond the areas that can efficiently be served, resulting in the characteristic problem of relatively poor, deprived and powerless 'tail-end' farmers with land located at the end of irrigation channels which in reality may rarely receive irrigation water; and relative underinvestment in drainage and in water-saving infrastructure like canal lining (Repetto 1986: 22–4).

In relation to the operation of irrigation systems, rent-seeking and financial irresponsibility produce: lavish and inefficient use of water by farmers whose fields are favourably located near irrigation channels, to the detriment of 'tail-enders'; incentives for such well-placed farmers to use water as a substitute for, *inter alia*, manual, mechanical, or chemical control of weeds (in rice production), precise land-levelling, or the cultivation of water-sparing crops;[10] weak farmer commitment to assist in or contribute to the cost of maintenance operations; and opportunities for management staff to corruptly favour some farmers, possibly by keeping all farmers in a state of uncertainty about the timing and volume of water deliveries. These incentives for managerial corruption and farmer irresponsibility can interact negatively with the relative dearth of water control facilities and poor maintenance of existing infrastructure to generate vicious circles of increasing anarchy, in relation to both physical water-control capacity and human relations (Repetto 1986: 24–7).

There is scope to challenge some of the premises upon which Repetto bases his analysis.[11] But as diagnosis his analysis appears very powerful. A relatively simple model which accords closely to the facts appears to explain a wide range of irrigation related phenomena: not just aggregate overinvestment and the high priority given to construction over water management, but also the extended phasing of construction activities, characteristic patterns of engineering design, and farmers' agricultural practices on irrigated land. It is difficult to justify any attempt to diagnose broad issues of irrigation policy which does not at least begin by exploring the validity of Repetto's analysis. And that in turn implies that rent-seeking analysis is a useful diagnostic tool. Whether it as useful for prescriptive purposes is the subject to which we now turn.

3. The Functions of Irrigation Fees[12]

There is little doubt that, for a range of reasons, most large-scale irrigation schemes in the Third World will continue to be owned and managed by public agencies of some kind. We are after all dealing with a natural monopoly. Repetto does not advocate privatization, but arrangements which make the main actors responsible for the financial implications of their resource use decisions. This entails in practice: (*a*) that farmers' demands for water should be significantly constrained by the obligation to pay water charges which reflect the cost of providing the water they receive; and (*b*) that these same service fees should constitute at least a significant proportion of the income of the irrigation management agency, and thus fund both the agency's recurrent operations and its capital investments.

How might the introduction of such a financing system improve the efficiency of irrigation policy and irrigation management in the Third World? The general answer is that it could substantially curb rent-seeking behaviour but would be of limited use in tackling other, more technical causes of inefficiency in the operation of irrigation projects. Indeed, it is generally impossible to operationalize principle (*a*) above, i.e. to levy fees which reflect the cost of the service requested and/or received by the individual user. To answer the question more precisely it is essential to treat separately two major sets of decisions: capital investment; and recurrent activities (or operations and management, henceforth O&M). The issues involved are substantially different.[13]

In relation to capital investment decisions, Repetto's analysis and prescriptions have a great deal of plausibility. Investment in large-scale irrigation systems is apparently excessively and inefficiently subsidized, at least in comparison with other agricultural investments. This has undesirable consequences for the level and nature of investment, for project design, and, indirectly, for O&M (see above). Any increase in user fees, at least if firmly and consistently implemented, should have the effect of easing political pressures for new investment from farmers, especially in areas where the likely returns to that investment are low. Equally, if the irrigation development agency were given a degree of financial autonomy and obliged to (partially) fund new investments through future fee collections, it would have to devote more attention to the issue of the returns to that investment.[14] Because of present irrigation user fees generally cover such a small proportion of the real costs of irrigation provision, and because 'commercial principles' rarely impinge significantly on the activities of irrigation development agencies, there is a general presumption in favour of Repetto's recommendations.[15]

In so far as it is desirable to levy or to increase fees to curb rent-seeking behaviour affecting capital investment decisions, the mechanics of fee assessment are relatively straightforward. In such cases fee payments are intended to fulfil two purposes: to provide revenue for the irrigation development agency; and to act as a disincentive against farmer political agitation in support of socially unprofitable investments. There is no need to tailor individual user fees closely to the quality of irrigation service (e.g. the amount of water) which each user receives. Indeed there are strong pragmatic arguments relating to the cost of fee assessment and collection for keeping tariff structures as simple as possible. Probably the most common system is a uniform rate on the acreage formally registered as irrigable. The same rate may be set nationally or varied for each irrigation scheme. Slightly more sophisticated systems vary the rate according to the crop for which the land is registered and/or according to the crop season.[16] There are thus a range of fee assessment systems which should in principle serve to curb the effect of rent-seeking on capital investment decisions, all of them characterized by the fact that neighbouring farmers growing the same crops are likely to pay the same per hectare rates.

The relationship between the introduction of 'financial responsibility' and the attainment of economic efficiency is more complex in the case of recurrent O&M activities than in the case of capital investment. The causal linkage is also weaker. The three main sets of mechanisms through which financial responsibility might improve O&M are best treated separately.

First, as has been suggested in the summary above of Repetto's argument, improved investment decisions stemming from the application of commercial financing principles to capital investment projects can be expected to improve O&M by: discouraging projects and designs which are unlikely to be profitable; encouraging improvements in project identification, design, and construction, which will increase the capacity of users to afford fees; and reducing overall levels of construction activity, thus redirecting the professional energies of engineering staff toward O&M. These arguments linking capital decisions with recurrent operations appear convincing.

Second, the introduction in relation to recurrent operations of financial autonomy and responsibility for the irrigation management agency can reasonably be expected to increase the amount of effort which the agency puts into O&M. It will wish to increase the farmers' capacity and willingness to pay fees.[17] The only real test of this claim lies in the experience of the National Irrigation Administration in the Philippines since 1980. In 1976 the National Irrigation Administration was deprived of all O&M subsidies from the government and, in response to government fiscal crises in the early 1980s, was also asked to begin repaying its foreign development loans. The Philippines experience to date appears to support the argument for financial responsibility. One of the more visible results has been that, in the effort to reduce costs, the National Irrigation Administration has (successfully) devolved the management of some small irrigation schemes and parts of larger schemes into water-users' associations. There has, however, also been considerable progress in other areas, including: devising incentive systems for staff and farmers to improve the overall level of fee collection; improving services to farmers; introducing performance evaluation and bonuses for staff; and devolving more operational responsibility to local levels and to system managers.[18]

The third and final mechanism through which the application of commercial principles to recurrent activities might be expected to improve efficiency lies in the effect of fees on the way in which farmers use water. The existence of a charge should encourage economy in the use of what is after all generally a scarce and rare commodity. It is, however, here that, excuse the pun, the case for fees gets into deep water.

4. Irrigation Fees and Water Pricing

At first sight there appears to be nothing exceptionable in the assertion that, were they obliged to pay irrigation fees, farmers would tend to use less irrigation water. Even if farmers cannot for some reason be made to pay according to the volume of water they use (much less according to the real scarcity value of a unit of water at different times of the day, season, or year[19]), payments which vary according to whether or not one uses water at all or according to the type of crop grown must surely, all our instincts and experience tell us, have an impact on farmers' water demands? In many cases these are quite valid expectations. The simple but basic point is that these are almost never valid expectations for the bulk of the Third World's irrigation systems—large-scale gravity flow schemes serving small farmers (henceforth LSGFSs)[20]. There are very specific technical features of LSGFSs which invalidate claims that volumetric water pricing can be practised on them because it is practised, for example, in pump irrigation schemes worldwide, or large-scale commercial farming in Europe and North America (Repetto 1986: 30). While one can levy an *irrigation service fee*, one cannot adopt *volumetric water pricing* (Small 1987).

The reasons for the unfeasibility of volumetric water pricing lie in the interaction of a number of physical and economic characteristics of water and of LSGFSs. We need to recall in the first place that water is an unusually mobile physical commodity. It has a high predisposition to flow, to seep vertically and horizontally through soils, to evaporate and transpire. On surface irrigation systems one has also to consider the way in which rainfall adds to aggregate supplies in a variable and unpredictable fashion and the correspondingly unpredictable losses which may result from the erosive effect of flowing water on the predominantly earthen physical infrastructure (Chambers 1988, chapter 2; Young 1987). This mobility is not a major problem for domestic water supply and pumped groundwater irrigation schemes, at least not for the agency responsible for conveying water from the reservoir (surface or subsurface) to the user. The water is generally safely encapsulated in pipe systems which contain a range of devices to control its flow. In such circumstances the delivery of water appears no more difficult than, for example, the delivery of electricity. Domestic water and electricity supply systems are however, *pace* Repetto (1986: 30), very misleading models for LSGFSs. The reasons why analogous charging systems are unfeasible can best be presented through separating out four main consequences of the physical peculiarities of LSGFSs. It is, however, important to bear in mind that these physical features and their consequences interact mutually in quite complex ways which exacerbate the problems of charging farmers for water.

1. Perhaps the most graphic contrast between electricity/domestic water

supply and LSGFSs is that the latter is not 'demand scheduled', where demand scheduling means that consumers are supplied with the resource as and when required (and then charged accordingly). Further and more importantly, irrigation water users are typically not even supplied according to the (imprecise) supply schedule laid down by the management agency.

Even the most reliable supply schedules, like those provided for most of the irrigation schemes in Taiwan, do not specify the volume of water to be delivered to particular points.[21] They cover (*a*) the kind of crop for which particular tracts of land will be supplied; (*b*) the dates when aggregate supply levels will be modified to fit changes in the crop calendar (e.g. a reduction in supplies when transplanting rice seedlings is scheduled for completion); and (*c*), where and when practised, the pattern of rotating supplies between different irrigation areas.

In other countries supply schedules are typically less detailed. More importantly, they are from the farmers' perspective far less reliable. The main reason for the unpredictability of deliveries lies in the interaction between (*a*) unpredictable and variable supplies from the irrigation sources (reservoirs, rivers, direct rainfall) and (*b*) the incomplete capacity of system managers to control and direct the water they have. The latter is the result of several interacting factors, most of them identified by Repetto as consequences of rent-seeking and/or already mentioned above: extensive development patterns leading to a dearth of water control (and measurement) structures on channels; the relative neglect of both maintenance and water management by the irrigation agency; the deliberate introduction of uncertainty into the supply schedule with the intention of eliciting bribes from farmers for the delivery of water; the activities of favourably located 'head end' farmers who take excess supplies by opening outlets at unscheduled times, pumping directly from canals, and breaking channel banks and control structures; the high degree of instability inherent in largely uncontrolled hydraulic systems; and the erosive effects on (poorly maintained) physical irrigation structures of partially uncontrolled and variable water flow levels. It is little wonder that LSGFSs have been described as 'very high entropy systems' in which 'order tends to rapidly decay into disorder' (Seckler 1981: 21).

Farmers suffer not only through the non-availability of water when they need it—or, when they might reasonably expect it. They also sometimes receive a damaging excess in the form of flood and drainage water. Water may be deliberately dumped from, or simply spill over from, main canals partly designed, in the interests of capital cost minimization per unit of irrigated area (see above), to serve as both supply and drainage channels. Equally, and with similar consequences for crop production, a substantial proportion of farmers under Asian irrigation schemes are not directly and individually served by irrigation channels, but depend on water which has first passed through neighbours' fields (and perhaps from there through field drains). This may be the result of: economies in the original design; faults in surveying, design, or construction which have rendered field channels useless; excessive water use by 'head end' farmers, which results in drainage ways from their fields bearing the water which should have flowed in supply channels to 'tail-enders'; and the expansion of the irrigated command area through private initiative. Whatever the season, farmers sometimes have to deal with greater inflows than they need or can cope with. Leaching away of agro-chemicals, washing away of young plants, deposition of silt on growing crops and waterlogging are among the costly consequences.

One way of expressing the implications of these kinds of points is that, as is now very widely accepted, the dominant and urgent water management problem on LSGFSs is to achieve greater and better managerial control of the main canal system rather than worry about changing farmers' water use patterns—the latter is mainly dependent on the former (Wade and Chambers 1980). One is making much the same point in saying that it is unrealistic to think of resource pricing to shape user resource demands if the supplier can neither deliver according to a schedule nor protect the user against excess supplies.

2. It was explained immediately above that there is 'hydraulic interdependence' among farmers in relation to surface water flows. Some depend on others for supplies. The same interdependence exists in relation to subsurface flows. Especially in rice irrigation systems, where the subsoil is kept saturated throughout the cultivation season, irrigation water is a public good in the economists' sense, i.e. potential beneficiaries cannot be excluded. One cannot deprive a farmer of irrigation water if he fails to pay his water bill even if one has complete control of the channel system. If the defaulter is not sufficiently lucky to be able to grow a crop on the moisture which enters his soil through lateral percolation, he could simply pump groundwater from his own land, knowing that the level would be continually recharged all the time his neighbours were willing to go on paying their bills and therefore receiving supplies through the channel system. Because the latter condition would not hold for long, the prospects of water pricing seem remote for this reason alone, especially in rice areas.[22]

3. Measuring water flows on LSGFSs is in a narrow sense technically feasible in almost any circumstances. The costs will, however, be prohibitive. Let us begin with the extreme case in which it is decided to measure flows to each individual (registered)[23] farm plot, bearing in mind that, at least in Asia, average farm sizes on irrigation schemes are frequently around one hectare. Such an exercise would incur four major costs: the capital (and maintenance) cost of constructing or rehabilitating the channel system to make possible the direct supply of water to each farm plot; the capital (and maintenance) cost of installing flow measurement devices (weirs, flumes, gauges, etc.); the loss of irrigation system efficiency resulting from the fact that measuring devices interfere with water flow; and the recurrent cost of measuring actual flows over weirs and flumes.[24] The later cost would be

enormous if main channel flows were not already under control and stabilized: variable flows would entail very frequent measurements. A high level of irrigation water control is a prerequisite for the existence of water pricing on gravity flow systems. We are, however, well into the realms of fantasy. Even ardent advocates of water pricing see the obstacles to charging each user individually on LSGFSs (e.g. Repetto 1986: 31). They turn to an apparent short-cut: the 'wholesaleing' of water to groups of farmers sharing the same distributary network (see below). While this does begin to make measurement of flows more feasible in principle, it still leaves open the question of achieving control of the main irrigation system.

4. Because water pricing is nowhere practised on LSGFSs there is no experience to help us estimate the likely cost of assessing and collecting charges. The fact that currently the costs of collecting irrigation service fees sometimes more or less equal the revenue collected is in one way misleading because service fees tend to amount only to a fraction of real service costs (Small *et al.* 1986 p. x; and Svendsen 1986: 12). Conversely, the costs of assessing individual water charges—and 'negotiating' with users over disputed assessments—would clearly be enormous. We are once again in fantasy land. And, once again, it is only the promise of wholesaling water to farmer groups which makes any further consideration of the issue seem justified (Small 1987: 7 and Svendsen 1986: 8).

In the face of such obstacles an insistence on water pricing can appear absurdly doctrinaire. It is clear that it is only the prospect of wholesaleing water to farmer groups which makes it possible for knowledgeable people to talk seriously about water pricing on LSGFSs. The logic behind the proposal appears to be that local farmer groups, unlike irrigation agencies, have or can develop the information networks, the organizational capacity, and the authority to: collect and aggregate data on water requirements; liaise between individual farmers and the irrigation agency; and enforce a fair and efficient system for distributing water and a corresponding system for assessing and collecting charges.[25] Unfortunately, the evidence suggests very poor prospects for such arrangements.

Contrary to Repetto's assertions (1986: 30–1), such arrangements are vanishingly rare. Some claims for the existence of the phenomenon are unproven.[26] The most solid claims actually turn out to be based on a brief and highly non-replicable experience with a single and very privileged water co-operative in Gujarat, India. From this there arose a whole myth about the prevalence, spread, and success of wholesaling of water to co-operatives in Gujarat or even in India more generally.[27] There are perhaps two major reasons why such arrangements are rare and unlikely ever to become widespread. The first is that they place very heavy demands on an organism known to be very fragile and unable to perform more than a fraction of the functions people would like to impose on it—farmers' organizations. Water wholesaling requires intensive, continuous organizational activity and authoritative intervention to allocate water, settle disputes, enforce the performance of maintenance work, and both allocate and collect charges. Yet all this is to be achieved by an organization representing a group of farmers who have no membership choice and who will be divided over many issues, not least the central issue of privileged and relatively wealthy top-enders versus relatively deprived and poor tail-enders.[28] Fair and efficient resolutions of this conflict of interest (i.e. arrangements that do not simply confirm or extend the dominance and privileged access to water enjoyed by top-enders) within a general context of institutional stability are to be striven for but not depended upon.[29]

The second main reason why water wholesaling is rare has already been indicated at more than one point above. There is a central paradox in this and in every other proposal for water pricing on LSGFSs. Water pricing is not feasible without a substantial degree of management control over the system in order to permit water deliveries according to some kind of schedule. Yet the existence of such water control capacity would in itself be an indication that the major irrigation management problems has been solved (Small *et al.* 1986: iii–v). There would be no case for incurring the very heavy transaction costs involved in water pricing in order to tackle those management problems remaining.

As the Taiwan experience illustrates, there are effective mechanisms for *directly* tackling the problem by using incentives and sanctions which encourage irrigation management staff to put effort into managing water and ensuring some degree of consumer satisfaction. Despite relatively favourable conditions for their introduction—a well-established system of levying relatively differentiated irrigation service fees; high levels of water control; and a dense network of authoritative farmers' and water-users' organizations—neither water pricing nor water wholesaling have been seriously considered in Taiwan. The water supply system is very much supply scheduled. The incentive system concentrates on improving supply directly rather than on attempting to work through pricing systems that might in turn influence consumer demand.

5. Politics and Management Accountability in Taiwan[30]

Taiwan's physical environment has not provided irrigation water managers with an especially easy task. The gravity flow systems which provide most of the irrigation capacity are intended and used mainly for rice cultivation. This imposes special constraints on any attempt at finely tuned water delivery. Water flows almost continuously in the irrigation channels during the crop season. It is virtually impossible to discipline farmers by depriving them of supplies of water. Yet rice farmers, in Taiwan as elsewhere, face compelling temptations to steal water in excess of their needs. The reason lies in the unusual way in which rice yields respond to varying levels of water supply. A deficit supply produces immediate and relatively severe yield decreases. By contrast, over a wide range, an excess supply does not harm the plant at all (e.g. Abel 1975: 16–18). It makes a great deal of sense for the rice farmer to seize any opportunity to appropriate more water than he is likely to need. He can store it in his flooded field for several days, and feel that he has done his best to provide for his crop if for some reason canal supplies prove deficient. In addition, Taiwan's topography and climate combine to produce highly variable and unpredictable flow levels in the rivers which constitute the main source of water for the irrigation schemes. Rivers are short and fall steeply from the central mountainous spine to the mainly narrow coastal plains. Their flow levels respond rapidly to unpredictable and seasonally concentrated monsoon rainfall, and irrigation system supplies are correspondingly unreliable.

Were the standards of irrigation management in Taiwan poor, it would be easy to find an explanation in the hostility of the natural environment. Instead, Taiwanese irrigation management is widely admired and is perhaps the most efficient in the world.[31] This is not the place to enter into a general discussion of the reasons for this good performance. There are complex questions about the mutual causal relationships between, respectively (*a*) good institutional arrangements and the increasingly elaborate physical irrigation infrastructure[32] which has been financed by the growth of agricultural production; and (*b*) Taiwan's success in irrigation management and in so many spheres of economic activity. Further, no general evaluation could sensibly treat Taiwan in isolation. For the country shares with Japan and South Korea a pattern of irrigation-related institutions which is distinctive and perhaps unique to East Asia (Wade 1988). The key feature is the institutional separation of major irrigation construction, which is the responsibility of national agencies, from routine operation and maintenance of irrigation systems. The latter is the responsibility of relatively small and locally rooted organizations, which have characteristically emerged incrementally from the amalgamation or expansion of local farmer associations, and which retain considerable autonomy and have parastatal rather than full government status. In Taiwan a series of reorganizations over this century have amalgamated numerous localized irrigation institutions into fourteen relatively large but still partly autonomous Irrigation Associations (henceforth IAs). These account for 80 per cent of the total irrigated area and each serve between 10,000 and 85,000 irrigated hectares, the average being 30,000 hectares.[33]

Without entering into an extended discussion of the causes of effective irrigation management in Taiwan, it is possible to identify some of the institutional mechanisms which stimulate IA staff to do a good job in O&M. However, because something of a myth has developed in the outside world about the causes of good irrigation management in Taiwan, it is useful first to say what does not happen.

In its most simple form the myth runs as follows. IAs are co-operative institutions owned by their farmer-members, directed by Representative Assemblies elected by members, and financed through the fees paid for irrigation services by members. The staff are therefore doubly responsible to the membership through both electoral and financial channels, and obliged to work well to satisfy the members. Unsatisfactory individual staff members can lose their jobs through the mediation of Representatives, and the collective salary fund of the staff is derived from the fees paid by satisfied members. The picture is completed with the claim that individual members who try to 'free ride' by withholding fees without valid reason may be deprived of water.[34]

The facts run directly contrary to the myth. Farmers who default on irrigation fees are not deprived of water. This is physically and administratively impossible (section 4 above; and Ko and Levine 1972: 58). Defaults on fee payments are rare. Defaulters are taken to court, and almost all pay up finally. Possible non-payment of fees by members is not a significant threat to IA finances, or therefore to the jobs and salaries of staff. This was true even before the government began to pay *large* recurrent subsidies to IAs in the early 1980s and before the government-imposed limits on the level of irrigation fees became as irksome to IA managements as they have done in recent years.[35] IA staff members are very rarely dismissed because of inadequate job performance. A staff job with an IA is almost a guaranteed job for life. And even the merit commendations and awards given to staff members are distributed so generously that receiving at least one per year is the norm rather than the exception.[36] Finally, the Representative Assembly is neither an autonomous decision-making body nor much concerned with irrigation issues. Its main function is political (Moore 1989).

It is then a myth that in IAs managerial efficiency is stimulated by management accountability to members operating through the two mechanisms of social control dear to liberal doctrine: the 'dispersed competition' inherent ideal models of the market and of electoral democracy respectively (Streek and Schmitter 1985). The actual mechanisms for controlling management are more exclusively political and less 'dispersed' and democratic, depending as they do on the existence—and balancing—of concentrations of institutional power. Yet the myth does have some roots in reality. To some degree it correctly identifies the tools used to stimulate managerial performance. It is wrong in its account of the way in which these tools are wielded.

A serious omission from the myth is that the only relationships considered are those between the client (IA member) and the service supplier (the IA). The implications of wider relationships are explored below. Even within the limited context of the client-supplier relationships there are two mechanisms for representing client concerns to management which I believe to be more important than the elected Representative Assemblies.

One such mechanism is the existence of elected Irrigation Group Chiefs responsible for the general supervision of water distribution, conflict management, and infrastructure maintenance at the level of the so-called 'rotation area', which covers between about 50 and 150 hectares, and a similar number of farmers. Irrigation group chiefs generally appear to be farmers from the higher strata of village society who exercise considerable 'natural' authority. There is little overt competition for the post, at least in the sense that incumbents are rarely challenged when elections are held, and the rate of turnover is relatively low.[37] In contrast to the election of representatives, party/national political alignments do not appear to impinge very heavily on the choice of irrigation group chiefs. Indeed, two factors indicate an implicit separation between the realms of 'politics' and of irrigation: the elections for representatives and for irrigation group chiefs are totally separate; and there is no formal mechanism for representing the irrigation group chiefs at levels in the IA structure higher than the individual rotation area. Farmers certainly tend to see representatives and irrigation group chiefs as very distinct categories of people.

Irrigation group chiefs do play significant roles in irrigation management and have a close relationship with the staff of their local IA Working Station. They are institutionalized within the IA system and are allocated some material resources to conduct small-scale maintenance tasks. They assemble annually or more frequently at the local Working Station for meetings which are largely orientated to socializing and entertainment, but which also provide farmers with opportunities to bring social pressure to bear on IA staff—and presumably vice versa.

The second mechanism for representing client interests is even more diffuse: the dense network of social relationships which exist among IA staff and IA members. For IAs are overwhelmingly manned by people who were born in the locality, have lived there all their lives, and, in many cases also farm there.[38] Further IA staff are not sharply differentiated from their members in terms of education or income levels. I have a strong overall impression that IA staff are so much part of local society that they can neither easily escape uncomfortable censure if they are conspicuously seen to be performing poorly at their work, nor ignore representations made to them by members in the context of regular and frequent social interaction.[39]

There seems little doubt that the localism of the IA structure and the institutionalization of the elected irrigation group chiefs provide opportunities for members to exercise some influence, albeit largely reactive rather than strategic, over management. Yet, even were the members permitted more electoral and financial power of the kind described in the myth above, there is reason to suspect that they would still face considerable difficulties in wresting strategic control of IA affairs from the professional IA staff. For experience from elsewhere suggests that numerous, dispersed, small-scale clients cannot normally organize effectively to control monopolistic public utilities run by highly organized bureaucracies with privileged access to technical knowledge. It is for this reason that direct state regulation of such utilities is common. But even the better equipped regulation agencies are frequently 'captured' and rendered impotent by the bureaucracies they are intended to oversee (Wilson 1984). Even if clients are given potential countervailing power of a political or financial nature, this can similarly be nullified by the management, especially through privileging a few influential clients who command wide political support among the client population more generally.

The post-war history of Taiwan's IAs reveals clear tendencies towards the realization of professional bureaucratic privilege at the expense of members' interests. The assumption of direct control of IA affairs by the government (Provincial Water Conservancy Bureau) in 1975 (see above) was motivated mainly by concern that, at least in some IAs, cliques of local politicians and staff members had entrenched themselves such that they were able to use IA resources for personal ends. One result was increasing farmer dissatisfaction as the quality of irrigation service appeared to be deteriorating. This led to worrying levels of default on fee payments in the early 1970s.[40] The take-over of IA management by the Provincial Water Conservancy Bureau[41] led to some immediate improvements in management and finances. For example, the number of IA members eligible to pay fees increased by 6 per cent in one jump in 1975. The government cleared a backlog of legal cases relating to fee defaults and, as has been explained above, soon assumed major responsibility for financing the IAs. Yet the IA staff were still in 1983 having some success in delaying reform proposals, especially plans for reducing staff numbers in line with the continuous decline in irrigated areas (Moore 1983).

This experience of the power of locally rooted bureaucracy seems to have led the Provincial Water Conservancy Bureau to place even more emphasis on what was perhaps already the main single mechanism for evaluating and stimulating IA management performance: the close monitoring of the speed with which members pay irrigation fees when they fall due. While fees are almost always paid eventually,[42] delay in payment has become an institutionalized mechanism, albeit an unpublicized one, through which farmers express dissatisfaction with the service they receive.

These signals are typically transmitted through delays which last days rather than weeks. During the two periods of the year when fees are due, most of the IAs' institutional machinery appears to be devoted to completing collections as expeditiously as possible. The same Working Station staff who provide a farmer with irrigation services come along to him encourage him to part with his money if there is any sign of delayed payment.[43] Each Working Station is required to make daily telephone reports about collections in their area to superiors. The same was true of the Management Stations which, in the larger IAs, formerly stood between the Working Station and the headquarters. And the headquarters are obliged to report regularly to the Provincial Water Conservancy Bureau. At each level, delays in fee payment are taken as prima facie evidence of a problem which requires attention. This particular signalling device fits into a system in which each unit in the IA system—the individual employee, the Working Station, (formerly) the Management Station, and the IA—are subject to a detailed annual performance evaluation covering a range of specified activities. These evaluations result in gradings which directly or indirectly affect salary increments, promotions, and access to additional resources. For the IAs and their Working Stations, speed in fee collection is one element in the formal grading system. IAs' published reports include tables giving information about the success of Working Stations in collecting fees according to the stated deadlines. In reality fee collection performance plays a specially important role in the evaluation system. Because overall fee collection levels are high, a rather small number of recalcitrant farmers can embarrass their local Working Station through delaying payment.[44] At least when it works well, the system seems to shift the balance of local bargaining power significantly in favour of clients.

6. Conclusion

The use of delays in fee payments as a signalling and monitoring device in Taiwanese irrigation management is possible only because it is enforced by a central government agency. An important part of the motivation lies in the incentive which the government of Taiwan has to forestall the emergence of any concrete grievance likely to mobilize the farming population. For that population is not generally disposed to accept the legitimacy of the regime.[45] This signalling/monitoring system is feasible only because the central (Mainlander-dominated) government has considerable autonomy in relation to local, Taiwanese-dominated instititutions like IAs. A more pluralistic political system might easily prevent the government from maintaining some kind of balance of power between the staff and management of IAs and the farmers they are supposed to serve. Taiwan therefore does not provide a direct model for transfer to most other environments. However, it does illustrate the possibility of using indirect quantitative indicators of clients' expressed grievances as mechanisms for monitoring management performance in circumstances where neither commercial nor electoral incentive and signalling systems are fully feasible or adequate.[46]

There are a wide range of reasons, varying for example from the hydraulic peculiarities of tropical irrigation systems to the highly bureaucratized nature of most contemporary polities and economies, why it may not always be feasible to rely upon market or market-like mechanisms to regulate the way in which public resources are managed. One may have to continue to rely not only on political mechanisms in general, but on political mechanisms which are fired less by the individualistic notion of 'dispersed competition' inherent in pluralist democracy than by exploitation of structural tensions between different concentrations of institutional power. There comes a point at which neo-liberalism, with its strong biases in favour of the market and of individualistic competition more generally, becomes impractical doctrine.

Notes

1. Rent-seeking analysis is sometimes subsumed under a broader field inelegantly termed 'the analysis of directly unproductive activities' (Colander 1984). The path-breaking work in the establishment of rent-seeking analysis as a distinct scholarly field is generally held to be Krueger 1974.
2. The term 'rent' is derived from economics and refers to the difference between the actual return obtained from bringing a resource into productive use and the minimum return at which the owner would bring the resource into use if that resource were in larger supply. The term was originally applied to the analytic problems arising from the fact that the supply of (good) land is fixed by nature. It has been adapted to circumstances in which market supplies are held to be limited by human action—quotas, business establishment licences, trade union restrictions on job choice and employment practices, etc. The existence of a rent is normally held to indicate malfunctioning in the competitive market system, and the term itself has pejorative overtones.
3. For a brief introduction see Staniland 1985. Other sub-fields of the rational choice paradigm include 'collective choice' and 'the new institutionalism'.
4. Bates (1983, conclusion) provides a balanced account of the methodological dimensions of rent-seeking analysis. My own views are summarized in Moore 1990.
5. Colander (1984: 4–5) provides some indication of the way in which rent-seeking analysis was nurtured to bolster strong presumptions against state involvement in the economy which, it was becoming increasingly clear, could not be validly supported by scholarly application of the apparatus of neo-classical economics. A critique of the biased and implausible *contingent* assumptions employed by scholars such as Krueger (1974) in the application of rent-seeking analysis is to be found in Lipton 1986.
6. In so far as this chapter has overt affinities with any particular approach to social science, this is to A. O. Hirschman's work on 'voice' as an alternative, political mechanism to market-orientated 'exit' for exercising sanctions over inadequate institutional performance (Hirschman 1970, 1981: chs. 9–12).
7. It is worth mentioning that Repetto is a theorist of rent-seeking, not an irrigation specialist, and that he turned his analytical toolkit toward irrigation after doing a similar exercise on the issue of pesticide use in the Third World (Repetto 1985).

8. Repetto's analysis is in fact general. Here I deal only with the question of its applicability to the Third World.

9. For some recent additional evidence on this point see Small 1987.

10. The points about weed control and land levelling are not made by Repetto.

11. For example, the assertion that it is generally more efficient to restrict the command area of irrigation schemes to the area which can be guaranteed a reliable supply of irrigation water is not proven, and may be false if one has the equalization of income as a policy objective. Equally, the question of the actual level of returns to irrigation investment is confused by the use of world cereal prices to value irrigation outputs. These prices are unstable, reflect transactions in a relatively small and highly imperfect market, and are thus imperfect indicators of the real value of agricultural output. Relatively favourable cost–benefit ratios for irrigation investment have been calculated using the temporarily high cereal prices obtaining in the early and mid-1970s (Yudelman 1985: 16).

12. As a result of the general resurgence of interest in 'market-mediated' economic strategies in recent years there has been an explosion of interest in the question of irrigation fees in the Third World. See Carruthers 1986, Coward and Martin 1986, Easter 1985, Small 1986, 1987, Small *et al.* 1986, and Svendsen 1986.

13. I ignore here the real-world substitutability between recurrent maintenance and rehabilitation investment.

14. The only evidence available on the plausibility of these expectations derives from the recent experience of the Philippines National Irrigation Administration (see text). Here increased financial dependence of the agency on user fees has not so far had a market effect on investment policy. New construction is still in the agency's interest because of the management fees it earns for supervising construction (Small *et al.* 1986, annex 6).

15. There are limits to the levels of fees which may be charged because, as Repetto himself explains, past rent-seeking behaviour has yielded a stock of irrigation projects which are uneconomic. The scope for brand new irrigation schemes is now very limited. The direction of capital investment activity is currently shifting to the rehabilitation of existing schemes. It will often be impossible to impose full financial responsibility for rehabilitation investment on users and the development agency, for full-cost fees might often far exceed the value to the farmer of the improved facilities.

16. The Taiwanese system is unusually sophisticated in that farmers' requests for additional capital works are financed by allocating the cost among the beneficiaries in proportion to their estimated share in the benefit. A supplement is then added to irrigation fees. In the four financial years 1978–81 these 'additional irrigation fees' amounted to only 6% of all assessed irrigation fees paid by Taiwanese farmers. Their role is thus limited. The basic fee comprised 77%, and special pumping fees comprised 17% (Kuo 1982: 12).

17. However, one should not neglect the possibility that the agency will respond mainly by putting more effort into extorting fees from farmers.

18. My main sources of information on this experience are: Cruz and Siy 1985; Small *et al* 1986, annex 6; Svendsen 1986; and a personal visit in 1985. In some respects the environment in the Philippines was especially favourable. For since the latter half of the 1970s the National Irrigation Administration had been very actively experimenting with the establishment of responsible water users' associations on

small-scale irrigation schemes (Korten 1982). This initiative appears to have been mainly motivated by a desire to reduce the financial burden of managing many small schemes (Cruz and Siy 1985: 15). The National Irrigation Administration was later able to use this experience in devising ways of approaching farmers and establishing similar associations on a larger scale (see Bautista 1987). Water users' associations appear to have played a key role in increasing the rate of fee collections. But fee collections still cover only about 75% of O&M costs, and thus do not begin to meet capital costs (Small *et al.* 1986: p. ix).

19. There are in fact unusually severe problems in applying marginal cost pricing to irrigation water because of the difficulties of calculating 'true' marginal costs. These difficulties stem especially from differences between the long and the short run and between locations (differences on the same irrigation scheme and between schemes). For a brief review and references see Carruthers 1986: 7.

20. Using figures from the *FAO Production Yearbook* and his own considerable experience, my colleague Robert Chambers has kindly taken the trouble to make the following estimates for the proportion of the currently irrigated area in developing countries falling under the three main categories: large-scale gravity flow systems—60% to 70%; farmer-managed/small-scale gravity flow systems—5% to 15%; and lift irrigation—20% to 30%. Almost all land in the first category serves mainly small farmers.

21. In Taiwan, but in few other places in Africa and Asia, managers have guide-lines about volumetric flows to which they adhere in some degree. The more acute the water supply position, the more intensively are flows measured and adjusted.

22. They are all the more remote because, due in part to decreasing relative costs, pumpsets are increasingly common on surface irrigation schemes. Pumpsets are now, for example, widespread on LSGFSs in Taiwan, where they are used to give even greater flexibility and convenience in water control.

23. This qualification about registration of holdings is important. For the actual pattern of land rights is commonly both different and more complex than the official registered pattern and variable from crop season to crop season. Holdings are variously subdivided, mortgaged, sold, and leased out in complex patterns.

24. This problem is, once again, most acute on rice schemes because water tends to flow in most channels most of the time during the crop season (Small *et al.* 1986: p. v).

25. It is an interesting paradox that, *in extremis*, the practical viability of market principles should be perceived to depend on local, non-market patterns of social interdependence and hierarchy. For its devotees have elsewhere lauded the market as the saviour of the peasant from the suffocating tyranny of the local community (e.g. Popkin 1979, ch. 2).

26. Repetto's claim (1986: 30) that volumetric pricing is practised in China remains unsubstantiated (Small 1986: 5).

27. Chambers (1988, ch. 3) has investigated and documented in detail the reality and the spread of the myth. Among the special features of this single co-operative were: favourable location very close to Surat city, a national highway, and a sugar mill; near-monocropping with sugarcane; major government support in the form of infrastructural investment (including canal lining), concessional water rates, financial guarantees against losses, provision of administrative staff

at no cost, and general publicity and promotion; and a privileged supply of irrigation water.

28. This conflict tends to be found at all levels on a canal system, including at the level of the smallest distributory channel. By far the most detailed and reliable study available of water theft on LSGFSs was conducted on a relatively well-regulated canal system in Taiwan. Yet even here it was found that the incidence of theft correlated with the opportunity to steal rather than with any measure of the objective 'need' to obtain more water for agricultural purposes: it was concentrated among top-end farmers already well supplied with water (Vandermeer 1971).

29. Faith in the capacities of water co-operatives could be enhanced by Wade's discovery (1979) on a South Indian canal system of highly effective village level organizations able to raise large sums of money to bribe irrigation officials and provide water guards to monitor the distribution of water among farms. There is no evidence that such organization is common elsewhere. In general, experience seems to suggest that individual farmers' organizations find it very difficult to handle very different kinds of functions. The kind of organization and leadership needed to bargain with external agents over issues in which members share a collective interest (e.g. improved irrigation system maintenance by government) may be very different from those required of organizations like water co-operatives which are obliged to make allocation decisions which penalize some of their own members. The faith placed in the capacities of water users' associations appears to be based in part on questionable visions of single purpose organizations gradually taking on a wider and wider range of functions with increasing competence.

30. This section is based in large part on the research I conducted while resident in Taiwan for three months in 1983 (for more details and evidence see Moore 1983, and 1989). It is not easy for the outsider to investigate the functioning of Taiwanese institutions. I was lucky to obtain support and approval to design and execute my own research programme with my own interpreters. This permitted a substantial degree of cross-checking of information. Nevertheless, much remains obscure. My perspectives and the confidence I have in certain conclusions owe a great deal to papers and personal communications from Anthony Bottrall and Gil Levine, who are among the very few outsiders to have conducted research on Taiwanese irrigation management. I also benifited enormously from the simultaneous presence in Taiwan of my colleague, Robert Wade.

31. Levine (1977: 41) provides relatively authoritative figures on one technical measure of efficiency—water use efficiency. He has elsewhere questioned whether Taiwan has not overinvested in irrigation water control, pursuing water use efficiency at the expense of economic efficiency.

32. Concrete canal linings, field channels serving individual farmers, and a dense network of structures to control water flow are now the norm in Taiwan, and the exception in poor Asia.

33. Wen 1980: 24. I have excluded from all of these statistics two very small IAs which now lie within the administrative boundaries of the capital city. One might note that the irrigated area is falling quite rapidly as farmland is converted to other uses.

34. The most credulous written account of the myth of which I am aware is in Abel

1975. Bottrall (1977) fell for the myth before he actually visited Taiwan. In fairness it should be pointed out that the myth is solicitously propagated by the government of Taiwan.

35. There appears always to have been at least an element of public subsidy to the capital projects of IAs. But in the early 1980s, and as a result of assumption of direct state control of IAs in 1975, government assumed major responsibility for financing IAs' current operations. In 1981, the largest IA, Chianan, received 47% of its income in the form of government subsidies and only 33% in the form of irrigation fees (Chianan Irrigation Association 1981: 145). By contrast, operating subsidies to the small Nantou IA accounted for only 15% of revenue in the same year, and fees accounted for 75% (Nantou Irrigation Association 1982: 15). These subsidies to IAs were one aspect of the increasing public subsidization of Taiwanese agriculture generally (Moore 1988). Some details of subsidies are provided in Kuo 1982.

36. In 1981, 92% of the staff of the Chianan IA had served for nine years or more, and 26% for thirty years or more. In that year 78% of staff members received some kind of merit award, and the total number distributed amounted to an average of 3.3. awards per recipient. By contrast, less than 1% of staff members received any kind of de-merit or punishment (Chianan Irrigation Association 1981: 176–7).

37. When elections were held for Irrigation Group Chiefs in the Chianan IA in 1975, there were 1.12 candidates for each post (Chianan Irrigation Association 1981: 12). When elections were next held seven years later, only 18% of posts changed hands. There was an average of 2.54 candidates for each post which did change hands (data kindly supplied by the IA).

38. Evidence on the permanence of IA staff has already been given above. In 1981 88% of the permanent staff of the Chianan IA originated from the three main administrative areas served by the scheme—Tainan City and Tainan and Chaiyi Counties. The proportion was exactly the same for the 35% of staff in the top two staff grades (Chianan Irrigation Association 1981: 173).

39. The significance of this enmeshment in local social networks was brought home to me vividly when I paid an unscheduled visit to an IA Working Station and was told that it would be a little difficult to meet the Station Chief because he had only just moved into the post from another area and would naturally have to spend his first two or three weeks paying social calls on the important officials and citizens of the locality. There are other reasons, beyond this 'social enmesh-ment', for believing that the East Asian model of locally rooted, parastatal irrigation management organizations is conductive to efficiency (Wade 1988). My observations in Taiwan supported this view. I was especially impressed with the deep familiarity of senior IA engineers with the physical properties of the systems they managed and their ability to calculate quantitative answers to questions about irrigation and water flows on the basis of figures they held in their heads.

40. Defaulting was concentrated in what is now the Yunlin IA. At the time this was part of the massive Chianan IA, and became a trouble spot in part because its unusual technical irrigation problems tended to receive low priority while it was part of a larger entity.

41. This reform was partially reversed in 1982: the Representative Assemblies were

reintroduced, albeit with reduced powers; and, formally at least, the General Managers (i.e. chief executives) were henceforth to be selected by the IA Assembly from a shortlist furnished by the Provincial Water Conservancy Bureau, rather than be appointed directly by the latter.

42. Between 1978 and 1981, fee collections nationally varied between 98.08% and 98.77% of dues (Kuo 1982: 12).

43. There is a diversity of means of collecting fees; IA staff are not necessarily involved if payments are made promptly.

44. For example, in the Chianan IA, over eighteen fee collection seasons in 1973–81, only in four cases did any of the nine Management Stations fail to collect at least 98% of fees by the deadline. With such intense competition between Stations, their relative rankings were rather fluid (Chianan Irrigation Association 1981: 137).

45. The weakness of this hold was demonstrated by the large-scale involvement of farmers in political demonstrations and riots in mid-1988.

46. There are many other examples of such systems. One is voting in the USSR. Until recently at least, voters have rarely faced a choice of candidates. They have, however, some choice about whether or not to vote. This appears to have been used to bargain with local Communist Party cadres about the provision of services of various kinds. Desperation about, for example, house repairs, could turn into embarrassing abstentions from the polls. Rates of voter turnout have in turn been used by the party hierarchy as indicators of the performance of local cadres.

References

Abel, M. E. (1975), *Irrigation Systems in Taiwan: Management of a Decentralized Public Enterprise*, Staff Paper P72-15, Department of Agricultural and Applied Economics, University of Minnesota, St Paul.

Bates, R. H. (1983), *Essays on the Political Economy of Rural Africa*, Cambridge University Press, Cambridge.

Bautista, H. B. (1987), *Experiences with Organizing Irrigators Associations: A Case Study from the Magat River Irrigation Project in the Philippines*, IIMI case-study no. 1, International Irrigation Management Institute, Digana, Sri Lanka.

Bottrall, A. F. (1977), 'Evolution of Irrigation Associations in Taiwan', *Agricultural Administration*, 4/4: 245–50.

—— (1978), 'Field Study in Yunlin', mimeo, London.

Carruthers, I. (1986), 'Approaches to Financing Irrigation', paper prepared for Expert Consultation on Irrigation Water Charges, Food and Agriculture Organization, Rome, 22–6 Sept.

Chambers, R. (1988), *Managing Canal Irrigation: Analysis and Lessons from South Africa*, Oxford University Press and IBH, New Delhi.

Chianan Irrigation Association (1981), *Chianan Irrigation Association: Statistical Outline* (in Chinese), Tainan.

Colander, D. C. (1984), 'Introduction', in D. C. Colander (ed.), *Neoclassical*

Political Economy: An Analysis of Rent-Seeking and DUP Activities, Ballinger Publishing Company, Cambridge, Mass., 1–13.

Coward, E. W., and Martin, E. (1986), 'Resource Mobilization in Farmer-Managed Irrigation Systems: Needs and Lessons', paper presented for Expert Consultation on Irrigation Water Charges, Food and Agriculture Organization, Rome, 22–6 Sept.

Cruz, M. C. J., and Siy, R. Y. (1985), 'Issues in Irrigation Water Management in the Philippines', mimeo, University of the Philippines at Los Banos, Centre for Policy and Development Studies.

Easter, K. W. (1985), *Recurring Costs of Irrigation in Asia: Operation and Maintenance*, Water Management Synthesis II Project, Cornell University, Ithaca, NY.

Hirschman, A. O. (1970), *Exit, Voice and Loyalty: Responses to Decline in Firms, Organizations and States*, Harvard University Press, Cambridge, Mass.

—— (1981), *Essays in Trespassing: Economics to Politics and Beyond*, Cambridge University Press, Cambridge.

Ko, H. S., and Levine, G. (1972), 'A Case Study of On-Farm Irrigation and the Off-Farm System of Water Delivery in the Chianan Irrigation Association, Taiwan, Republic of China', mimeographed paper prepared for Seminar on Management of Irrigation Systems at Farm Level, Cornell University, Ithaca, 16 Oct. 1972.

Korten, F. (1982), *Building National Capacity to Develop Water Users' Associations: Experience from the Philippines*, World Bank Staff Working Paper No. 528, Washington, DC.

Krueger, A. O. (1974), 'The Political Economy of the Rent-seeking Society', *American Economic Review*, 64/3 (June): 291–303.

Kuo, C. H. (1982), 'Financial Structure Concerning the Maintenance of Watercourses for Watercourses for Water Management in Taiwan, R.O.C.', mimeo, Council for Agricultural Planning and Development, Taipei.

Levine, G. (1977), 'Management Components in Irrigation System Design and Operation', *Agricultural Administration*, 4/1: 37–48.

—— (1981), 'Irrigation Development and Strategy Issues for the Asian Region', in *Irrigation Development Options and Investment Strategies for the 1980s: Bangladesh*, Water Management Synthesis Report 3, USAID, Washington, DC, pp. A1–A19.

Lipton, M. (1986), 'Agriculture, Rural People, the State and the Surplus in Some Asian Countries: Thoughts on Some Implications of Three Recent Approaches in Social Science', mimeo conference paper, Institute of Development Studies, Brighton.

Moore, M. (1983), 'Irrigation Management in Taiwan', mimeo, Institute of Development Studies, Brighton.

—— (1988), 'Economic Growth and the Rise of Civil Society: Agriculture in Taiwan and South Korea', in G. White (ed.), *Developmental States in East Asia*, Macmillan, London, 113–52.

—— (1989), 'The Fruits and Fallacies of Neo-liberalism: The Case of Irrigation Policy', *World Development*, 17/11: 1733–50.

—— (1990), 'The Rational Choice Paradigm and the Allocation of Agricultural Development Resources', *Development and Change*, 21/2 (Apr.): 225–46.

Nantou Irrigation Association (1982), *Introduction to Nantou Irrigation Association*, (in Chinese), Nantou.

Popkin, S. L. (1979), *The Rational Peasant: The Political Economy of Rural Society in Vietnam*, University of California Press, Berkeley and Los Angeles, Calif.

Repetto, R. (1985), *Paying the Price: Pesticide Subsidies in Developing Countries*, Research Report 2, World Resources Institute, Washington, DC.

—— (1986), *Skimming the Water: Rent-Seeking and the Performance of Public Irrigation Systems*, Research Report 4, World Resources Institute, Washington, DC.

Seckler, D. (1981), 'The New Era of Irrigation Management in India', mimeo, Ford Foundation, Delhi.

Small, L. (1986), 'Water Charges: A Tool for Improving Irrigation Performance?', paper prepared for Expert Consultation on Irrigation Water Charges, Food and Agriculture Organization, Rome, 22–6 Sept.

—— (1987), *Irrigation Service Fees in Asia*, Overseas Development Institute/International Irrigation Management Institute, Irrigation Management Network Paper 87/1c, London.

—— Adriano, M. S., and Martin, E. (1986), 'Regional Study on Irrigation Service Fees: Final Report', mimeo, International Irrigation Management Institute for the Asian Development Bank, Digana, Sri Lanka.

Staniland, M. (1985), *What Is Political Economy? A Study of Social Theory and Underdevelopment*, Yale University Press, New Haven, Conn., and London.

Streek, W., and Schmitter, P. C. (1985), 'Community, Market, State—and Associations? The Prospective Contribution of Interest Governance to Social Order', in W. Streek and P. C. Schmitter (eds.), *Private Interest Government: Beyond Market and State*, Sage Publications, London, 1–29.

Svendsen, M. (1986), 'Irrigation System Recurrent Cost Recovery: A Pragmatic Approach', paper prepared for Expert Consultation on Irrigation Water Charges, Food and Agriculture Organization, Rome, 22–6 Sept.

Tiffen, M. (1987a), *Cost Recovery and Water Tariffs: A Discussion*, Overseas Development Institute, Irrigation Network Management Paper 11e, London.

—— (1987b), *The Dominance of the Internal Rate of Return as a Planning Criterion and the Treatment of O&M Costs in Feasibility Studies*, Overseas Development Institute/International Irrigation Management Institute, Irrigation Management Network Paper 87/1b, London.

Vandermeer, C. (1971), 'Water Thievery in a Rice Irrigation System in Taiwan', *Annals of the Association of American Geographers*, 61: 156–79.

Wade, R. (1979), 'The Social Response to Irrigation: An Indian Case Study', *Journal of Development Studies*, 16/1: 3–26.

—— (1982a), 'The World Bank and India's Irrigation Reform', *Journal of Development Studies*, 18/2: 171–84.

—— (1982b), 'The System of Administrative and Political Corruption: Canal Irrigation in South India', *Journal of Development Studies*, 18/3: 287–328.

—— (1988), 'The Management of Irrigation Systems: How to Evoke Trust and Avoid Prisoners' Dilemma', *World Development*, 16/4: 489–500.

—— and Chambers, R. (1980), 'Managing the Main System: Canal Irrigation's Blind Spot', *Economic and Political Weekly*, 15/39: 107–12.

Wen, L. J. (1980), 'Improvement of Irrigation Systems and Water Management in Taiwan', mimeo, Council for Agricultural Planning and Development, Taipei.

Wilson, G. K. (1984), 'Social Regulation and Explanations of Regulatory Failure', *Political Studies*, 32/2: 203–25.

Young, R. A. (1987), 'Market versus Nonmarket Management of Irrigation Water: A Review of the Issues', in W. R. Jordan (ed.), *Water and Water Policy in World Food Supplies*, Texas A. & M. University Press, College Station, 205–14.

Yudelman, M. (1985), *The World Bank and Agricultural Development: An Insider's View*, Research Report 1, World Resources Institute, Washington, DC.

14
Politics and the Neo-liberals

JAMES MANOR

The neo-liberal paradigm or approach, as defined in the introduction to this volume, has come to prominence at a time when those of us who study the politics of Asia, Africa, and Latin America are unusually receptive to new modes of analysis. This is because the two paradigms or schools of thought that have dominated the study of Third World politics over the last quarter-century have encountered serious difficulties.

The first of these—the 'political development' school—yielded important insights, but its expectations of a unilinear pattern of change, and of convergence among less developed nations, were misplaced. It also tended to create models which presumed more equilibrium and fewer contradictions in polities and societies than were there. If often emphasized stability at the expense of change and social justice. Many in this school made simplistic contrasts between 'tradition' and 'modernity', and tended to underestimate the diversity among Third World nations, the importance of political economy and of the international economic order.

The second, 'dependency' school also taught us much that was valuable, but it emphasized the importance of economic forces—especially international forces—at the expense both of politics and of the varied cultural and historical particularities within nations. Its preoccupation with class as an analytical category underplayed the importance of indigenous or hybrid social institutions. It was useful in analysing small countries which depended heavily on the export of one or two primary commodities, but it was less adequate at assessing larger, more complex political economies. It neither anticipated nor explained the rise of newly industrializing countries on the 'periphery' of the international economic system, or the re-emergence of liberal political regimes in places like India after the Emergency of the mid-1970s and Brazil, Uruguay, Argentina, and Chile in the 1980s (Smith 1985).

So students of Third World politics have been in the market for alternative paradigms at the very time when the neo-liberal approach has commanded great attention in the field of development studies. We might therefore have expected political scientists—whether they stand to the left or the right of centre—to have made some attempt to generate a new mode of enquiry based on the neo-liberal approach. The purpose of this chapter is to explain why this has not occurred. This chapter should be read in tandem with John Toye's which follows it and which assesses in more detail the political presuppositions of the neo-liberals, the political implications of many of their prescriptions, and the political circumstances that helped them to gain influence within institutions like the World Bank.

The first thing to say is that the neo-liberal approach is attended by some of the difficulties that have assailed the 'political development' and 'dependency' paradigms. Many neo-liberals either imply or openly present a set of prescriptions which are intended to lead towards a certain desired end, so that their analysis is often teleological in character. Students of Third World politics have tended to react against this of late, because in their experience teleologies have a way of impeding rather than assisting them in their essential task which is to understand what has been happening in Third World polities. The neo-liberals, like the 'political development' school, tend to underestimate the importance of the international economic order in determining outcomes within less developed countries. And like both paradigms, their approach presumes too much cultural, social, historical, and political homogeneity among the less developed countries. They therefore tend to assume that their prescriptions will produce roughly similar results in all Third World settings. This is true within limits, when they are proposing changes in economic policy at the micro-level, but the limits are reached far sooner than they think.

These comments point to a more fundamental problem. For students of Third World politics, the neo-liberal approach greatly underestimates the complexities within and the variations among political regimes in the less developed countries. A recent set of studies concluded that much of the political science literature on these regimes—which offers a far more complicated picture than the neo-liberal approach allows for—has seriously understated the complexity that actually exists in the polities in question. One writer argued, for example, that too many studies oversimplify by concentrating on sets of two-dimensional relationships: between socio-economic development and democratic politics, between things 'traditional' and 'modern', between 'democratic' and 'non-democratic' systems, etc. This inclines analysts to view the process of change as a series of dyadic conflicts leading eventually to syntheses, which again oversimplifies. He proposes that at least three dimensions need to be assessed—regimes' concerns with security, development, and participation—which substantially complicates the analysis. And he argues that in many Third World settings, the interplay of these three factors leads not to neat syntheses, but to incongruous hybrids in which apparently contradictory elements exist uneasily alongside one another (Chai-Anan 1991).

A consensus emerged from the same set of studies that many previous assessments of 'strong' and 'weak' states in the Third World had oversimplified somewhat by failing to distinguish carefully enough between types of strength and weakness. Strength can flow from the use, or the potential use, of coercive power, from a state's willingness to govern even-handedly, from its capacity to entice or co-opt key social groups by drawing them into transactional relationships and from other things. A particular state or regime may possess one or two of these things, but lack others—so that it is strong in some ways and weak in others. What we therefore encounter most of the time are not 'strong' or 'weak' states, but ambiguous 'strong/weak' states in which the admixture of strengths and weaknesses will probably differ from other cases. These complications need to be understood if we are to make sense of political reality in the countries that we study.

This set of studies also found that scholars have tended to underplay the importance of the theatrical and imaginary dimensions to politics in many Third World countries. This emerged from assessments of such different cases as mainland China and Togo. Much of the interaction between social forces and the state in China has been played out—not least in the period up to and since the Tiananmen killings—in highly theatrical terms, in an artificial, symbolic discourse. This has such importance that it has acquired a certain material substance, and it cannot be ignored by students of the Chinese polity (Wagner 1991). To understand popular perceptions of regimes in Togo, Cameroon, and certain other West African cases, it is essential that we grasp—among other things—images of devouring and other notions derived from witchcraft which predominate in many people's mental constructions of the state, and which politicians seek to cultivate to sustain themselves in power (Tulabor 1986, Bayart 1988, Mbembe 1991).

All of these examples indicate that those who specialize in the study of Third World politics are tending to broaden the nature of their enquiry, to take in dimensions of the political process that have been under-studied, and to reach beyond politics to adjacent areas of activity. This is also apparent in the work of other teams of political analysts that have recently addressed the subject (Chabal 1986, Weiner and Huntington 1987, Diamond *et al.* 1989, O'Donnell *et al.* 1987). They vary somewhat in their approaches, but they share this tendency to widen the field of enquiry. In so doing, they are moving in the opposite direction from the neo-liberals who—when they are not omitting politics from their discussions—focus on an extremely narrow range of things.

The neo-liberals usually ignore elements of the political process which are downright fundamental to a grasp of events in less-developed countries. They scarcely recognize, for example, that a single state or regime can play varied roles at the same time. Consider the case of independent India, where the state has played three broad roles. It was first a relatively neutral arena within which relationships between various social groups were constantly renegotiated. It also played the role of protector, a guarantor that the sensibilities of the vast array of subcultures in this heterogeneous society will not be unduly disrupted, and a bulwark against unduly precipitate change. It therefore acts much of the time as a guardian of the status quo. And yet its third role often stands in contradiction to its second, for it also has acted as a liberator, mitigating or removing certain injustices, seeking—especially since 1947—to reform society (Nandy 1982). Only if we understand these ambiguities can we form an accurate view of that decidedly untidy phenomenon, the modern Indian state. The neo-liberal approach cannot accommodate these complexities, and descriptions of India as a rent-seeking society (Krueger 1974) accurately depict only a small part of this variegated story.

The same message emerges from a study of China since 1978, when the dramatic liberalization of the rural economy began. Until then, the Chinese Communist Party and state had succeeded very substantially first in remaking and then in controlling the agrarian socio-economic order through the use and the threat of coercion. Power was mainly used to smother market forces. Since 1978, those forces have been allowed a much freer rein, so that small and not-so-small capitalist enterprises have burgeoned all across rural China.

But this process has not entailed a simple shrinkage of the state and an equal and opposite expansion of the private sector. This is no zero-sum game. The state and party as coercive instruments have certainly contracted, but the state has had to grow quite markedly in other respects, to perform tasks that were unnecessary before liberalization. A new corpus of contract law had to be created, and since a legal system barely existed before 1978, a set of new judicial institutions has had to be generated to administer the new laws. As new enterprises arose and economic growth gathered momentum, the state also developed new instruments to regulate and, more especially, to abet market forces. Economic liberalization in China has thus been attended by the shrinkage of certain party and state agencies and roles, but also by the very substantial growth of the state, both as an arena within which capitalism can operate and as an enabler of private enterprises (Zweig *et al.* 1987). The latter changes have occurred because, to operate most effectively, capitalism requires the presence and assistance of the state. This crucial point tends to be missed amid the neo-liberals' over-reaction against the state.

They also tend to overlook the enormous variations which exist among the states of Asia, Africa, and Latin America—variations that are so marked that they inspire doubts about the universal efficacy of any single economic strategy. The set of studies mentioned above placed Taiwan at one extreme and Togo at the other. The Taiwan government has long possessed formidable coercive powers, but in recent times it has demonstrated a capacity to assist the private sector in achieving spectacular export success. Still more recently, it has begun to develop a somewhat more accommodating posture towards civil society—which itself has changed in complicated ways unacknowledged in the writings of most neo-liberals—while retaining very substantially its position of command.

In Togo, by contrast, one encounters a little cursory clientelism and more than the occasional smack of autocratic governance, but the regime depends so heavily upon theatricality that leading specialists are inclined to describe it as a 'show state'. The main device which maintains the legitimacy—or perhaps we should say the hold—of the regime is a voodoo cult based on the national leader's survival of an air crash in which his two French pilots were killed. The leader is regarded as someone who has returned from the dead, and the cult that has been built on that belief provides the state with its main underpinnings (Tulabor 1986, O'Brien 1991). This regime—and others of this sort, such as Papa Doc Duvalier's in Haiti and Bokassa's in Central Africa—are incapable of assisting the private sector, or of generating more than the most rudimentary accommodations with civil society.

Between these extremes, we find a broad array of regime types which differ from both of them. India's political institutions have undergone considerable decay since the early 1970s, but they still have considerable substance, and have shown that they are susceptible to regeneration in the right circumstances. Their strength resides partly in their potential coercive power, but their ability to entice social groups into accommodative relationships by offering them political patronage has almost always counted for more than mere clout. The state has seldom sought to pervade, control, or homogenize India's highly variegated society. Society is usually seen to be prior to the state, which implies that regimes should adopt a restrained posture towards society. This has led to state–society relations which differ markedly from those of places such as Taiwan (or mainland China) on the one hand and Togo on the other.

The same set of studies found the current regime in Ethiopia to possess an effectively centralized system of control, consisting mainly of coercive instruments. This needs to be stressed, lest the discussion of Togo be read as a blanket comment on all African regimes. The difficulties that one encounters in Ethiopia arise from the regime's continued pursuit of Stalinist collectivism of a kind now rejected in China and the USSR, rather than from an inability to implement any policy, as in Togo (Clapham 1988 and 1991). Tropical Africa offers plenty of variety beyond these two cases, as of course does Latin America. These kinds of variations and complexities lie quite outside the scope of neo-liberal enquiry, and this inclines students of Third World politics to look beyond the neo-liberal paradigm in their search for new approaches.

Another part of the explanation for the uneasiness of students of Third World politics with the work of neo-liberal economists arises out of differences between the study of economics and politics. Some of the comments which follow can be applied to most development economists, and not just to the neo-liberals, but the problems cited below tend to assail the latter more consistently and with particular force. This is mainly because they assume such a radical opposition between states and markets, and because their dismissal of the state as a creative force leads them to dismiss so much of the logic of politics from their discussions that they end up producing especially extreme and—for political scientists—unsatisfactory analyses.

Consider the problem of people's perceptions of their interests. Students of Third World politics constantly encounter evidence that such judgements are subjective (Leys 1970). What may seem as objectively rational perception of material self-interest to an economist may have little appeal to a rural dweller in a less developed country. Cultural biases often incline people to pursue goals other than welfare maximization, and other considerations may persuade them to pursue different avenues to that end from those an economist might prescribe. Even when a person accepts that a prescription may increase his or her wealth, it may be seen to entail consequences which are unacceptable—a violation of religious or ethical codes, or the rupture of group solidarity which can take precedence over an individual's welfare, partly (but not merely) because it provides material support in hard times. We see here not the irrationalities of the people in question, but a more complex and subtle form of rationality than the neo-liberal approach recognizes.

The problems do not end with the perceptions of ordinary individuals. People in authority in Third World political systems—politicians and bureaucrats—generally accept the need for economic growth, but they often have other, more compelling political concerns that take precedence. They are usually more anxious about the security of their regime and sometimes of the state than about development (Chai-Anan 1991). They have networks of supporters to cultivate, whose interests may be threatened by economic prescriptions. State structures, political institutions, or even ruling cliques often possess considerable complexity and material substance, which means that they generate their own imperatives and possess their own internal logic. This understandably preoccupies power holders, often at the expense of economic concerns.

There is also an extensive literature, stretching back through Machiavelli to Aristotle and Kautilya, which is erected on the highly plausible proposition that 'the ruler's first imperative, and his most urgent desire, is to retain his position at the apex of government' (Wriggins 1969). The recent study mentioned above which argues that politicians' concerns with security take precedence over their interest in development and participation (Chai-Anan 1991) resonates with that literature. The neo-liberal paradigm has little to say on these matters. It is hardly surprising, then, that political scientists find it wanting.

To say these things is not to claim that politics usually enjoys primacy in determining outcomes. That happens some of the time, but not most of the time. But it is to deny that economic considerations usually predominate. Other things—political and social considerations, cultural prejudices, mis-perceptions, errors of judgement—also play their part on many occasions. We live in an untidy world, and the excessive neatness of economists' explanations—and none are neater than those of the neo-liberals—needs to be treated with suspicion.

The neo-liberals' distaste for state intervention often causes them to overlook a great deal of evidence of mutually supportive relations between states and markets. We have already noted how economic liberalization in rural China has necessitated the expansion of the state's role as arbiter in contractual disputes. We have referred to the potent role of the state in Taiwan in abetting the development of private sector industry there. The same could be said of South Korea—which has a 'tradition of centralized government control over the private sector' which is 'pervasive' (Toye 1987: 87)—and, in an earlier phase, of Japan. Indeed, across much of continental Europe, Scandinavia, and beyond, the state has commonly played an important role as protector and enabler of private sector development.

We hear little acknowledgement of this from the neo-liberals. They tend to over-react so sharply against the state that they lose sight of its creative potential. This is especially true of P. T. Bauer, the most forthrightly polemical of the neo-liberals. He has a keen eye for easy assumptions, exaggerations, and internal contradictions in the writing of those who do not share his views, which means that we have plenty to learn from him. But when he uncovers a weakness in the arguments of an adversary, he tends to leap to extreme conclusions which his earlier discovery does not justify.

We can accept his view that the growth of the state sector in a less developed country can retard economic growth, and that sometimes it may even promote greater inequality, but it is quite another thing to conclude that the state should be minimized more or less invariably. We can agree—and some of us have agreed (Manor 1989)—that, after independence, many Asian and African nationalist leaders were naïvely optimistic about social engineering and other state-led experiments. But this need not incline us to see all such experiments as perverse. We can share his disagreement with the view that only planned economic development can achieve a rate of growth capable of commanding popular enthusiasm (Bauer 1984) without concluding that there is only the most minimal role for the state in less developed economies.

Given their tendency to underestimate the state, it is very curious to see that neo-liberals frequently overestimate it in one important respect. Miles Kahler and Thomas Callaghy have reminded us that structural adjustment programmes which the International Monetary Fund and the World Bank have derived mainly from neo-liberal theories usually assume that Third World governments possess the administrative capacity to implement complex sets of changes which produce severe political dilemmas. Political scientists

—especially those who study Africa—know from long experience that many governments lack these capabilities, and that the neo-liberals lack the analytical tools to estimate state capacity (Kahler 1990, Callaghy 1989).

This is not the only example of the neo-liberals' regrettable disregard for both the political implications of their economic prescriptions, and the political contexts within which they must operate. Bela Balassa has produced a set of economic case-studies (Balassa 1985) in which the state appears only occasionally and fleetingly. He focuses on a strictly limited set of questions. He asks how a particular economy works. He assesses the changes that were made in economic policy during a particular episode, and the results in economic terms of those changes. He then discusses other changes which might have been made, and the economic results that would have followed from them.

This means, at one level, that his work has a kind of integrity when taken on its own terms. But at another level, it entails serious and curious omissions. For example, he has produced a study of economic liberalization in China after 1978 which makes no mention of the political context, the political compulsions that caused these policy changes to be made, or their political ramifications. These cannot be dismissed from the discussion without risking a misunderstanding of the economic changes that have occurred. If the effort to liberalize encounters major difficulties or fails, it is very likely that this will occur partly for economic reasons, but mainly because it proved incompatible with the logic of the political system and with the political perceptions of key groups. If it succeeds, its main significance and much of the explanation will again lie in the political sphere.

Other, related limitations are apparent in his essay on Chile between 1973 and 1983. The name Pinochet never appears in this study, nor is there any remote suggestion of the draconian nature of the regime. We are told at one point that Chile had 'a military government' (p. 161), but that rather neutral remark is all that we get. This case-study appears among essays on France before and during the Mitterand years, Portugal after 1983, and Mexican trade policy, and is treated in the same manner as they are.

This is, at one level, understandable and appropriate. After all, each of these episodes raises a set of economic issues which can be and need to be subjected to an economist's critical eye. But if one regards them only at that level, one fails to consider other—and in the case of Chile, more compelling —concerns. Balassa's paper gives no inkling of the extreme sentiments that clearly lay behind the reign of terror which the Pinochet regime unleashed. Nor does he say that the particular economic strategy adopted in Chile required, as a prerequisite, a regime that was prepared to use political repression. To discuss the benefits of those economic policies without mentioning the costs that repression entailed is analytically unsatisfactory. If Balassa had considered such issues, then it is hard to believe that his judgements about the optimality of the policies selected would have remained the same. His failure to do so suggests either a surpassing political naïvety or a willingness to sanitize a vile regime.

Similar cause for concern arises from the writings of other neo-liberal economists. Lord Bauer, commenting on 'appropriate political arrangements for economic achievement' (Bauer 1981: 189), commends to us the example of Hong Kong, where elections have had an exceedingly minor role to play. 'The absence of election promises, together with an open economy and limited government, have much reduced the prizes of political activity and hence the interest in organizing pressure groups' (p. 187). Citizens' voluntary associations and an open political system which responds to them must not, it seems, be permitted to retard the free play of market forces.

His sentiments are echoed by Deepak Lal, writing about the lobbies which spring up when governments issue licences and permits in the trade and manufacturing sectors. Lal writes that 'A courageous, ruthless and perhaps undemocratic government is required to ride roughshod over these newly-created special interest groups' (Lal 1983: 33). Such bellicose language makes one wonder whether any sort of political participation can be tolerated in the neo-liberal scheme of things. It is also worth noting that a 'ruthless' state which 'rides roughshod' over interest groups is something other than the minimalist state that the neo-liberals claim to prefer. This in turn makes one wonder whether the tendency of some neo-liberals to exclude things political from their analyses is not intended to distract attention from the inconveniently draconian political implications of their prescriptions.

In Chapter 4, Naila Kabeer and John Humphrey tackled this problem by offering a critique of Hayek's theory of politics, on the assumption that it underpins much neo-liberal thinking. They may be correct to assume this, but since the neo-liberals scarcely mention Hayek, Kabeer and Humphrey may be crediting them with a more fully developed understanding of politics than they possess. To clarify things, this writer asked four leading neo-liberals for readings that would explain their conception of the state. All of them very kindly responded, but—with one exception—they referred entirely to their own work, to economic studies which fall short as political analysis. The exception was Anne O. Krueger, who suggested the writings of a well-respected political scientist, Robert H. Bates.

This, however, raises new problems for the neo-liberals, since Bates has mounted a formidable attack on their approach (Bates 1988). He offers three main criticisms. He first objects to the uses which some neo-liberals make of the criterion of Pareto optimality. They sometimes 'employ it to compare allocations made by politicians with those that would be generated by the market', and at other times they use it normatively, to criticize governments' actions by weighing the social cost of political decisions. In Bates's view, neither procedure is legitimate. He is especially unhappy with its normative use, since this 'presumes that economic efficiency provides a measure of what is socially best'. This cannot be true amid marked disparities in wealth, since in those circumstances, bargaining occurs between decidedly unequal agents—a common feature in the Third World.

In fairness, it should be said that Bates's complaints about Pareto optimality do not apply to much of what the neo-liberals have written, but his other two criticisms are much more generally applicable to their work. His second objection is to a problem that has already arisen in this discussion—their disinclination to engage in serious analysis of things beyond their narrow economic concerns. They are so preoccupied with what they see as the social costs incurred by institutions other than the market that those institutions are 'more condemned than studied' in their writings. Since individuals who depart from the logic of the market in allocating resources 'are often branded as "irrational" . . . their behavior is placed beyond the scope of systematic enquiry'. Bates believes that there is some validity in the neo-liberal view 'that political activity imposes economic costs upon society', but this idea 'so dominates the analysis that it obscures deeper political questions'.

Finally, Bates turns to 'the problem of aggregation'. The neo-liberals' analysis is anchored in micro-economic theory which provides 'a method of aggregating individual preferences into collective outcomes, [by which] voluntary exchange in markets . . . yields predictable results; it generates an equilibrium'. Bates notes, however, that 'markets behave this way only under very special circumstances'. Market failure is often bound up with strategic behaviour. 'In strategic environments, rational choices by individuals no longer aggregate in well-behaved ways. Equilibrium may no longer exist; if they exist, they may no longer be unique.' In such conditions, 'market-based reasoning may no longer give insight into collective outcomes'.

Less developed economies also require the formation of public goods. 'Law, order, justice and security, as well as roads, health and education, are relatively scarce in developing societies, and are highly desired.' In such an environment, 'maximizing behavior by private individuals simply will not yield the market equilibrium' so that 'market based reasoning therefore cannot explain how individually rational choices generate collective outcomes'. Thus, Bates concludes that the neo-liberals offer 'an inadequate theory of how the choice of individuals will yield collective outcomes'. Coming from the only recognized political analyst cited by them as a source for their view of the state, these judgements raise grave doubts about the validity of that view.

Bates is better able to criticize their work than are most political scientists who study the Third World because his mode of political analysis stands so close to their mode of enquiry. His 'rational choice' approach is substantially derived from micro-economics, as is the neo-liberal economic paradigm. By locating Bates's work in the larger field of Third World political studies, we can illustrate in yet another way the severe limitations which most people in the field of Third World politics find in the neo-liberal paradigm.

These comments may, incidentally, serve other purposes. They may help development economists of many different perspectives to see that it is a mistake to believe that political scientists who use the 'rational choice' approach cover most of the ground in the field of Third World political studies. They may also suggest some important differences between economic and political analysis, and offer some insight into the problems that assail the study of politics in the Third World.

The work of political scientists who use 'rational choice' methods is greatly valued by most others in the field. But it needs to be understood that they represent a relatively small subgroup within the broader guild of political analysts. They address a rather limited set of issues within the discipline, as most of them readily admit. One hears them say, for example, that they are mainly concerned with questions that are susceptible to rigorous analysis. They are inclined to say that if they face a choice between a hugely important question that is not susceptible to such analysis and a smaller, less compelling question that can be so analysed, they prefer to take on the latter. This is a perfectly respectable posture, but it leaves many crucially important political issues underexplored. Or, to put it differently, the number of interesting questions that can be studied in such a rigorous manner is quite limited.

It is also worth stressing that the number of such questions is more limited in the study of politics than in economics. This is mainly because reliable quantification is far easier in economics where expenditures, deficits, etc. are commonly and usually accurately quantified, whereas things like political interests, political perceptions, the power to coerce or to entice, etc.—the stock in trade of political analysts—are far more difficult to measure, even in the best of circumstances.

Scholars, especially Western scholars, who study politics in Asia, Africa, and Latin America are not working in the best of circumstances. Westerners face enormous cultural barriers which can never be entirely overcome and which can only be substantially removed after years of hard labour. They also face immense difficulties developing an understanding of people who lead vulnerable lives amid conditions of scarcity. They often have huge problems gaining access to data, and if they are inclined to pursue rigorous quantitative analysis, the data that they obtain are often highly dubious.

It is partly for these reasons that so few political scientists have attempted to apply 'rational choice' methods to Third World cases. In the United States today, we find a sizeable army of scholars using these techniques to analyse American politics, but in the study of Asia, Africa, and Latin America, there is only Robert H. Bates and a rather limited circle of colleagues. Their achievements are impressive, but they operate under such severe constraints and they tackle a sufficiently narrow range of issues that it would be wrong to view their work as covering the entire field of Third World political studies.

Three points emerge from this discussion of Bates's critique and of 'rational choice' methods that are relevant to a political scientist's assessment of the neo-liberals. First, any mode of analysis derived from micro-economics —whether it be that of the neo-liberal economists or of the 'rational choice' political analysts—has serious limitations as a means of developing a broad understanding of Third World politics. Second, even those students of Third World politics who stand closest to the neo-liberals—the 'rational choice' school—believe that the particular approach offered by them is assailed by major difficulties. Finally, given the limited set of political issues which 'rational choice' specialists address, and given the serious disagreements which separate the 'rational choice' school from the neo-liberals, a considerable gulf separates the latter from mainstream political studies of the Third World.

It should by now be clear that there is no shortage of reasons for the disinclination of students of Third World politics to make use of the neo-liberal paradigm. The teleological character of the neo-liberals' approach, and their tendency to contract the scope of enquiry at a time when political analysts are broadening it, are both unwelcome. So is their inclination to offer a single set of economic prescriptions amid the enormous variations which characterize Third World polities—a strategy which will often produce unintended and unwelcome results when those prescriptions are adopted. Political scientists are hardly likely to be attracted to a mode of analysis which excludes fundamental elements of the political process, such as politicians' intense anxiety to maintain or enhance their power. By ignoring this and many other fundamentals, the neo-liberals' economic analyses operate with a certain kind of integrity within a broader irrationality.
  Students of politics are also bound to be concerned about the possibility that some neo-liberals may harbour an unspoken preference for draconian political strategies which carry heavy costs in human terms, and which are so extreme as to be politically unsustainable over the long term. The neo-liberals' over-reaction to the exaggerated optimism about state intervention which typified the 1950s and 1960s also makes them unconvincing to political scientists. Among other things, they fail to recognize that, far from being essentially antagonistic, states and markets are often mutually supportive. All of these problems are compounded by the difficulties that arise when we seek to cross the line between economic and political analysis. Those difficulties are intensified when micro-economics loom as large as they do in the case of the neo-liberal paradigm. This formidable list of impediments is virtually certain to prevent the neo-liberals from exercising any meaningful influence over studies of Third World politics.

The contributors to the present volume offer a range of approaches to development issues which are likely to be more acceptable to political scientists, because they deal more adequately with patent political realities.

Some of them draw upon the work of neo-liberals, but seek insights from scholars whose writing is anchored in other paradigms as well. Robert Chambers favours a 'stance of eclectic pluralism'. He derives prescriptions both from neo-liberal views of what the state should not do and from neo-Fabian views of what the state should do. For example, he argues that we need to operate on a case-by-case basis when considering whether parastatal marketing organizations make things better or worse for the rural poor, and he finds that the answers differ in different countries. Mick Moore finds that rent-seeking analysis offers explanations and prescriptions which are broadly correct at a high level of generality. But he also argues that it has serious limitations. These include the practical difficulties that assail attempts to apply commercial principles fully to the financing of recurrent irrigation operations in Third World settings, and the inflexibility of the neo-liberal approach in the face of political and technical particularities that one encounters in individual cases.

Other contributors concentrate more fully on the limitations of the neo-liberal paradigm, and often point to its tendency to overlook important political elements. Hubert Schmitz and Tom Hewitt remind us that the enabling state has played a major role in several successful attempts at export-led development in East Asia. By curtailing the free play of market forces—by, for example, making access to the domestic market contingent upon good export performance—the South Korean state constitutes a strong case for 'hands-on economic policies'. Reginald Green finds that the neo-liberals scarcely discuss war or spending on armaments and defence as important variables in the economies of Third World nations. And yet one or both of these things, which emerge from the realm of politics, impinge mightily upon a great many of the less developed economies. Charles Harvey calls attention to the complex array of political difficulties which assail attempts by African states to implement structural adjustment programmes and which the neo-liberals tend to ignore. And so it goes on. Studies such as these—which pay attention to the varied, complex, ambiguous roles played by the state and by things political—are much more likely than the work of the neo-liberals to prove convincing to specialists in Third World politics.

References

Balassa, B. (1985), *Change and Challenge in the World Economy*, MacMillan, Basingstoke.

Bates, R. H. (1988), 'Macro-political Economy in the Field of Development', Working Paper no. 40, Duke University Program in International Political Economy, Durham, NC.

Bauer, P. T. (1981), *Equality, the Third World and Economic Delusion*, Weidenfeld & Nicolson, London.

—— (1984), *Rhetoric and Reality: Studies in the Economics of Development*, Weidenfeld & Nicolson, London.

Bayart, J.-F. (1988), *L'État en Afrique: La Politique du ventre*, Fayard, Paris.

Callaghy, T. (1989), 'Toward State Capability and Embedded Liberalism in the Third World: Lessons for Economic Adjustment', in J. Nelson (ed.), *Fragile Coalitions: The Politics of Economic Adjustment*, Overseas Development Council/ Transaction Books, Washington, DC.

Chabal, P. (1986) (ed.), *Political Domination in Africa: Reflections on the Limits of Power*, Cambridge University Press, Cambridge and New York.

Chai-Anan, S. (1991), 'The Three-Dimensional State', in J. Manor (ed.) 1991 (forthcoming).

Clapham, C. (1988), *Transformation and Continuity in Revolutionary Ethiopia*, Cambridge University Press, Cambridge.

—— (1991), 'State, Society and Political Institutions in Revolutionary Ethiopia', in J. Manor (ed.), 1991 (forthcoming).

Diamond, L., *et al.* (1989), *Democracy in Developing Countries*, 4 vols., Adamantine Press, London.

Kahler, M. (1990), 'Orthodoxy and its Alternatives: Explaining Approaches to Stabilization and Adjustment', in J. Nelson (ed.), *Economic Crisis and Policy Choice: The Politics of Adjustment in Developing Countries*, Princeton University Press, Princeton, NJ, 33–62.

Krueger, A. O. (1974), 'The Political Economy of the Rent-Seeking Society, *American Economic Review*, 64/3 (June): 291–303.

Lal, D. (1983), *The Poverty of 'Development Economics'*, Institute of Economic Affairs, London.

Leys, C. (1970), 'Political Perspectives', in D. Seers and B. Joy (eds.), *Development in a Divided World*, Penguin, Harmondsworth, 106–38.

Manor, J. (1989), *The Expedient Utopian: Bandaranaike and Ceylon*, Cambridge University Press, Cambridge.

—— (ed.)(1991), *Rethinking Third World Politics*, London (forthcoming).

Mbembe, A. (1990), 'The Imaginary Dimensions and the Construction of Political Arenas: The Case of Cameroon' in J. Manor (ed.) 1991 (forthcoming).

Nandy, A. (1982), 'The State of the State', *Seminar* (New Delhi), 57–61.

O'Brien, D. C. (1990), 'The Show of State in Francophone Africa', in J. Manor (ed.) 1991 (forthcoming).

O'Donnell, G., *et al.* (1987), *Transitions from Authoritarian Rule*, Johns Hopkins Press, Baltimore, Md.

Smith, T. (1985), 'Requiem of New Agenda for Third World Studies?', *World Politics*, 37/4: 532–61.

Toye, J. (1987), *Dilemmas of Development: Reflections on the Counter-Revolution in Development Theory and Policy*, Blackwell, Oxford.

Tulabor, C. (1986), *Le Togo sous Eyadema*, Karthala, Paris.

Wagner, R. (1990), 'Institutions and the Imaginary in the Politics of China', in J. Manor (ed.) 1991 (forthcoming).

Weiner, M., and Huntington, S. P. (eds.) (1987), *Understanding Political Development*, Little Brown, Boston, Mass.

Wriggins, W. H. (1969), *The Ruler's Imperative: Strategies for Political Survival in Asia and Africa*, Columbia University Press, New York.

Zweig, D., *et al.* (1987), 'Law, Contracts and Economic Modernization: Lessons from the Recent Chinese Rural Reforms', *Stanford Journal of International Law*, 23/2: 319–64.

15
Is There a New Political Economy of Development?

JOHN TOYE

As Christopher Colclough notes in his Introduction, some exponents of the neo-liberal economic philosophy of the 1980s see themselves as creators of a whole new social scientific paradigm based on the application of the methods of economics to the study of politics in developing countries. This New Political Economy of development uses the assumptions of neo-classical micro-economics—methodological individualism, rational utility maximization, and the comparative statics method of equilibrium analysis—to explain the failure of governments to adopt the 'right', i.e. neo-liberal, economic policies for growth and development. In this way, neo-liberalism presents not merely 'a body of settled conclusions immediately applicable to policy', but also, in the form of the New Political Economy, an account of *why* its own prescriptions over forty years of the practice of development have until recently found so little political favour. At their most ambitious, the neo-liberals strive for the unification of economics and politics—both in normative and in positive modes—under the banner of rational choice theory. Since Colclough's Introduction does not attempt an assessment of the New Political Economy (henceforth, NPE), except its postulated link between rent-seeking and the need for a minimal state, it may be worthwhile to conclude this volume with a commentary on the NPE in its wider aspects.

For this purpose, we need to begin by sketching some of the characteristic features of the NPE, noting where appropriate variant versions. This is attempted in the following section. We argue that major features are an unrelievedly cynical view of the state and a sharp disjunction between that view and the political requirements for the adoption of liberalization policies in the economic sphere. The inherent pessimism of the NPE is problematic in itself, but it also in turn draws attention to another problematic feature, namely the exclusion of *international* economic and political causal factors from the frame of analysis.

In order to explain the features of the NPE which have been highlighted, a third section of this chapter takes a more detailed look at the origins of some of its constituent ideas and, finally, offers an alternative view, both of the political process in developing countries and of the politics lying behind the NPE approach itself. The answer to the question posed in the chapter title— 'Is there an NPE?'—is both 'yes' in a literal sense, and 'no', in that both the newness of the NPE and its status as good political economy can easily be exaggerated.

By now, a vast and quite variegated literature has accumulated which might be packaged with the label of 'the new political economy'. No attempt is made here at a comprehensive survey. We note only the very broadest distinctions between its main variant types. However, the reader will need to know some of the examples of the NPE literature which are taken as especially representative of the genre. Its flavour is well conveyed by both Buchanan, Tollison, and Tullock 1980 and Colander 1984. Surveys of results from the work in the NPE vein can be found in Bhagwati 1982 and Srinivasan 1985. The relevance of the NPE to developing countries is asserted enthusiastically by Findlay (1989); its limitations in this regard are stressed by Meier (1989).

The NPE is characterized first of all by a profoundly cynical view of the state in developing countries. To say, as exponents of the NPE do, that people in political positions are typically motivated *only* by individual self-interest is, and should be, shocking. It is shocking because it denies and disparages all the norms and values of political life no less dramatically than those ancient philosophers who pretended they were dogs in order to demonstrate their scorn for the ideals of the Greek *polis*. However one defines the public interest, and however much scope one grants to the protection of private interests as part of the definition of the public interest, the unbridled pursuit of self-interest by rulers belongs to the pathology of politics—to tyranny or dictatorship or, ultimately, to anarchy.[1] To attribute individual self-interest as their exclusive motive to politicians in developing countries is to deny their sincerity, their merit, and, ultimately, their legitimate right to govern. While this is appropriate criticism for particular rulers or regimes, in the developing no less than in the developed areas of the world, as a general characterization of the state in developing countries, it is breathtaking in its scope and pretensions. The NPE is not merely saying unflattering things about Third World politicians—that they are misguided, myopic, or cowardly. Its claims are much more extreme: that their unbridled egoism makes them constitutionally unfit for any political role whatsoever.

Why so extreme? The NPE contrasts its negative view of the state with the assumption of the benign or benevolent state which (the NPE claims) underpinned the literature on social democratic planning and, by extension, much of the development planning literature of the 1950s and 1960s. Indeed that assumption has at times proved misleading and unrealistic, especially when used in combination with another assumption frequently implicit in those discussions of planning—that the state was also omni-competent, i.e. it had access to all the information and policy instruments that it needed to achieve its objectives, whether benign or otherwise. But there is a puzzle here. Would it not have been better tactics for the neo-liberal challenge to focus on the myth of the omni-competent state in developing countries, rather than the myth of the benevolent state? Given that the prescriptions of neo-liberalism are represented as the true embodiment of the public interest of LDCs would not it have been advisable to doubt politicians' competence, while suspending disbelief in their good intentions? Then at least one would not have produced a theory where prescription and description are so seriously at odds as they are in the NPE, where the body of settled policy conclusions is so readily (too readily, in truth) to hand, while the political process is damned as incapable of serving *any* conception of the public interest.

The political hypotheses of the NPE are too cynical, too extreme, and it is this extremism (the reason for which we will speculate on in the penultimate section) which creates the second major feature of the NPE, its pessimism. For the major prediction of the new political economy in its positive mode must be that significant changes towards the 'right' neo-liberal policies will not, or will hardly ever, take place. Where the interests of rulers and ruled conflict, personally self-interested politicians will not make arrangements which secure the legitimate interests of citizens. In the absence of a natural harmony of interest, rulers serve themselves better by using their power to exploit others, and political arrangements which limit rulers' pursuit of self-interest are the only constraint on this exploitation. If such arrangements do not exist or have been subverted—which is the scenario in developing countries, according to the NPE—then the adoption of 'good' policies becomes an impossible dream. An inherent inability to implement policies that are taken to be obviously socially desirable amounts to more than just gloom about the prospects for reform. It is much more deterministic and much more pessimistic than this. It is (as it has been dubbed elsewhere) 'an economistic hypothesis of equilibrium unhappiness'—or an EHEU theory (Toye 1987: 122–7).

That the NPE is indeed an EHEU theory has been recognized by Grindle (1989: 31–2), who states that:

while the new political economy provides tools for understanding bad situations and for recommending policies that will engender better situations, it provides no logically apparent means of moving from bad to better . . . Locked into an ahistorical explanation of why things are the way they are and the notion that existing situations demonstrate an inevitable rationality, it is hard to envision how changes in such situations occur.

If a conceptual taboo did not prevent it, neo-liberals might accurately describe their political diagnosis as one of the *structural* frustration of sound public policy. They are in any case vulnerable to the riposte that such a diagnosis gestures in the direction of long-run dynamic theory, but does not actually specify any dynamics.

In an interdependent world with an unequal distribution of political power, it is only to be expected that some of the dynamics of policy changes in poor, developing countries will be international in character. But the NPE typically pays much less attention to international influences on public policy in LDCs than to national influences. Its frame of reference for analysis is the individual developing country. This is either analysed as a unitary entity, as in theories of 'the predatory state' (or 'the Leviathan state') which has its own rational self-interest; or as an arena in which outcomes result from the pursuit of rational self-interest by individual LDC politicians, bureaucrats, and other actors. In the best examples of the NPE, for example Repetto's analysis of irrigation projects which Moore discusses in Chapter 13, other actors do include international influences like multinational construction companies and international aid agencies. But this is not usually the case. The international actors are kept typically beyond the framework of analysis. The desirable policies are desirable domestic policies for developing country governments. Usually no complementary policy changes are demanded by NPE theorists from the developed countries' governments, or from the international institutions which they largely control. Ironically, in view of its heavy emphasis on international trade and investment, the NPE usually takes a very 'closed economy' approach to policy-making in developing countries. This in turn renders it particularly defective for illuminating actual policy changes in the 1980s, when the debt crisis and internationally sponsored structural adjustment programmes were responsible for so much of the policy change that did—NPE pessimism to the contrary notwithstanding —occur in developing countries.

Why are a profoundly cynical view of Third World states, a rigid pessimism about the prospects for reform, and a country-focused analytical framework such prominent features of the NPE? The answer to this riddle, it will be argued here, is to be found not in the intellectual sphere, but in the realm of rhetoric.

The NPE is an economic theory of politics, and uses the assumptions of neo-classical micro-economics. But nothing in those assumptions, or in the economic theory of politics as such, requires or determines the three major features of the NPE that have been identified. In the transposition of the economic theory of politics from its earlier reference to developed countries (and particularly, the United States) to its present reference, via the NPE, to developing countries, a number of significant component parts have been removed and replaced with something different. Such flexibility of the content of the economic theory of politics emphasizes that neo-classical micro-economics is not so much a doctrine as a method. It is a particular brand of logic, within which a great variety of different models of reality can be constructed, but not *any* model of reality. It is even more like a set of Meccano or Lego than the 'tool-kit' with which it is usually compared.

It is worth noting just how flexible the economic theory of politics has been over the years, in order to avoid the mistaken view that the conclusions of the NPE can simply be read off from its neo-classical starting-points. Three examples are discussed, concerning the nature of interest group pressure in the political process, the origin of social rigidities, and the optimal size of the government sector.

Originally, the pressures of interest groups in the political process were evaluated positively: they were a good thing. Interest group pressures were interpreted as equivalent to a competitive process in the political arena. The political need to achieve a broad consensus for the government's programme of measures ensured that extreme demands would be moderated by compromises, while the reasonable expectations of minorities would be respected in the process of coalition-building. The political competition of interest groups thus served not only to protect, but actually to construct, the public interest. In the NPE, all this has changed. Interest group competition has become *destructive* of the public interest (identified with liberalization policies) and symptomatic of a political fragmentation which occurs when politicians and administrators (illegitimately) as well as ordinary citizens (legitimately) pursue their individual self-interest (Grindle 1989: 13).

An even more dramatic change has occurred on the question of the origin of social rigidities, because here the shift of emphasis occurs between the earlier and later works of the same author—Mancur Olson. In the revised edition of his path-breaking *The Logic of Collective Action*, Olson summarizes its key finding as follows: 'even if all of the individuals in a large group are rational and self-interested, and would gain if, as a group, they acted to achieve their common interest or objective, they will still not voluntarily act to achieve that common or group interest' (1971: 2). This finding, that, paradoxically, rational individuals will not organize themselves to achieve their common interests, is then used as a critique of writers in the pluralist tradition who assumed not only that interest group pressures were benign, but that they would indeed manifest themselves. It was not the benign nature of interest group pressure which Olson questioned in 1971, but the logical inconsistency of assuming that self-interested individuals will voluntarily sacrifice in order to promote group aims (ibid. 126). But a decade later, the story-line has been completely reversed. In *The Rise and Decline of Nations* (1982), notwithstanding the difficulties of group collective organization, such groups are argued not only to exist, but also to 'reduce efficiency and aggregate income in the societies in which they operate and make political life more divisive' (1982: 47). Interest groups' activity is then used to explain the relatively slow growth performance of Britain, India, China, and the South African apartheid system. Not only have interest groups changed from being unproblematic to being the critical source of socio-economic ills, but the logical flaw which Olson originally spotted in interest group theory has dropped progressively out of sight.

A third example of the changing content of the economic theory of politics concerns the role of government. Anthony Downs, the pioneer of the economic theory of politics, used the theory to argue that the government sector would be inevitably *underextended* (1960: 341–63). His argument turned on the cost to citizens of acquiring information about remote dangers which could, if they occurred, cause massive damage, and which the government could potentially prevent. His example was the possible threat from improved Soviet space capability, but global environmental problems would be a clearer contemporary illustration. However, by the 1980s, the NPE is concerned exclusively with the *overextension* of government, and the argument used is the power of interest groups to vote themselves increases in public expenditure while diffusing the resultant costs through rises in general taxation.

The purpose of indicating these three major voltes-face in the content of the economic theory of politics is not to pass an opinion on whether the early version is better than the later one, or vice versa. Two points are relevant to our argument about the NPE. One is well put by Hindess (1988: 20–1), who remarks 'how radically different conclusions can be generated from the same set of abstract principles as a result of different assumptions about the conditions in which they are supposed to apply'. The other is that all three changes are consistent with each other. They together represent a dramatic shift away from a pluralist, participatory ideal of politics and towards an authoritarian and technocratic ideal based not on big government, but on small and highly efficient government. In the longer perspective, they signal the return in the 1980s to dominance of the non-participatory strand of Western liberal political theory (Hexter 1979: 293–303).[2] One can argue that the economists of politics are absorbed in the technical ingenuity of their models, so that their work merely reflects the larger shift in the political mood that occurred in the 1980s. They may not have been aware how conveniently their new conclusions suited it; and there is certainly no evidence that they deliberately altered them to gain political favour with the New Right. But it is not necessary to claim this. All that is necessary is to make the negative point that there is nothing about the practice of the economics of politics which inevitably generates the cynicism, pessimism, and contracted domestic focus of the NPE.

Nor, when one comes right down to it, is there anything about the theory of rent-seeking which drives one inevitably towards these features of the NPE. The original analysis of government economic controls did not provide a new political economy. Its author, Anne Krueger, explicitly declined to draw any political conclusions from her discussion of rent-seeking (1974: 302). Its significance in the doctrines of neo-liberalism was economic, not political. It was aimed at showing that trade controls are much more costly in terms of economic welfare than they had previously been taken to be. Empirical estimates of the size of the loss inflicted by the use of trade restrictions have, over the years, normally been small. Typically the gain in efficiency to be derived by the removal of trade controls has been estimated to be around 3–5 per cent of GNP—an amount equivalent to one year of growth in the case of many developing countries. If governments of LDCs believed that trade controls could be used to improve their growth rate in the medium and long term, they might well be willing to trade off static efficiency losses of this kind of size against their expected increase in long-run growth. Trade liberalization as a policy was handicapped because its pay-off was stated, even by its own advocates, to be relatively small. Krueger's rent-seeking theory was an attempt to address this problem, in the belief that the true economic costs of protection must be higher than had previously been calculated.

Krueger identified an additional source of static welfare loss from protection, namely the resources which are used up by economic agents in competing for an allocation of administratively allocated import licences. Such resources produce nothing and, at the limit, could equal in size the economic rents which the licensing regime creates. Thus the *potential* costs of using quantitative restrictions on imports were shown to be much greater than had previously been considered. This was a fundamental neo-liberal insight and it has not been gainsaid. But its implications for political economy remain to be fully assessed. They are not at all as straightforward a confirmation of the tenets of the NPE as it might appear at first blush.

The additional welfare losses arising from a trade regime characterized by quantitative restrictions result from an unproductive, but resource-consuming, competitive scramble for import licences that bring windfall gains to those who acquire them. For these additional losses to be realized in practice requires such a process to exist. But does it exist? It does not exist when the competitive scramble which we actually observe in developing countries is conducted by those who would be otherwise unemployed; clerks who fill in forms, leg-men who stand in queues at government offices, are consuming largely their own time and effort, and it is often sadly true in developing economies that these do not have any alternative productive use, and therefore no economic value. But more importantly for the NPE, a competitive rent-seeking process does not exist when licences are allocated by a process of pure patronage of the sort which self-interested political leaders use to reward their cronies. When a military ruler instructs officials of the Foreign Trade Ministry to issue import licences to his chief henchmen and lieutenants, there is *no* competitive process and *no* resource cost involved. This point is usually overlooked. In neo-liberal discussions of 'the politicization of economic life', the scramble for spoils and patronage are lumped together as if they were slightly different aspects of essentially the same phenomenon, whereas for the purpose of gauging the real significance of rent-seeking theory they have diametrically opposite implications.

The cynical view of Third World states, that self-interested state rulers, lacking much in the way of institutional constraints, maximize their own welfare at the public's expense, fits most easily with the scenario of patronage, rather than with that of the competitive scramble for spoils. The competitive scramble theory assumes that rulers are indifferent about the identities of the winners of the spoils. If this were true, it would be difficult to explain why the authorities would continue to oppose an auction of import quotas. An auction, after all, captures the rents of the import licences for the ruler's own treasury, while eliminating their dissipation on unproductive activities. Its crucial disadvantage, from the self-interested politician's viewpoint, is that it also abolishes clandestine political control over the distribution of unearned benefits. And, on that criterion, the competitive scramble is no different from an auction.

It is difficult to argue in the light of these considerations that it is the logic of the theory of rent-seeking that has produced the characteristic features of the NPE. The theory of rent-seeking has no specific theory of political economy built into it, and, to the extent that it is based on the idea of impersonal competition for rents, stands at some distance from the cynical account of Third World rulers' behaviour which the New Political Economy offers. (It also has some surprising implications for standard neo-liberal prescriptions of trade policy—concerning the policy ranking of QRs, tariffs, and domestic subsidies—but these would take us too far from our present theme to explore here.)

An important hiatus thus exists between the neo-classical roots of the NPE (whether in the economic theories of politics which existed before 1980 or in the original theory of the rent-seeking society) and the actual form and content which characterize the NPE of the 1980s. To elucidate the NPE solely in terms of its genealogy in economic science would be inadequate and confusing. The rhetorical uses of economic theory must also be brought in to any explanation of why the NPE is as it is. Economic theorizing always takes place within a specific changing historical context. Our assumption here is that two-way interaction can take place between economic theories and their changing context. Larger-scale change in the political mood, such as occurred in the 1980s, can affect what is theorized and the substance of the conclusions of theory. Influence can also flow in the reverse direction, as theorists deliberately seek to alter the stances of public policy-makers. If these assumptions are valid, one should not expect to be able to confine the intellectual history of the NPE just to its lineage in logic: there may well be strange logical leaps of the kind which have been noted above. We need to turn elsewhere to investigate why one kind of intellectual tool is produced from the tool-kit at one moment, and another kind of tool at another time, or why the same tools produce opposite policy conclusions in succeeding periods.

It may be worth emphasizing a corollary of the assumption of two-way interaction between theorizing and its historical context. It is that the economic theory of politics (of which the NPE is an offshoot) itself rests on too narrow foundations. 'To take account of the role of ideas (influencing, and being influenced by, public policy) must require, at the very least, a more complex model of the individual actor than Downs and the public choice school appear to offer' (Hindess 1988: 22). Although this chapter does not offer a detailed critique of the internal logic of the NPE, this is one major point which such a critique would have to include.[3]

But leaving that aside, what was the historical context of the emergence of the NPE, and what were the extra-scientific factors that shaped its development? These are large questions, and what follows is the merest sketch. Let us start from one further puzzle of the 'new political economy', its title. Why does the NPE refer to itself as 'new'? The standard answer to this is that it is new because it rejects the naïvety of the development economists and others who in the 1950s and 1960s believed that the state was an agency that promoted social welfare—the assumption of the benevolent or do-gooding state. But this is to respond to one naïvety with another. To suggest that all that was needed to give birth to the NPE was a process of gradual disillusion with the benevolence of the state in developing countries has the same simple-minded quality as the benevolent state assumption has itself.

One could put another case. It is that very few development economists forty years ago believed that the state in developing countries was concerned unreservedly to maximize social welfare. Quite a lot of economic work is technical and requires no particular view of the state. The assumption of the benevolent state, when it appeared without qualification, was usually more a matter either of pure diplomacy or of 'reformist hope'. It is vital to recall that the development economists of that time were largely foreigners to the developing countries, where they operated with either explicit or implicit sponsorship of their home governments. They wanted to assist their adopted country in their capacity as professional 'improvers', but not to get entangled with local politics. As professional economists seeking to promote reforms, they assumed the existence of certain institutions and attitudes, as it were trying to coax them into life while aware that they were often not in fact there. *Saying* that they were not there in public would, however, have been easily interpreted as a political act. The benevolent state assumption in developing countries was thus a convenient myth for those in a false position, not their firm belief. Many felt morally uncomfortable in their inability to explore openly the reasons for their professional frustration, but most of these loyally respected the diplomatic imperative.

What the orthodox could not acknowledge publicly in the 1950s and 1960s surfaced as dissent. Specifically, it appeared in the neo-Marxist political economy of development. In the work of Paul Baran (1973), this combined a cynical view of the LDC state with strong and critical emphasis on the role of foreign capital in frustrating rational development. Gradually this tradition bifurcated, with some neo-Marxists retaining the stress on the determining pressure of foreign capital ('capital logic') and others locating the source of distorting pressures in the domestic class system above all ('class logic'). The class logic version of the Marxian political economy of development is morphologically almost identical with that version of the NPE which concentrates on the problematic role of interest groups. Both have political processes which guarantee economically irrational outcomes. The only important difference is that the former attributes the pressures for economic irrationality to an exploitative class, while the latter attributes it to the activities of self-interested groups. And both, of course, keep out of sight the international pressures which a capitalist system generates on developing countries. It is thus highly misleading to ignore the influence that neo-Marxism exerted on the NPE. The success of neo-Marxism in discrediting the assumption of the benevolent state paved the way down which the New Right moved triumphantly in the 1980s. The NPE is new specifically in succession to the 'old' political economy of neo-Marxism.

The decisive events in ensuring this succession took place, as usual, in the sphere of high politics. Some time at the end of the 1970s, at the end of McNamara's time as President of the World Bank, diplomacy no longer seemed to require tact and tongue-biting, but instead a justification for a much more active intervention in the local politics of developing countries. Neo-classical economists, many of whom were then still producing project appraisal manuals with shadow prices and income-distribution weights, went back to the box of Lego and produced instead various sanitized versions of neo-Marxian political economy, sanitized in that they were deducible from individual rational self-interest rather than anything so unorthodox as 'class'. (The neo-Marxists were having sufficient difficulty with class themselves![4])

The move from the 'old' neo-Marxism to the new political economy can be traced both in academic discourse and in practical affairs. Among academics, some have simply abandoned the conceptual vocabularly of neo-Marxism in favour of that of public choice analysis, on the basis that the latter furnishes a more consistent and powerful set of hypotheses about the political economy. Others have tried to blend neo-Marxism into rational choice theory, analysing long-term historical developments in terms of a predatory state acting under constraints of bargaining power, transactions costs, and discount rates (Levi 1988). This is essentially an attempt to modernize a Marxist analysis of the autonomy of the state that goes back to Engels's *Origin of the Family, Private Property and the State*.

In practical affairs, one classic study in the switch from Marxism to the NPE is the trajectory of David Stockman, who was responsible for putting the supply side revolution in US economics on the conservative political map, and was President Reagan's Budget Director during his first term. His early student Marxist politics; his discovery of a 'Grand Doctrine' in the corruptions of the welfare state, if post-F.D.R. America could be so called; his conviction of the high moral quality of a thoroughgoing anti-statist revolution; and his bitterness at the 'triumph' of [US] politics' which defeated that revolution as soon as it had produced a Republican electoral victory—all of these things mark him as a bell-wether of a generation that succeeded, but only briefly, in foisting on conservatism an ideological position. The transition from the old to the new political economy found in David Stockman its representative figure (Stockman 1985).

The revamping of the neo-Marxist class logic story with the aid of methodological individualism left its major rhetorical features unaffected. The introduction of rational self-interest as the sole motive of politicians and bureaucrats did not change the neo-Marxist view of the state as an entity merely pretending a real concern for the public interest and national welfare. Like neo-Marxism, the NPE makes strong normative claims, essentially taking it as obvious that a certain set of social and economic arrangements is right. The conjunction of a cynical view of the politics of existing regimes and strong normative claims leads both to produce a bleak and deeply contradictory pessimism about the possibilities of progress. But the aim in both cases is not so much to interpret the world as to change it, and for that purpose cynicism and pessimism (when further combined with a vision of a liberating crisis) are powerful ideological instruments of persuasion.

The NPE found in the profound economic shocks of the 1970s a catastrophe that served as a revolutionary crisis. The liberation was to be provided, not by classless intellectuals, but by international economic experts. Dudley Seers, who postulated (1979) 'the congruence of Marxism and other neo-classical doctrines', provided the clue to these and other parallels. For in both neo-Marxism and the NPE, what is attempted is no less than the unity of theory and practice.

On this interpretation, it makes no sense at all to try and refute the cynicism and pessimism of the NPE about the governments of developing countries by pointing to current examples of successful reform programmes in Africa and Asia (as Grindle (1989) does). For it is here that the economic catastrophe has taken place, and the international economic experts of structural adjustment have arrived. Most of the empirical evidence from the 1980s on policy reform is contaminated (from a scientific point of view) by the very rhetorical success which the NPE theorists have achieved in underwriting international action in support of liberalizing reform. The appearance of contrary cases represents failure for the scientist, but signals success for the soothsayer. But the comparison of the new political economy with the neo-Marxism and the indication of the strong soothsaying element in both should not be taken to imply that the intellectual achievements of the

NPE have been negligible. Apart from Krueger's theory of rent-seeking, the NPE has provided enlightening explanations of how micro-economic incentives can sustain particular types of projects and programmes which are meant to be, but are not in fact, developmental. These may look oddly similar to the now despised 'vicious circle of cumulation causation' theories of the past, but they are welcome because they are more thoroughly grounded in the analysis of individual behaviour. It is the large-scale analyses of the NPE which are flawed—by exaggeration, self-contradiction, and *arrière-pensée*.

What changes are needed if our thinking is to be released from these flaws? The NPE is one of those branches of modern economics which, in the words of A. K. Sen (1984: 7), seem 'indeed to be based on the corset-maker's old advice: "If madam is entirely comfortable in it, then madam most certainly needs a smaller size." ' The assumptions of methodological individualism are painfully restrictive (Meier 1989: 20–2). Social, political, and indeed economic *structures* have to be reintroduced into the analysis. In doing so, however, it is very important—and this is one other vital legacy of the NPE—not to do so to the exclusion of individual agency and the single person's power of self-determination. A structuralism which treats people only as determined by structures is no less objectionably reductionist than an individualism which treats society, polity, and economy only as the aggregates of self-determined individual action. A consensus is now emerging that agentless structure versus structureless agency is a false dilemma and that this long-standing dualism has now to be set aside in favour of theories that permit reciprocal interaction between the individual and the social setting. The argument here is owed to Giddens (1984), but many others, including Lawson (1985), Hodgson (1988), and Dearlove (1989), have endorsed it.[5]

By way of illustration, let us consider the problem of nationalism. Nationalism, the denial of legitimacy to regimes where political rule is not coextensive with one language or culture, presents difficulties of explanation both for the economic theory of politics and for neo-Marxism. It seems to be such a powerful force in the modern world—whether we look to its First, Second, or Third incarnations. Yet both neo-liberalism and neo-Marxism, if they do not ignore it altogether (in the manner of Olson, whose book on *The Rise and Decline of Nations* is innocent of any index entry for nationalism), represent nationalism simply as a product of economic interests, either individual or class interests. The individual economic interest route collapses in self-contradiction for the same reason as does the analysis of voting in terms of rational choice: there is a paradox of national identification exactly analogous with the paradox of voting. The fate of the nation is so little affected by the moral or material investment of a single nationalist in its well-being, that no nationalist would make that investment (Barry 1970: 45–6). The class economic interest route collapses when called upon to explain the persistence of nationalism in officially classless societies like the USSR (Kolakowski 1978: 103–5).

Any explanation of nationalism, its growth, and its consequences must have recourse to certain *structural* features of the social world. These features may include class, but are not restricted to class as neo-Marxism might claim. Relevant structural features of social life for an analysis of nationalism would be the pattern of social stratification, the form and functions of the education system, the level of literacy, the degree of secularization, and the nature of migration and other contacts with more developed countries (Gellner 1983). In that long run in which we are all dead, it is the changes in these features of society which produce the rise and decline of nations. But in the short and medium run, they act as the parameters of individual choice. Any individual is free to choose to become a revolutionary nationalist hero or heroine. He or she is equally free to renounce the nationality of birth and to assimilate to an alien culture. Nothing prevents some people from deciding to do *both* of those things. Finally, nothing prevents other people from deciding to do neither, perhaps because they agree with Santayana that 'nationality is . . . too implicated in our moral nature to be changed honourably, and too accidental to be worth changing'. Even in the short run, the existence of structural determinants does not abolish individual choice.

It is important to insist also that choice is not necessarily exercised only after a process of economic calculation. 'In the growth of nationalist feeling and agitation, there is no need to assume any conscious long-term calculation of interest on anyone's part . . . It would be genuinely wrong to try to reduce these (nationalist) sentiments to calculations of material advantage or social mobility' (Gellner 1983: 61–2). As Barry (1970: 45) has put it, national identification leads to certain kinds of actions which lie outside the framework of economic calculation, and the most useful response is to work out the circumstances in which it does so. Yet the fact that nationalism lies somewhere beyond rational calculation should not permit neo-liberalism to brush it aside, as of little significance. After all, the 'erroneous' domestic economic policies which the NPE attributes to the cynical self-interest of LDC rulers are also frequently interpreted as the policies of economic nationalism (Burnell 1986: 37–9). If that were true, one would surely want to be equipped with a form of political economy broad enough to analyse nationalism and its economic policy impact, in the variety of shapes in which it appears in different developing countries. The realization by the international financial institutions that structural adjustment has a 'missing political dimension' may be a reflection of their own previous willingness to view economic liberalization through the prism of the NPE, when this boldly excludes, by assumption, the considerations which might make economic nationalism intelligible.

If a renewed emphasis on social structure is accepted, then the institutions of political life take on an expanded significance.[6] They are no longer seen merely as a set of constraints (unchanging and unexplained) within which individual politicians and bureaucrats rationally maximize their utility. Their role in conferring legitimacy, authority, and power on those who participate in them can be understood, as can the associated concept of institution-building and institutional decay. If the problem is that self-interested behaviour by rulers of developing countries has increased, one must enquire how structures have changed to weaken the institutional constraints on opportunistic self-aggrandizement in the realm of politics. One could go further and argue that the real problem is the inability to reconstruct institutional constraints in some LDCs once the externally imposed colonial institutions have been swept away, or once traumatic external interventions have destabilized old societies. Politicians have responded to this empty institutional space in many diverse ways. Some, like President Mobutu of Zaïre, have been a byword for rampant corruption. Others, like Flight-Lieutenant Jerry Rawlings, are not corrupt, but are driven by a (sometimes violent) messianic puritanism to save their country. In some cases, such as Pol Pot and the Khmer Rouge in Kampuchea, chiliasm turns atrocious: the rulers do not accumulate wealth, only the piled-up human skulls of the killing fields.

It is impossible to discuss how different politicians in the Third World react to what Lucy Mair (1965: 34) once called 'the breathless speed with which historical circumstances have extended the room for manœuvre' without addressing the moral factor in politics—its absence in certain instances of anarchy or tyranny; the particular kinds of constraints which are imposed on politicians and bureaucrats in hypocritical regimes, where considerations of political 'visibility' become important, and the instances where, *mirabile dictu*, LDC rulers actually are benevolent, although possibly also misinformed about how best to tread the road paved with good intentions. Thus the reintroduction of structuralist ideas is not just a device to revert to the assumption of benevolent LDC governments, which, as has been argued, was in any case previously advanced with considerable mental reservations even by those who espoused it. It is a proposal to inject into political economy a much richer and more refined analysis of politics than the NPE permits. It is also an invitation to apply a more refined understanding of politics not only to governments of developing countries, but also to the international actors in political economy.

As for the validity of the NPE's 'body of settled conclusions immediately applicable to policy', the reintroduction of structures and institutions to the debate helps to explain why an automatic presumption in favour of free market solutions may not be warranted. Markets themselves are institutions. Michael Lipton's chapter argues, among other things, that markets for agriculture often have to be developed, that this is costly and that the costs often have to be borne by the state. The cutting back of state activity may, in plausible circumstances, actually hinder the desirable goal of greater scope for economically rational pricing of rural inputs and outputs. Kaplinsky draws essentially the same lesson for the growth of small-scale industry from his Botswana case-study. David Evans argues from an inherent imperfection in labour contracts to the need for institutions to moderate the welfare losses inflicted by authoritarian managers of work: the growth of these labour unions is rarely encouraged and often actively discouraged by neo-liberal advocates of economic liberalization. Yet their healthy development is necessary both to protect employees from exploitation and unfair discrimination and to contribute to pluralism in the political arena. Women as a gender are exposed to widespread and persistent discrimination and devaluation, which their access to the labour market does not itself dissolve. Kabeer and Humphrey conclude that women must have strong grass-roots organizations to confront these persistent disadvantages, and that the key issue is how they can harness some of the power of the state to sustain their struggle for appropriately equal treatment with men.

What the state can do to promote rural markets, to foster small-scale industry, to respond intelligently to the pressures of labour unions and women's organizations, and to address a great range of other legitimate tasks of development depends upon how well the government's own institutions are working. Why insist, with the neo-liberals, on minimal government, if better government is a possibility? Government budgeting institutions are crucially involved in any agenda for better government. Yet, as Reg Green suggests, even those (like the World Bank) who recognize the need for *more* government expenditure lack a clear vision of how the selection and management of rational expenditure programmes can be institutionalized. On the revenue side of the budget, neo-liberal emphasis on fees and user charges diverts attention from the reconstruction of progressive tax systems, which Colclough points to as preferable for the financing of education.

Finally, international institutions can help or hinder the government's attempts to address the tasks of development. This is true in two particular senses illustrated in earlier essays. If the policy prescriptions of the IMF or the World Bank are too standardized and are attempted to be pressed home without due consideration for local institutional variations, the effects (as Charles Harvey's African cases show) will be unhelpful. At the same time, there is no innate requirement that the international financial institutions should always behave in this Procrustean way. They, too, are a terrain for learning and innovation. The innovations of the 1980s have been significant, though not all of them have delivered what their inventors believed that they would. Much scope remains for further learning and new institutional departures, in the spirit of Stephany Griffith-Jones's suggestions for the IMF, that will provide a better combination of incentives and disciplines for developing country governments than has been achieved so far.

Notes

1. It may be of interest to explain why the statement that 'politicians and bureaucrats are motivated only by individual self-interest' is shocking. First, it is assumed that the proposition is not tautological, that is, it does not mean that whatever these actors do must be self-interested in some sense, because otherwise they would not do it. Second, if the statement is not empty because tautological, it means that these actors when faced with any conflict between their own individual interest and the interest of any other person will infallibly prefer the former. Third, it is assumed that conflicts of interest do occur, and that a natural harmony of individual interests does not prevail. When conflicts of interest occur between individuals in *economic* life they are arbitrated in the market-place by the 'invisible hand' of the price mechanism which, on given assumptions, can achieve an 'efficient' reconciliation of conflicting interests. But even Adam Smith did not suppose that market-generated outcomes could be efficient without an over-arching framework of law and regulation to maintain the socio-political parameters within which markets can work efficiently. Now if the politicians and bureaucrats, who are responsible for enacting laws and enforcing regulations, use their *political* power to advance personal and private interests when they conflict with the public interest, they betray their duty to the general public and that is, and ought to be, shocking. The application of the neo-classical self-interest assumption to politics is, therefore, something much more fundamental than the simple 'extension' of a behavioural assumption from one arena of social life to another.

2. The participatory strand in Western political theory starts from Aristotle and runs through Machiavelli and Guicciardini, Harrington, Ferguson, and Rousseau. The non-participatory strand starts with the Stoics and runs through the Roman legists, Magna Carta, Coke, Blackstone, Bentham, and James Mill.

3. For an earlier attempt to discuss the basic logical difficulties of certain economic theories of politics, see Toye 1976. A good recent discussion is Dearlove 1989, as well as Hindess 1988.

4. In this regard, they follow closely in the footsteps of Marx himself. The *Communist Manifesto* speaks of two classes, bourgeoisie and proletariat, but in his other writings three-layered models of class structure are to be found; and when Marx discusses class in what was later to become vol. iii of *Capital*, the manuscript breaks off before the definition has properly begun (Prawer 1978: 146–7).

5. Strictly speaking, it is the recent revival of this argument that is owed to Giddens. It has long been a commonplace of the anthropological literature. Malinowski (1926: 56) wrote that 'the savage is neither an extreme "collectivist" nor an intransigent "individualist"—he is, like man in general, a mixture of both'. The anthropological discussion has focused on the question of how, if society is continuously re-created by the transmission (through socialization, education, etc.) of social roles (husband, parent, teacher, judge, ruler), social change can occur. Emmet (1960) suggested that change was the product of individuals deciding (rather in the manner of an actor's ad-libbing) marginally to reinterpret their roles. (The recent adsorption of some of the anthropological literature by students of Third World politics, especially in France, has led to the reappearance of the theatrical metaphor as a key to political understanding.)

6. Bates (1989) also emphasizes the importance of institutions, but from inside the methodological individualism tradition. His argument is that while rational individuals should constitute the unit of analysis, 'they compete within a set of political institutions; and the structure of these institutions shapes their interactions so as to determine the outcome that will hold in equilibrium' (ibid. 10–13). While criticizing market-based theories of politics, he advocates further work in the same tradition as the literature on the theory of committees and elections.

References

Baran, P. A. (1973), *The Political Economy of Growth*, Penguin, Harmondsworth.

Barry, B. M. (1970), *Sociologists, Economists and Democracy*, Collier-Macmillan, London.

Bates, R. H. (1989), 'Some Skeptical Notes on the "New Political Economy" of Development', Duke University (mimeo), Durham, NC.

Bhagwati, J. N. (1982), 'Directly Unproductive Profit Seeking (DUP) Activities', *Journal of Political Economy*, 90/5 (Oct.): 988–1002.

Buchanan, J. M., Tollison, R. D., and Tullock, G. (1980) (eds.), *Towards a Theory of the Rent-Seeking Society*, Texas A. and M. University Press, College Station, Texas.

Burnell, P. (1986), *Economic Nationalism in the Third World*, Wheatsheaf Books, Brighton.

Colander, D. C. (1984), *Neoclassical Political Economy*, Ballinger, Cambridge, Mass.

Dearlove, J. (1989), 'Neoclassical Politics: Public Choice and Political Understanding', *Review of Political Economy*, 1/2: 208–37.

Downs, A. (1960), 'Why the Government Budget is Too Small in a Democracy', *World Politics*, 12/4 (July): 541–63.

Emmet, D. (1960), 'How Far Can Structural Studies Take Account of Individuals', *Journal of the Royal Anthropological Institute*, 90: 191–200.

Findlay, R. (1989), 'Is the New Political Economy Relevant to Developing Countries?', PPR Working Papers (WPS 292), World Bank, Washington, DC.

Gellner, E. (1983), *Nations and Nationalism*, Basil Blackwell, Oxford.

Giddens, A. (1984), *The Constitution of Society*, Polity Press, Oxford.

Grindle, M. (1989), 'The New Political Economy: Positive Economics and Negative Politics', mimeo, Cambridge, Mass.

Hexter, J. H. (1979), *On Historians: Reappraisals of Some of the Masters of Modern History*, Harvard University Press, Cambridge, Mass.

Hindess, B. (1988), *Choice, Rationality and Social Theory*, Unwin Hyman, London.

Hodgson, G. M. (1988), *Economics and Institutions: A Manifesto for a Modern Institutional Economics*, Polity Press, Oxford.

Kolakowski, L. (1978), *Main Currents of Marxism*, Oxford University Press, Oxford.

Krueger, A. O. (1974), 'The Political Economy of the Rent-Seeking Society', *American Economic Review*, 64/3 (June): 291–303.

Lawson, T. (1985), 'Uncertainty and Economic Analysis', *Economic Journal*, 95/380 (Dec.): 909–27.

Levi, M. (1988), *Of Rule and Revenue*, University of California Press, Berkeley, Calif.

Mair, L. (1965), 'How Small-Scale Societies Change', in J. Gould (ed.), *Penguin Survey of the Social Sciences 1965*, Penguin, Harmondsworth.

Malinowski, B. (1926), *Crime and Custom in Savage Society*, Routledge & Kegan Paul, London.

Meier, G. M. (1989), 'Do Development Economists Matter?', *IDS Bulletin*, 20/3 (July): 17–25.

Olson, M. (1971), *The Logic of Collective Action: Public Goods and the Theory of Groups* (rev. edn.), Schocken Books, New York.

—— (1982), *The Rise and Decline of Nations: Economic Growth, Stagflation and Social Rigidities*, Yale University Press, New Haven, Conn., and London.

Prawer, S. S. (1978), *Karl Marx and World Literature*, Oxford University Press, Oxford.

Seers, D. (1979), 'The Congruence of Marxism and other Neo-classical Doctrines' in K. Q. Hill (ed.), *Towards a New Strategy for Development*, Pergamon Press, New York, 1–17.

Sen, A. K. (1984), *Resources, Values and Development*, Basil Blackwell, Oxford.

Srinivasan, T. N. (1985), 'Neoclassical Political Economy, the State and Economic Development', *Asian Development Review*, 3/2: 38–58.

Stockman, D. A. (1985), *The Triumph of Politics: The Crisis in American Government and How it Affects the World*, Bodley Head, London.

Toye, J. (1976), 'Economic Theories of Politics and Public Finance', *British Journal of Political Science*, 6: 433–48.

—— (1987), *Dilemmas of Development: Reflections on the Counter-Revolution in Development Theory and Policy*, Basil Blackwell, Oxford.

Index

Index compiled by Frank Pert